Jean-Francois
KOENIG
Architect

teNeues

CONTENTS

Preface — 4
by Gaetan Siew

Introduction — 6
Jean-Francois Koenig: The Architect Who Designs to Bridge Cultures, Form, Space, and Time
by Dr Nnamdi Elleh

Jean-Francois Koenig and Multidisciplinary Architecture — 18
by Jan Heynike

Jean-Francois Koenig and Arup Associates — 19
by David Thomas

Jean-Francois Koenig, a Mauritian Architect — 22
by Sylvie de Leusse

A Few Random Thoughts and Stories — 23
by Jean-Francois Koenig

Projects

Chapter 1 Residential — 30
Chapter 2 Hotels — 132
Chapter 3 Public, Educational, Industrial — 204
Chapter 4 Offices — 242

Future — 298

Chronological List of Projects — 302

Curriculum Vitae — 318

Credits — 319

Imprint — 320

Preface
by Gaetan Siew

Architecture, as an expression of art and creativity, is the language that builds and shapes societies. Once an architect infuses creativity in a building, it is ingrained and inevitably influences the design of other surrounding structures. An architect has the power to shape societies and the view of the populace about the built environment.

Such power has diffused over time, as the world has seen a rapid appreciation, through globalisation, of homogenous design principles. As every building is now more or less the same, the work of architects is more important than ever. Their task is to renew creativity in design and function, to bridge the gap between society and people, to restore a sense of belonging to people, and to bring back glory to cities.

As we browse the pages of this book, we realise that architecture and talent knows no borders, and that creativity can be sourced from unlikely and remote places. The works of Jean-Francois Koenig have received increasing global acclaim, and I am even more delighted that this source of inspiration comes from the small tropical island of Mauritius, an island that stands as a leader in the African world, and faces the numerous challenges of global warming.

As the world turns towards homogenisation, we see the impacts of global warming fuelled by the building industry. It is of such great importance to re-evaluate our ethos, so positioning ourselves as designers of a better future.

As Jean-Francois Koenig showcases his work, we learn that ideas for sustainable design can emerge from unlikely places. We need to keep an open mind about the role of architecture as a shaper of cities, architecture as a catalyst for economic growth, and architecture as a tool for social regeneration. In this respect, we need to acknowledge the role of time, context, and place.

Gaetan Siew
UN Habitat – CP Representative
Former President – Union Internationale des Architectes
Mauritius, 2017

Right: The Mauritius Commercial Bank, Ebène, Mauritius (2006–2012). South face.

Introduction
Jean-Francois Koenig: The Architect Who Designs to Bridge Cultures, Form, Space, and Time

by Dr Nnamdi Elleh

Jean-Francois Koenig is one of the few architects whose designs bridge cultures, form, space, and time. It is exciting to explore these themes in his work. The Mauritius Commercial Bank Building that Koenig completed in 2012 is an elliptical bronze-like structure that sits on its site in Quatre Bornes like an ornamental landscape brooch. The building shows how Koenig's oeuvre incorporates the cultures, formal expressions, spatial needs, and the temporal experiences of the contemporary era in a symbiotic design.

As a formal representation, the Mauritius Commercial Bank is placed on giant semi-circular shaped piers that symbolise how the most prominent mountain peaks that define the island's jagged landscapes, such as the Pieter Both, Le Pouce, Le Lion in Grand Port, Les Trois Mamelles, and Le Rempart, define the undulating bowls and slopes where the inhabitants dwell, cultivate, and make their living. Visually, the peak of the Pieter Both appears like a human head on a pedestal. Koenig was aware of the significance of this powerful symbol to the people of Mauritius when he was designing the bank building and he interpreted it in a form that appears like a natural landscape formation on the island.

The culture and spatial arrangements of the bank building supported each other. Koenig understood that the bankers who would occupy the Mauritius Commercial Bank would be dealing with transactions on a global scale. For that reason, and although the Island's physical geography presented him with national physical symbolisms, he met the needs of banking cultures by placing the employees, regardless of rank, in a large space with equivalent desk sizes and

Right: The Mauritius Commercial Bank, Ebène, Mauritius (2006–2012). North face.

cubicles. This democratised spatial arrangement recalls the type of organisation we saw at Frank Lloyd Wright's Johnson Wax Building (1936–1939) in Racine, Wisconsin, USA.

The contemporary experiences of the era in which Koenig completed the building are marked by environmental awareness, so emphasising that our earth has limited resources and needs to be protected from pollution and degradation. Koenig produced a design that synchronised the needs of our time with the building's form by using large glazed window panels to bring light into the elliptical structure, thus reducing energy consumption during office hours. Another example of Koenig's contemporary design is the use of solar panels to produce electricity and the collection of rainwater as well as recycling run-off rainwater.

The versatility of Koenig's work is evident in the Mauritius Commercial Bank at Trou aux Biches (1990–1992). It is a homely cottage structure that evokes the traditional Victorian era of architectural ironwork production in Mauritius. In comparison to the large-scale and technical installations, for example, solar panels applied in the design of the Mauritius Commercial Bank at Ebène, as well as the glazing set in metalwork in the form of an old grille and the recycled teak shingles of the structure at Trou aux Biches emphasise the understanding of how buildings function in the tropics to improve climatic conditions. How did Koenig learn to build with sensitivity to the climate in the tropics on a large and small scale, and with diverse design tectonics as shown in these two bank buildings? The path he followed before establishing his practice provides the answers to our question. Koenig's cosmopolitan education exposed him to the English and French systems and languages; he is grounded in the culture, fauna, and knowledge of the architecture and landscapes of his beautiful homeland, Mauritius, where the different cultures of the world coexist. He studied architecture at Thames Polytechnic, London, from 1973 to 1980, under the supervision of Dr Jacques Paul who was a leading authority on the Bauhaus.

He began to make his mark on the design scene while still a student when his design won third place in the international competition "An Image for Britain" organised by the Royal Institute of British Architects (RIBA) in 1979.

It was judged by the eminent architects Charles Moore, Derek Walker, and Norman Foster.

Top: The Mauritius Commercial Bank, Trou aux Biches, Mauritius (1990–1992). Front façade and gable end.
Left: The Mauritius Commercial Bank, Trou aux Biches, Mauritius (1990–1992). Banking Hall.

In 1979, Jean-Francois Koenig entered the Architectural Competition "An Image for Britain" organised by the Royal Institute of British Architects (RIBA) on the Hampton Site adjoining the National Gallery in Trafalgar Square, London. The competition drew 132 entries from across the United Kingdom.

His design went 'beyond the brief' to include a pedestrian link between Trafalgar Square and Leicester Square. The building, containing an information centre, cafes, and restaurants is placed to one side of the site leaving two thirds open to the sky to create an urban space. It thus forms the link between the two popular London Squares. A pedestrian subway connects Trafalgar Square and St Martin's Street, which is pedestrianised, and leads to Leicester Square. The building has a rooftop restaurant giving onto large open terraces with views. It celebrates and pushes the limits of the glass technology of the day

and aims to be as transparent as possible with the inclusion of internal planting. A full-height glazed façade with structural glass fins is hung from a column and beam structure clad in Portland stone. A glass barrel vault of giant sheets of glass extends the restaurant over the pedestrian street and sits on a bridge structure that frames the view of the classical façade of Canada House seen when walking down St Martin's Street from Leicester Square with a Henry Moore bronze sculpture underneath.

Jean-Francois Koenig was the only student to win a prize. He was placed third behind architect Eva Jiricna, the current President of the Royal Academy of Arts and the Chrysalis Group, comprised of Alan Stanton, Mike Davies, and Ian Ritchie. His drawings, some of which are shown here, formed part of the exhibition of the first 10 entries of the competition which was held at the RIBA Headquarters in Portland Place, London.

The competition was judged by American architect and author Charles W. Moore (1925–1993), recipient of the American Institute of Architects (AIA) Gold Medal, Dean of the Yale School of Architecture, Professor at the Universities of California Berkeley, Los Angeles, and Texas; British architect Derek Walker (1929–2015) responsible for the planning of Milton Keynes, and Norman Foster.

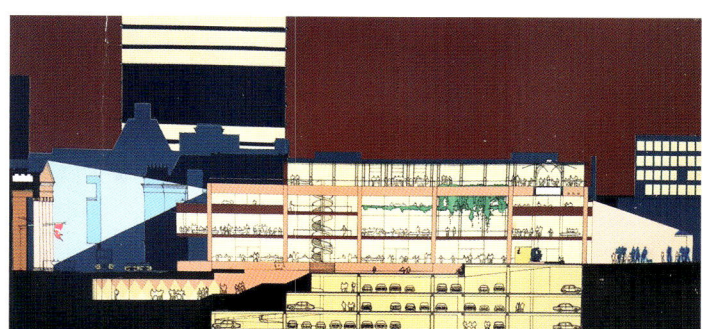
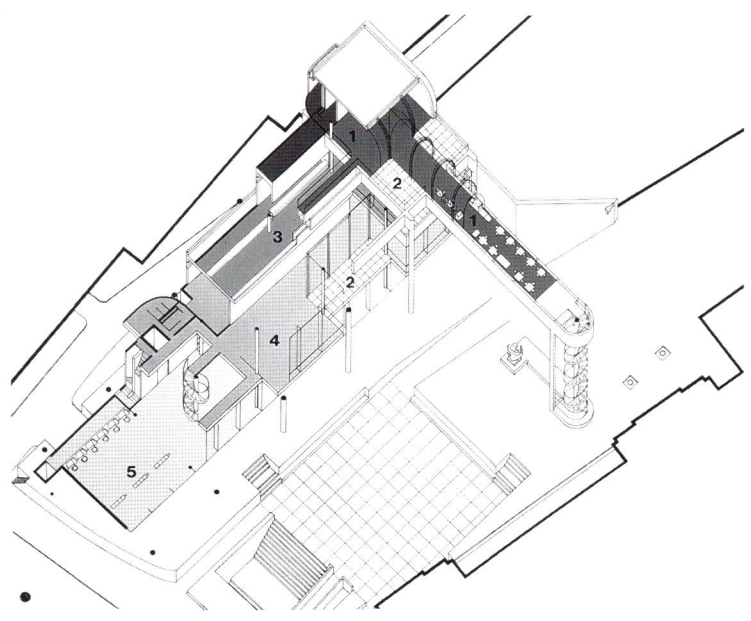
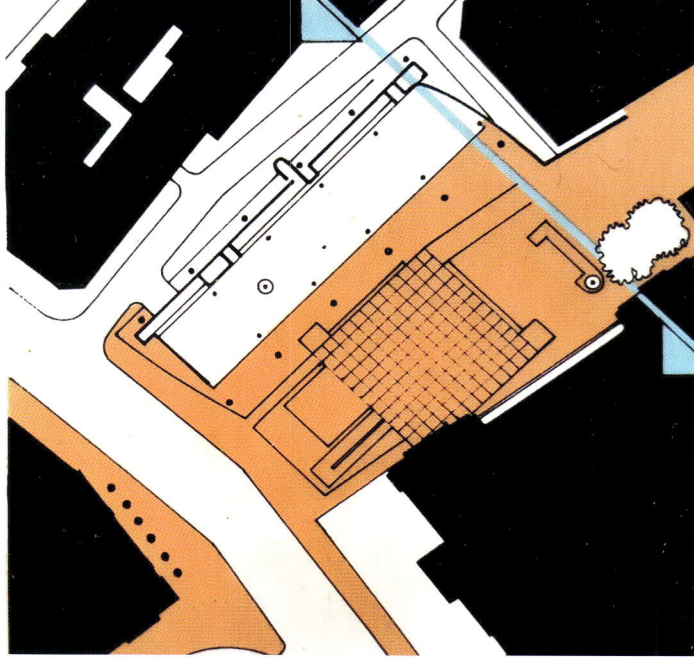
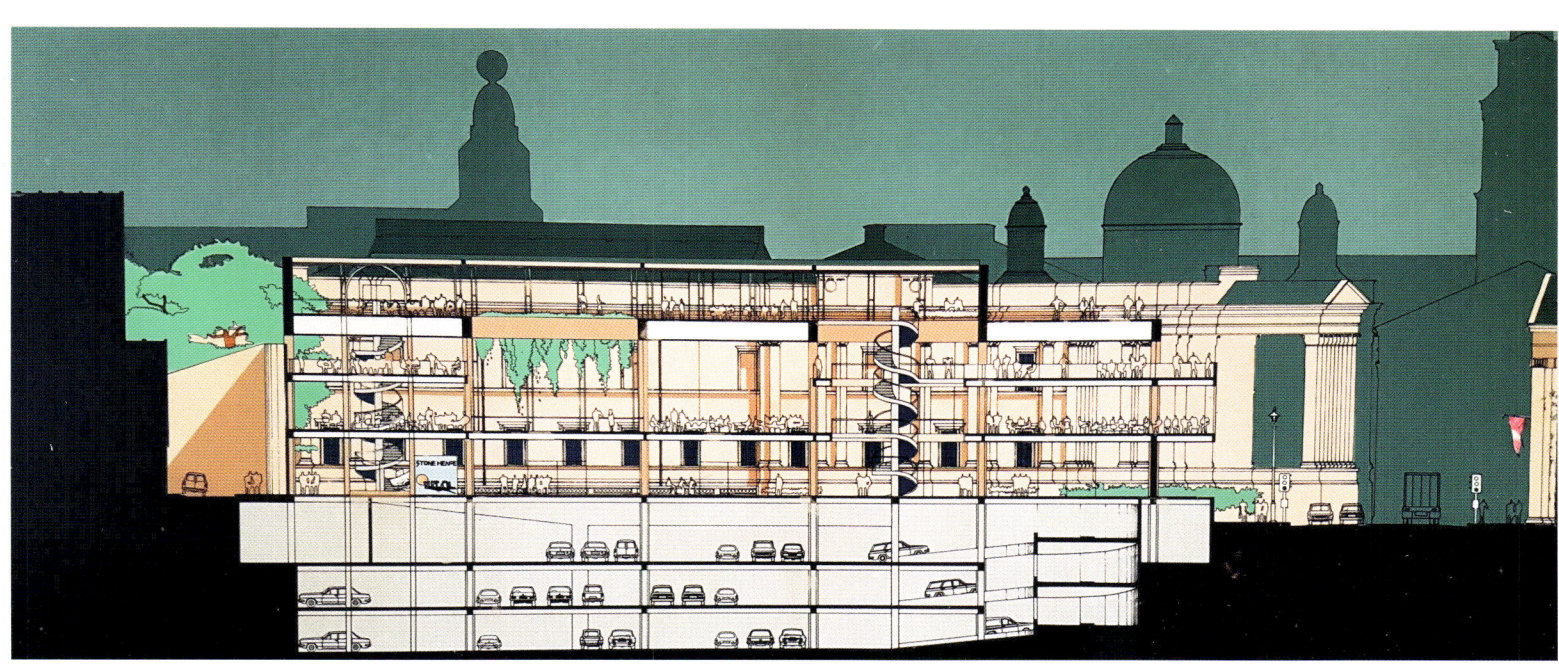

During this period, he developed an interest in the work of Frank Lloyd Wright, Norman Foster, Le Corbusier, as well as Japanese traditional architecture, and the classical proportion of façade composition.

He has travelled widely. Moreover, his broad-based cultural and international outlook on design was further enhanced when he worked for the multidisciplinary offices of Rhodar in Johannesburg and for the parent firm, Arup Associates in London. He has worked on a large design portfolio including offices, houses, hotels, apartment and industrial structures, educational and public buildings, as well as a number of restoration and renovation projects, all incorporating landscape designs. He started his practice in Mauritius in 1987. In 2012, Koenig was confirmed as one of the "100 Architects of the Year" in an international competition organised jointly by the Korean Institute of Architects (KIA) and the International Union of Architects (UIA).

One of the tallest buildings on the Island by Koenig is the Mauritius Telecom Tower in Port Louis, designed and built between 1992 and 1995. Today, 'telecom' has multiple meanings beyond the telephone and telegraph gadgets from which it evolved in the late nineteenth and early twentieth centuries. It encompasses Internet accessories, fast communication tools, and the social media infrastructures that drive the growth of global market and socio-cultural experience. The Mauritius Telecom building was the first glass curtain wall construction on the Island and its design symbolises the contemporary cultures of rapid information and data transfer from the island to where they are needed around the world. As a government-owned structure, the form of the building projects both corporate and governmental power in an international context with a glistening façade and communication infrastructure similar to those of other firms operating in such buildings in different parts of the world.

Top: Sotravic Office building, Coromandel, Mauritius (1992–1995).

Top right: Mauritius Telecom Headquarters, Port-Louis, Mauritius (1992–1995).

Bottom right: Le Ruisseau Rose, Les Mariannes, Mauritius (1990–1995).
House and office of Jean-Francois Koenig.

Koenig envisaged the needs of our digital communication age and the potential for the future in the form of the Mauritius Telecom building by designing multifunctional spaces that easily facilitate the upgrade of rapidly and continuously changing communications infrastructure. The building's form also reveals the influences of futuristic designs by Norman Foster and I.M. Pei. Koenig has designed numerous office structures besides the Mauritius Telecom building. The pleasure of reviewing such buildings derives from how he applied his background to design for the tropics. His greatest strength is his gift of interpreting architectural language in exploiting shading from solar effects as well as protection from excessive rainfall. For example, the United Basalt offices, Trianon, Mauritius, 1988–1990, is reminiscent of the wide overhanging eaves and roofs of Frank Lloyd Wright buildings.

The CIEL Ebène Centre, Mauritius (2005–2009), uses extended perforated grille fins over glazed windows to allow in filtered light while shading the structure.

The Sotravic Building, Coromandel, Mauritius, completed between 1992–1995, draws from minimalist linear and rectangular steel structures from the high modernist period to articulate shaded glazed surfaces. Unlike the buildings where he used verandas and extended roof eaves to shade a structure, at Sotravic, Koenig has recessed the windows to achieve the same goals. The effect was subtle, but it nevertheless realised the objective of solar reduction.

The basis for Koenig's tropical building style is a combination of eighteenth century French and late nineteenth century Victorian architecture. For example, the house on the East Coast completed between 1993 and 1996 demonstrates his ability to draw from the Islands' rich cultural and architectural heritage. The structure shows how cast-iron columns support the shallower sloping concrete roof overhang of the verandas, which are wrapped around the structure like a skirt, to provide shade and rain protection. The house on the East Coast shows how Koenig responds to culture, and uses form to meet the needs of each client on different sites and with timeless architecture.

Koenig's interest in cultural heritage is demonstrated in his many design projects. Le Ruisseau Rose, Les Mariannes, completed between 1990–1995, is where his practice is located and where he also resides. The Roman villa-type layout of the plan uses the pool, colonnaded arcade, and terraces to provide shade and reduce heat.

The wide glazed corner windows and doors, without mullions, take advantage of the surrounding undulating vistas, while the extended roof and eaves facilitate shading and accentuate shadows. In addition, the extended eaves and the landscape of the elevated courtyards evoke Frank Lloyd Wright's and traditional Japanese architecture and gardens.

The buildings designed by Koenig, notable for their exploration of Western and Eastern architectural heritage, and the French and Victorian traditional architecture of Mauritius, an island representative of Pluriculturalism, could be tectonically interpreted and translated for contemporary and future generations. His houses have wide roofs and extended verandas, rafters and posts, pools, courtyards, and surrounding vegetation. The House at Moka (1989–1991), Les Salines (1988–1989), Pereybere (1990–1993), and the hotels, Indian Club Resort at Le Morne, Mauritius (1997–2002), Voile D'Or at Bel Ombre, Mauritius (2002–2004), are some examples that demonstrate the characteristics mentioned here and they show how Koenig explored the relationships between culture, form, space, and time in tropical architectural design.

Koenig's schemes for apartment buildings, for example, Queen Mary Gardens, Floreal,

Left: Indian Resort and Spa, Le Morne, Mauritius (1997–2002).

Top right: Ruisseau Hortensia, Les Salines, Mauritius (2004–2011). Master plan drawing by Jean-Francois Koenig.

Centre right: Ruisseau Hortensia, Les Salines, Mauritius (2004–2011). View of villas and pond.

Bottom right: House at Les Salines, Rivière Noire, Mauritius (1988–1989).

Pages 16/17: Le Ruisseau Rose, Les Mariannes, Mauritius (1990–1995). House and office of Jean-Francois Koenig.

Mauritius (2013–2015), and Beau Vallon Beach, Mahé, Seychelles (2006–2013), also respond to tropical climate conditions, often turning constraints into advantages. Long before the concept of sustainable design became commonplace in the circles of architectural education and production, design in the tropics always required sensitivity to the environment, and Koenig recognised this responsibility in his masterfully planned landscapes and developments such as, for example, Ruisseau Hortensia, Les Salines, Mauritius (2004–2011).

Jean-Francois Koenig drew from his diverse cosmopolitan architectural education and experience to create the design of the Mauritius Commercial Bank Building. Despite the high-tech nature of the project, it reinforces the role of culture, form, space, and time in tropical architecture in an era when we are becoming more conscious of global environmental degradation and the need to conserve natural resources. The architectural tectonics of Koenig are diverse, but harmoniously unified with respect for the needs of tropical design which include sensitivity to solar aspects and protection of the structure from excessive moisture. Koenig's work is a contribution to the endeavours of predecessors who championed sensitivity to design in the tropics. Moreover, his portfolio will benefit those who are generally interested in architectural books – the readers, students, scholars, and practitioners of the present and future.

Dr Nnamdi Elleh,
Cincinnati, Ohio, USA, 2017

Jean-Francois Koenig and Multidisciplinary Architecture

by Jan Heynike

Jean-Francois joined Rhodar one year after university graduation in 1981. Rhodar was established as a Multidisciplinary Design Practice in 1980 servicing industrial clients in southern Africa. The company was established by Ove Arup and Partners, London, with a core philosophy inspiring gifted talent to design beyond Façadism.

Jean-Francois then returned to London to join Arup Associates in 1985, a practice that uses osmosis and exchange of ideas throughout the design process. Arups was the first fully integrated design practice exploiting materials and new construction techniques with teams of architects and engineers. Each member was an equal contributor in the joint pursuit of building excellence and intelligent buildings.

Jean-Francois' design mission has always remained faithful to those informative years working at Rhodar and Arup Associates. He has worked endlessly and passionately to excel in design, as the breadth and diversity of his outstanding portfolio of work testifies.

Jan Heynike
Architect and Engineer
Rhodar and Arup Partner 1960–1985
Switzerland, 2017

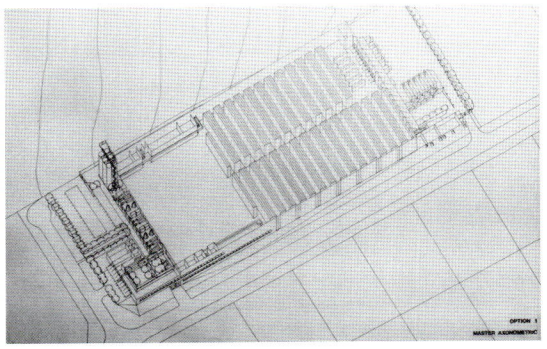

Jean-Francois Koenig and Arup Associates
by David Thomas

Arup Associates, Architects, Engineers, and Quantity Surveyors is a multidisciplinary architectural practice which was founded in 1963 having grown out of the 'building group', an offspring of the world-renowned engineering practice of Ove Arup and Partners. It was the brainchild of Ove Arup – a philosophical, brilliant engineer, and Philip Dowson – a romantic modern architect – who both passionately believed that to meet the needs of constantly developing modern technology in the construction world, the best architecture could only be achieved when all those designers involved in its creation come together in the same space and work as a team.

These teams or groups as they became known, consisted of Architects, Interior Designers, Structural Engineers, Mechanical and Electrical Engineers, Quantity Surveyors, and an Administrator. Each group is responsible for its projects from the very first meeting with the Client right through design, working drawings, and site works to the day of handover, and the settling of the final account, so creating in all members a strong sense of ownership for the projects. The core members of the Group are permanent and learn to appreciate the needs and aims of their colleagues in the different professions.

All projects need a leader and in most cases the leader will be an experienced architect, but there will be cases when an engineer (structural, mechanical, or electrical) takes on the leader's role. The projects of the six design groups, as they evolve, are presented to the whole practice at formal meetings for critical and helpful assessment to maintain the design ethos of the practice. The aim is to produce designs that are sensitive to the environment, to human needs, and that exploit advances in technology.

As an offspring of the sister practice Ove Arup and Partners, Arup Associates can call upon sources and skills shared with O A P such as the technical library, research & development, acoustic engineering, fire engineering, geo-technics, and traffic engineering, etc.

It was into this integrated practice – one that produced innovative design solutions in concrete, steel, and timber – that Jean-Francois Koenig arrived in 1985 to join Group 3 and work on several important projects including the prestigious UK Headquarters of Hasbro-Bradley, the American Toy manufacturers, at Stockley Park west of London.

After two formative years of learning about Arup Associates' way of working and contributing to the designs he worked on, Jean-Francois left Arups to return to Mauritius and start his own highly successful practice – Jean-Francois Koenig Architect.

David Thomas BArch (Hons L'pool) RIBA
Retired Architect Director of Arup Associates
Oxfordshire, UK, 2017

Top left: Rhodar, Metal Box Flagship Factory, Midrand, Witwatersrand, South Africa. The building is 400 m long x 100 m wide. Isometric drawing by Jean-Francois Koenig.

Centre top left: Rhodar, Baldwins Steel, Canteen, Brackpan, Witwatersrand, South Africa. Corner detail.

Centre bottom left: Jean-Francois Koenig in Rhodar.

Bottom left: Rhodar, B&J Mechanical Workshop, Alrode, Johannesburg, South Africa.

Below: Arup Associates – Hasbro Bradley UK Headquarters, Stockley Park, UK. Elevations in pencil and ink drawn by Jean-Francois Koenig in 1987 at Arup Associates.

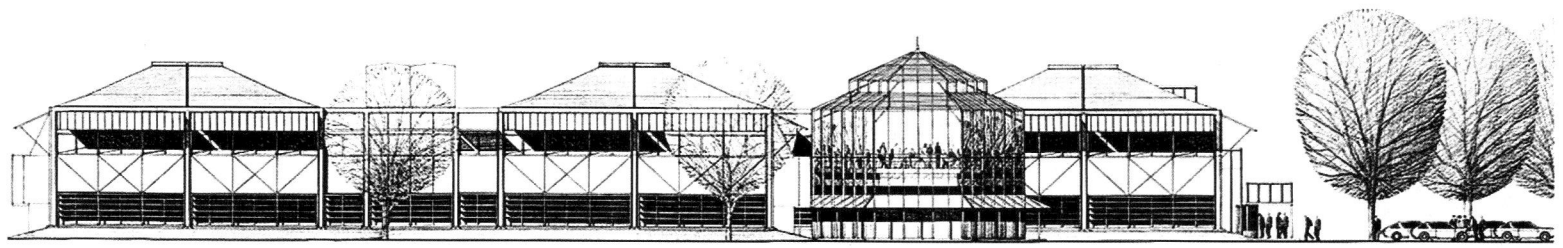

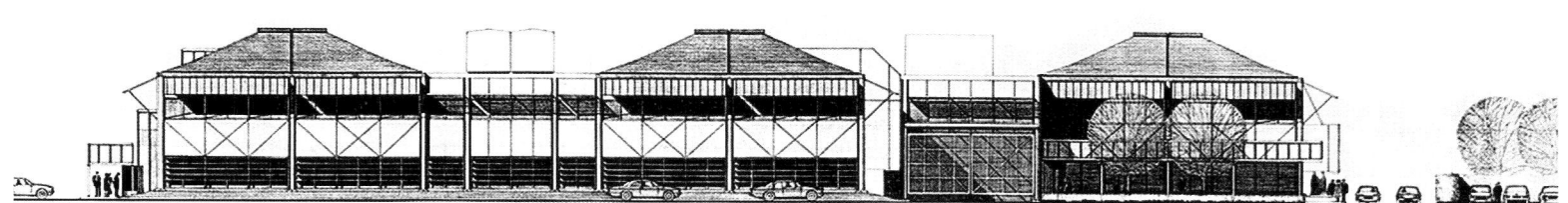

Jean-Francois Koenig, a Mauritian Architect

by Sylvie de Leusse

After qualifying as an architect in London in 1980, Jean-Francois Koenig became the 31st member of the Mauritius Association of Architects (MAA), formed in the early 1960s. He served on its executive committee for two years, before and during the time that the MAA was recognised by the laws of Mauritius as an independent Association of Professional Architects in November 1988. The MAA became a member of the Union Internationale des Architectes (UIA) in 1990 through the initiative of Gaetan Siew who subsequently became its President (2005–2008).

In the context of an ever-increasing population in Mauritius, there was a demand for low-cost housing that was often built without the services of an architect. At a time when concrete flat roofs were common construction, Jean-Francois Koenig advocated the preservation of traditional local architecture through his housing projects and renovations. During a period when the old architecture in timber was being demolished, he contributed to heightening public awareness for their preservation with his book "La Vie en Varangue" and the English version "Living in Mauritius" (Editions du Pacifique, 1989).

Jean-Francois Koenig incorporates concrete, timber, and steel with new technology adapted to tropical architecture with sustainable solutions.

He has stamped his own personal imprint on the local architectural scene. The respect that he commands in Mauritius is reflected in his ongoing role as mentor besides his influence on young architects who study his works.

During my tenure as President of the MAA, I gave proof of Jean-Francois Koenig's membership, as a precondition of entry, for the submission of his project of the Mauritius Commercial Bank to the UIA and the Korean Institute of Architects (KIA), the two institutions jointly responsible for the organisation of the International Competition "100 Architects of the Year 2012". It is good for architecture in Mauritius that Jean-Francois Koenig, a Mauritian Architect, has won this global award.

Sylvie de Leusse, Architect DPLG (Marseille)
Former President of the
Mauritius Association of Architects
Mauritius, 2017

Right: The Mauritius Commercial Bank, Ebène, Mauritius (2006–2012). Detail of East façade.

Pages 20/21: The Mauritius Commercial Bank, Ebène, Mauritius (2006–2012). East and North façades.

A Few Random Thoughts and Stories

by Jean-Francois Koenig

Architects live, design, and build, in 'a period in time' on a calendar. 'Periods' or 'movements' or 'styles' in Architecture are all relative to each other and have come and gone and reappeared in ebbs and flows. For example, Classical Greek and Roman resurfaced during the Renaissance about 1,400 years later and resurfaced again with Neo-Classicism about 400 years after that. Sometimes, the first question a potential client will ask me is: "what is your 'style'?" and invariably my reply is: "I don't have any". An architectural solution does not begin with a 'style' and is rather assessed on many factors such as the site, its historical context, what the building is used for, etc. The best buildings are founded on technical, functional, environmental, and conceptual grounds and not on the fashion of an architectural 'period'. Good architecture will endure and transcend 'periods'. What is important is for Architecture to be timeless.

It would be impossible to describe Architecture in a few words, because it is a life living it, embracing it, and breathing it for every second of the day. Architecture is visual and everything that surrounds us is related to an architect's life and consequently to Architecture itself. We live in it. We use it. Architecture does not exist on its own. It is inherently and inextricably part of our landscape and our infrastructure which makes up our whole environment. Architecture is responsible for the quality of life that shapes our villages, our cities, our counties, and architects have an opportunity to improve the quality of life of people to make our world a better place to live, including the cultural dimension. I am convinced that this is the role of the architect in society.

Designing relatively small projects with relatively low budgets in Mauritius is just as much a responsibility for an architect as designing the tallest or largest showcase building on the planet.

Top: Typical modest Mauritian house, Notre Dame, Montagne Longue, Mauritius. This house was demolished in the 1990s. Painting by Jean-Francois Koenig, "La Petite Maison au Toit Jaune", 2015, acrylic on board, 40 × 55 cm.

Bottom: "La Carrière", Moka, Mauritius. A fine example of the preservation of the traditional architecture of Mauritius. These houses are built in timber on a raised basalt stone base with front and back verandas flanked by turret roofs. Photographed by Jean-Francois Koenig in 2017.

I have been fortunate to get a good start in architecture. I had great teachers when I started studying in London in 1973. Dr Jacques Paul, the head of the University, was an expert on the Bauhaus and there was a strong connection with the Modern Movement. It was an exciting time to be a student in the 1970s in London when it was brimming with new ideas and great architecture was being produced by young 'high tech' architects whose work labelled the term and influenced the world. Norman Foster was one of them. I followed him ever since and consider him as the greatest living architect. I remember going, several times, to his first office in Fitzroy Street, a tinted glass façade with 'invisible' glass structural fins and trying to see inside. I went to see the Willis Faber Dumas building (Norman Foster, 1971–1975) in Ipswich and the Sainsbury Centre (Norman Foster, 1974–1978) in Norwich twice in 1978. Those two buildings left a deep impression. Their glass technology was unseen before and fascinated me.

I was also fortunate to work in multidisciplinary teams of the highest standard at Rhodar in Johannesburg and Arup Associates in London (1981–1987). Rhodar was formed in the early 1980s in the image of, and supported by, the pioneering multidisciplinary Architectural practice Arup Associates. Working there allowed me to meet, be around with, listen to, and work with some great engineers like Jack Zunz[1], Michael Lewis[2], Bob Hobbs[3], Peter Warburton[4], and Peter Rice[5] to name but a very few. I also had the privilege to work with great architects like Philip Dowson[6], David Thomas[7], Jan Heynike[8], and others. Those times provided a solid foundation for a holistic approach to design, grounded in sustainability as a given standard of conceptual thinking. It was before sustainability accreditations such as BREEAM in the United Kingdom and LEED in the United States came into being in 1990 and 1994 respectively, but it was part of the ethos of these two multidisciplinary practices that informed design decisions.

Starting my professional life in a multidisciplinary office designing factory buildings that are all about function, process, efficiency of structure, and services has been a great learning experience. There was no expectation on behalf of the client for aesthetics. Budgets were tight. This grows a strong functional approach to design and a thorough understanding of structural and mechanical engineering. I was very aware of what had, and was being produced in Office design and Industrial Architecture and the buildings of Arup Associates in particular, to which I had internal library access, were a great source of learning.

Top and centre left: Ludwig Mies van der Rohe (1886–1969) – The Barcelona Pavilion (1929). The German Pavilion for the Barcelona Exhibition of 1929 became an icon of the Modern Movement in Architecture. It was demolished in 1930 and rebuilt in 1986. These photographs were taken by Jean-Francois Koenig in 1986, just after its reconstruction.

Bottom left: Norman Foster – Willis Faber & Dumas Headquarters, Ipswich, England (1971–1975). This building became the youngest Grade I Listed Building in Britain in 1991. Photographed by Jean-Francois Koenig in 1978.

[1] Sir Jack Zunz was chairman of Ove Arup and Partners and guided "Arup" in becoming the global firm it is today.

[2] Michael Lewis was a senior partner of Ove Arup and Partners responsible for the structural design of the Sydney Opera House and the setting up of the Arup Australia office. Both he and Jack Zunz started with Ove Arup at the Johannesburg office where they came regularly and where I met them.

[3] Bob Hobbs (1923–2006) was one of the founding structural engineers of the multidisciplinary office Arup Associates and later became Chairman of Ove Arup and Partners.

[4] Peter Warburton is a leading mechanical engineer and retired Director of Arup Associates. He worked on the Mauritius Commercial Bank building in Ebène, Mauritius in close collaboration with me.

Travelling as much as possible to visit buildings, old and new, and reading books on architecture and architects were my pastime. Visiting Fallingwater (Frank Lloyd Wright, 1936) twice in 1991 and 1993, arriving into the atrium and going up the lifts of the Hong Kong and Shanghai Bank (Norman Foster, 1980–1985) in 1988, walking up the road with a rucksack to Ronchamp (Le Corbusier, 1954), and hitchhiking from Florence to Munich to visit the Olympic Stadium (Frei Otto, 1972) in 1974, was exciting. Everything Architecture interested me: for example, walking on the roof of the Pont du Gard (19 AD), oblivious to danger in 1974, or climbing over the fence to access the then abandoned villa of Eileen Gray and Jean Badovici at Cap Martin to get a closer look at Le Corbusier's mural paintings on a Sunday morning after New Year in 1979, were just done from the excitement of seeing beautiful structures built for infrastructure and the incorporation of Art on buildings that all relate to the architectural world we live in.

The list is long and cannot be all told here, but how can one not mention the Acropolis and the Parthenon (447–438 BC), or the Temple of Poseidon (444–440 BC) at Cape Sounion overlooking the Mediterranean with the profile of the coastline and islands beyond. The site, its environment, and its architecture is all encompassing. Light beige marble in strong sunlight, seen against a blue sky and blue sea, is never quite the same when re-interpreted in an urban environment of grey skies in temperate climates. They grew my understanding of climate, context, place, and time.

Other parts of the world that offer different architectural influences to Western Architecture, but which are just as essential to acquire a balanced and global view of the built world, include the East, from Istanbul up the east coast of the Asian Continent to Japan. For example, a first-time view of the Taj Mahal seen from 'the back', on the other side of the Yamuna River, as it slowly emerges from the invisibility of pitch black darkness of night through to dawn, leaves a lasting impression of beauty. The Korean and Japanese philosophy of perfection of detailing and their respect for, and integration with, nature in their architecture and gardens, is a great source of inspiration.

Two places designed and built by non-architects which have made a lasting impression are: Jim Thompson's Thai house in Bangkok (1959) and Axel Munthe's Villa San Michele (circa 1900) in Anacapri. Both designed with nature in mind and both contextual in their setting. Both have plenty of sculpture and artwork. Both have timeless interiors and are integrated in their gardens. They do not have windows, only shutters that are frameless openings on views of landscapes or seascapes. The words of Physician Axel Munthe about Villa San Michele: "My house must be open to the sun, to the wind, and to the voice of the sea, just like a Greek temple and light, light, light everywhere" is a powerful architectural statement of design intent made by a non-architect who understood what Architecture is all about.

Top: Arup Associates – Trebor, Colchester Factory, England (1978–1980). This building won an RIBA award in 1983. Photographed by Jean-Francois Koenig in 1985.

Centre: The Taj Mahal, Agra, India (1632–1648). Painting by Jean-Francois Koenig, "The Taj Mahal, View from the Yamuna River". Acrylic on board, 27 × 41 cm.

Bottom right: Dr Axel Munthe (1857–1949) – Villa San Michele, Anacapri, Capri, Italy. Built at the turn of the 20th century. Photographed by Jean-Francois Koenig in 2016.

[5] *Peter Rice (1935–1992) was a senior partner of Ove Arup and Partners and responsible for the structural design of the Pompidou Centre in Paris. He is one of the few engineers to receive the Royal Institute of British Architects (RIBA) Gold Medal in 1992.*

[6] *Sir Philip Dowson (1924–2014) was the founding architect of the pioneering multidisciplinary office Arup Associates. He received the RIBA Gold Medal in 1982 and was President of the Royal Academy of Arts (1993–1999), one of the first Visual Art Institutions in the world founded in 1768, encompassing Painting, Sculpture, and Architecture.*

[7] *David Thomas is a leading architect and retired director of Arup Associates. He headed Group 3.*

[8] *Jan Heynike is a leading architect and structural engineer. He headed design at Rhodar.*

The Alhambra in Granada is where I spent the most time in a single place. Not because I preferred it, but because I gave myself the time: five consecutive days over the Christmas period of 1986 when the crowds were absent and the courtyards and the gardens were almost to myself.

Reflective pools and garden design like at Tivoli, Versailles, or Taranto on Lake Maggiore, to name a few, are marvellous examples of the significance of the garden in Architecture.

The surrounding exteriors of a building, its landscaping, the way one enters, how it is planned to include rather than exclude the landscape like Hadrian's Villa near Rome or traditional Japanese houses and gardens are references of note.

Those and the above are just a few examples of visits I made that make up the commutation of images that imprint the mind to contribute to one's never-ending architectural education in the visual world we live in.

The tropics pose some specific challenges to architects. For example, catering for cyclones is constraining and more specifically so when introducing glass curtain walls for the first time in Mauritius. Specifications for weather tightness and wind pressure become more stringent than normal. There is a need to understand climate and more particularly the effect of mould growth on materials exposed to humidity. Sun and rain control achieved whilst preserving natural ventilation, a requirement for comfortable living in hot and humid climates, is best solved with large overhangs and deep verandas.

Many of these answers are found in the traditional architecture of

Above: Taranto Gardens, Pallanza, Lake Maggiore, Italy (1931–1940). Photographed by Jean-Francois Koenig in 2012.

Top left: The Court of the Myrtles – The Alhambra, Granada, Spain (1330s–1350s). The reflective pool measures 7.1 m wide × 34 m long. The façade of The Court of the Ambassadors is viewed at the end of the reflective pool. Photographed by Jean-Francois Koenig in 1986.

Bottom left and right: The Gardens of the Alhambra, Granada, Spain. Designed and built between 1302 and 1324. The present-day gardens were completed between 1931 and 1951. Photographed by Jean-Francois Koenig in 1986.

Mauritius. But the expensive cost of imported timber and the relatively cheaper and more robust local use of block work and reinforced concrete have forced the re-invention of new shapes which are more appropriate to solve the problems that flat roofs and parapets cannot. Moreover, the tropics are the antithesis of the dense urban environment. One builds in, and with, nature. Trees, flowers, plants in their garden settings are an integral part of a building just as much as are interiors.

Upon my return to Mauritius in 1987, after what was effectively a fourteen-year absence, there was a need to preserve and rebuild the traditional architecture of the Island.

Twenty years after Independence, the Country was being developed at a frantic pace, and much of the architectural heritage, including old trees, were being lost to make space for new buildings.

I initiated the book "La Vie en Varangue" (English version "Living in Mauritius", Editions du Pacifique,1989) to try to bring National awareness to this problem. I also designed several houses and hotels in the spirit of the old in a hope of a revival of an architecture that not only works for the tropics and is beautiful, but is representative of the Country's multicultural population. Some of them are illustrated in this book.

In the last thirty years of practising Architecture in Mauritius, I had no architects working with me in the office. I operated alone, with draughtsmen. Although there were times when I longed to discuss an idea or a design with peers, or going to listen to a colleague that the distance separation of working in Mauritius did not permit, this isolation forced a focused attention on the aims and ethos of the design process and the production of an architecture that has meaning. As the world moves to new contractual agreements where the architect sometimes loses his prime role of lead consultant, I remain convinced that the best results are obtained when the architect leads. Architecture is not only about improving the lives of people; it is also about creating beautiful buildings that uplift the spirit. Architecture is Art. An architect designing alone, like an individual painter or sculptor, also has its advantages.

Jean-Francois Koenig
Mauritius, 2017

Le Ruisseau Rose, Les Mariannes, Mauritius (1990–1995). House and office of Jean-Francois Koenig. Sliding doors and large overhangs open the house to the outside converting interior spaces into verandas.

CHAPTER 1
RESIDENTIAL

St Aubin Plantation House	32
House and Apartment-Garage Conversion	36
House on the East Coast	40
House at Moka	52
House at Pointe aux Canonniers	56
House at Poste Lafayette	58
House at Swan Properties	62
House at Grand Baie	64
Le Ruisseau Rose	68
Two Houses at Roches Noires	84
Apartments at Pointe d'Esny	100
Sables d'Or	104
Queen Mary Gardens	108
Beau Rivage Golf Estate	113
Petite Victoria – Le Café des Arts	116
Le Vieux Moulin	126

St Aubin Plantation House
Mauritius
1992

Situated in the south of Mauritius, in the heart of a sugar plantation, is a traditionally grand and typical Mauritian house resting in the middle of large lawns surrounded by century-old trees. Its renovation in 1992 to convert it into a restaurant open to the public included new timber shingles on the roof, replacement of the internal wooden flooring, part of the timber roof beams, and part of the timber boarding on the outer façades. The veranda floor was redone entirely in a chequered pattern of dark grey local basalt stone and white Namibian marble and its balustrade was redesigned and replaced in the spirit of traditional Mauritian architecture. The interiors were remodelled to include a new professional kitchen.

Car parking is kept out of sight outside the site, retaining the landscape and the approach view of the house unchanged in its natural setting, preserving the character and charm of the place. The renovation makes a seamless passage of time from the past to the present.

The house and garden. The original approach road is left untouched with its century-old trees.

Above: The front façade. The pedestrian arrival walkway in hand cut basalt stone and fountain are new.

Left: The front veranda. The floor and balustrades are new.

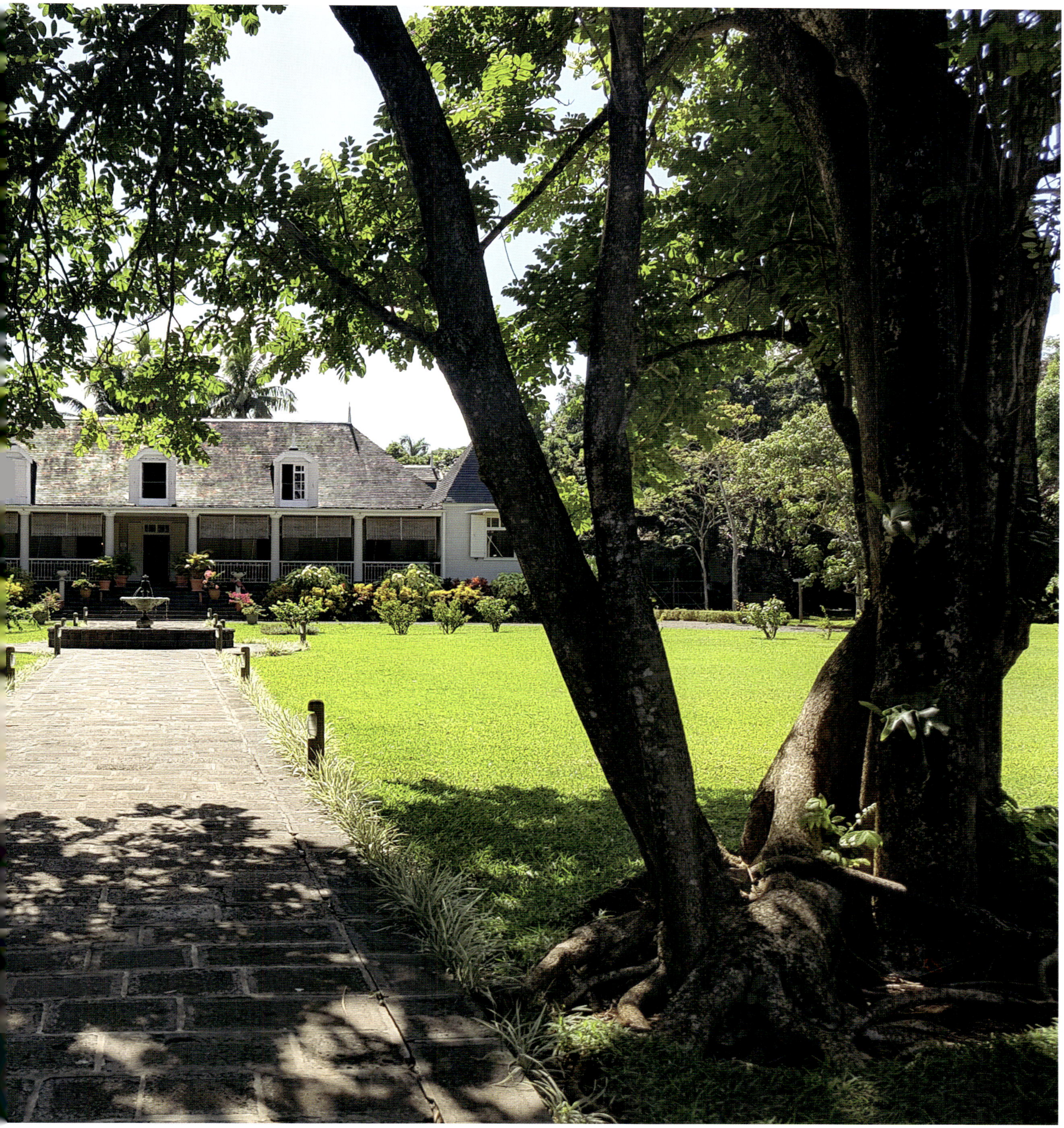

House and Apartment-Garage Conversion

Vacoas, Mauritius
2015

The conversion of an existing house and store was completed in 2015. The original house, built in 1962, had a flat roof in reinforced concrete. An extension of the ground-floor veranda occurred in 1984. The 2015 conversion consists of a new insulated copper roof with lower angled overhangs supported by timber double brackets. It transforms the architecture and returns the house to its identity of place and context. With the new conversion, the house becomes integral with the traditional architecture of Mauritius in its tropical setting of rolling lawns, gardens, and old trees.

At the back of the property, an existing store was converted into an apartment and a garage. A hipped copper roof with overhangs was added and detailed in the same manner, and in architectural unity with the main house.

The house sits in a tropical garden with mature trees and a rolling front lawn, created in the early 1960s.

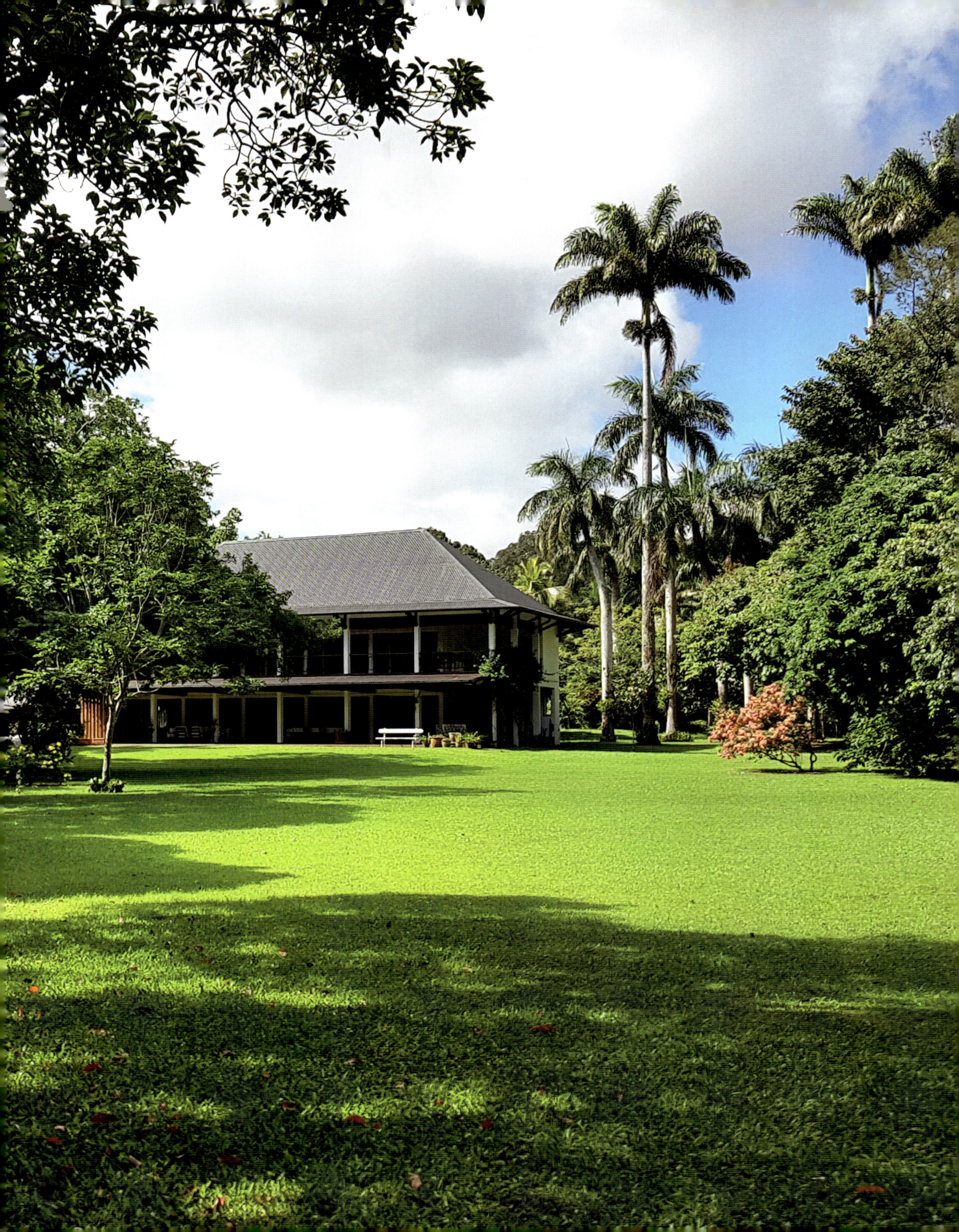

Above: The apartment and garage out-house with its insulated sandwich panel copper roof in the back garden.

Top right: The main house. Side view.

Bottom right: Still in perfect working order, a 1929 Rolls-Royce in the new garage.

39

House on the East Coast
Mauritius
1993–1996

The house on the east coast is on a virgin piece of the Mauritian coastline, conceived with collection pieces of construction of rare availability and quality that were collected over the years by the client. They were inserted into a new construction to create the finished building. Classical columns of Ionic order in cast iron are used all around the front, back, and side verandas. The floors of the verandas are hand cut basalt stonework in a pattern that had to be carefully reassembled on site like a jigsaw puzzle. The ornate wrought iron balustrade came from a demolished grand old house stored away for years before being reused. Long door lintels in hand cut stones were reused for the fireplace in the living room. The internal doors in teak with bevelled-edged frosted glass with motifs leading from the main space to the verandas were rescued from another demolished building. These elements set the tone for a re-interpretation of the vernacular Mauritian house but built in concrete. The roof is clad with flat cement tiles made from a special mould specifically factory produced locally for the job and which eventually became standard production in Mauritius. The wrought iron spiral staircase painted Chinese red was ordered new from England. The concept makes it difficult to date the building in an attempt to achieve a timeless piece of architecture.

Above: The house recedes into the landscape making a minimal impact on the environment.

Overleaf: Sea-facing veranda. The wrought iron columns and balustrades were recovered from demolished buildings and incorporated in the new house.

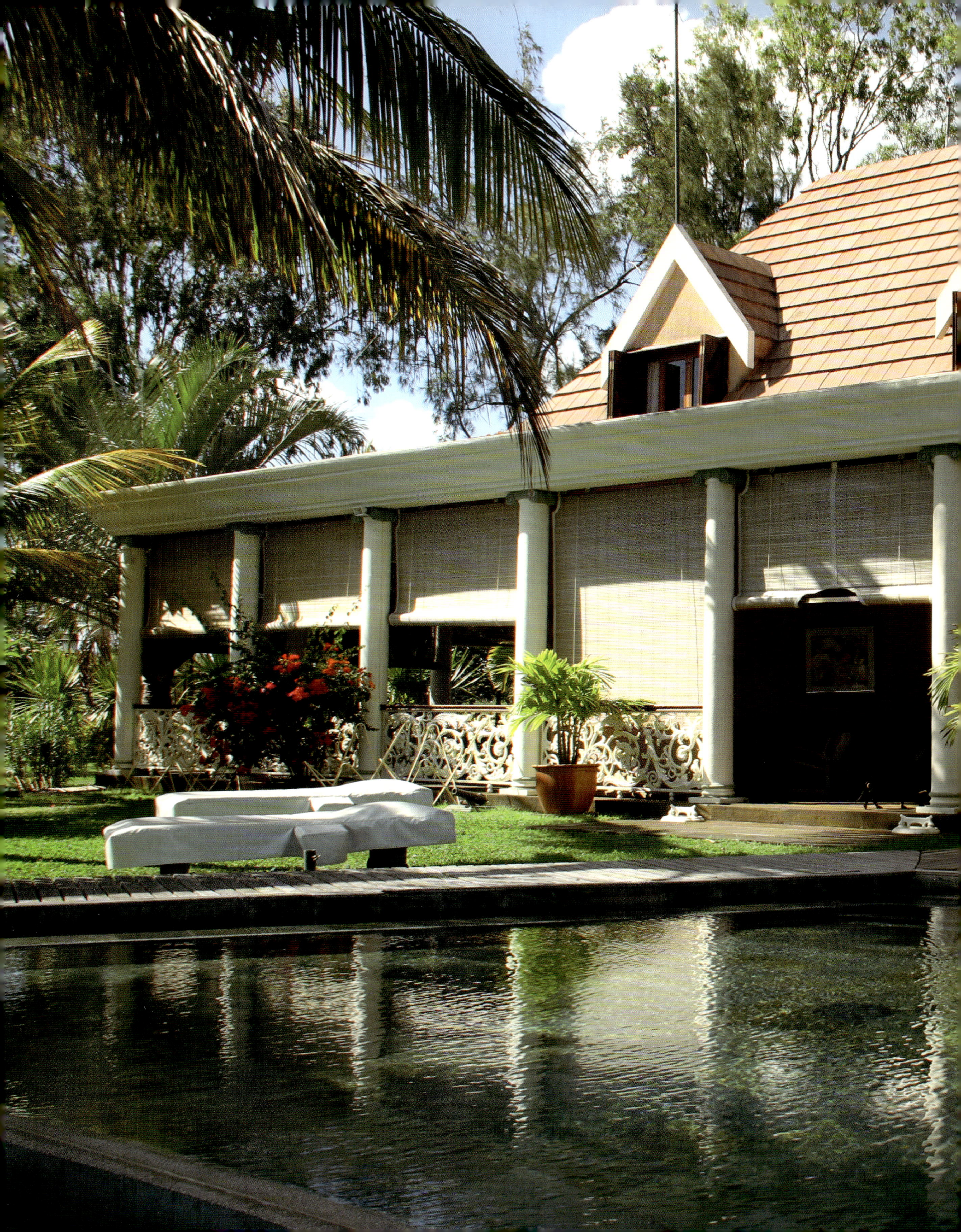

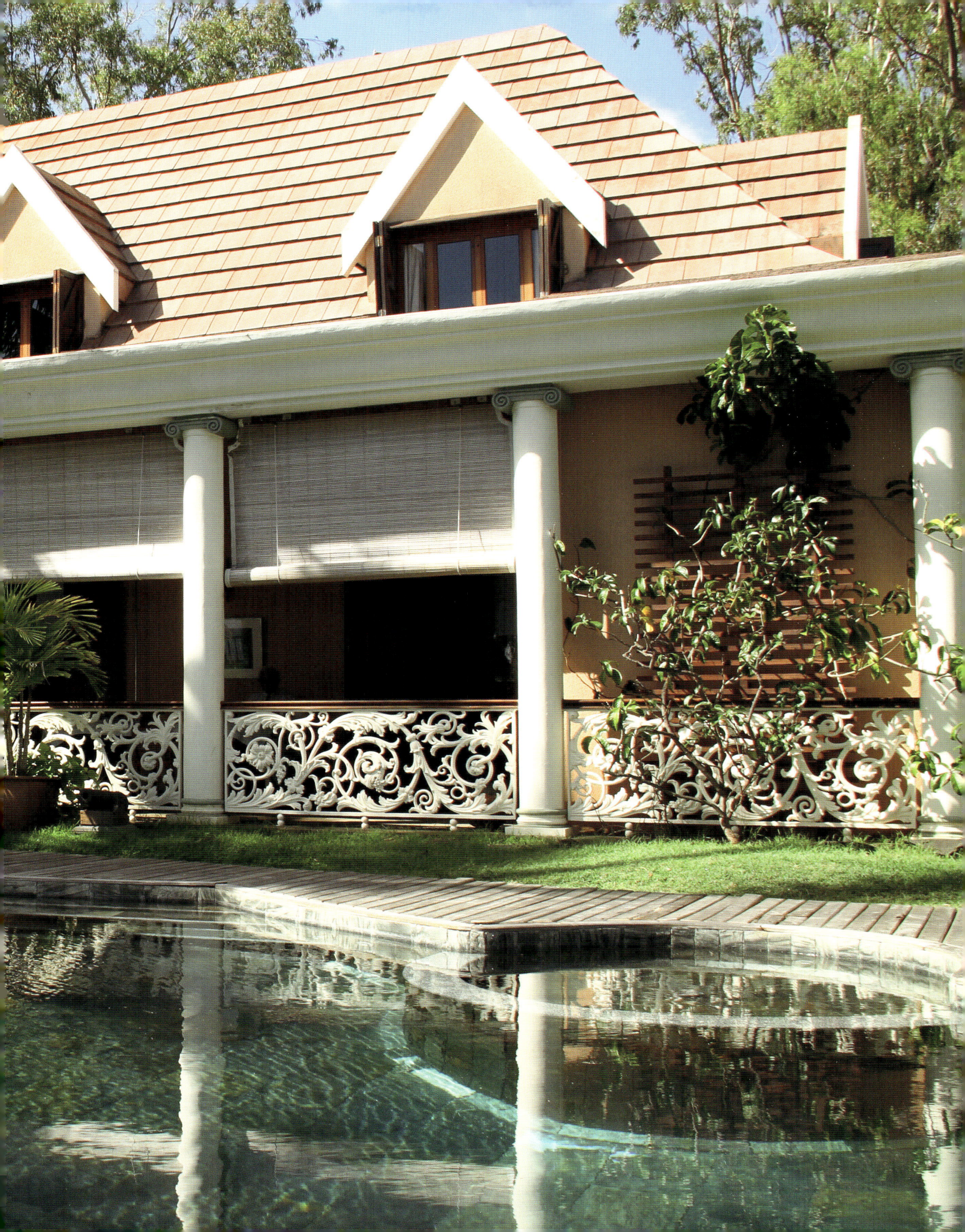

Top and bottom: Sea-facing veranda.

Top and bottom: Entrance veranda.

Sea-facing veranda. The hand cut basalt stone floor was recovered from a demolished building and reassembled on site like a puzzle.

Top and bottom: The living and dining room space.
Overleaf: Hand-cut basalt stone gate posts and low walls and the entrance roundabout driveway.

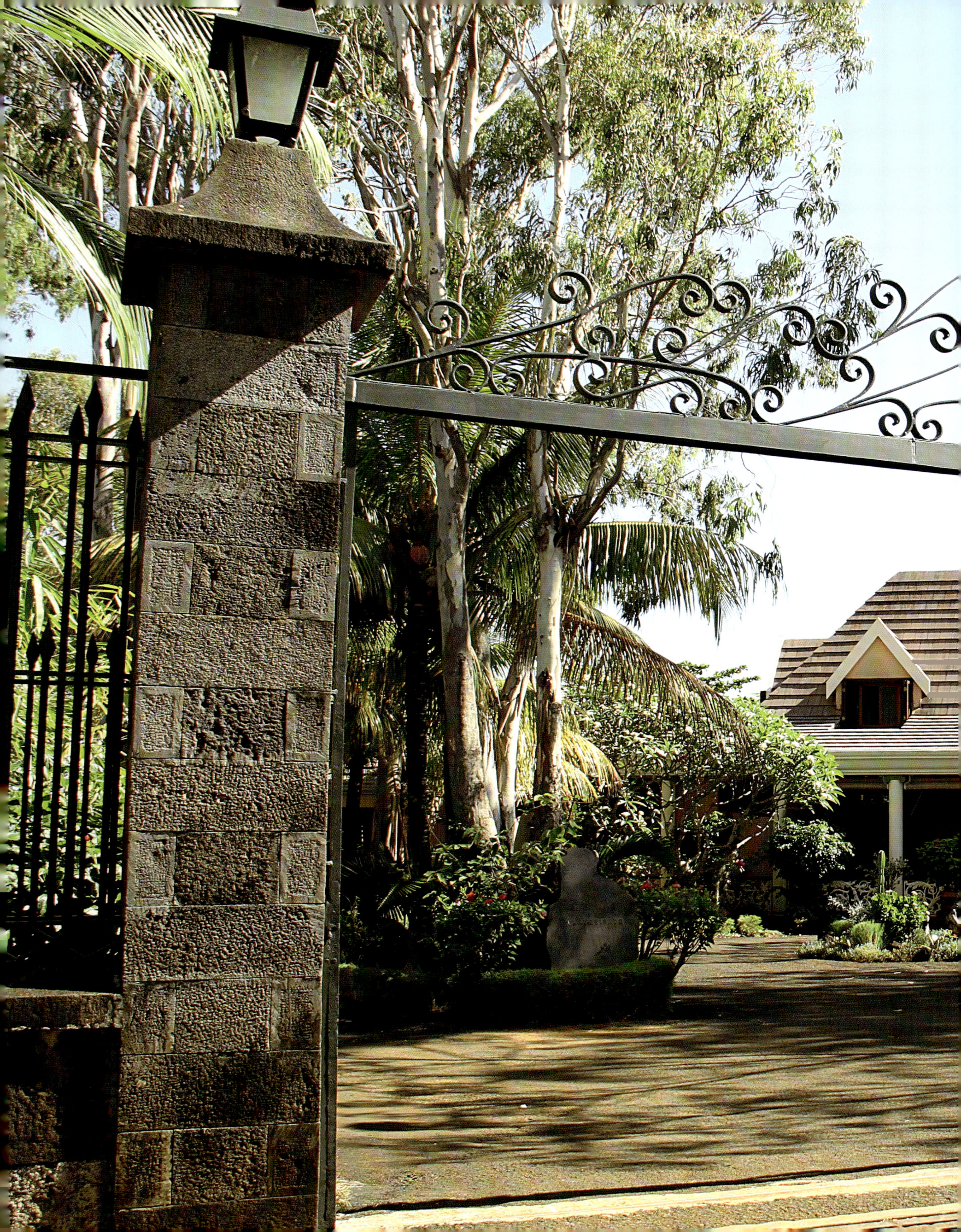

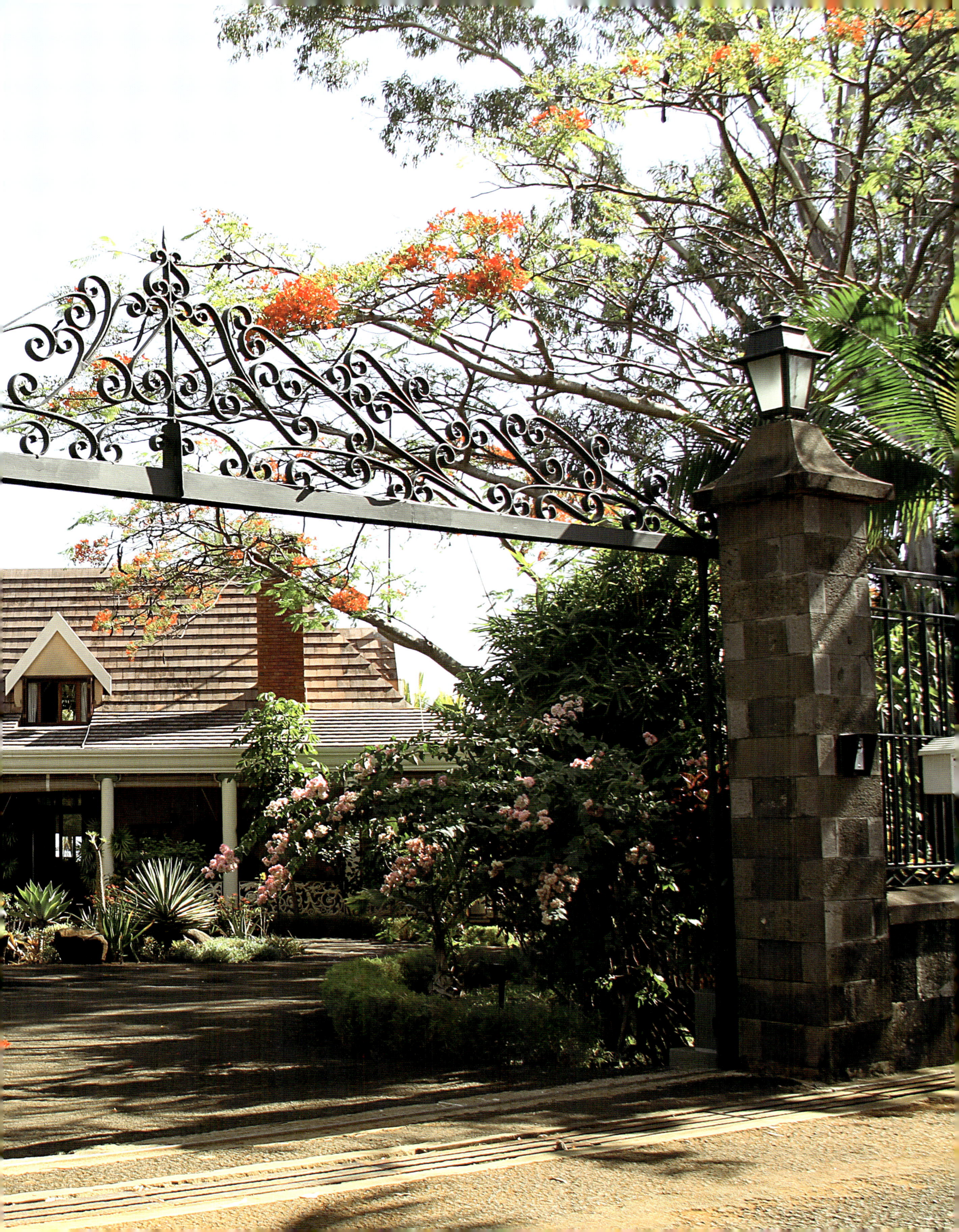

FACADE NORD - VUE DE LA MER

FACADE SUD - VUE DE L'ENTRÉE

PLAN - REZ DE CHAUSSÉE

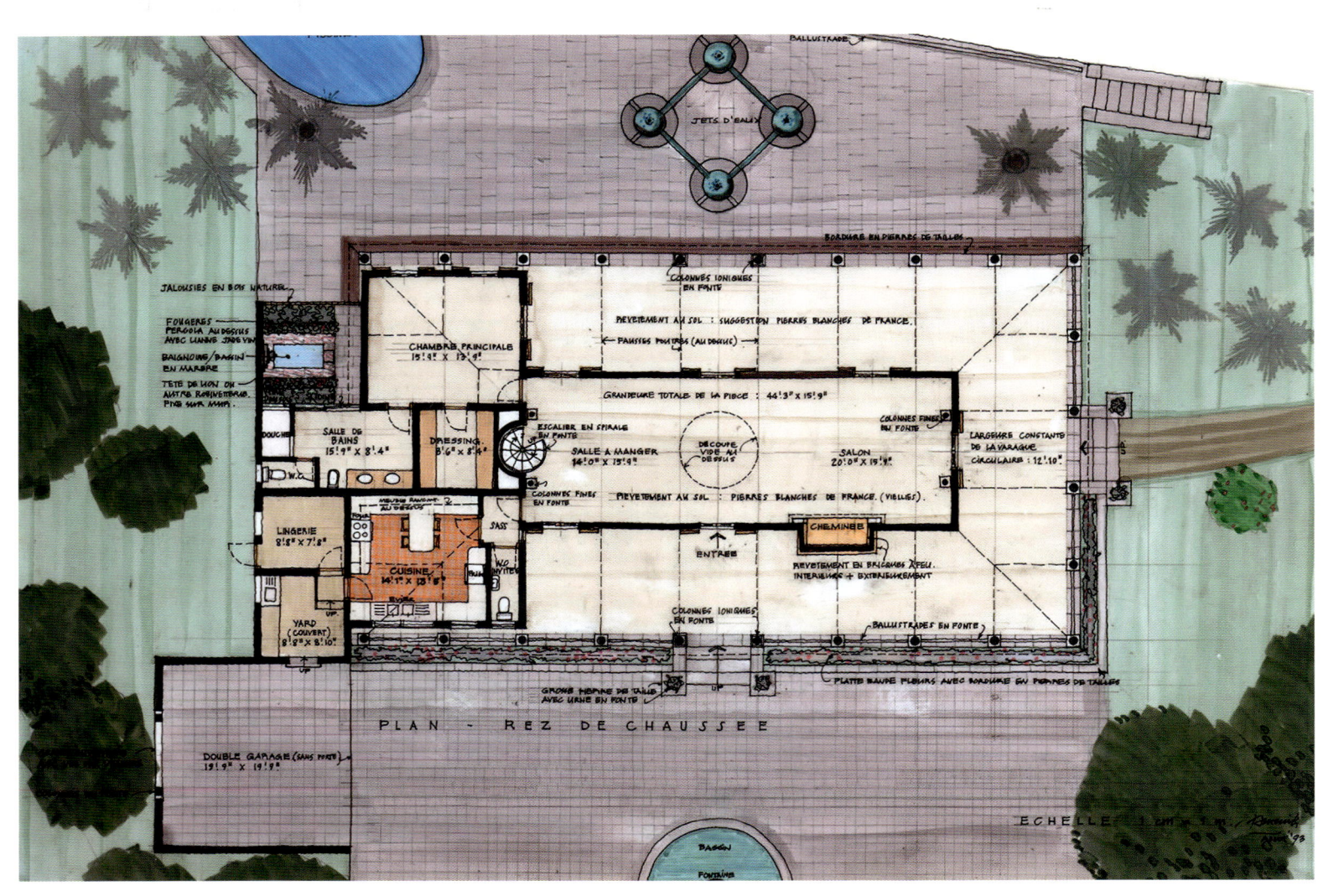

PLAN DE SITUATION

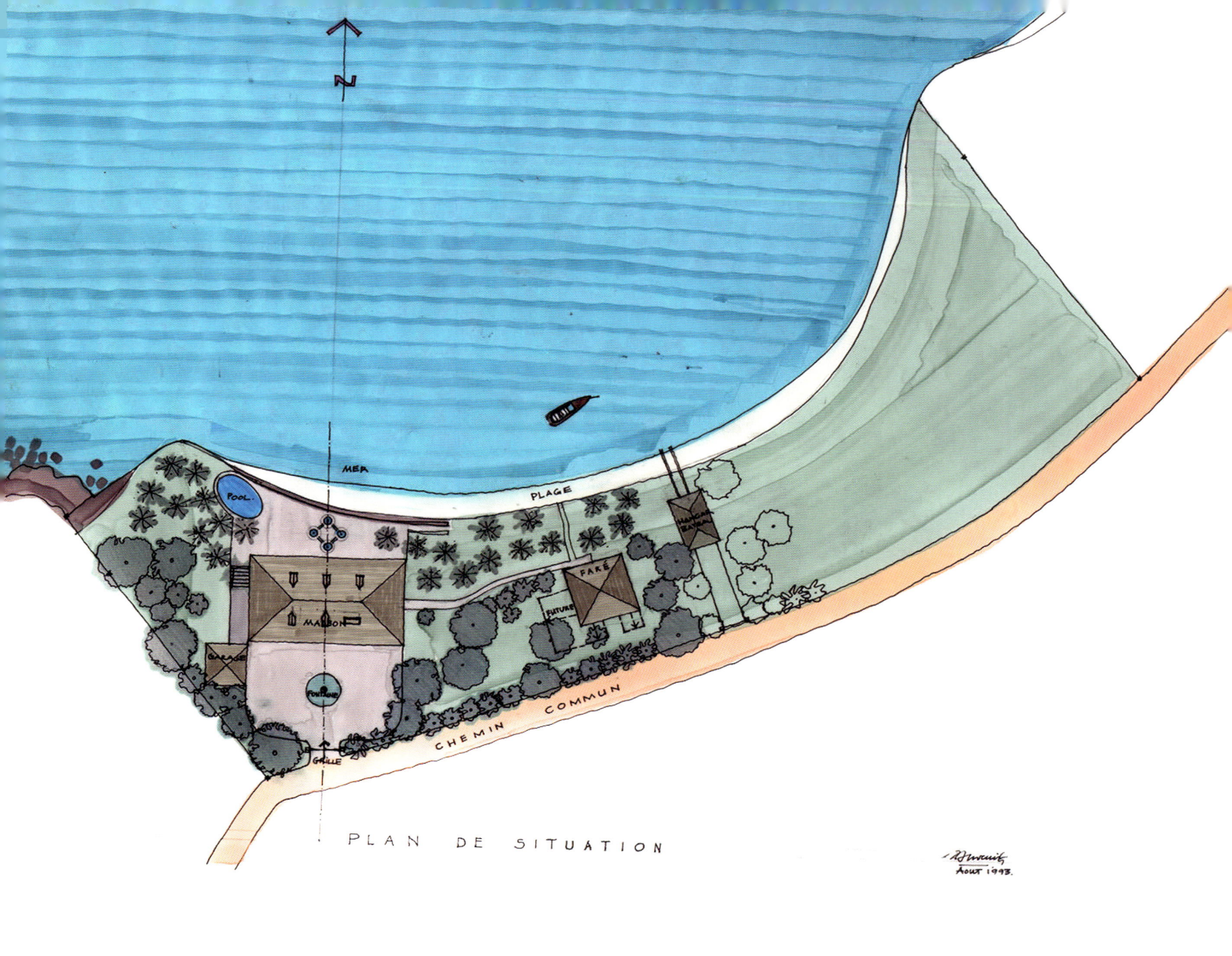

The presentation drawings by Jean-Francois Koenig are technical pen lines in china ink drawn freehand over scaled and ruled clutch pencil lines on tracing paper and background colouring in felt-tip markers.

COUPE TRANSVERSALE

FACADE EST - VUE DU FARE

House at Moka
Mauritius
1989–1991

The house was inserted within an unspoilt forest of trees and dense vegetation like an acupuncture operation leaving as much as possible untouched. Lawned spaces subsequently followed around the footprint of the new building, so opening vistas on the panorama of the mountain range of Moka, a residential neighbourhood on the central plateau of Mauritius.

A deep veranda on three sides and along the full length of the house is given priority of use and area as the primary living space. Facing north towards the sun and turning its back on the south-east trade winds, which are chilly in winter, this externally covered living space opens the house to the outside and extends the inside into the gardens.

Corrugated iron sheeting, as employed on old low-cost traditional buildings in Mauritius, is used as the roof covering. The veranda is an all timber construction built with attention to detail and achieved with simple means with a young local builder willing to embark on uncharted territory. The column bracing necessary in structural timber construction was turned into a work of highly skilled carpentry only found in the finest examples of the older traditional buildings of Mauritius.

Front façade.

Top: The back of the house with the glazed walls of the staircase.

Bottom: The main contractor, Jean-Francois Koenig and the client at a site meeting during the construction of the house.

Right: The veranda.

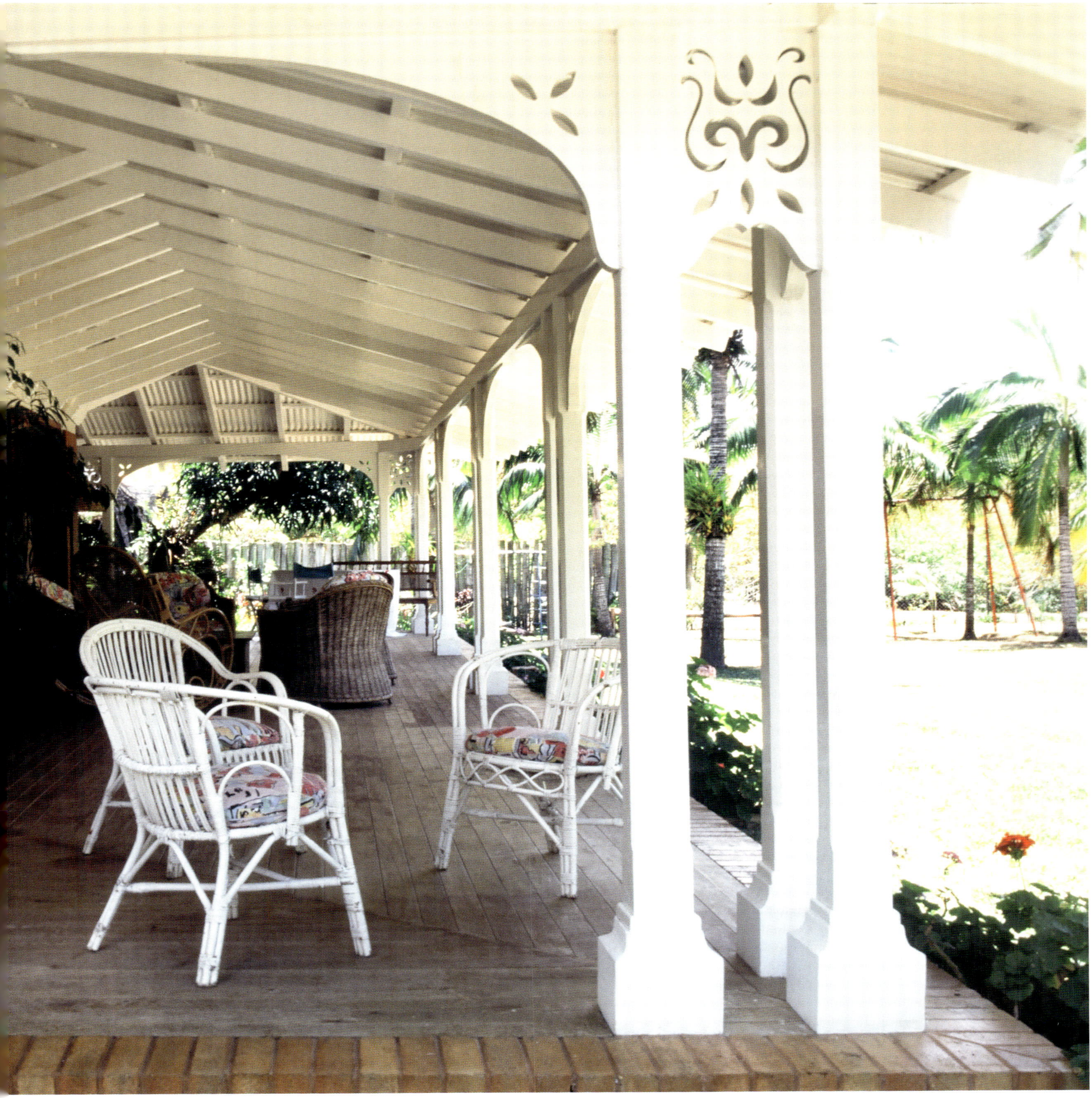

House at Pointe aux Canonniers
Mauritius
1987

Project number one in Mauritius intends to revive the local vernacular architecture. The architecture is a re-interpretation of the twin steeply pitched roof and the 'casquette' low pitched roof over a veranda. An existing garage in stone was converted as part of the house and its sturdiness brings contrast to the more lightweight new structures.

The pencil drawings were drawn on a small bedroom table with an A3 size T-square and set-square on tracing paper.

Presentation drawings in pencil on tracing paper by Jean-Francois Koenig.

Elevation Ouest.

Campement à Pte aux Canniers
1987

Campement à Pte aux Canniers
Elevation Sud.

'84

House at Poste Lafayette
Mauritius
1987–1988

Commission number two addresses the challenges posed by the narrow 12-m wide seaside plot facing the strong seasonal head winds of the east coast of Mauritius. The architectural solution is an elongated courtyard house.

The entrance door is positioned centrally between two windows in a symmetrical one-storey façade across the full width of the site. Upon entry one can see the sea through a series of orchestrated spaces. A central corridor divides the plan into kitchen on one side and bedrooms on the other. It opens on an inner courtyard with a dip pool. It is surrounded by a colonnade walkway reflecting in the pool which contains a coconut tree transplanted in the middle.

Small landscaped courtyards introduced along the perimeter walls under a lightweight pergola create intimate spaces with dappled light.

All pitched roofs in corrugated iron are orientated parallel to the beach. The only two-storey structure faces the sea to act as a high wind shield for the courtyard and living spaces behind. The en-suite master bedroom on the first floor offers prime views of the sea.

The intricate screens in the gable ends were machine-carved out of marine plywood in strict accordance with the drawings and executed under personal supervision. The pencil presentation drawings respond to the delicacy of the traditional architecture of Mauritius.

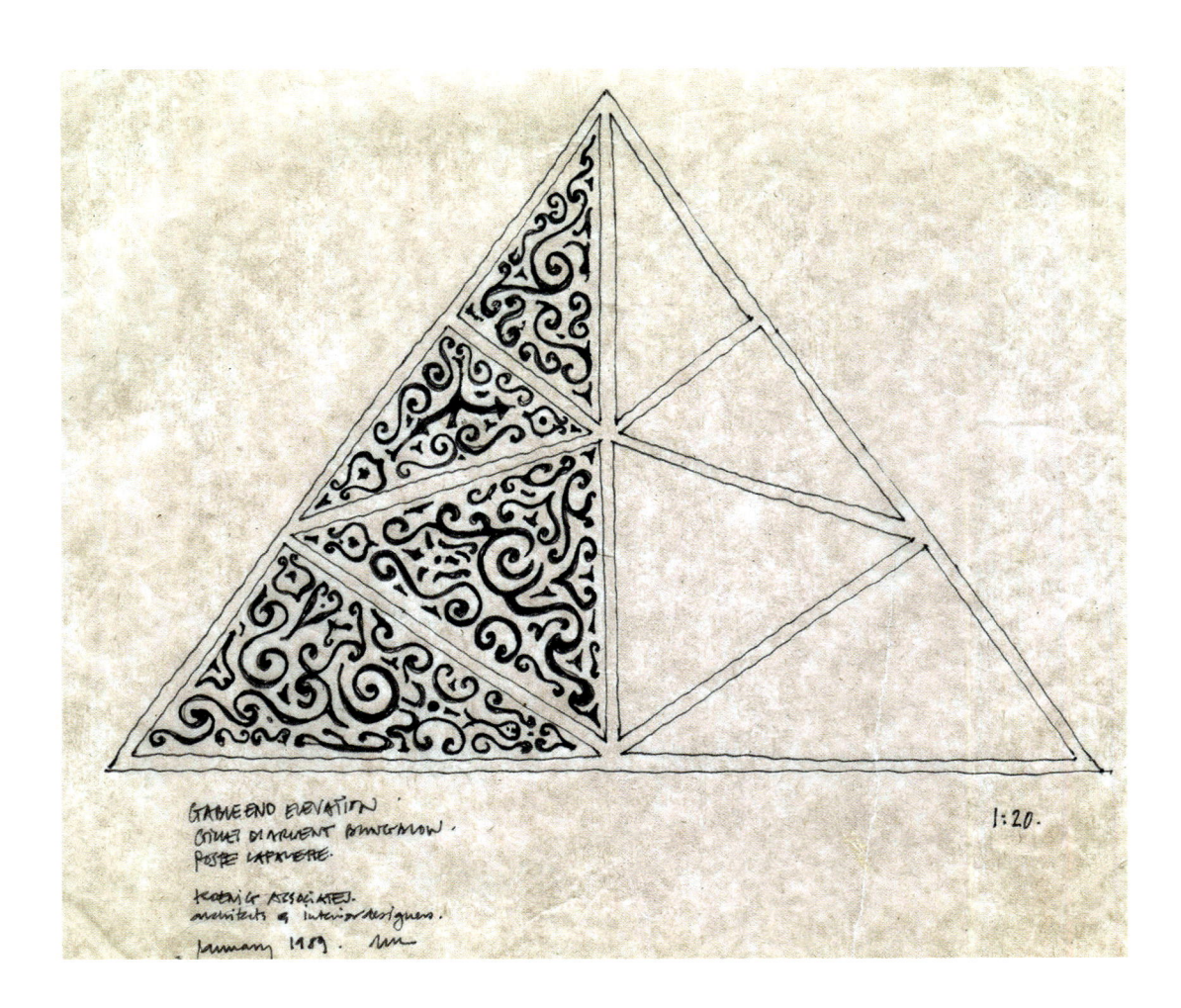

Above: Sketch detail of the gable-end screen. Drawing by Jean-Francois Koenig.

Right: The dining room as a protected veranda. Shadows cast by the gable-end screen. View of the protected planting zone along the boundary wall shaded by a pergola. The courtyard pool surrounded by a covered passage and timber colonnade in the background.

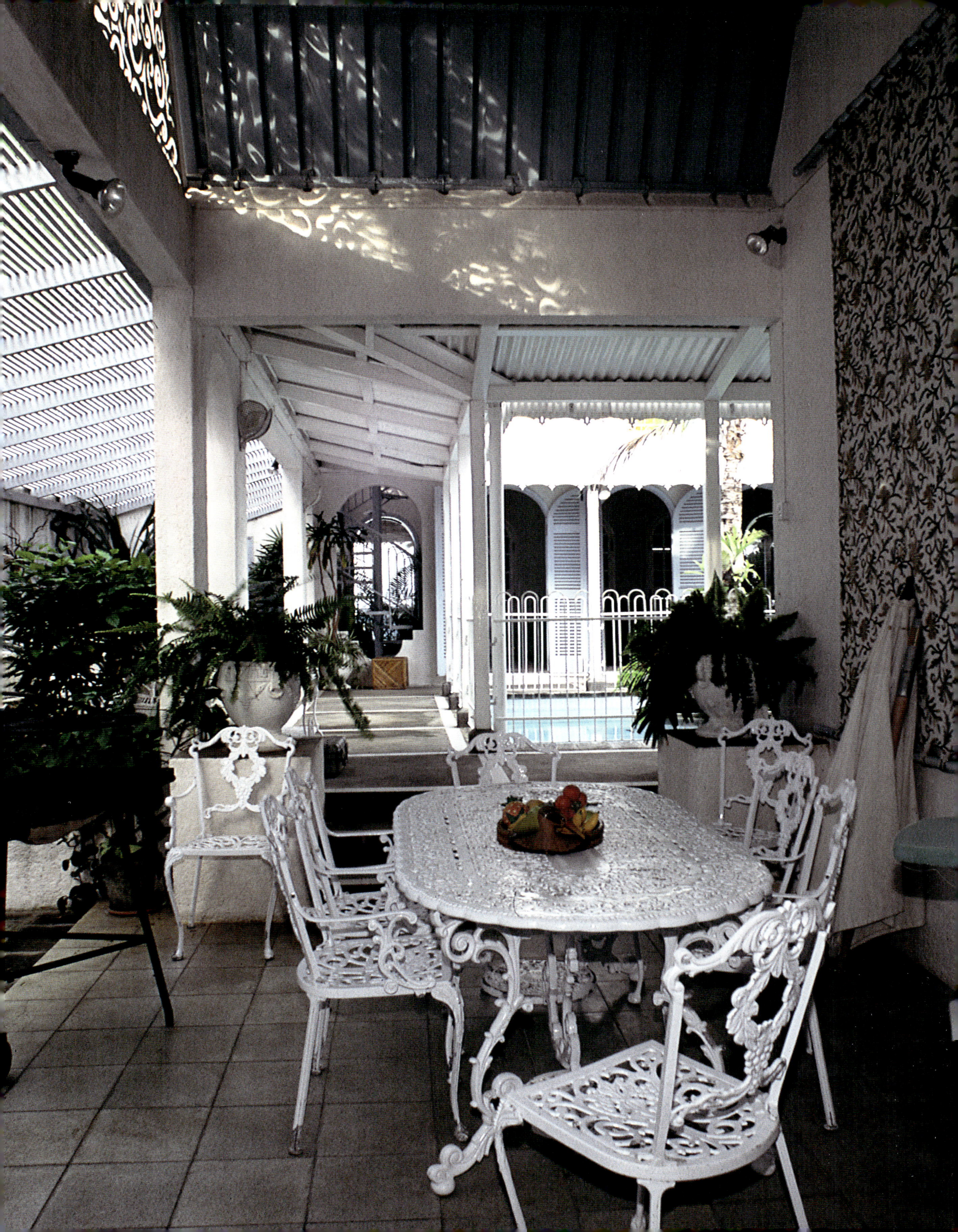

Left: The screen wall of the staircase well.

Right (from top down):
1. Seaside and entrance elevations.
2. Longitudinal section.
3. First-floor Plan.
4. Ground-floor Plan.
Drawings in pencil on tracing paper by Jean-Francois Koenig.

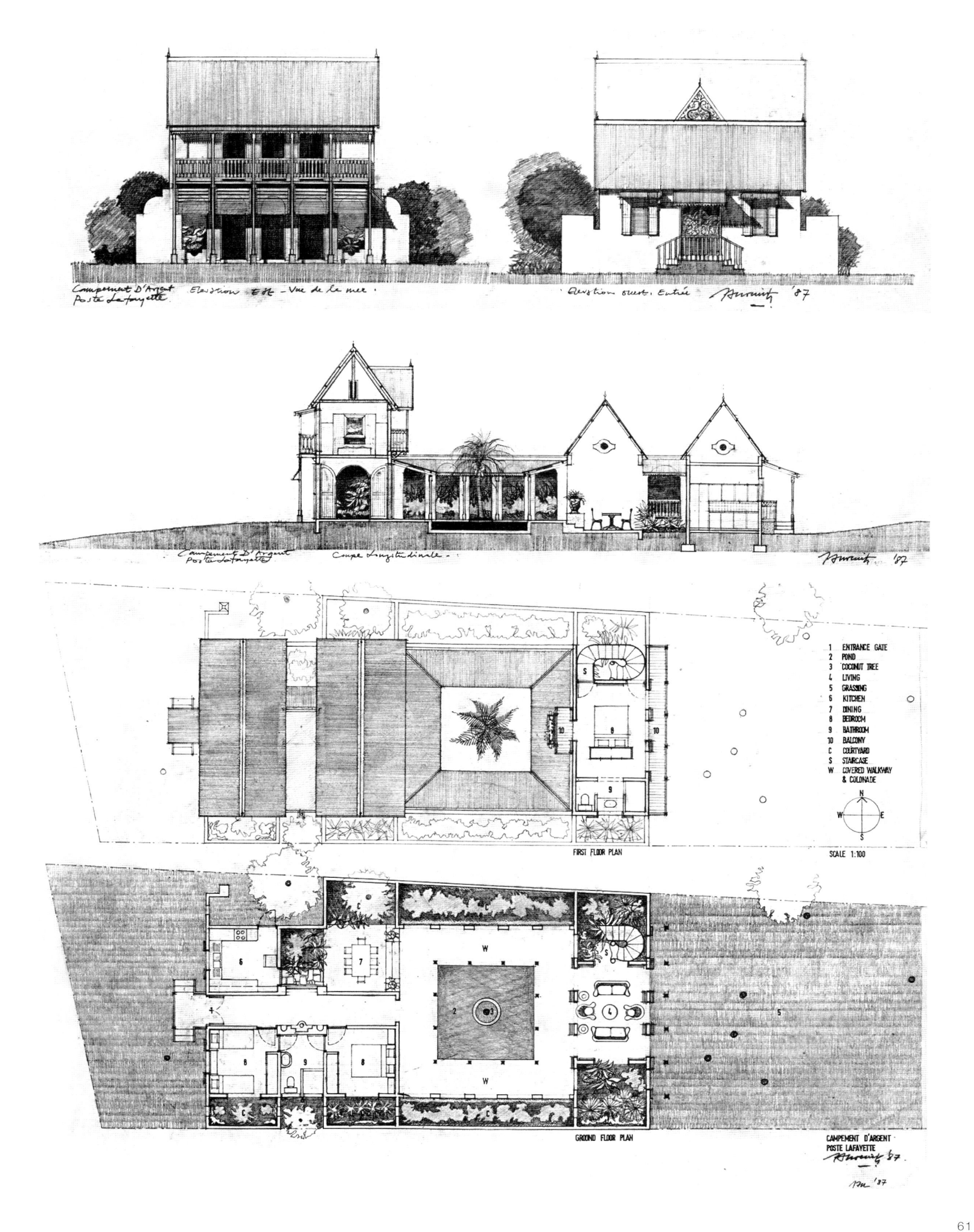

Campement D'Argent, Poste Lafayette — Elevation Est – Vue de la mer.

Élévation ouest. Entrée. '87

Campement D'Argent, Poste Lafayette — Coupe Longitudinale. '87

1	ENTRANCE GATE
2	POND
3	COCONUT TREE
4	LIVING
5	GRASSING
6	KITCHEN
7	DINING
8	BEDROOM
9	BATHROOM
10	BALCONY
C	COURTYARD
S	STAIRCASE
W	COVERED WALKWAY & COLONADE

FIRST FLOOR PLAN
SCALE 1:100

GROUND FLOOR PLAN

CAMPEMENT D'ARGENT
POSTE LAFAYETTE
'87

House at Swan Properties
Pereybere, Mauritius
1987–1988

On plan, the house at Swan Properties is a 10 x 10 m square, divided on one side into three equal parts. The first contains a small bathroom in the middle of two bedrooms. The second is the living-dining and kitchen. And the third is the veranda. Steep corrugated iron roofs are over parts one and two. A slightly sloping 'casquette' roof for part three is over the veranda. All the roofs are insulated with treated and varnished 'ravenal' leaves, a material obtained from the 'ravenal' palm tree which is dried, fumigated, and varnished or painted for protection. They were commonly used in the first seaside bungalows built in Mauritius at the beginning of the 1900s. The architecture is a simple, yet effective re-interpretation in the modern era of the typically modest Mauritian house and underlines the importance of the veranda as the most often used inside–outside living space in the tropics.

The living room.

Top and bottom: The veranda.

House at Grand Baie
Mauritius
1987–1989

Foreseeing the popular seaside village of Grand Baie in the north of Mauritius turning into a densely-populated town, the design was built around an existing tree found on site to create a square courtyard open to the sky. The courtyard protects its occupants from the urban neighbourhood and opens the living areas onto a space of privacy and serenity.

Similar in construction to several early houses, steep corrugated iron roofs are fixed on timber trusses and expressed internally.

The timber post colonnade of the courtyard is raised from the ground on concrete plinths. Typical Mauritian ornamentation of the eaves called 'lambrequins' were hand cut from specification drawings. The gable ends of the garage and veranda roofs are infilled with an ornate screen filtering light that cast intricate shadows on the walls and floors.

When all sliding, folding doors are open, the habitable spaces become like verandas themselves. They provide generous natural cross ventilation and a sense of openness and space around the tree which gives shade.

The Courtyard built around the existing tree.

65

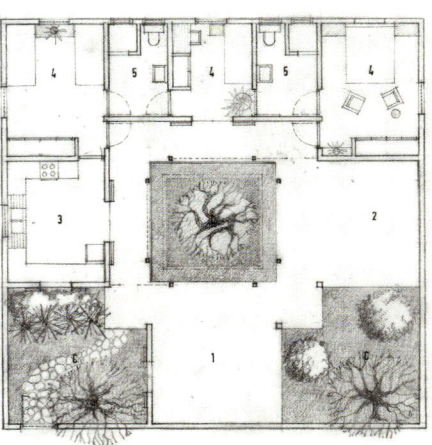

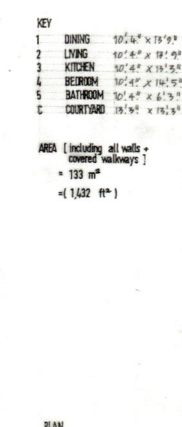

Top: View of the courtyard and the surrounding circulation space.
Above left: 'Raffia' blinds movable screens to internal spaces.
Above right: Plan. Drawing in pencil by Jean-Francois Koenig.
Top and bottom right: Gable-end detail viewed internally and externally.

67

Le Ruisseau Rose
House and Office of Jean-Francois Koenig
Les Mariannes, Mauritius
1990–1995

Le Ruisseau Rose, named after a small river running nearby, is situated in a once virtually unvisited area of Mauritius without telephone lines, on steep slopes offering unparalleled views of the Pieter. Both mountain ranges open, with a 270-degree sweeping view of the landscape, towards the sea and islands beyond.

The construction makes minimal impact on the site by hugging the ground and integrating into the brow of the hill. The land was carved to create platforms retained by walls built in stone recovered from demolished buildings and left with the old paint showing. It was the first time that local basalt stone was used in this way on the Island. A dark grey roof in concrete tiles, like the colour of shadows in the landscape, blends the architecture into its environment.

The house is joined to the office by a covered walkway and colonnade of dusty rose-tinted off shutter concrete columns. Together they form an elongated U-shape embracing the scenery. A 23-m long by 7-m wide black reflective pool containing three stones and one frangipani tree, is a re-interpretation of the Japanese garden on water.

Coming from the road through a simple gate and following a 60-m long driveway, which sinks to the parking level, a low-lying carport roof that serves as the office and house entrances, greet the visitor. A tiled concrete roof spanning 7.5 m rests on a beam in rose-tinted bush hammered concrete supported at one end by a pair of cast-iron columns, left rusty. They were bought from a demolished building. A timber lattice screen window under two stone lintels and corresponding stone sills, supported by a pair of off-white marble columns, punctuates the back wall.

The arrival is on an upper level above the office roof and the house remains invisible. It is discovered after walking through a simple teak door opening onto a Japanese garden made of finely crushed coral and carefully chosen basalt field boulders. Following the walkway of rose-tinted off shutter concrete columns along the Japanese garden, a staircase leads down to a pair of Chinese moon gates in rose-tinted off shutter concrete with views, over the reflective pool, of the mountains on the horizon. Only then is the house and office discovered.

Right: View of the reflective pool and office from the house.

Pages 70/71: Views of the mountains from the house.

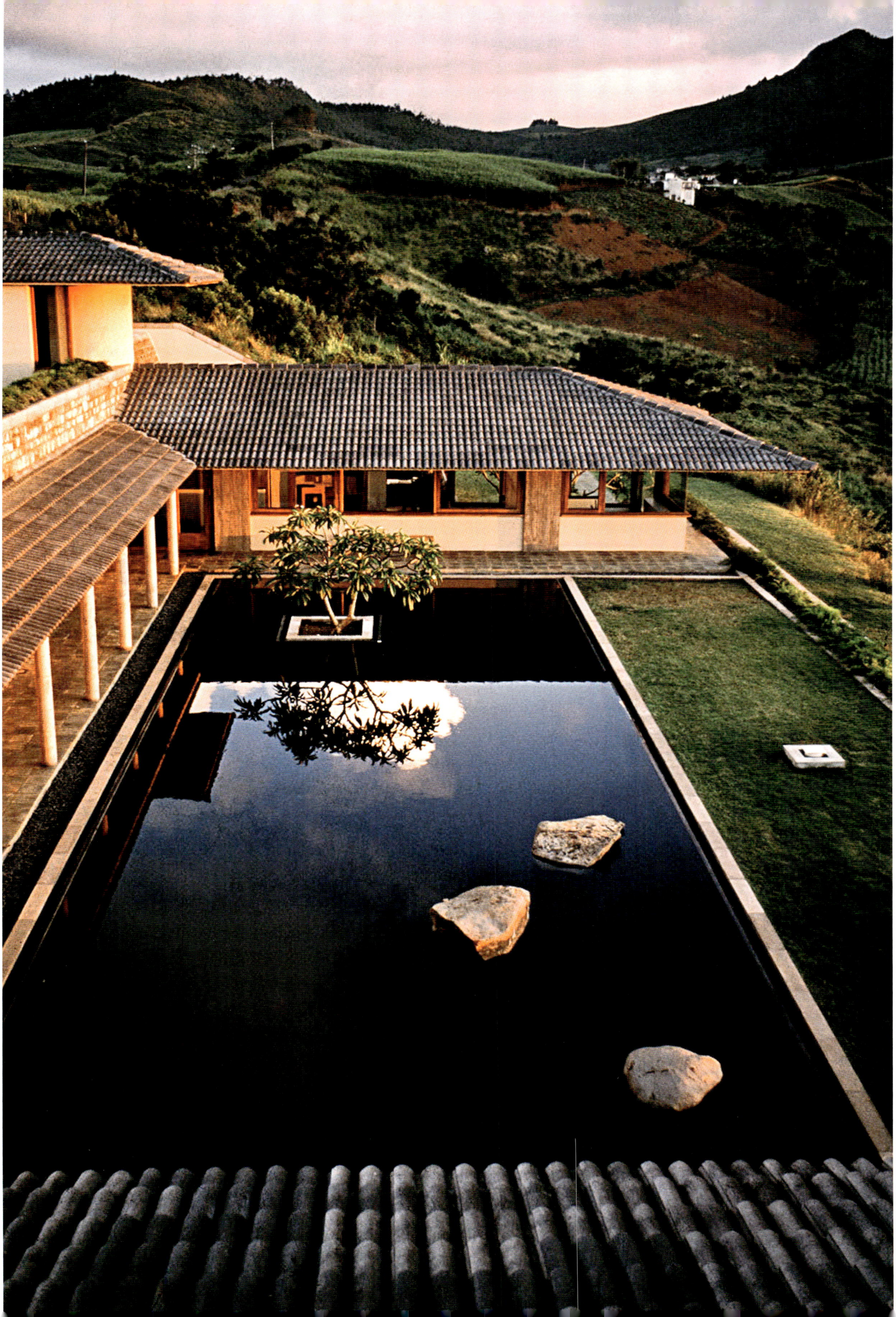

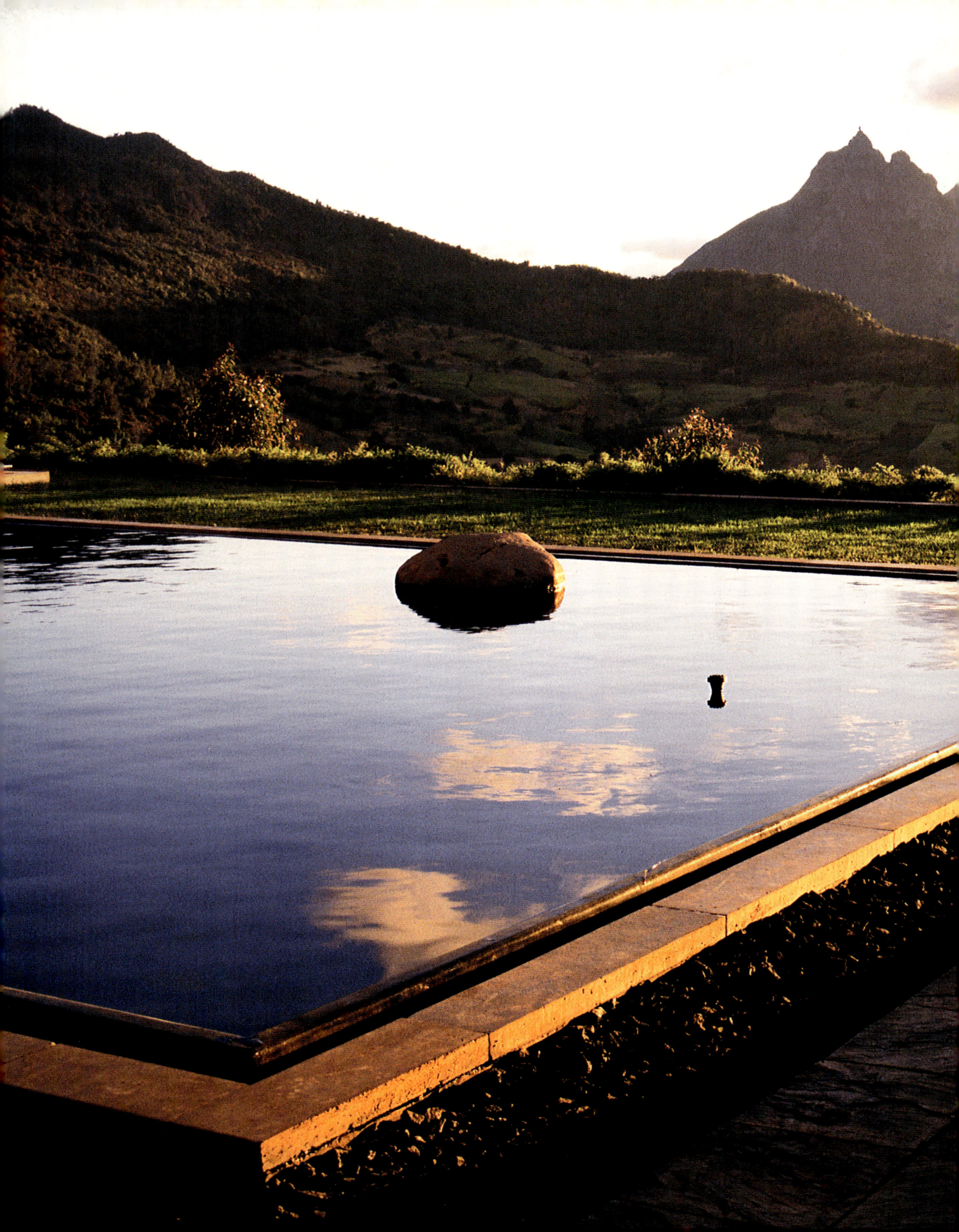

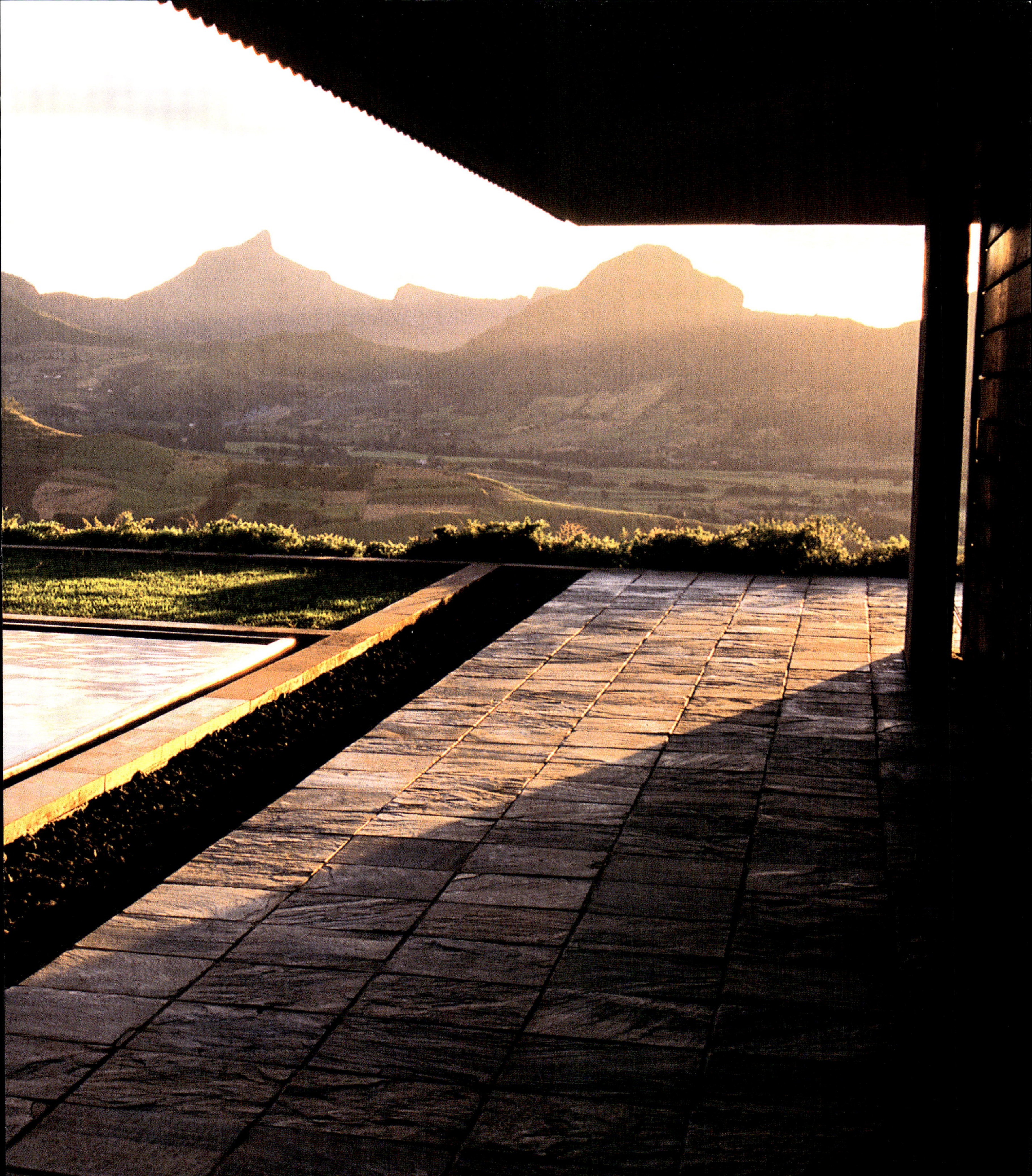

Tinted off shutter concrete colonnade, pool surround, and copings. The retaining wall is built from stones recovered from a demolished building which were originally painted and are left in their weathered state.

Top: View of the top entrance carport, offices, colonnade, and reflective pool, seen from the house.
Bottom: View of the entrance carport and the Japanese garden on the upper level, and the reflective pool and its frangipani tree on the lower level.

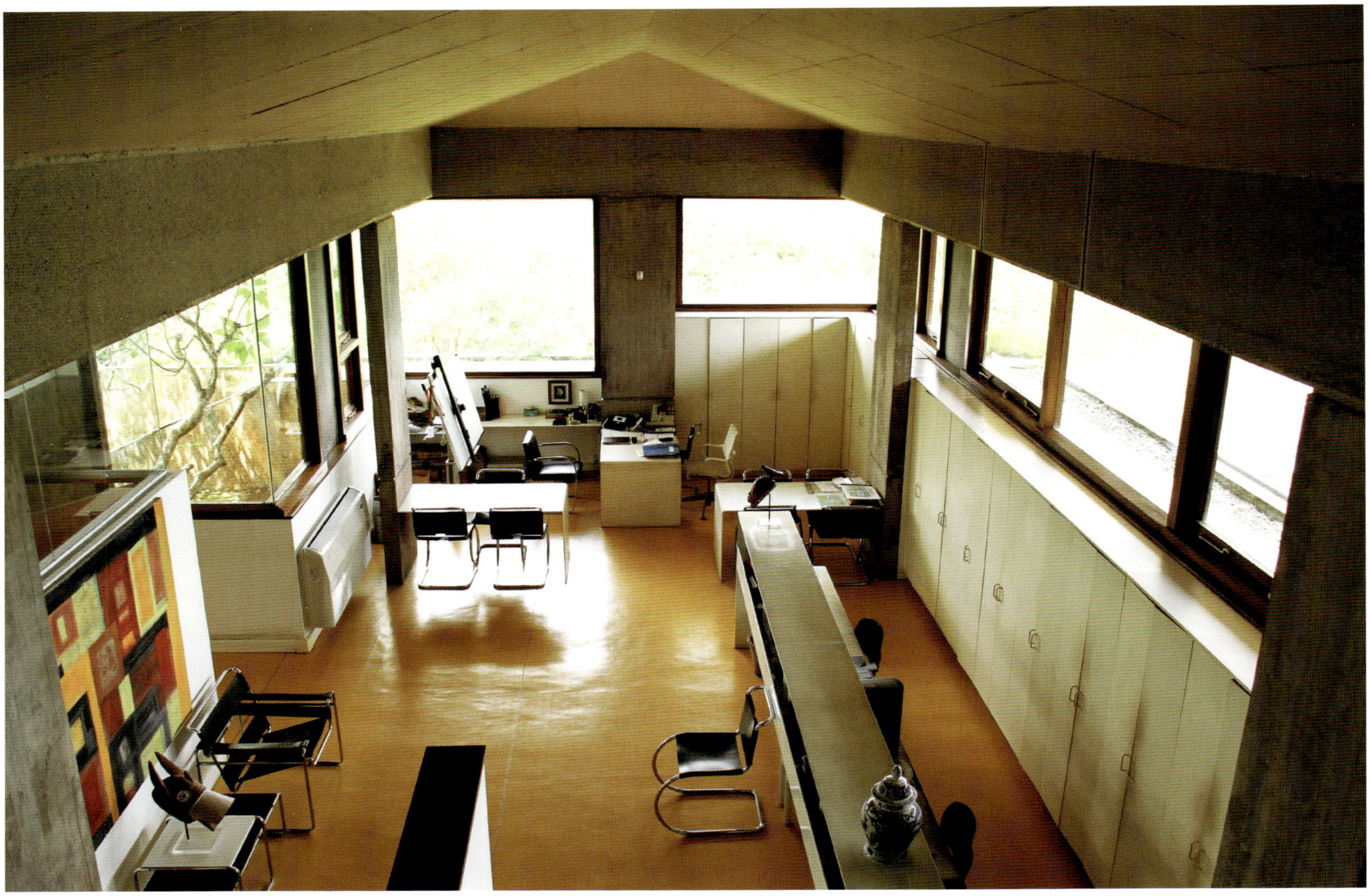

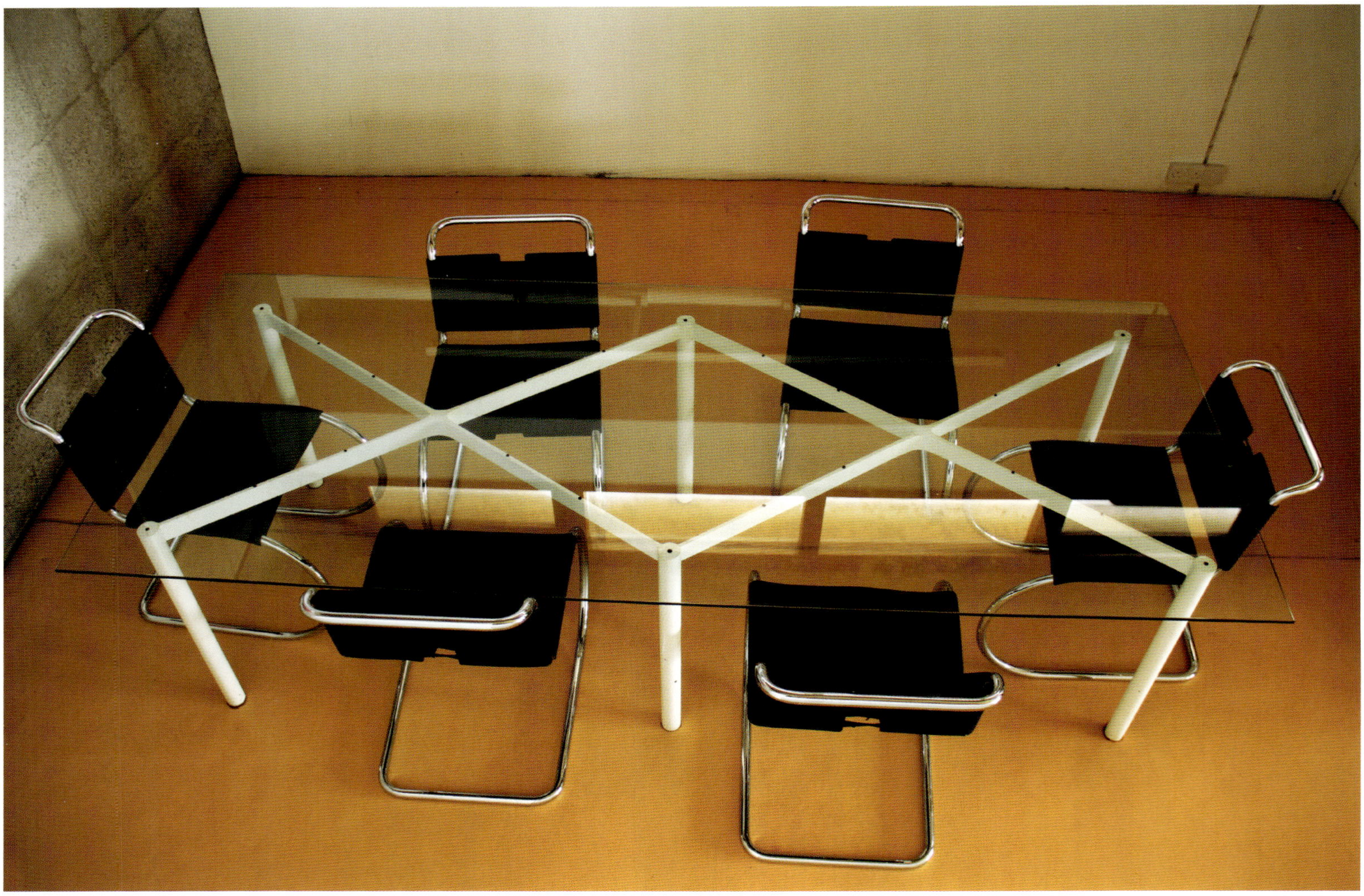

Top: External view of the office wing.

Right: Carport window timber lattice screen. Hand cut basalt stone lintels and sills recovered from a demolished building supported by white marble columns recovered from a disused church altar.

Top left: Office interior with steel tables and tinted off shutter concrete double columns and beams.

Bottom left: Yellow acoustic vinyl floor and steel and glass conference room table designed by Jean-Francois Koenig.

The house is a 12 x 12 m square plan with a pyramidal roof, culminating in a tinted glass pyramidal roof light. The façades, exactly similar on three sides, are the expression of the structure. Their elevations comprise two sets of twin 80 x 15 cm columns, 60 cm apart in rose-tinted off shutter concrete, at 6-m centres giving a balanced cantilever of 3 m at both ends. Thus, the corners are column free, and the addition of 2-m cantilevered overhangs results in 5-m floating roof corners. When the sliding cyclone doors are open, the internal spaces open to the outside dispensing with the traditional veranda. The house itself transforms into a veranda.

A dark green slate floor runs throughout, internally and externally, and the absence of a weather step on the threshold of the doors heightens the sense of the outside coming in and the inside going out.

All external timber is teak and iroko and internally oak and ash. All the furniture is modern classics and no distinction is made in the interior design between different spaces with different functions.

The project has weathered with dignity acquiring a patina which comes from the craftsmanship of good building construction and the ability to join materials together with good detailing. The large protective overhang is a key element in the protection against the elements in the moisture-laden atmosphere of the tropics.

View of the Pieter Both and Le Pouce mountains from the corner window of Jean-Francois Koenig's desk.

Top: Carport roof supported by twin cast-iron columns left rusty.
Bottom: The carport and timber screen window seen from the Japanese garden with local basalt field boulders and crushed coral.

Top: 5-m cantilevered corners of the house with tinted off shutter concrete double columns and timber sliding door shutters.
Bottom: House entrance with double Chinese moon gates in tinted off shutter concrete.

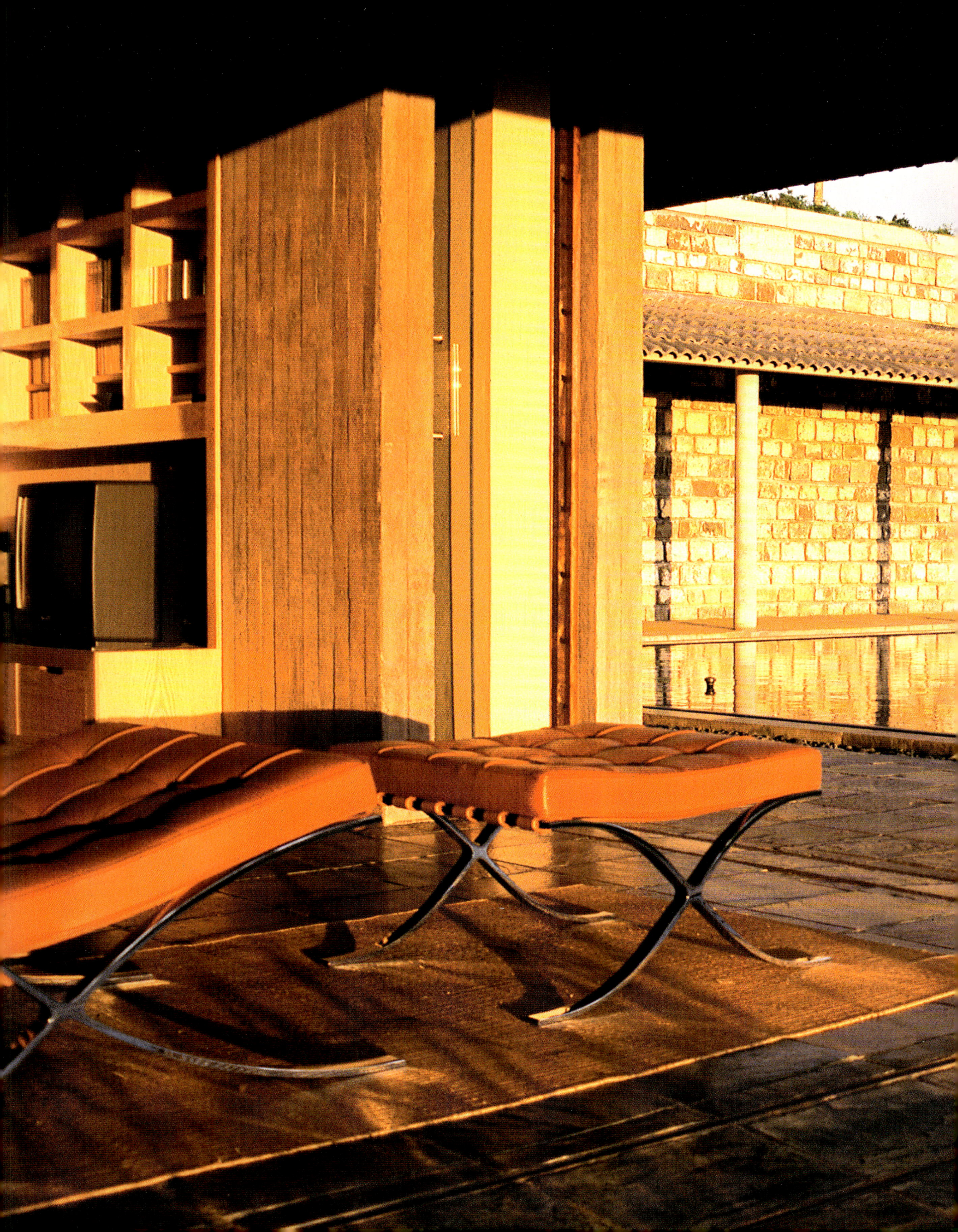

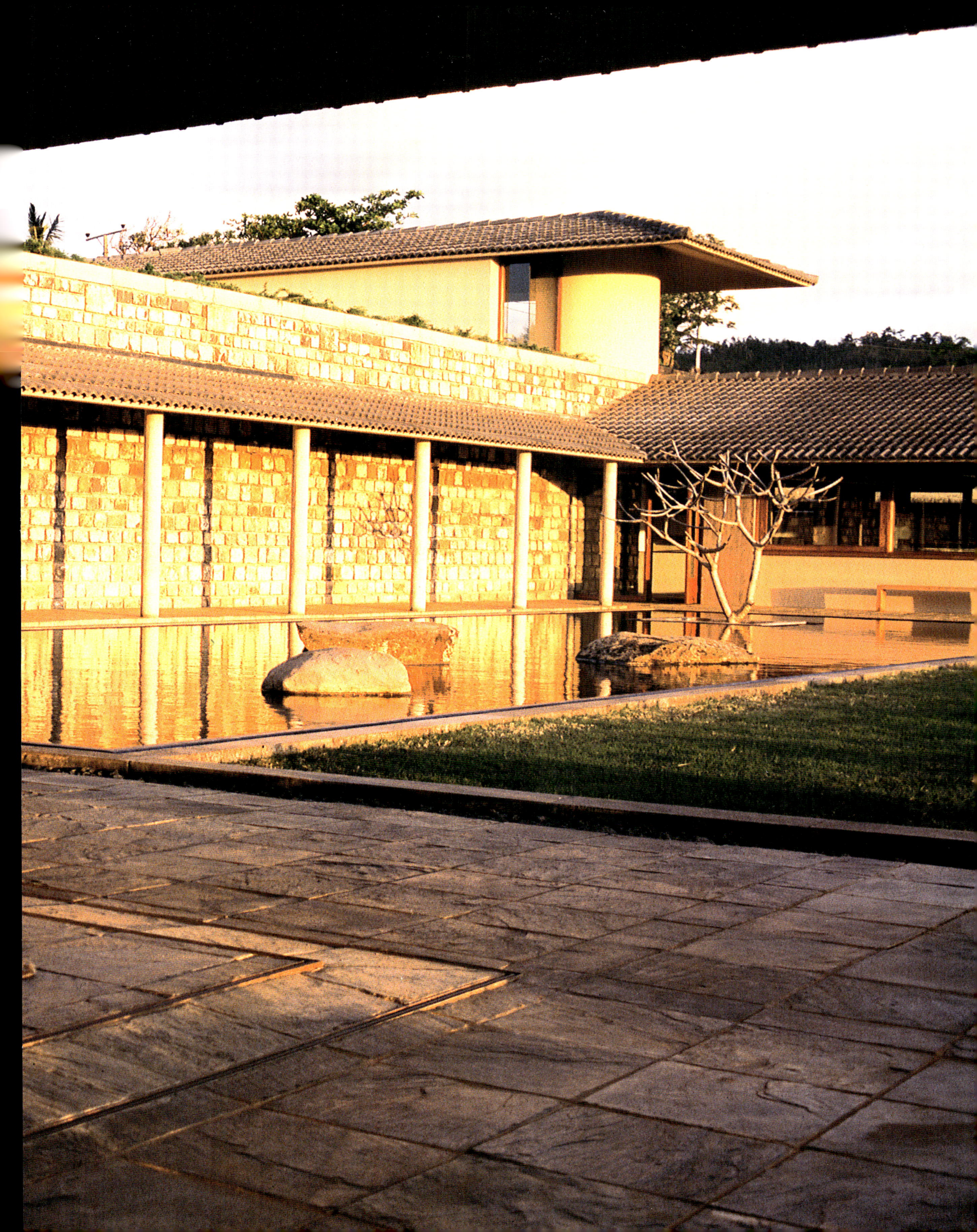

Above: House living room.
Pages 80/81: View from the library of the reflective pool and colonnade.

Top: House living room.
Bottom: House living room. The paintings are by Jean-Francois Koenig.

Two Houses at Roches Noires
Mauritius
1992–1997

Roches Noires is a seaside residential village on the east coast of Mauritius where two villas were built side by side.

The first house is square on plan with a central courtyard open to the sky through which all spaces are cross ventilated. It becomes the central focus of the house and contains a shallow reflective pool designed to cool. A covered, external walkway connecting all parts of the house surrounds the inner courtyard. Its timber shingled roof rests on circular tinted off shutter concrete columns cast flush in galvanised steel (top and bottom) structural shoes left unpainted. The space aims to provide an atmosphere of serenity within a pavilion structure.

The plan is separated down the middle with bedroom quarters on one side and living zones on the other. On the left-hand side are two guest rooms and a master suite. Its bathroom leads onto an external shower set in a private tropical garden and a large walk-in shower has an open entrance defined by a pair of beige marble Assyrian sculptures. The washstand basin is a single piece of tinted off shutter precast concrete with incorporated sleeves for taps and drains built to architectural specifications.

Designed with attention to detail a mix of old and new materials highlight their contrast but are in harmony with each other. The hand cut stone lintel of the living room 'passe-plat' window is recovered from a demolished building. The lintels and beams in bush hammered tinted off shutter concrete are built into smooth beige walls. Old cast-iron columns, which were recovered from a demolished building and left unpainted and rusty, support the concrete beam of the veranda and frame the view to the sea. A generously sized veranda serves as the connection space between the house and the garden. The house is well set back from the sea to leave space for a coconut tree plantation in a manicured lawn that gently leads to a white sandy beach.

House 1: The Courtyard with cooling pond and tinted off shutter concrete columns cast flush in galvanised steel shoes and top brackets.

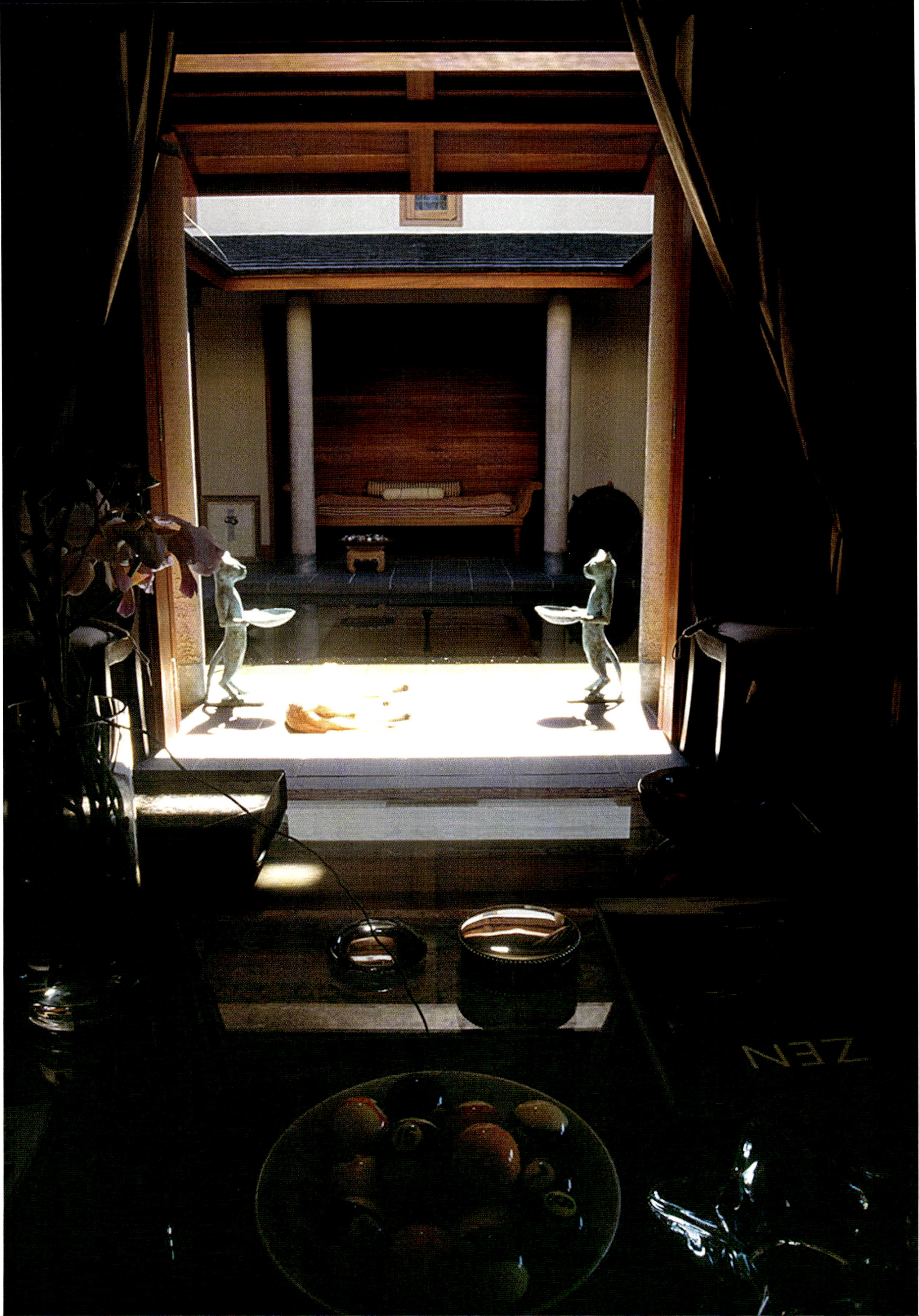
ZEN

*Top: The living room. Bottom: The veranda.
Left: The Courtyard seen from the living room.*

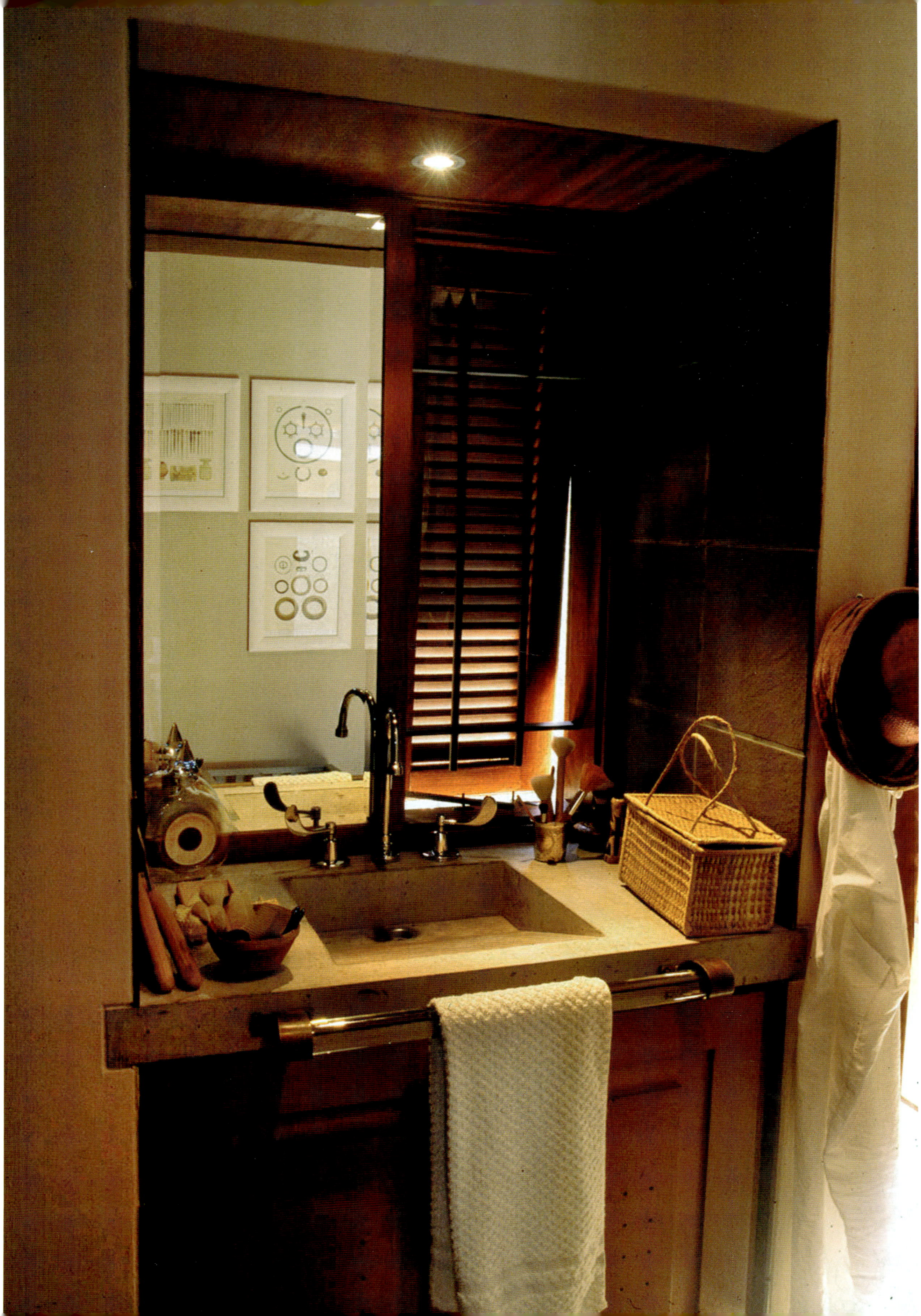

Above: Walk-in shower with a pair of marble Assyrian sculptures on an off shutter concrete base to mark the entrance.

Left: Alcove for the wash-hand basin in tinted off-shutter concrete.

Teak loungers in front of the veranda with 'raffia' blinds.

Top: Sea-facing façade. The veranda on the left. On the right, the door of the master bedroom and the windows of the walk-in shower in front of the newly planted coconut palm trees on the lawn. Bottom: The cultivated coconut grove.

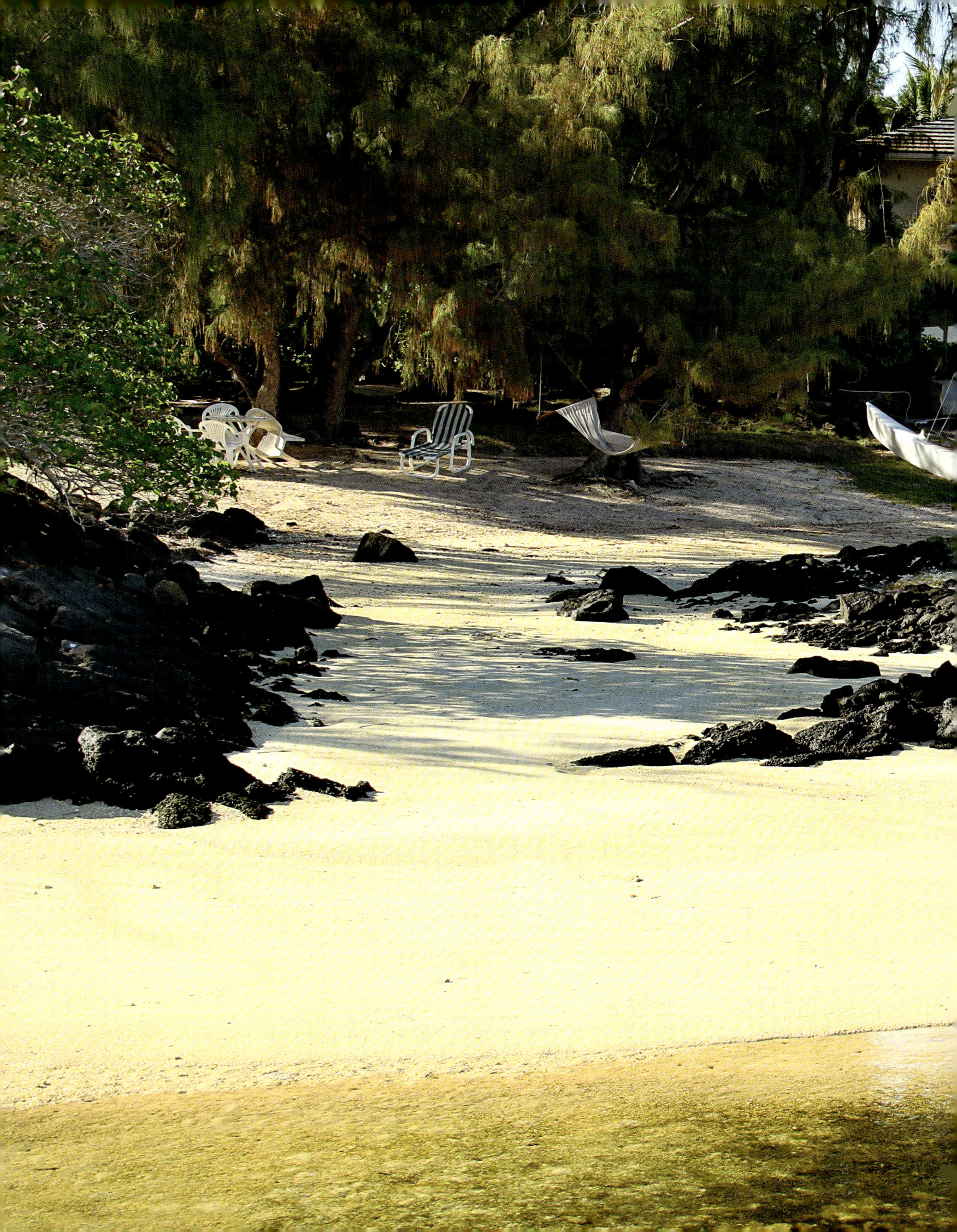

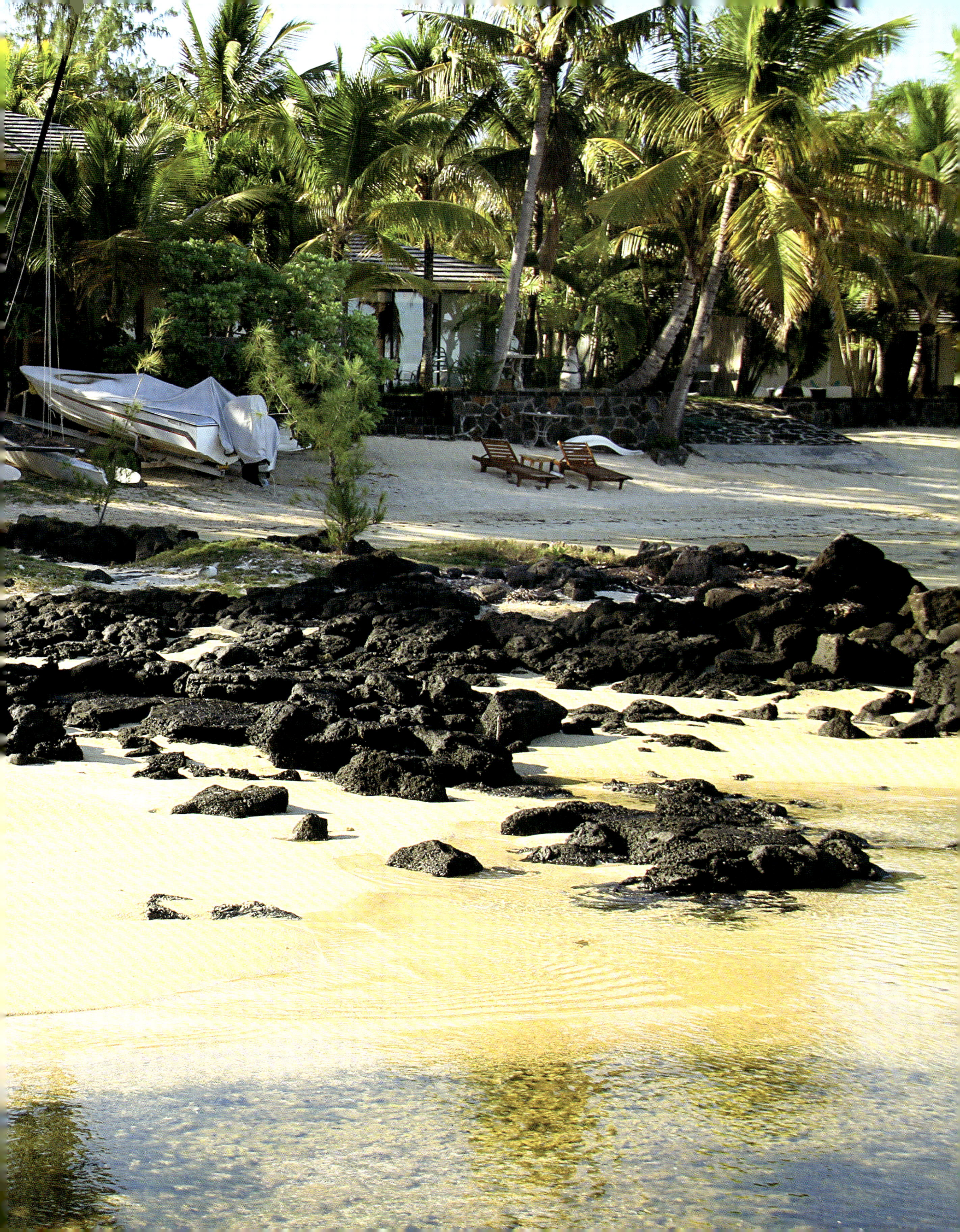

The second house is nestled in the landscape amidst existing coconut trees without intruding on the coastline. It is situated at the end of the sandy beach and at the beginning of Pointe Roches Noires, a position on the coast where the lagoon ends with black volcanic rocks from which the place takes its name.

The entrance is from a lush tropical garden where cars are absent. A spacious double volume entrance hall with a staircase of steps cantilevered from the wall leads to the first-floor master bedroom. All the wood used for the house is teak. A three-step change in level marks the transition between the entrance hall and the living areas. The dining room with large windows facing the sea is niched in a lower corner of the space under an all-encompassing sloping roof.

In keeping with traditional Mauritian architecture, the veranda acts as the transition space between inside and outside offering splendid vistas onto the white sandy beach, the black rocks, and the emerald lagoon.

Above: The main living space seen from the veranda with louvred shutters in teak.

Previous pages: House 2 set on the beach and integrated into the landscape.

Top: The entrance arrival walkway.
Bottom: The veranda with dining table and lounge.
Top right: The main living and dining room.
Bottom right: The entrance and staircase to the master bedroom. All the timber is teak.

Overleaf: View of the lagoon from the external breakfast and lunch table.

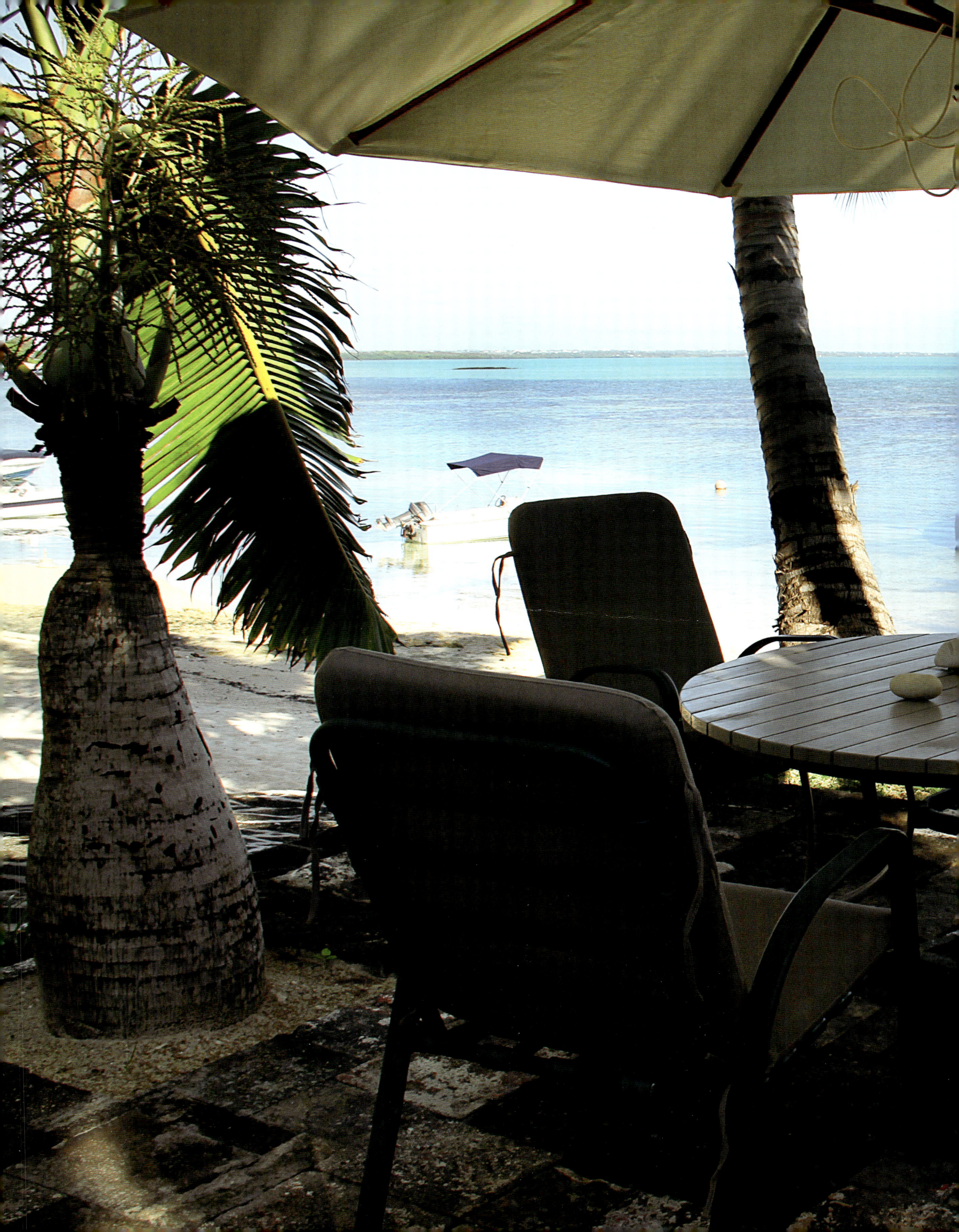

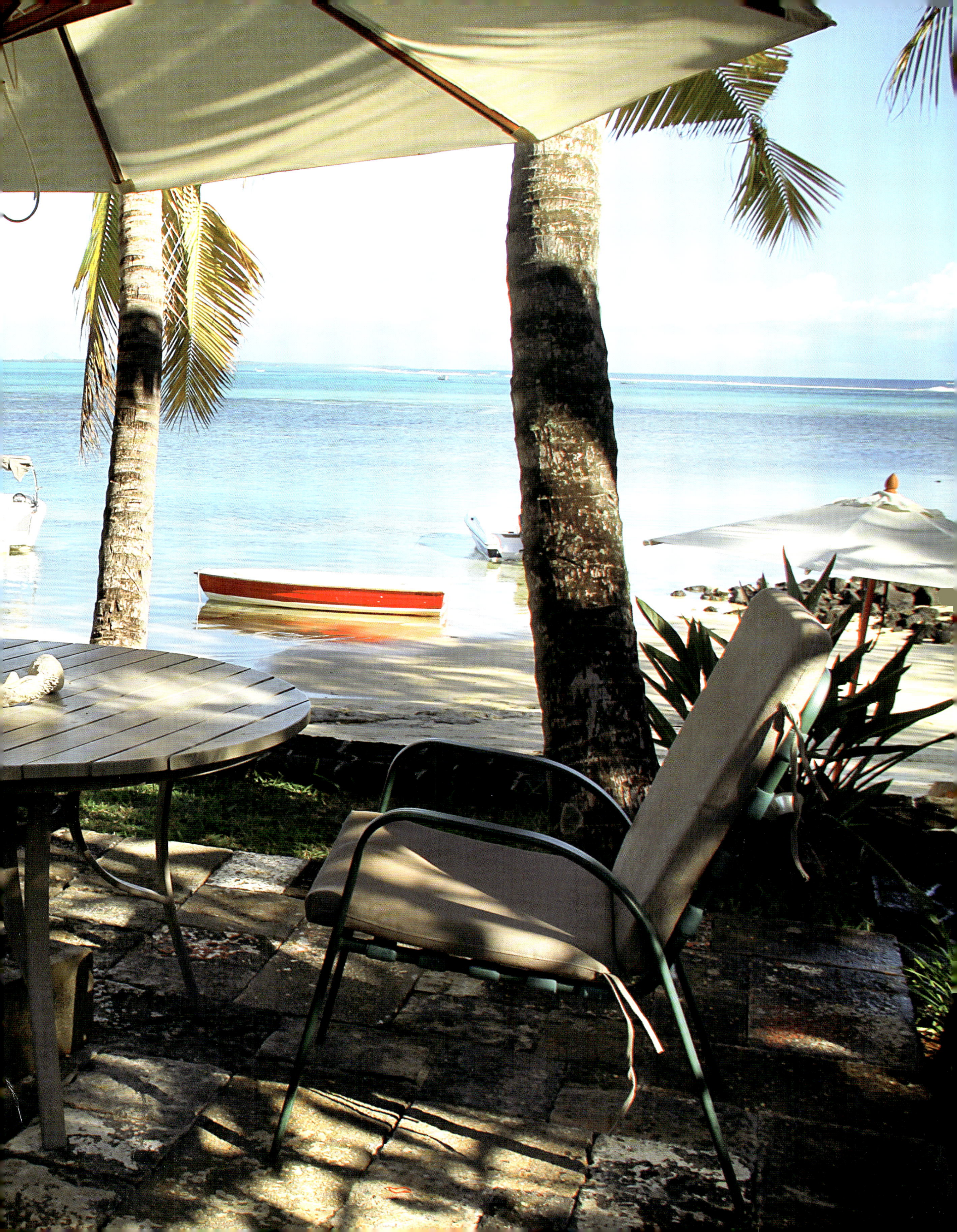

Apartments at Pointe d'Esny
Mauritius
1998–1999

This beachfront site in Pointe d'Esny on the south-east beachfront of Mauritius is unspoilt, wild, and wind-battered by the south-east trade winds. The brief to design four individual apartments raised concern that a new building of that size, where all four apartments required sea frontage, would dominate and impact the coastline's appearance which had not been densely developed, and certainly not with apartments, since the beginning of bungalow construction on the coast of Mauritius at the turn of the last century.

The resulting solution transforms four double storey apartments into what looks like two single storey houses. The down-scaling is achieved by A-framed gable roofs which incorporate within their height the bedrooms on the first floor. At the opposite end, used as the entrance to the apartments, steep roofs also scale down the building. They are sloped over double volume verandas that cross ventilate the bedrooms above which there are balcony doors looking down on the space.

This project was not built on a high budget. Cement screed floors, off shutter concrete, basalt stones obtained from the de-rocking of agricultural land, old hand cut stones recovered from demolished buildings used for the steps of the internal staircase and garden retaining wall, thatch made from dried sugar cane leaves after the yearly harvest, and treated pine poles used as structural timber left unpainted are the sustainable materials employed in creating a building requiring minimal maintenance. It weathers naturally to blend into the landscape of the windy coastline. The apartments are well recessed behind the existing tree line and, seen from the sea, integrate seamlessly with the surrounding vegetation resulting in successful design intent. At a later stage the thatch was replaced with natural timber shingles retaining the weathered appearance.

The first-floor veranda A-frame windows of each apartment seen from the beach. The timber roof shingles and timber structures and balustrades are left unpainted so as to weather naturally in harmony with its environment.

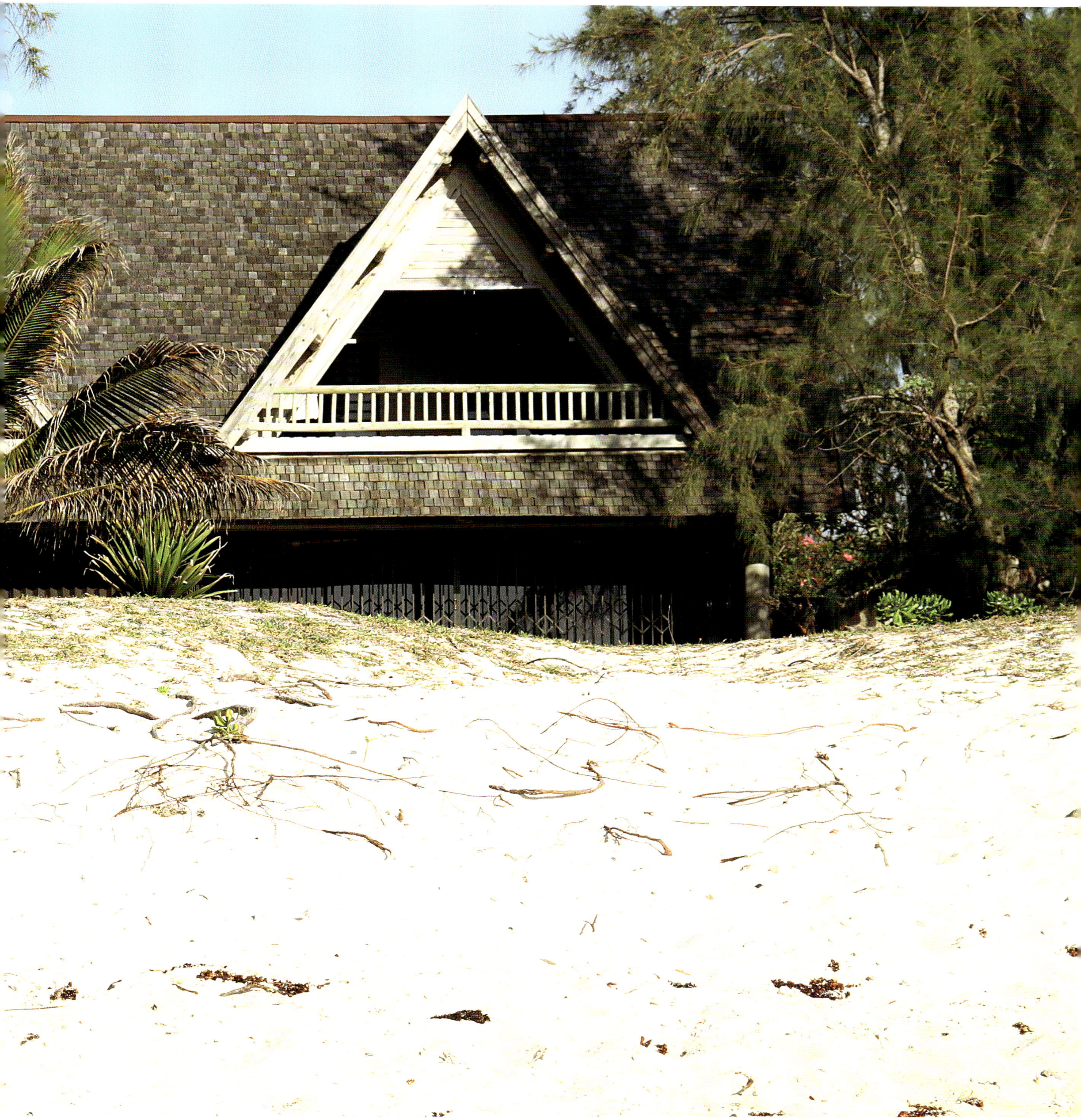

102

Top left: Sea-facing façade.

Bottom left: Back façade. The double storey apartments are made to appear as single storey houses.

Top right: The double volume back entrance veranda seen from the bedroom balcony doors above.

Bottom right: The living-dining room on ground floor seen from the open kitchen. The stairs on the right are in hand cut basalt stones recovered from a demolished building. The balustrades are treated pine poles, the floor is concrete screed, the beams and columns are bush-hammered concrete and tinted off shutter concrete.

Sables d'Or

Beau Vallon Beach, Mahé, Seychelles
2006–2013

Sables d'Or is four short stay apartments on two levels and a fifth apartment on three floors designed for the owners. They face the turquoise seas and give onto the beach of Beau Vallon, well known as one of the best swimming spots of the main island of Mahé in the Seychelles. As opposed to the usual balcony, each apartment has a proper veranda, the most comfortable place to live in the tropics. The pencil drawings on the following pages show the planning of the spaces with their furniture.

Above: Sea-facing and back elevations. Pencil drawings by Jean-Francois Koenig.
Right: View of the apartments from the sea.

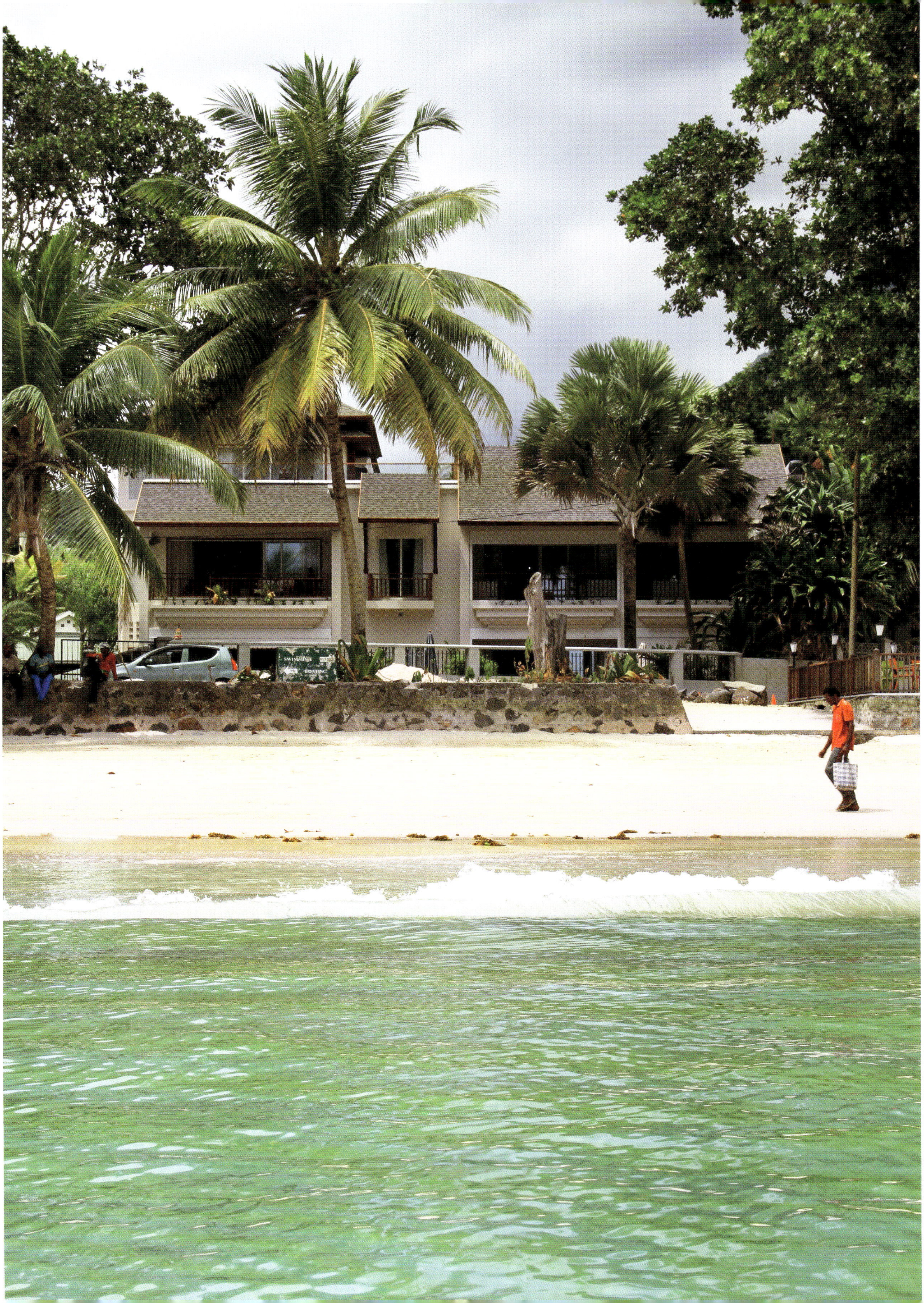

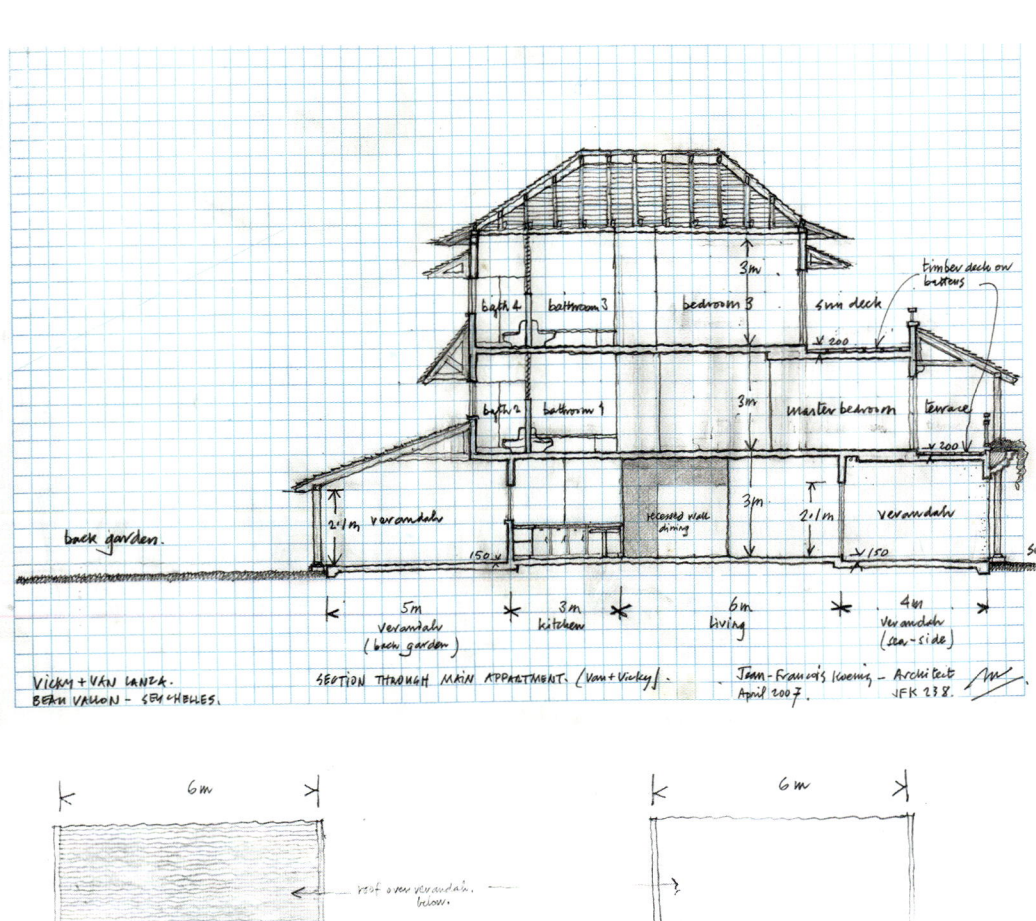

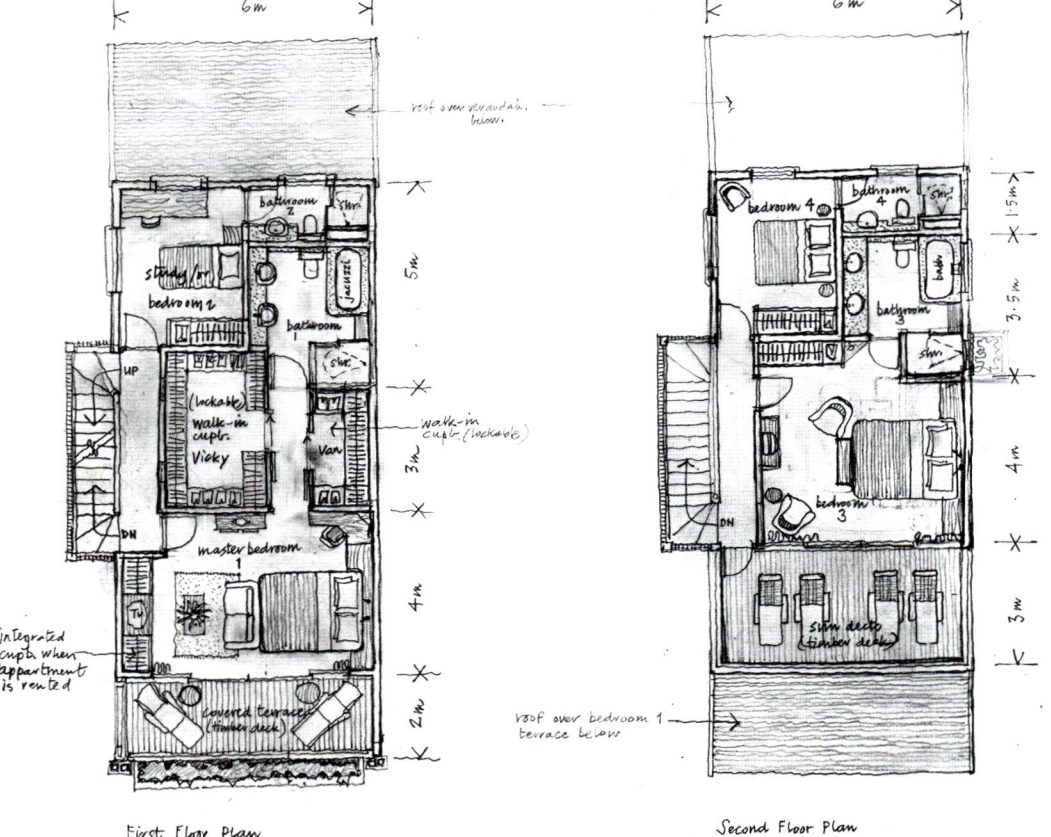

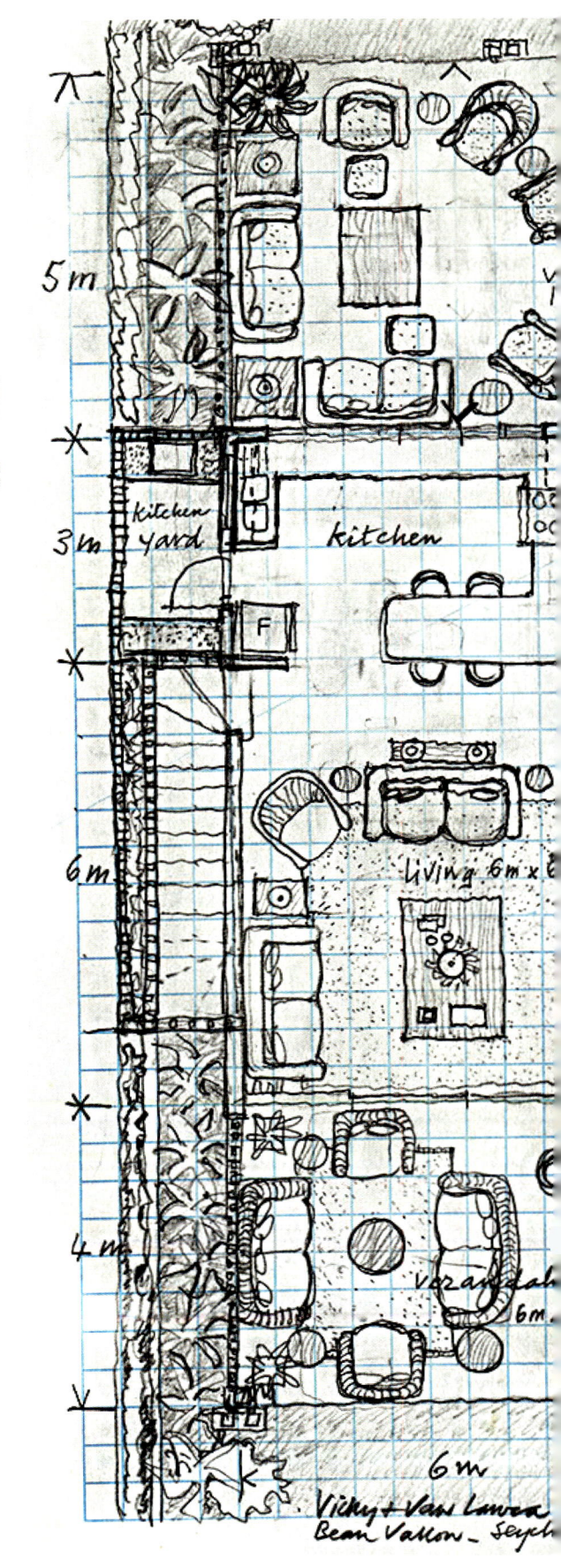

Top: Cross section.

Bottom: First- and second-floor plans.

Right: Ground-floor plan.

Pencil drawings by Jean-Francois Koenig.

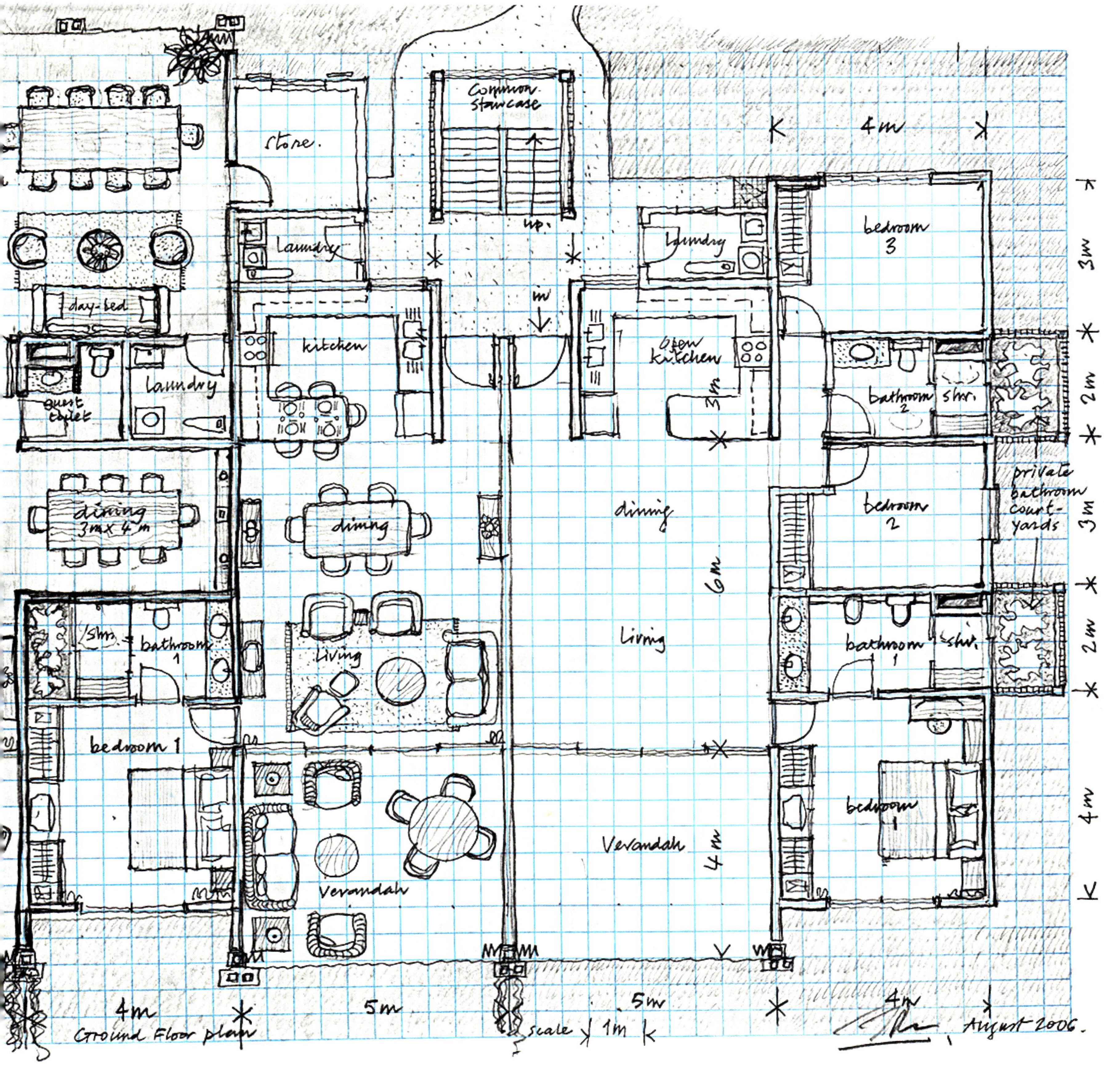
Common staircase
store
up.
in
Laundry
Laundry
bedroom 3
day-bed
kitchen
open kitchen
3m
guest toilet
laundry
bathroom 2
shr.
private bathroom court-yards
dining 3m x 4m
dining
dining
bedroom 2
6m
shr.
bathroom 1
Living
Living
bathroom 1
shr.
bedroom 1
bedroom 1
Verandah
4m
Verandah
4m
3m
2m
3m
2m
4m
4m
5m
5m
4m
Ground Floor plan
scale 1m
August 2006.

Queen Mary Gardens
Floreal, Mauritius
2013–2015

Floreal is a residential suburb situated on the central plateau of Mauritius on the slopes of the extinct volcanic crater of Trou aux Cerfs. It faces north with stunning views of mountains and sea. On clear days, Reunion Island can be seen 180 km away. The climate is milder than on the coast and has traditionally been a favoured residential place.

The building is seven storeys comprising 26 apartments with two-car private garages per apartment. The typical floor plan comprises four apartments divided into two wings of twin units, each with its own vertical core of twin lifts offering a personal lift for each apartment. The two middle and the corner apartments have 20-m and 24-m frontages respectively which are well above market norms in Mauritius.

The ground-floor apartments have a private heated swimming pool and the central ones have double storey volume living rooms along their full 20-m frontage. The four-bedroom apartments on the upper middle floors have 6-m high double storey volumes over the living room and give onto corresponding double storey planted party walls which improves sound insulation between apartments and brings healthy living in contact with flowering plants to the upper levels. The microclimate of Floreal lends itself, in shaded zones protected from wind, to the cascading ferns and orchids intended for the two-storey high separation walls as well as for the plantation of tree ferns called 'fandias', and 'hortensia' flowers in the deep floor planters provided in the project. The last two floors contain four double storey penthouses with double volume living areas under sloping glass, shaded by a large sunscreen along the full length of the façade. The lightweight screens are supported by 'Y'-shaped steel columns that rest on glass bottom strip pools that run along the full length of the building. There is a running–walking track on the roof to exercise whilst enjoying the views.

Above: View from the veranda of a 4th-floor apartment with its double height planted party wall and garden.

Pages 110/111: Night-time view of the building.

The front façade is a combination of recessed windows, full-height glass, balcony verandas, and perimeter planters shaded by deep sunscreens which are hung from white steel columns and beams forming a delicate lattice work of elegant proportions. They sit on an inclined basalt stone base which conceals a semi-underground parking garage. The architecture makes reference to a contemporary re-interpretation of the traditional Mauritian residence on a larger scale.

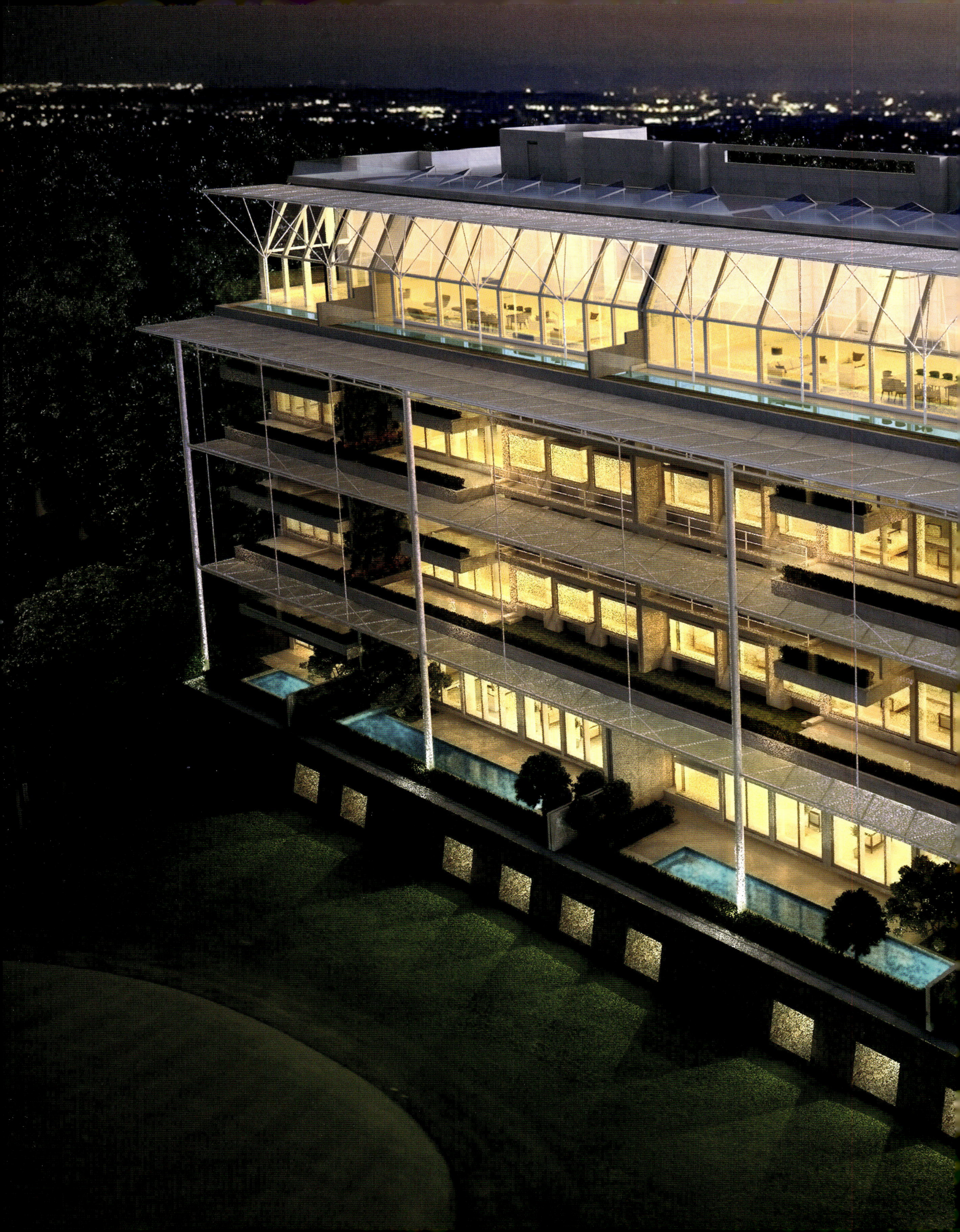

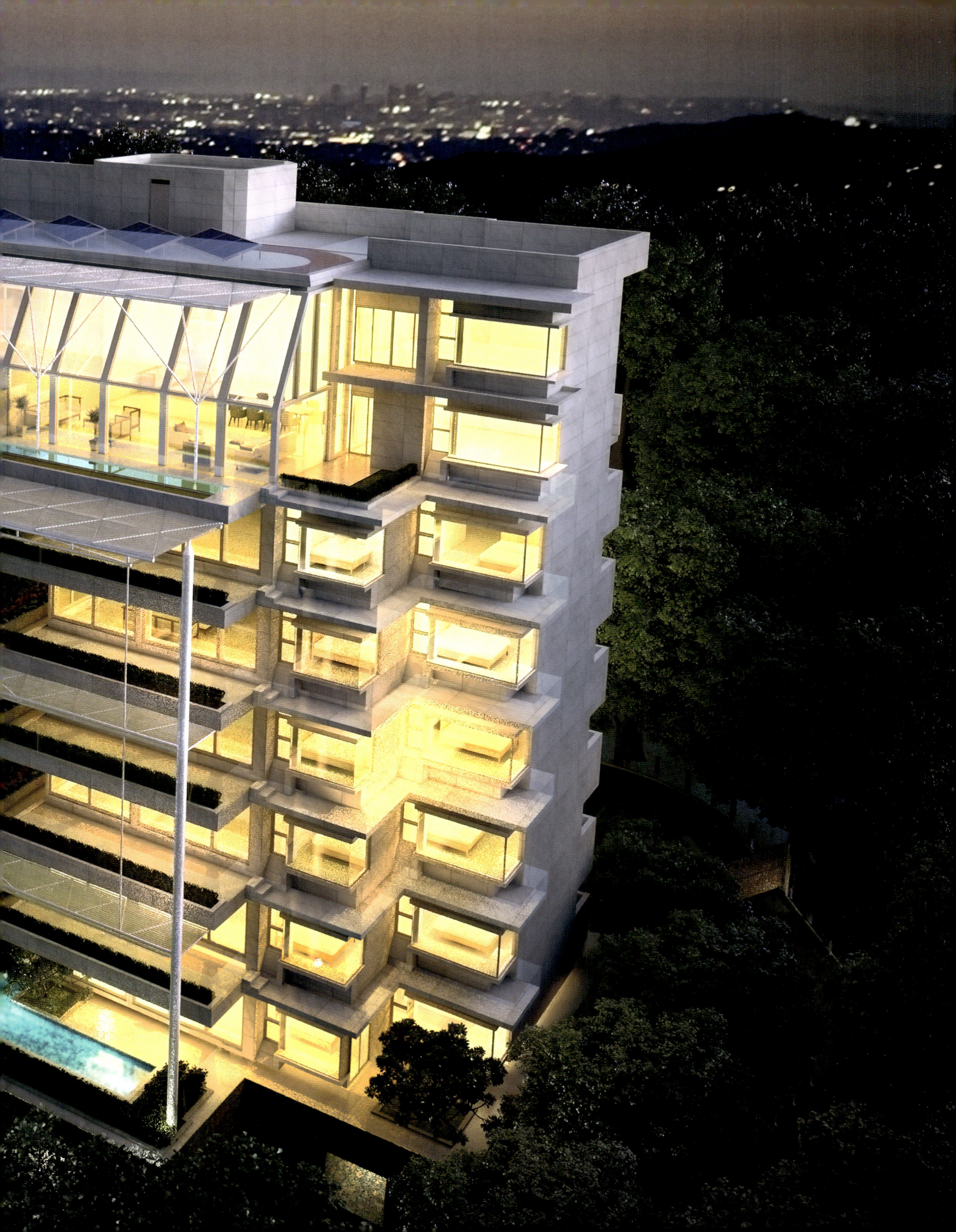

Top: Top-floor double volume penthouses.

Centre: Ground-floor double volume apartments with 17-m long private lap pools.

Bottom: Ground-floor apartments with a double volume living-dining space and planted party wall and garden for improved acoustic separation and healthy living in contact with nature.

Beau Rivage Golf Estate
Beau Rivage, Mauritius
2002

Beau Rivage is one of the first projects in Mauritius to integrate villas with a golf course. The plot sizes are 50-m deep and have a 30-m frontage on the golf course. The villas are different to each other but similar in character whereby the integration of house and garden on ground-floor level only avoids overlooking and plunging views over boundary walls, thus optimising privacy. This allows bathrooms to open freely onto gardens with external bathing facilities. The same privacy applies to all the other spaces stretched across the whole plot. They form a composition of open, semi-open, and closed spaces that meander around existing trees, orchestrated courtyards, and pools that blur the divide between inside and outside. The house is no longer a typical single entity and instead becomes a series of individual spaces offering a variety of planning options. All have hipped roofs with a 2-m cantilevered eaves line overhanging low for good sun and rain protection. The villas have a low roof line and make a minimal visual impact on the environment with which they totally integrate.

The freehand pencil drawing is drawn on one single sheet of A1 size tracing paper to a scale of 1:200. The drawing is not annotated so as not to disturb the graphic quality of the architecture and planning. One can imagine walking through them and experience their spaces. The plans are drawn with their furniture and trees in the belief that architecture, interior design, and landscaping are inseparable from each other.

Overleaf: Plans and elevations of multiple house proposal options.
Freehand pencil drawing on A1 size tracing paper by Jean-Francois Koenig.

BEAU RIVAGE GOLF ESTATE ~ MAURITIUS ~ PROPOSED

TCHES OF HOUSES ~ KOENIG ASSOCIATES ARCHITECTS

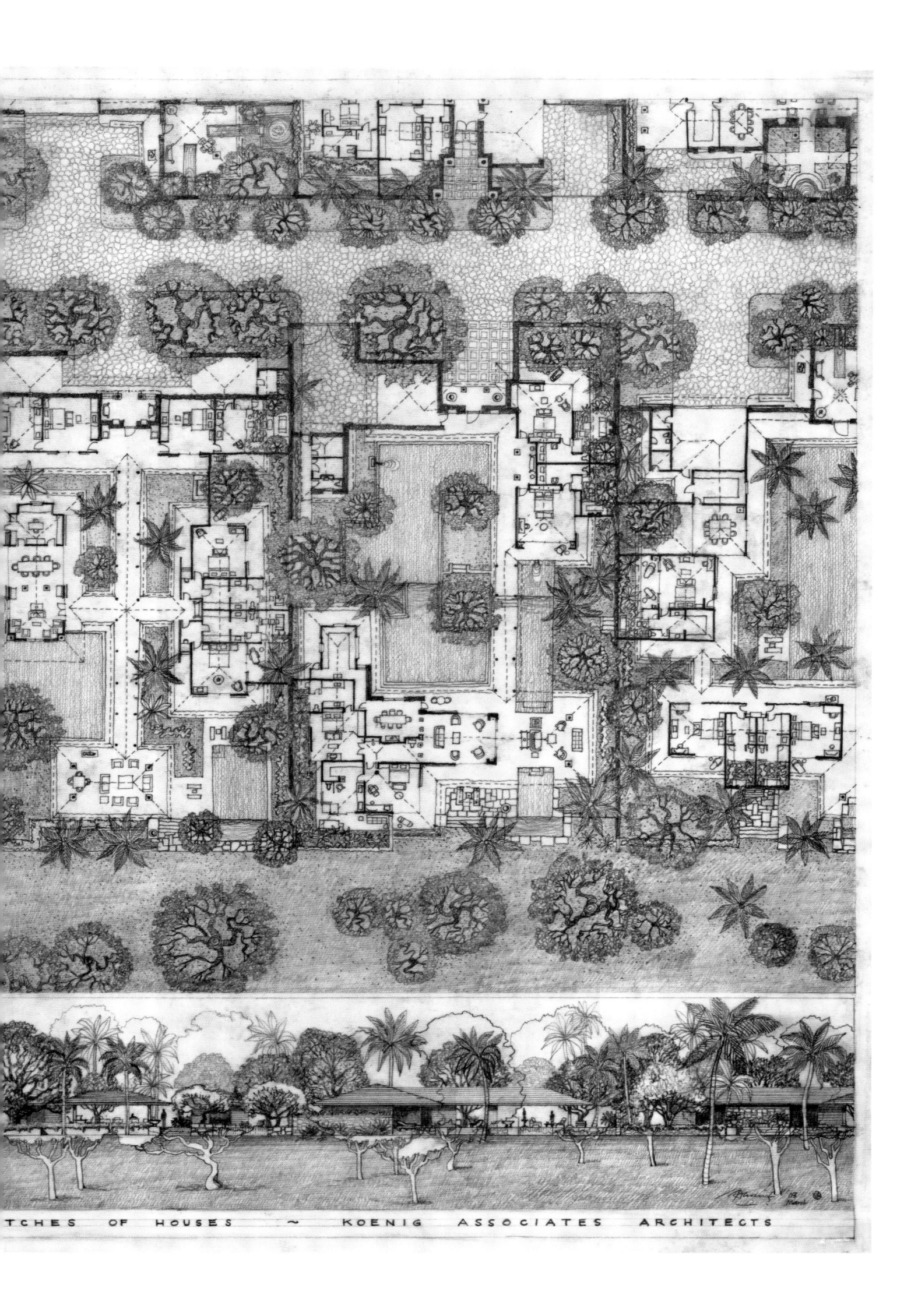

Petite Victoria
Le Café des Arts
Trou d'Eau Douce, Mauritius
1988–1990

Before and after photographs.

More than a refurbishment, this project is almost the complete reconstruction of the old sugar factory of "Petite Victoria" in Trou d'Eau Douce. The load bearing stone structure was left in a state of ruins with no roof and crumbling walls overgrown with wild vegetation. Its reconstruction was a major undertaking that gives a new breath of life to the old bones of the structure.

From the outset, the pencil drawings set out the reconstruction process from the master plan to the structural roof detailing. The factory was converted into a house with giant living spaces. The end space of crumbling walls was left open to the sky enclosing a contemplative Japanese garden. An external reflective pool with deeper swimming zones on two levels and a cascade corresponding and highlighting the existing change in level of the two main cores of the old factory, is placed along its length mirroring its walls and chimney. An international size croquet lawn levelled accordingly to absolute flatness with golf greens' quality grass continues the rectangular external landscaping and terminates with a new guest house built in stone to match the existing structures. That whole external proposal was unfortunately never built and the elegant timber and steel roof trusses with tension rods and turnbuckles were unfortunately changed to steel angle irons. A swimming pool was later added by the client, in the space originally intended for the Japanese garden.

KEY

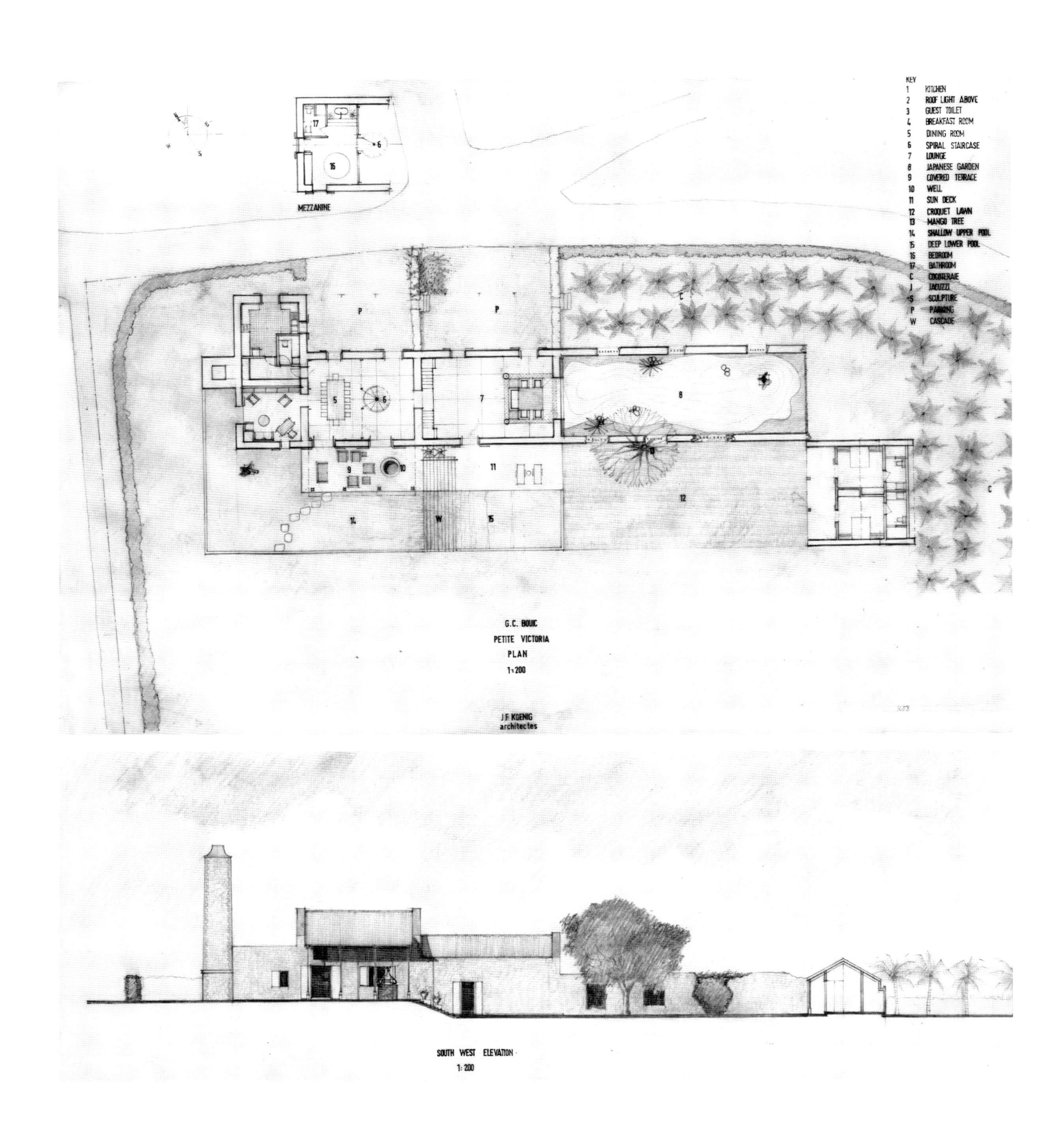

1	KITCHEN
2	ROOF LIGHT ABOVE
3	GUEST TOILET
4	BREAKFAST ROOM
5	DINING ROOM
6	SPIRAL STAIRCASE
7	LOUNGE
8	JAPANESE GARDEN
9	COVERED TERRACE
10	WELL
11	SUN DECK
12	CROQUET LAWN
13	MANGO TREE
14	SHALLOW UPPER POOL
15	DEEP LOWER POOL
16	BEDROOM
17	BATHROOM
C	COCOTERAIE
J	JACUZZI
S	SCULPTURE
P	PARKING
W	CASCADE

MEZZANINE

G.C. BOUIC
PETITE VICTORIA
PLAN
1:200

J.F. KOENIG
architectes

SOUTH WEST ELEVATION
1:200

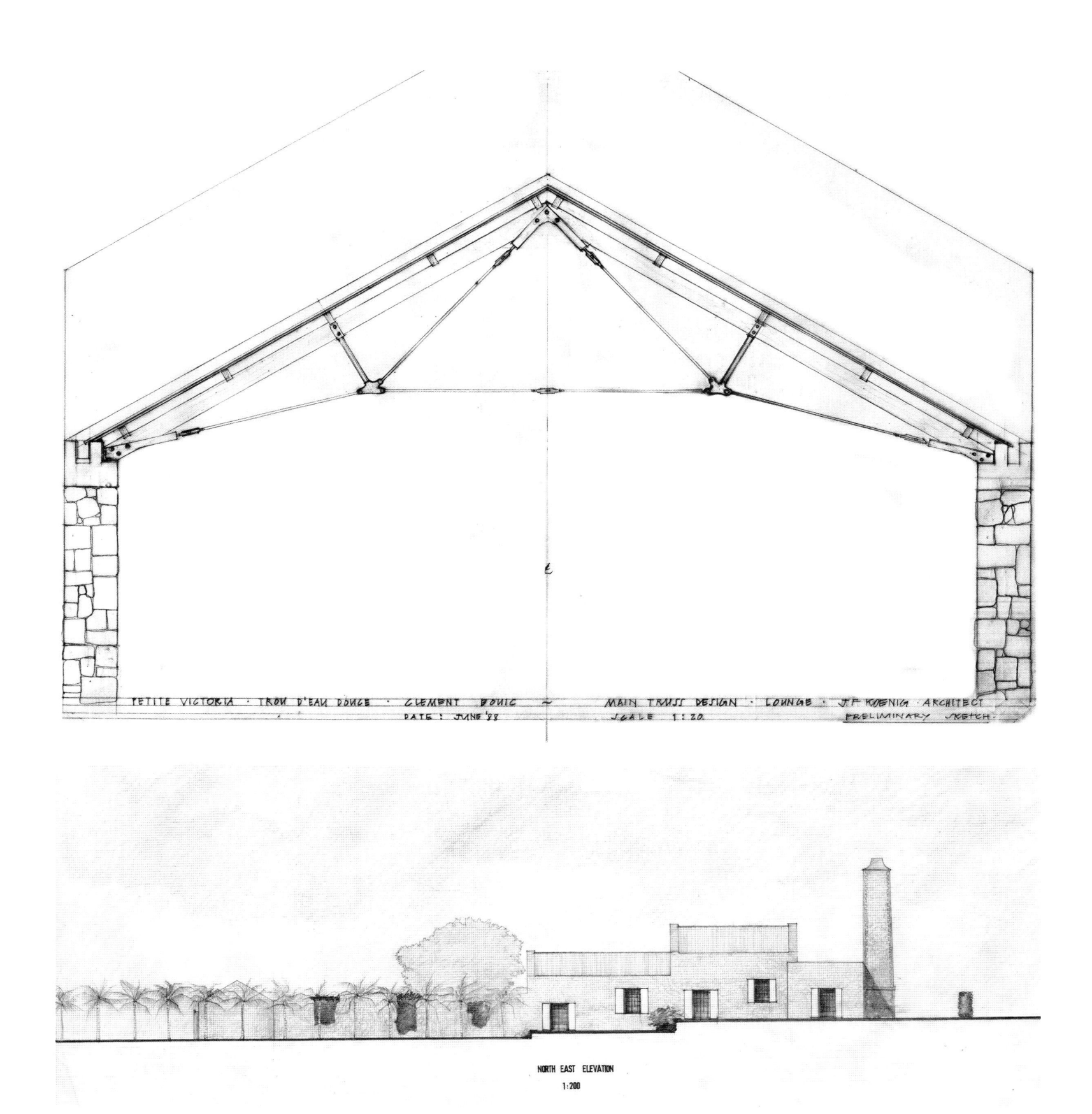

Presentation drawings by Jean-Francois Koenig. Pencil on tracing paper.

Dining room of the restaurant of the Café des Arts with paintings by Maniglier.

Top and bottom: The Reception room of the Café des Arts with paintings by Maniglier.

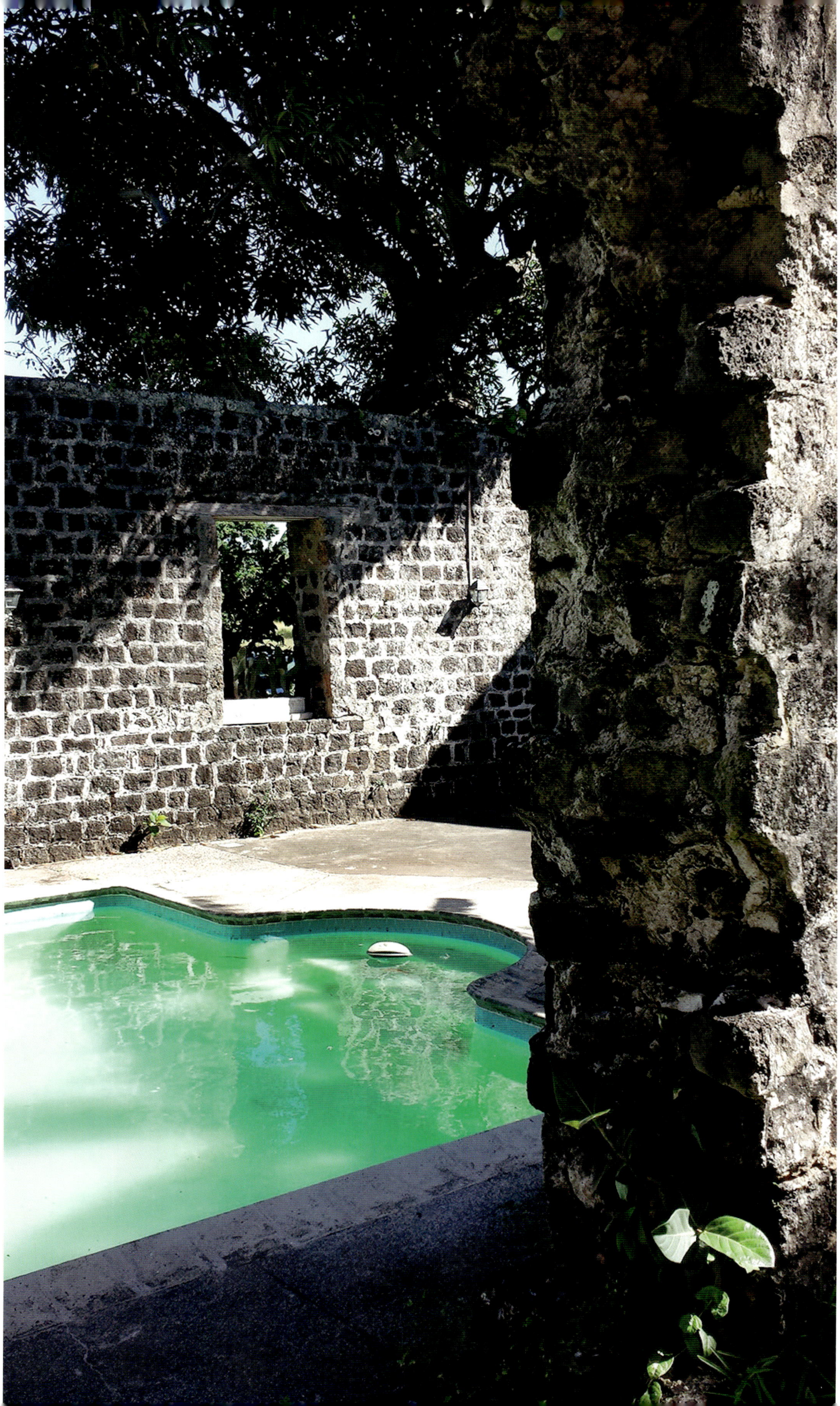

Today, "Petite Victoria" has been renamed "Le Café des Arts" and the owner, Jocelyn Gonzales, runs a high-class restaurant which caters to guests on reservation only. Of note is the collection of paintings by the French artist Maniglier, a lady who lived her remaining life in Mauritius amongst all her paintings that adorn the old factory walls. She had been the 'last' pupil of Henri Matisse. The result is a special place with plenty of character and a triumph of the rebirth of old stones.

The stone walls were rebuilt and the openings straightened, but sometimes the openings were left in their broken state.

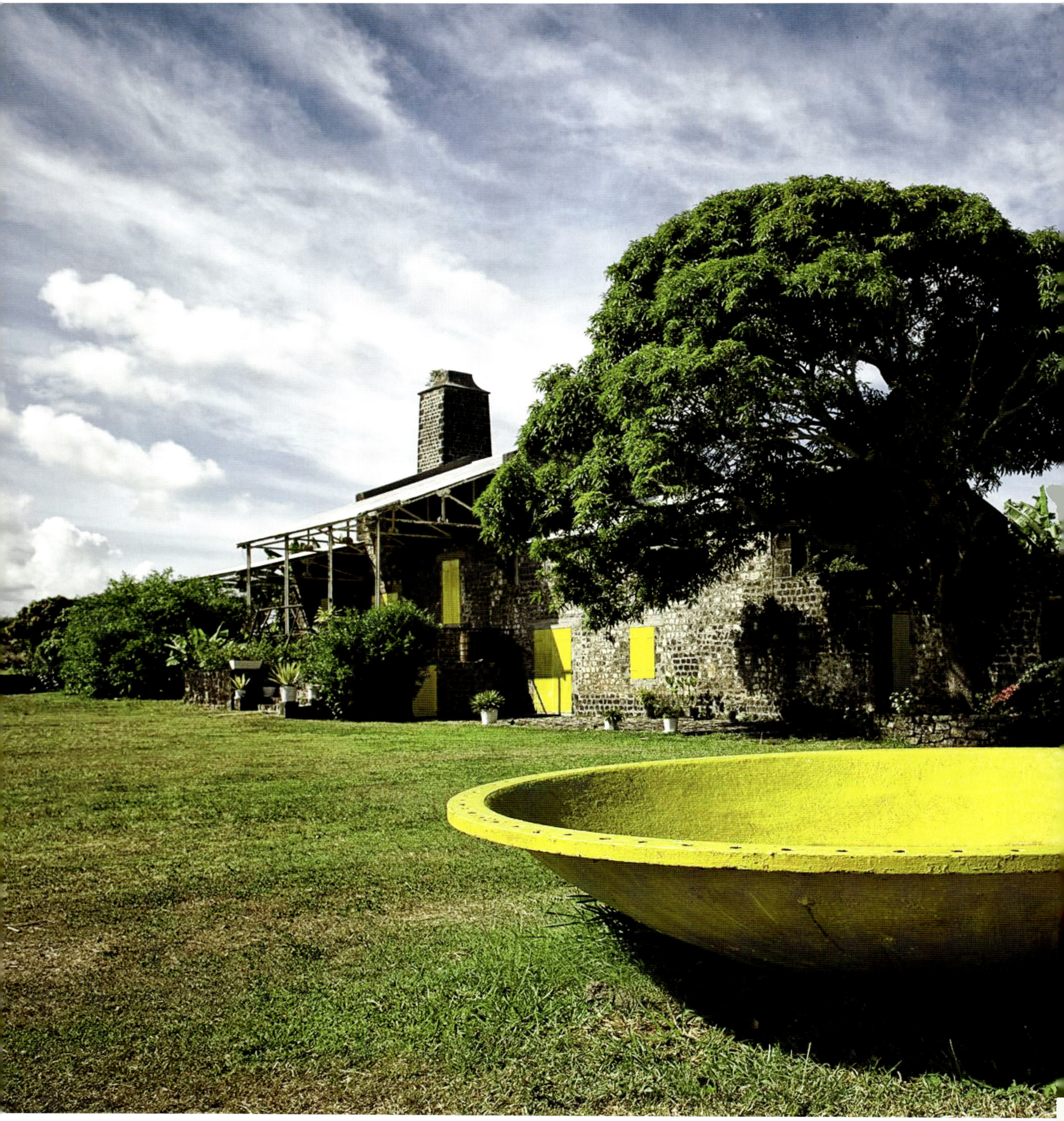

Before and after photographs.

Le Vieux Moulin
Pereybere, Mauritius
1996–2000

This project is the redevelopment of an old sugar factory which had been built with unusual barrel vaulted roofs. They were built with clay pots turned upside down and expressed internally over which concrete was poured to form the barrel vaults. The two larger vaults placed side by side had been rebuilt and converted in 1974 by Peter and Margaret White with the architect Geoffrey Bawa whom Jean-Francois Koenig knew, and met in Mauritius. The brief from the new owners in 1996 was to re-plan and add to the existing to create a permanent home.
Designed in the spirit of the old, the pencil and felt-tip drawing explains the intent of the master plan encompassing the whole site with large external reflective pools, a croquet lawn, and open veranda outhouses. Unfortunately, they were not followed entirely. The concept is one of blurring the edges of time whereby one cannot tell the difference between the new and the old, as if it never was added.

The barrel vaulted ceiling of the old factory was built with clay pots turned upside down and used as permanent shuttering for the concrete structure resting on stone walls.

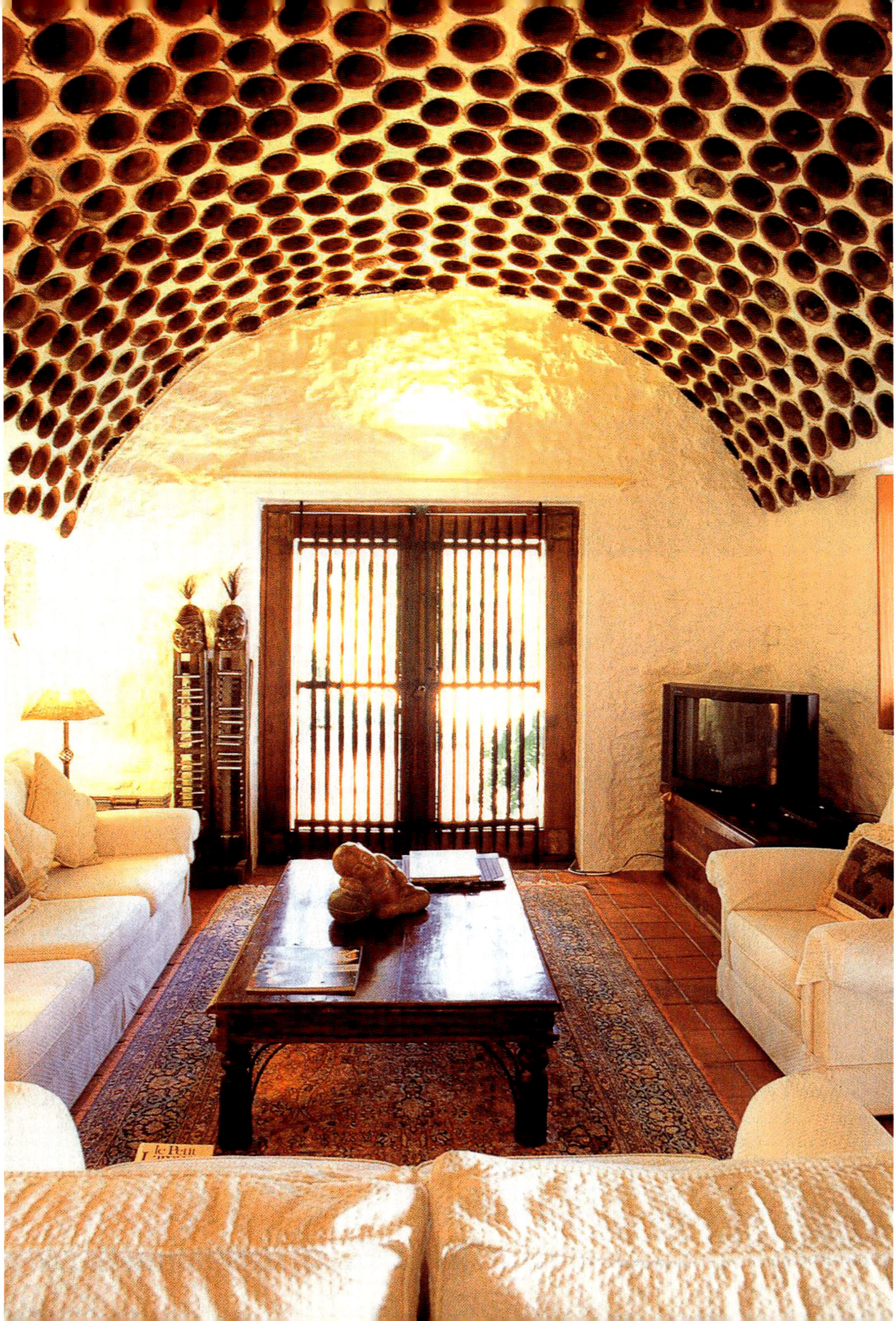

Left: The television room in the annexed structures converted into the living quarters.

Top: The external swimming pool separating the main factory and the annexed structures.

Bottom left: The existing and new annexed structures.

Bottom right: A doorway in hand cut basalt stonework connecting the two barrel vaults of the old factory.

Overleaf: Master plan. Freehand pencil drawing on tracing paper and background colouring in felt-tip markers by Jean-Francois Koenig.

130

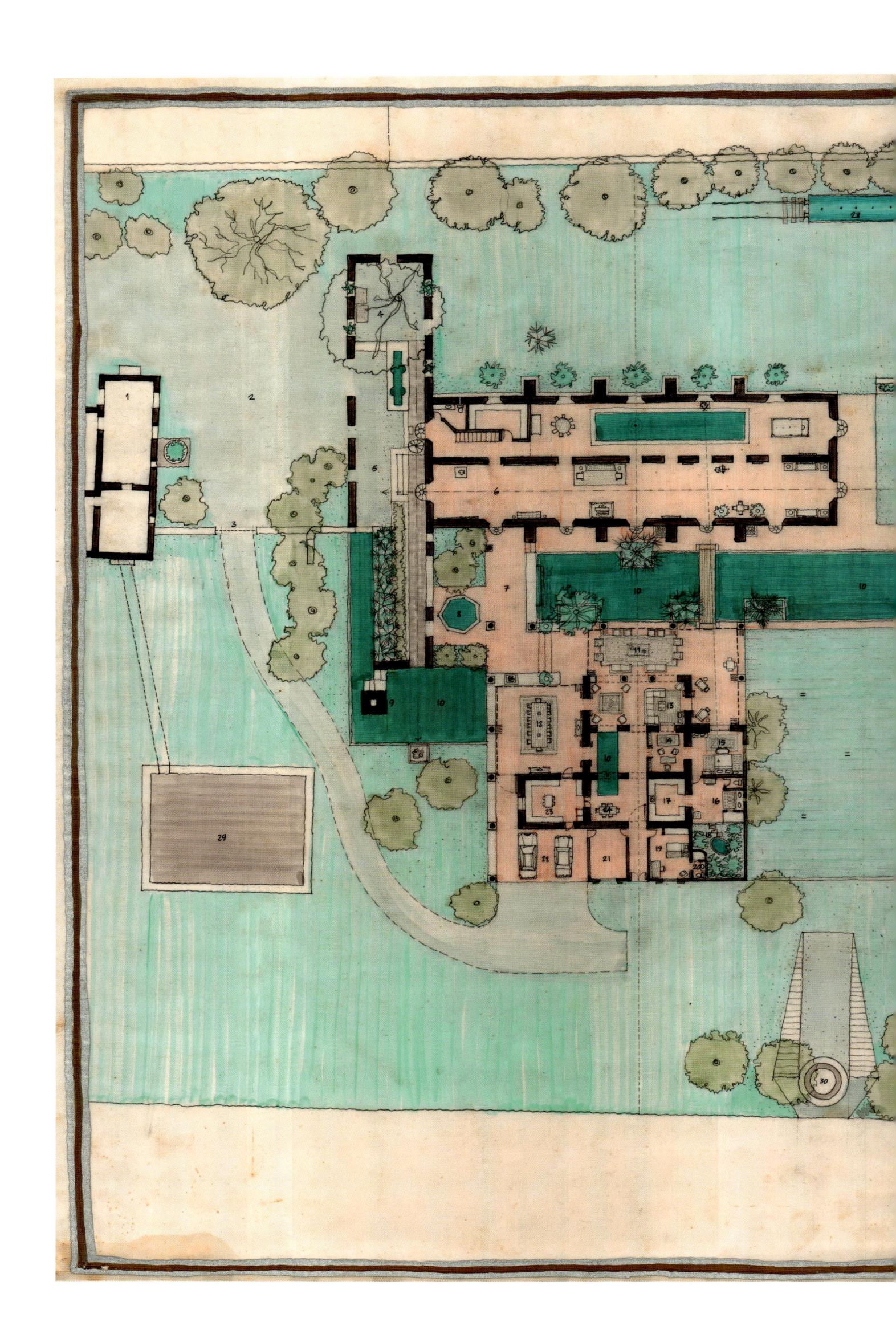

Le Vieux Moulin

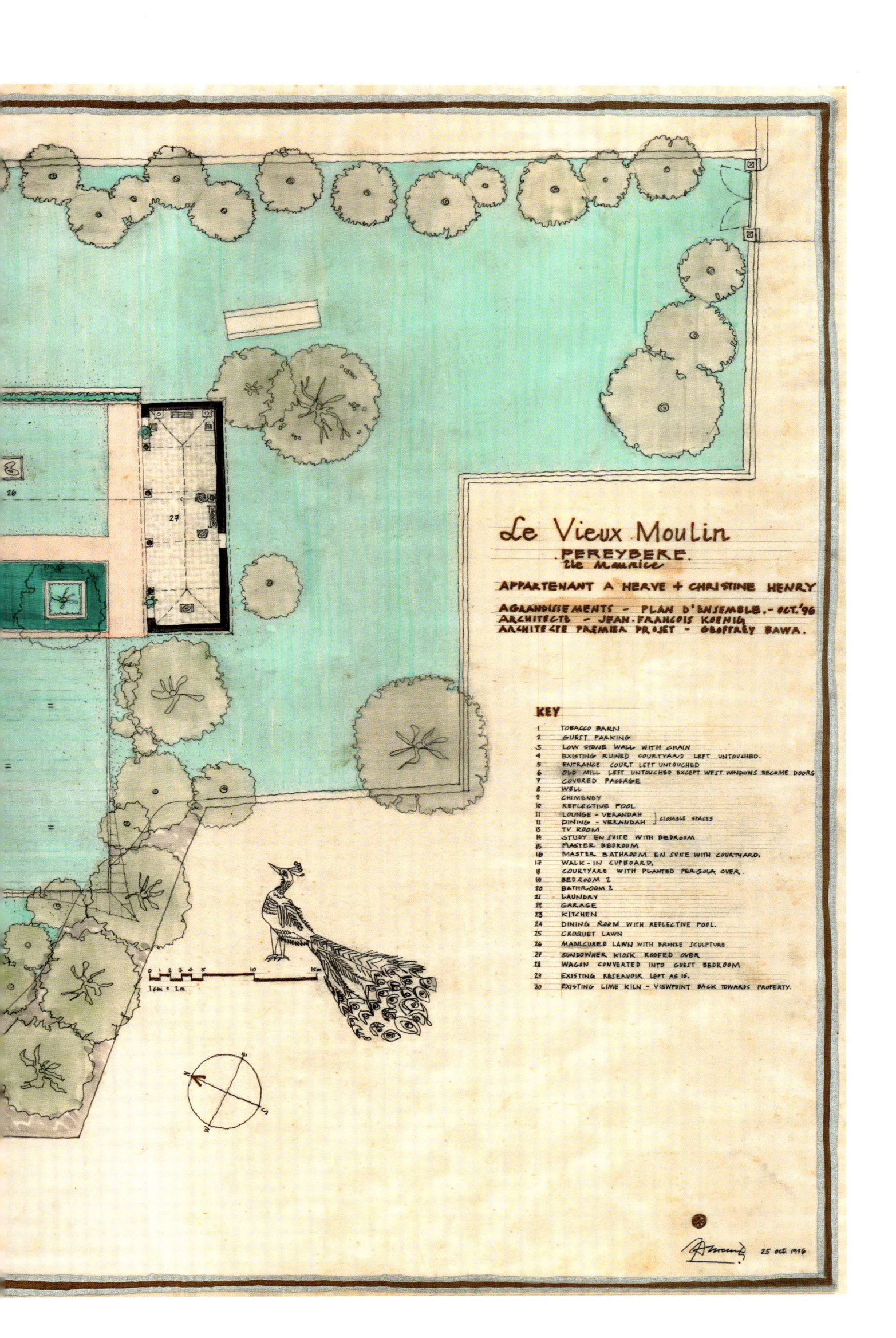

.PEREYBERE.
Ile Maurice

APPARTENANT A HERVE + CHRISTINE HENRY

AGRANDISSEMENTS - PLAN D'ENSEMBLE.- OCT.'96
ARCHITECTE - JEAN-FRANCOIS KOENIG
ARCHITECTE PREMIER PROJET - GEOFFREY BAWA.

KEY

1	TOBACCO BARN
2	GUEST PARKING
3	LOW STONE WALL WITH CHAIN
4	EXISTING RUINED COURTYARD LEFT UNTOUCHED.
5	ENTRANCE COURT LEFT UNTOUCHED
6	OLD MILL LEFT UNTOUCHED EXCEPT WEST WINDOWS BECOME DOORS
7	COVERED PASSAGE
8	WELL
9	CHIMENEY
10	REFLECTIVE POOL
11	LOUNGE - VERANDAH } CLOSABLE SPACES
12	DINING - VERANDAH
13	TV ROOM
14	STUDY EN SUITE WITH BEDROOM
15	MASTER BEDROOM
16	MASTER BATHROOM EN SUITE WITH COURTYARD.
17	WALK-IN CUPBOARD.
18	COURTYARD WITH PLANTED PERGOLA OVER.
19	BEDROOM 2
20	BATHROOM 2
21	LAUNDRY
22	GARAGE
23	KITCHEN
24	DINING ROOM WITH REFLECTIVE POOL.
25	CROQUET LAWN
26	MANICURED LAWN WITH BRONZE SCULPTURE
27	SUNDOWNER KIOSK ROOFED OVER
28	WAGON CONVERTED INTO GUEST BEDROOM
29	EXISTING RESERVOIR LEFT AS IS.
30	EXISTING LIME KILN - VIEWPOINT BACK TOWARDS PROPERTY.

25 Oct. 1996

CHAPTER 2
HOTELS

Voile d'Or Resort and Spa	134
Domaine du Chasseur	157
Hotel at Flic en Flac	160
Klondike Village Vacances	162
Sugar Beach	166
Ocean Lodge	170
Indian Resort & Spa	172
Les Creolias	182
Boutique Hotel and Golf	184
La Plantation Hotel	186
Holiday Villas	192
The Palace Hotel	196
Skystar	200

Voile d'Or Resort and Spa
Bel Ombre, Mauritius
2001–2005

The hotel Voile d'Or Resort and Spa is situated on the south coast of Mauritius. Guest experience starts at the entrance gate when a slight curve in the driveway creates an intimate external space. The gate house is camouflaged amongst lush vegetation and huge ficus trees planted to the architect's specifications on both sides of a long driveway. They form a grand vaulted ceiling of foliage filtering light and lead to a triple volume barrel vaulted porte cochère, which carries through to the reception lobby, whose axis runs through the entire site, open at both ends to sea views at entry and mountain views at the other. A 90-degree turn up wide marble stairs leads through a double volume space, square in plan and with high arches, opening in deep walls on a rectangular reflective pool framing views to the sea. This courtyard-on-a-roof is lined on both sides by golf-quality lawns and round timber columns that support the wood shingled roofs of the walkways. They terminate by two lounge gazebos and high palm trees. They were transplanted fully grown in planters that make use of the depth of the structure in the valleys between the barrel vaults of the restaurant below. At night, the pool has a double row of gas flames which appear to float on water reinforcing the notion of the elements: Earth, Wind, Fire, and Water.

Right: Arrival driveway and porte cochère.

Overleaf: The ground level reflective pool and beach bar.

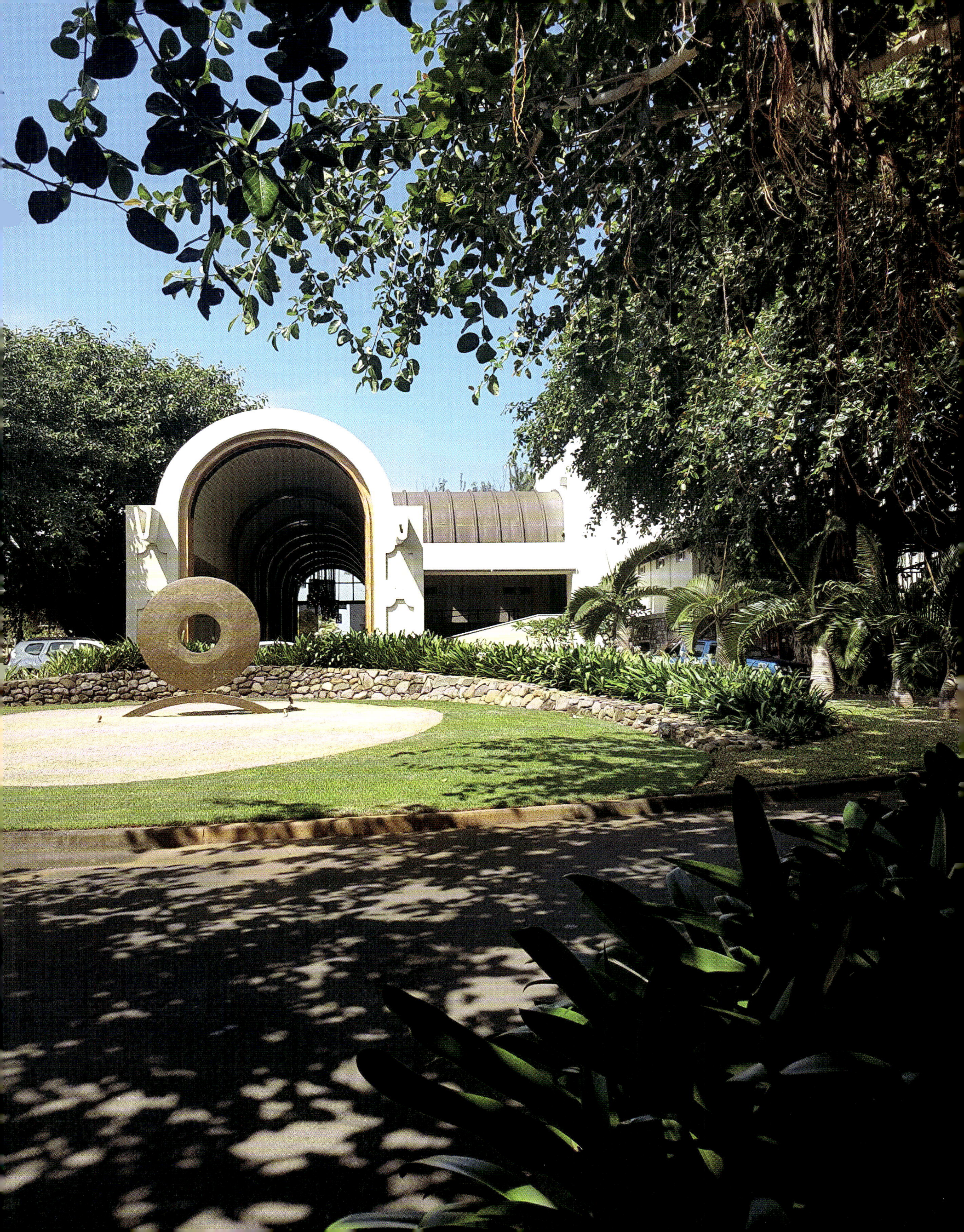

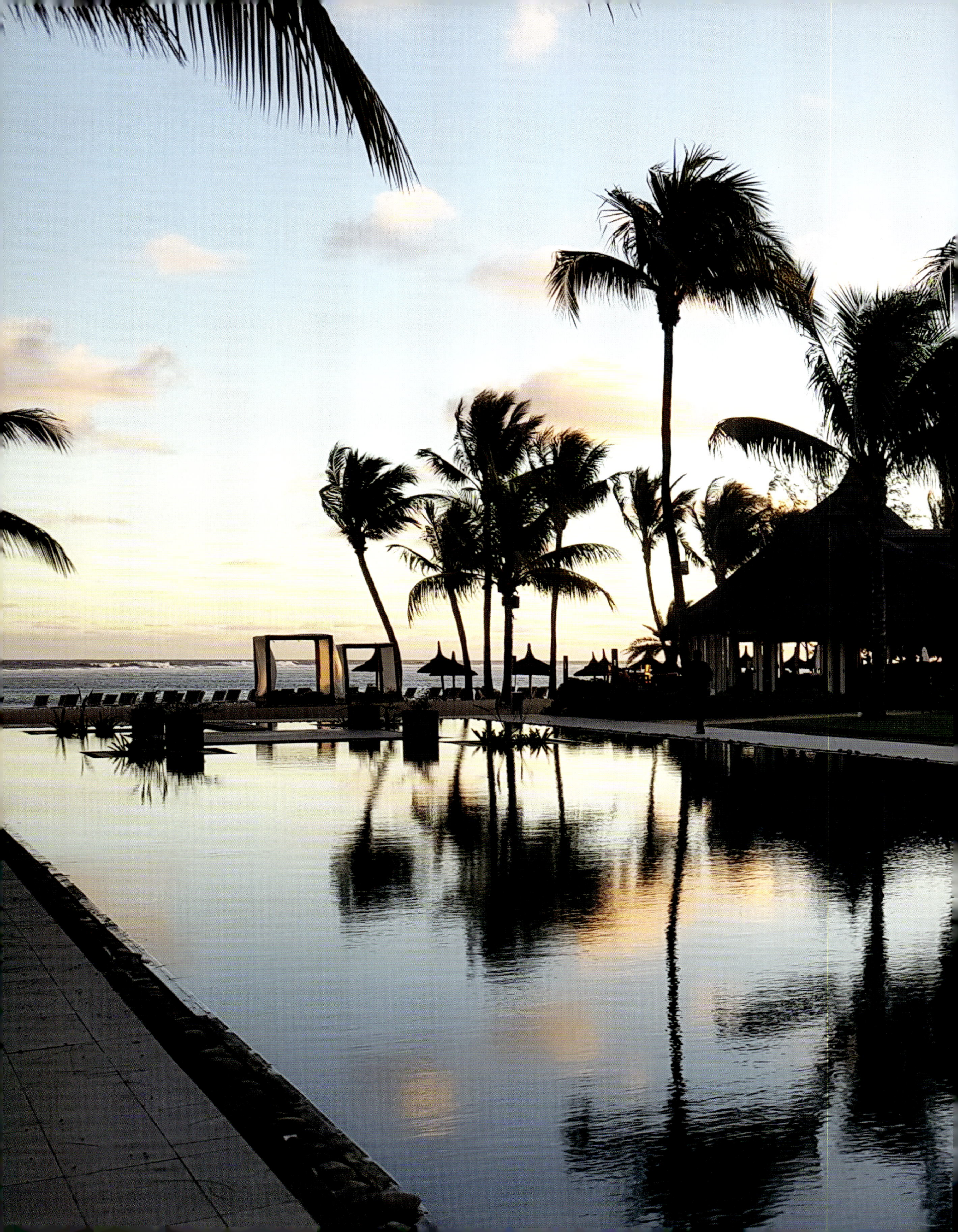

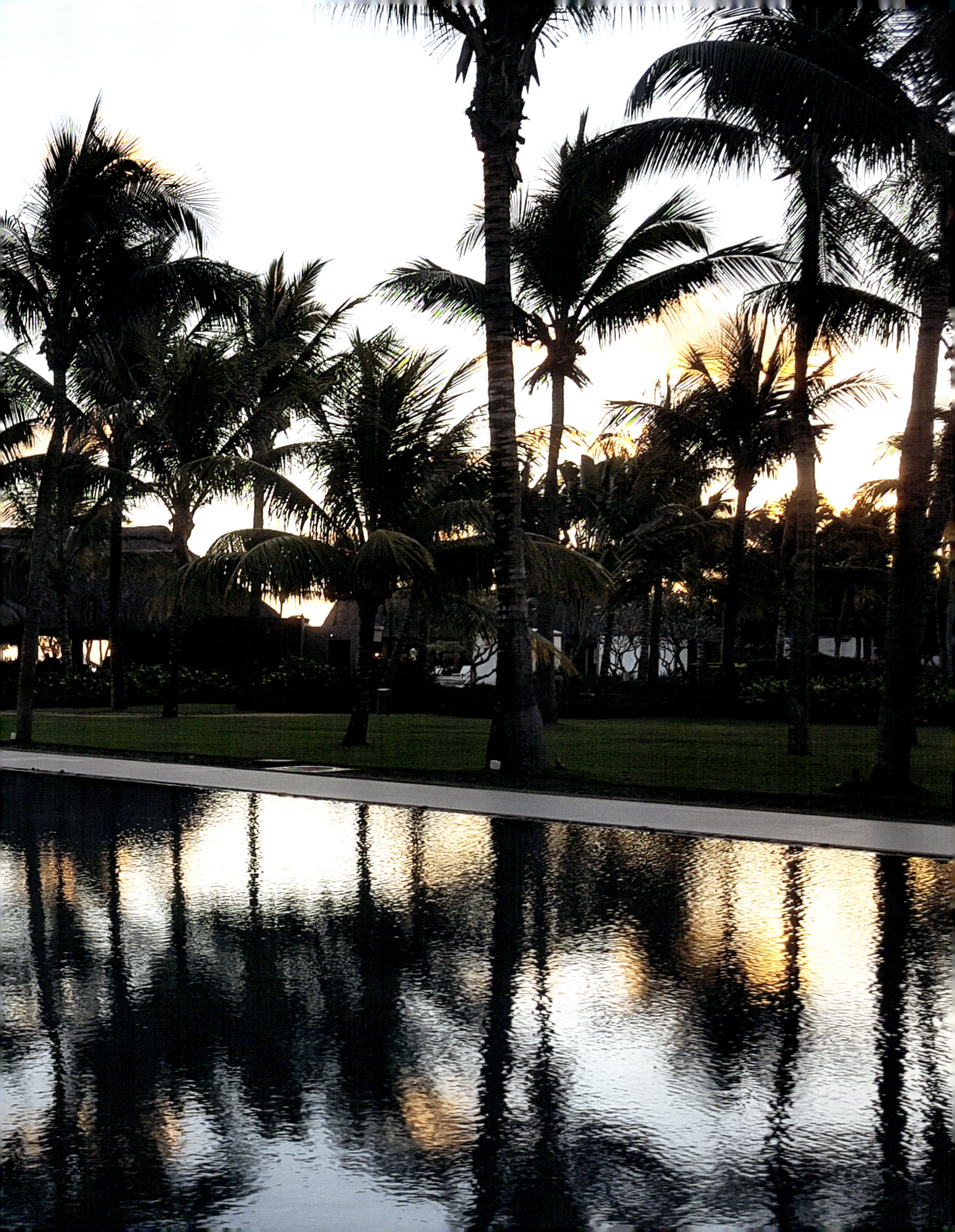

Above: Entrance lobby with marble stairs and barrel vault in clay pots.

Right: The main building and the double reflective pools on the roof and ground levels.

139

Above: The 'fire and water' of the reflective pool of the rooftop courtyard.

A long reflective pool on grade below completes the grand vista of the beach and sea. The building makes reference to Moorish architecture as a tribute to the Arab sailors who, it is believed, first discovered Mauritius when the Island appeared on the 1502 reproduction of an Arab map with the name Dina Arobi. The hotel is the construction of old stones on imaginary foundations left by the passage of the Arabs, which in truth never existed, but pertinent nonetheless to the history of Mauritius and its current existence as a hospitality destination with a multicultural population. A team was sent on a hunt for old stones from demolished buildings across the country to use in the construction of the walls. The circular tower, whose roof is the relaxation pool of the Spa, has viewing 'miradors' which were built on 17th-century Mauritian timber buildings as elevated watch-posts for viewing incoming ships called in the local language 'guette a li'. The desired effect, whereby the stonework looks dated, is a deliberate attempt to blur time.

Above: The roof level reflective pool at dusk with gas flame lighting on water.

Top: Perspective of the main building and restaurant. Pencil drawing by Jean-Francois Koenig.

Bottom: First sketch of the entrance arrival. Pencil drawing by Jean-Francois Koenig.

Right: External staircase leading to the upper level of the main building.

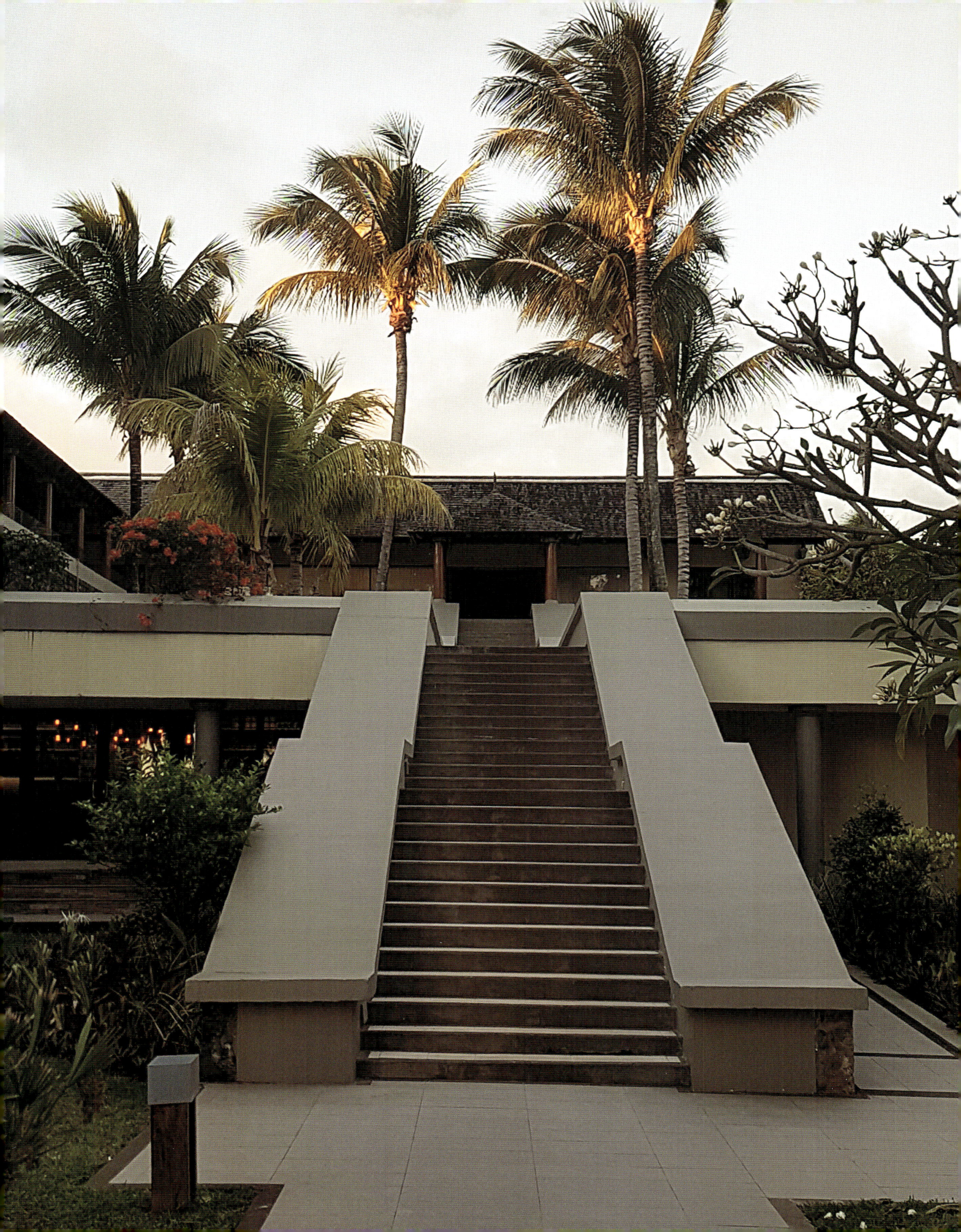

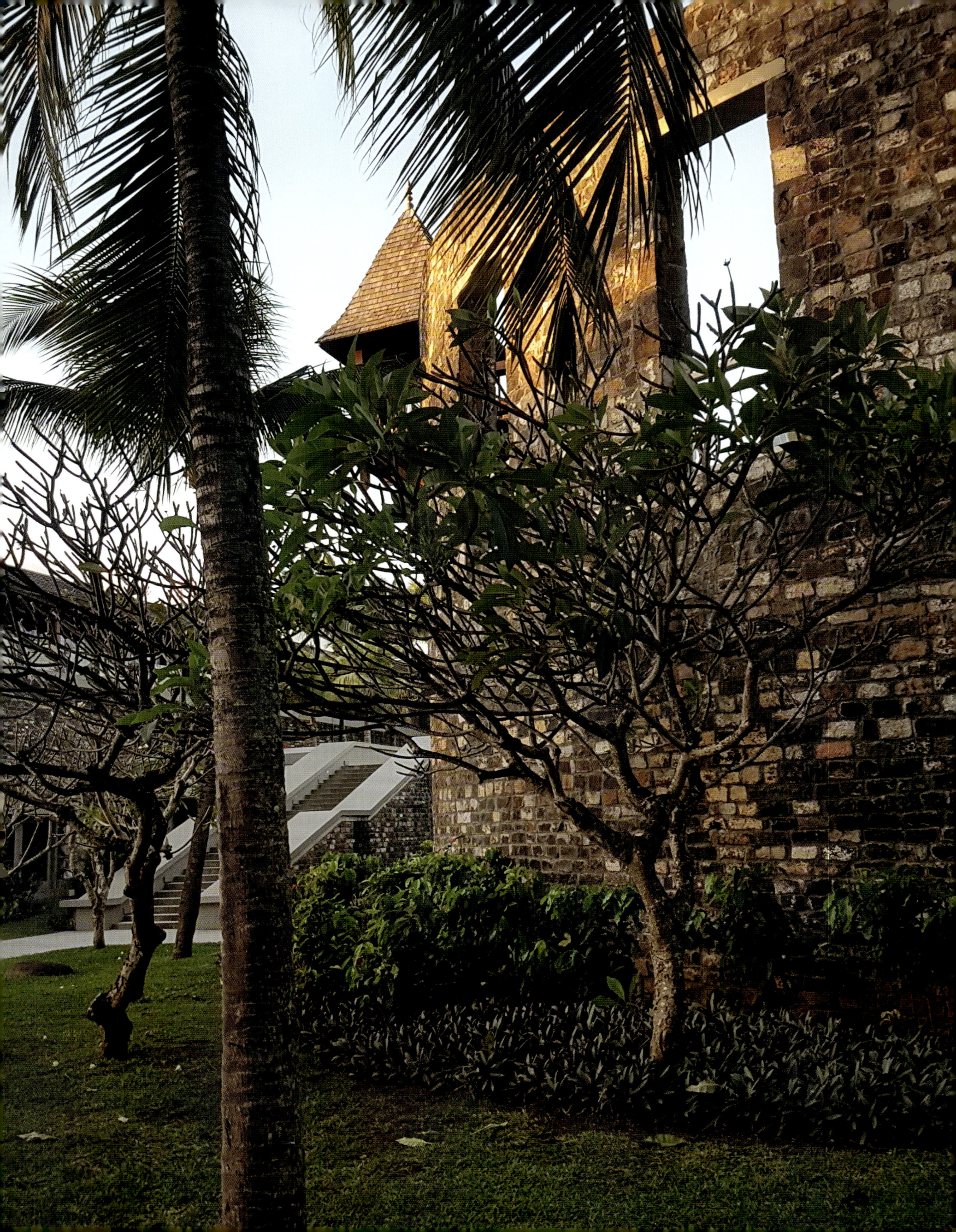

Left and top: Watch tower in stones recovered from demolished buildings left with the paint showing. The top floor of the watch tower is a private rooftop relaxation pool for the spa, and the ground floor is a nightclub sunken below grade.

Bottom: The garden and side walls of the restaurant with the timber colonnade walkway of the rooftop courtyard above.

Top: Garden, watch tower, and main building.

Bottom: The exterior of the Spa seen from the gardens.

Right: The timber shingled roofs of the Spa.

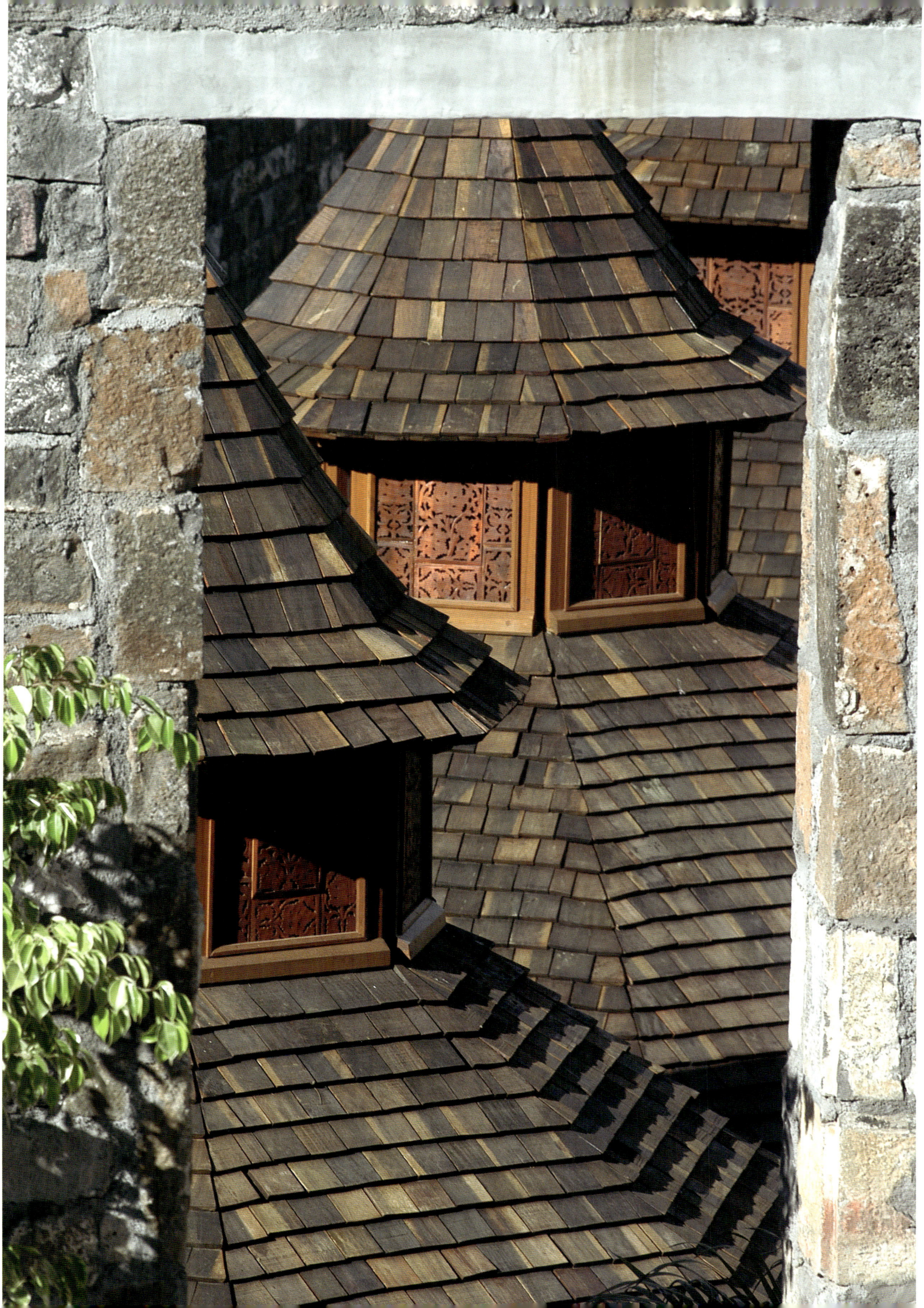

Top and Bottom: The single storey Junior Suites.

*Top left: The walkway leading from the main building to the bedrooms opens a vista to the sea. Top right: Landscaped guest walkway.
Bottom: The Junior Suites are well set back from the shoreline preserving the existing 'filao' trees of the original landscape.*

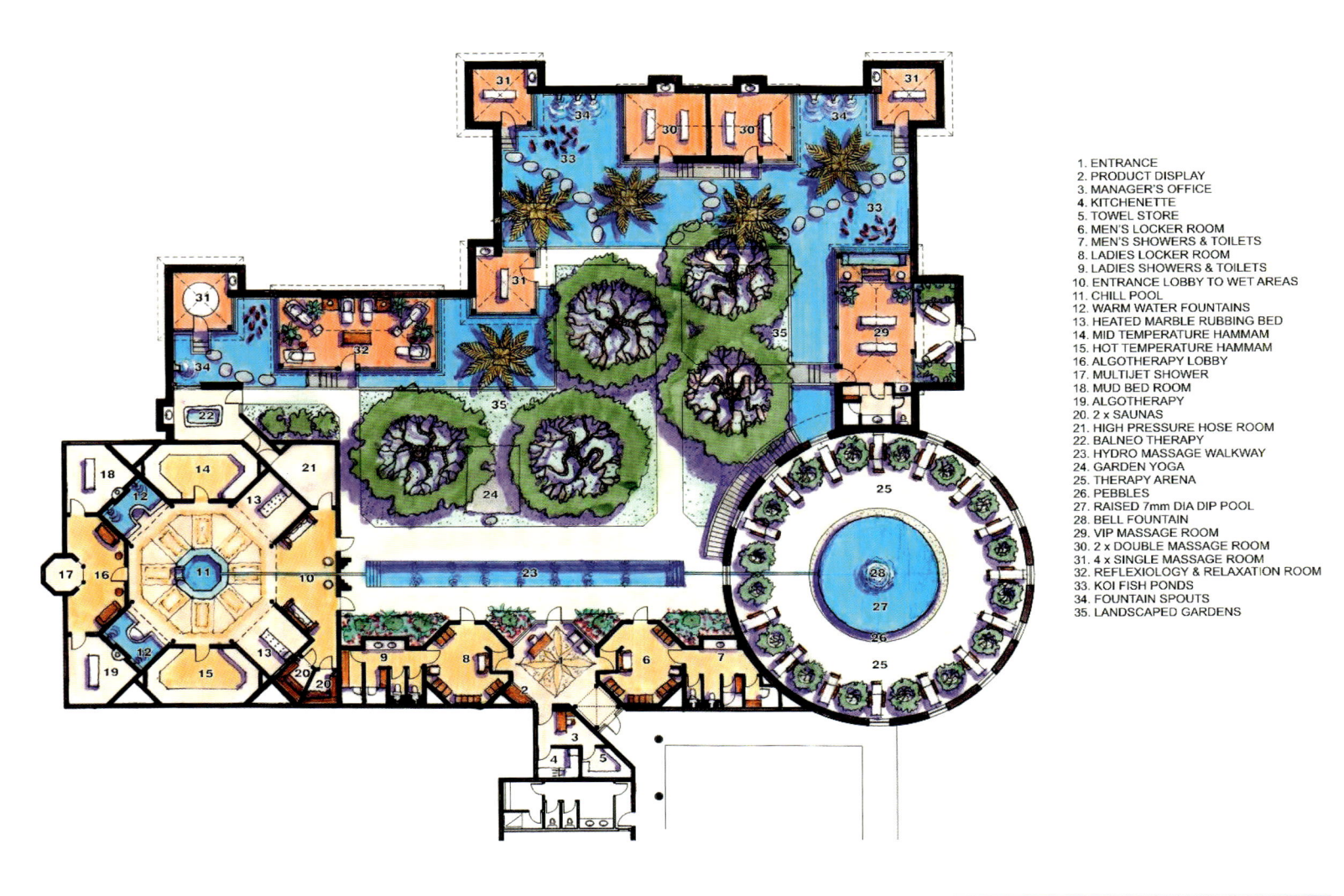

1. ENTRANCE
2. PRODUCT DISPLAY
3. MANAGER'S OFFICE
4. KITCHENETTE
5. TOWEL STORE
6. MEN'S LOCKER ROOM
7. MEN'S SHOWERS & TOILETS
8. LADIES LOCKER ROOM
9. LADIES SHOWERS & TOILETS
10. ENTRANCE LOBBY TO WET AREAS
11. CHILL POOL
12. WARM WATER FOUNTAINS
13. HEATED MARBLE RUBBING BED
14. MID TEMPERATURE HAMMAM
15. HOT TEMPERATURE HAMMAM
16. ALGOTHERAPY LOBBY
17. MULTIJET SHOWER
18. MUD BED ROOM
19. ALGOTHERAPY
20. 2 x SAUNAS
21. HIGH PRESSURE HOSE ROOM
22. BALNEO THERAPY
23. HYDRO MASSAGE WALKWAY
24. GARDEN YOGA
25. THERAPY ARENA
26. PEBBLES
27. RAISED 7mm DIA DIP POOL
28. BELL FOUNTAIN
29. VIP MASSAGE ROOM
30. 2 x DOUBLE MASSAGE ROOM
31. 4 x SINGLE MASSAGE ROOM
32. REFLEXOLOGY & RELAXATION ROOM
33. KOI FISH PONDS
34. FOUNTAIN SPOUTS
35. LANDSCAPED GARDENS

Top: Plan of the Royal Suite. Drawing by Jean-Francois Koenig.
Centre: Typical bedroom elevations. Drawing by Jean-Francois Koenig.
Bottom: Plan of a typical bedroom. Drawing by Jean-Francois Koenig.
Top left: Plan of the Spa. Drawing by Jean-Francois Koenig.
Bottom left: Computer-generated aerial perspective of the Spa.

Top and bottom: The fine-dining restaurant. Entrance view.

Right: Detail of the natural timber shingles of one of the four corner turret roofs of the building.

Below: The pathway coming from the beach to the fine-dining restaurant.

153

The restaurant is on grade under three barrel vaults in clay pots turned upside down, expressed internally and used as permanent shuttering. They rest on 1-m wide stone walls.

The spa sits in its own private gardens surrounded by stone walls and a circular structure resembling an old fort. The courtyard is an array of external pools, fountains, water running in floor channels, and lush ground covers with palm trees. The glazed walls of the massage rooms are sunk in pools up to massage table height level, allowing, in a lying down position, an eye level view of Koi fish swimming by.

The site faces south directly into the seaward south-east trade winds and the buildings are set well behind the existing trees leaving the wild aspect of the south coast untouched.

A private club with a fine dining restaurant in its own gardens and pool is tucked away in the far eastern corner of the property. The architecture refers to old Mauritian architecture with turrets and pitched roofs in timber shingles.

The fine-dining restaurant.

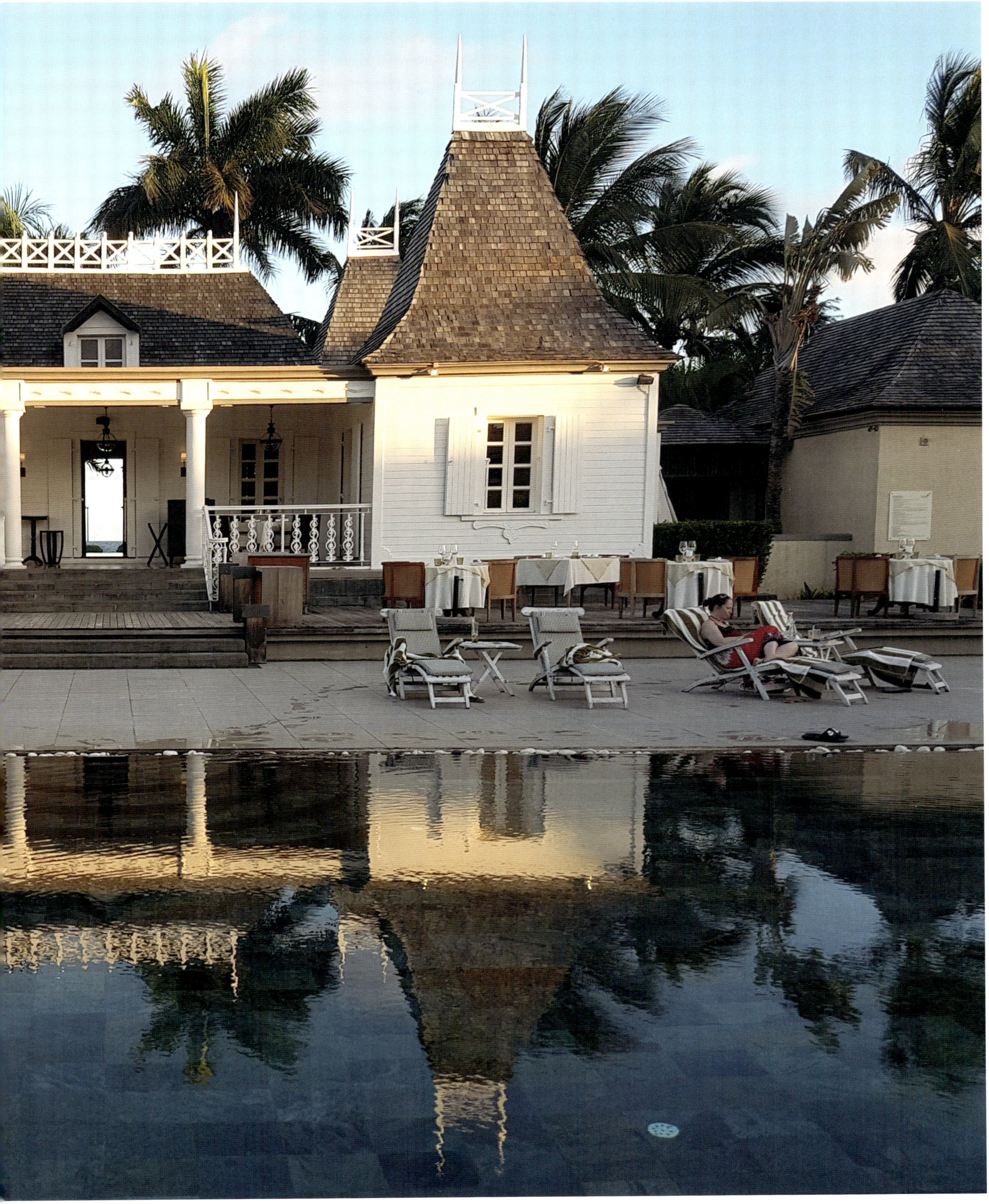

The ficus trees at the entrance garden in this picture, as well as all the landscaping on site were planted to Jean-Francois Koenig's instructions without a landscape architect.

Domaine du Chasseur
Anse Jonchée, Mauritius
2000

The 5-star boutique hotel as a quiet getaway in the tropics is best served when space is generous and free all around. This translates as: no bedroom suite should be below, above, or next to another. A bedroom suite providing solitude and peace is the best of luxury hospitality. The drawings for a bedroom suite amongst virgin vegetation on the mountain slopes of Anse Jonchée for the "Domaine du Chasseur" illustrate this concept. A series of independent small-scale structures on stilts and with individual roofs make up a typical bedroom suite. The architecture aims to make minimal impact on the environment leaving the flora and fauna of the mountain slopes untouched. The site is home to the Kestrel, a unique small bird of prey indigenous to Mauritius. This further reinforces the concept of peace and quiet.

LARGE 1.2 DIAMETER
EATING TABLE

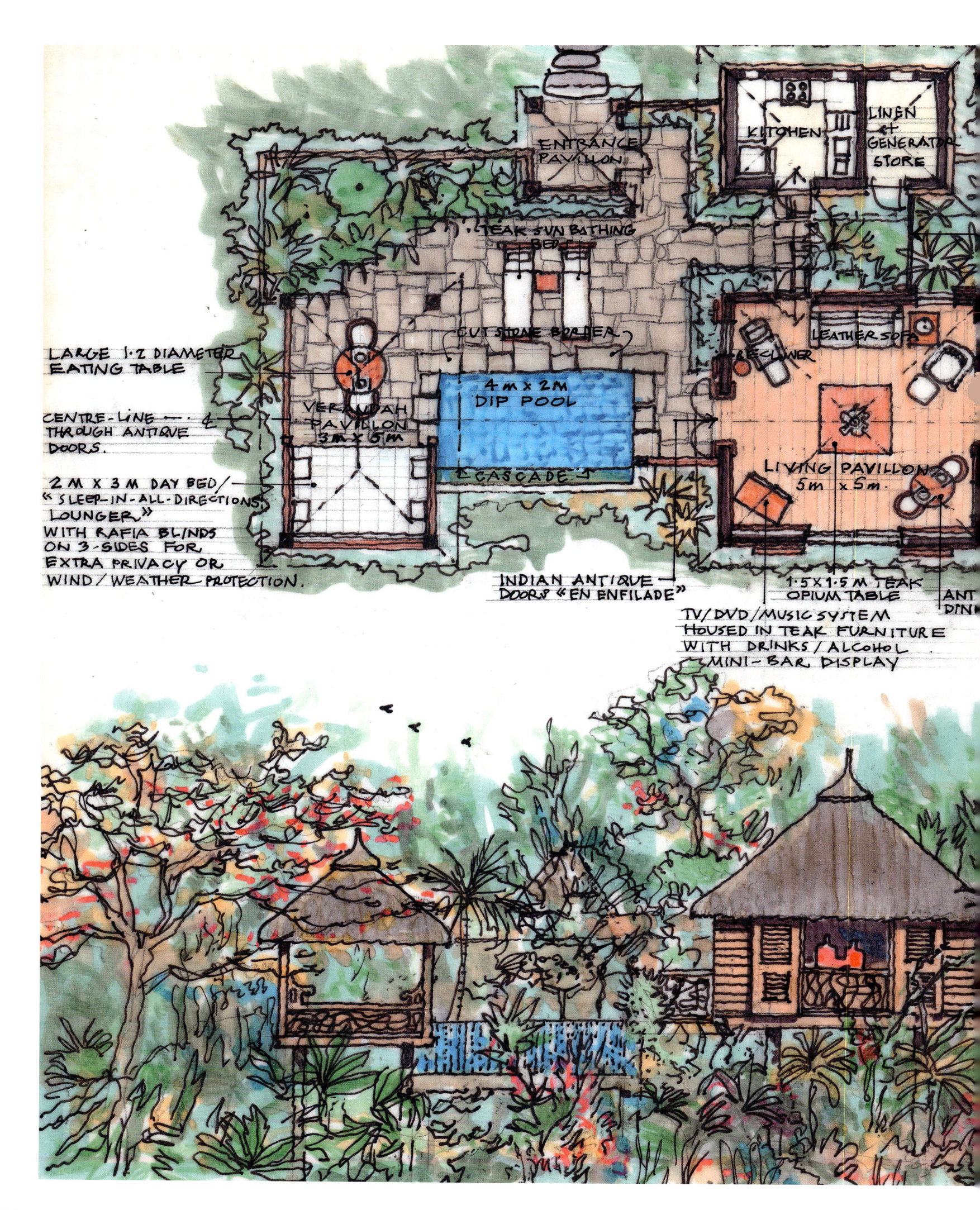

CENTRE-LINE
THROUGH ANTIQUE
DOORS.

2M X 3M DAY BED/
"SLEEP-IN-ALL-DIRECTIONS
LOUNGER"
WITH RAFIA BLINDS
ON 3-SIDES FOR
EXTRA PRIVACY OR
WIND/WEATHER PROTECTION.

ENTRANCE PAVILION

KITCHEN

LINEN & GENERATOR STORE

TEAK SUN BATHING BED

CUT STONE BORDER

RECLINER

LEATHER SOFA

4M X 2M DIP POOL

VERANDAH PAVILION 3M X 5M

CASCADE

LIVING PAVILION 5M X 5M

INDIAN ANTIQUE DOORS "EN ENFILADE"

1.5 X 1.5 M TEAK OPIUM TABLE

TV/DVD/MUSIC SYSTEM HOUSED IN TEAK FURNITURE WITH DRINKS/ALCOHOL MINI-BAR DISPLAY

Plan and elevation of a bedroom suite. Annotated freehand drawing in technical pen and ink on tracing paper, and background colouring in felt-tip markers by Jean-Francois Koenig.

Hotel at Flic en Flac
Mauritius
1988

This pencil elevation of the façade of a typical bedroom block for a small inland hotel with a low budget reinvents the traditional French-influenced steep turret roof found on the larger estate houses of Mauritius. They are used here, in a different function, as a roof for external staircases feeding the corridors of typical back entry bedrooms. They flank a typical bedroom block, but contrary to traditional architecture, whereby they are incorporated into the building, here they are detached. A two-sided recliner chair doubling up as a balustrade and covered with a traditional sun and rain canopy in steel, a traditional feature of the Mauritian house, replaces the typical bedroom balcony.

Typical bedroom block elevation. Pencil drawing by Jean-Francois Koenig.

Klondike Village Vacances
Flic en Flac, Mauritius
1988–1990

Klondike Hotel in Flic en Flac on the west coast of Mauritius was completed in 1998–1990. It is a low budget project on a site with no beach and elevated from the sea by a rocky cliff. In compensation, an infinity pool with a walk-in entry from a man-made beach in white cement and sand aggregate was created for the first time in Mauritius. The pencil drawings of the elevations reveal the original treatment of the gable ends of the roofs. Timber battens painted white bring shade, filtered light, and identity to the architecture. A deep veranda acting as a proper living space replaces the usual small balcony found in low budget hotels. This not only upgrades the standard of the hotel, but enhances the guest's experience with tropical living.

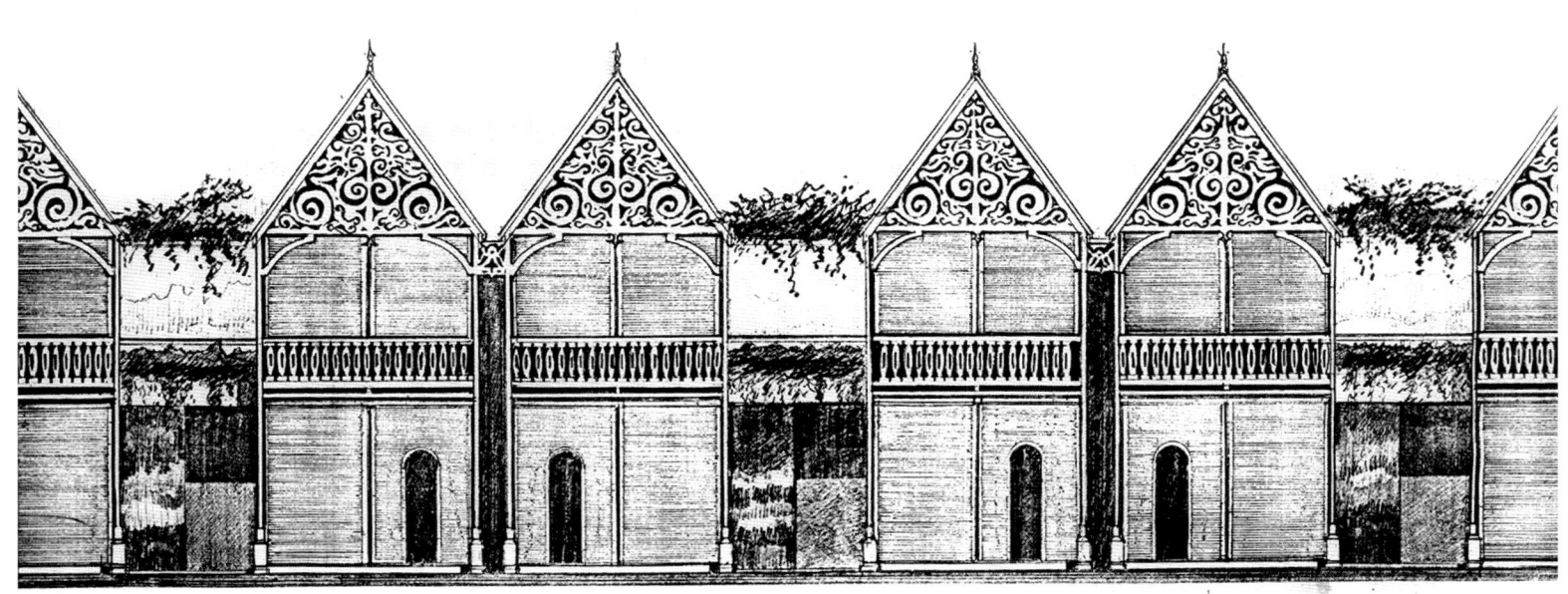

KLONDIKE VILLAGE VACANCES
FLIC EN FLAC

TYPICAL BUNGALOW UNITS
NORTH WEST ELEVATION
1:100

KOENIG ARCHITECTS   K 14 / B.401

Above: Bedroom elevations. Pencil drawing by Jean-Francois Koenig.

Right: Detail of the octagonal pool bar.

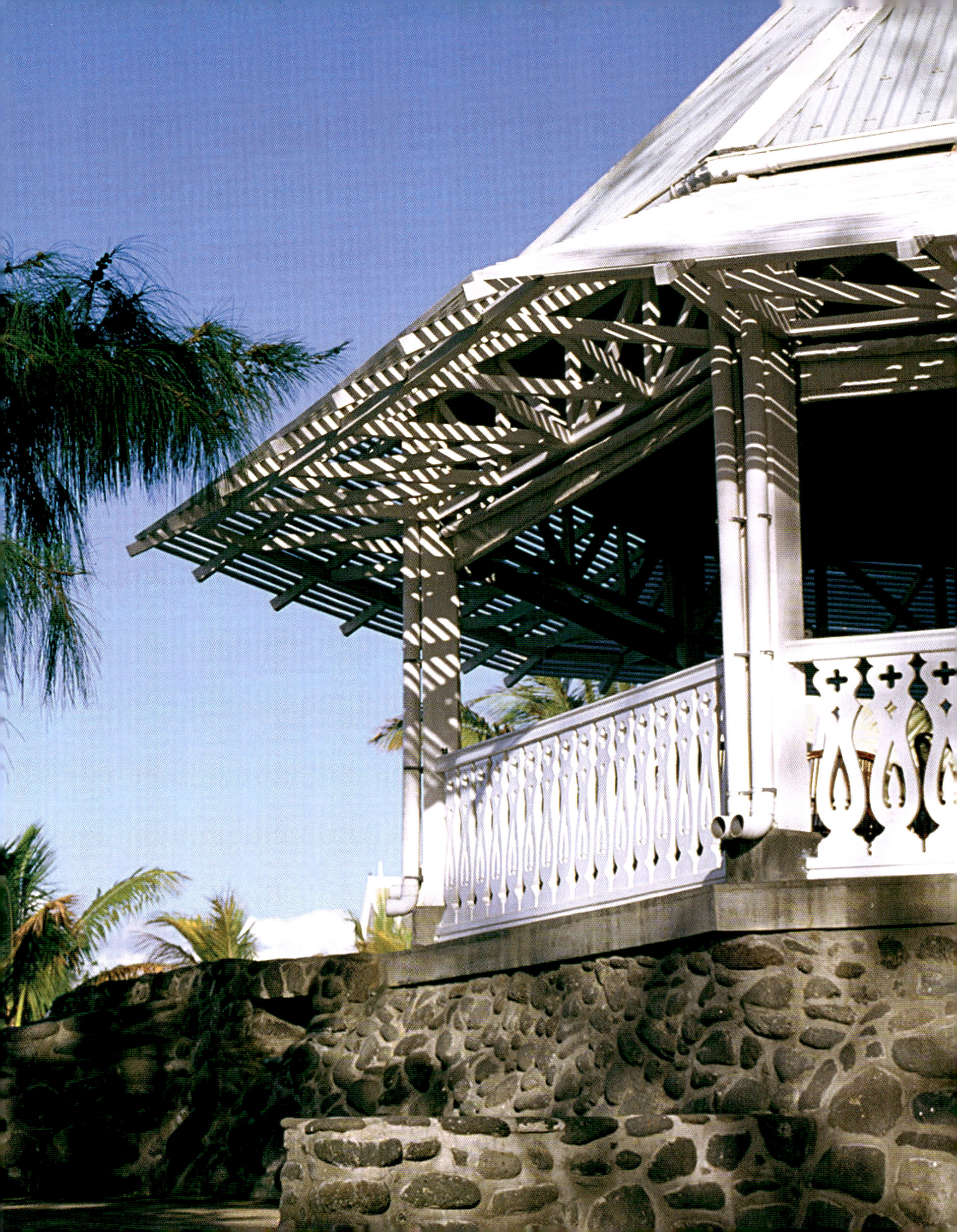

The curving façade of the restaurant with sunscreens.

Top: The gable-end roofs of the restaurant viewed from the pool bar.
Bottom: The restaurant open to the outside with views of the infinity pool merging into the sea.

Sugar Beach
Flic en Flac, Mauritius
1995–1996

Following in the footsteps of Klondike, Sun Resorts built a 4+ star hotel of 250 keys in the style of the traditional architecture of Mauritius to break away from the mould of luxury beach hotels that were repetitively similar at the time. The site is on one of the best beaches on the west coast with calm waters and views of Le Morne mountain. The architecture of the resort identifies guest experience with place and context. Landscaping is comprised, amongst others, of over 2,000 coconut trees transplanted from a nursery specially created for the job. Two large man-made ponds were also built where exotic birds and ducks live in and around them.

Top: Beachfront walkway.

Bottom: View of the main building at nightfall.

Right: The main staircase leading from the reception hall.

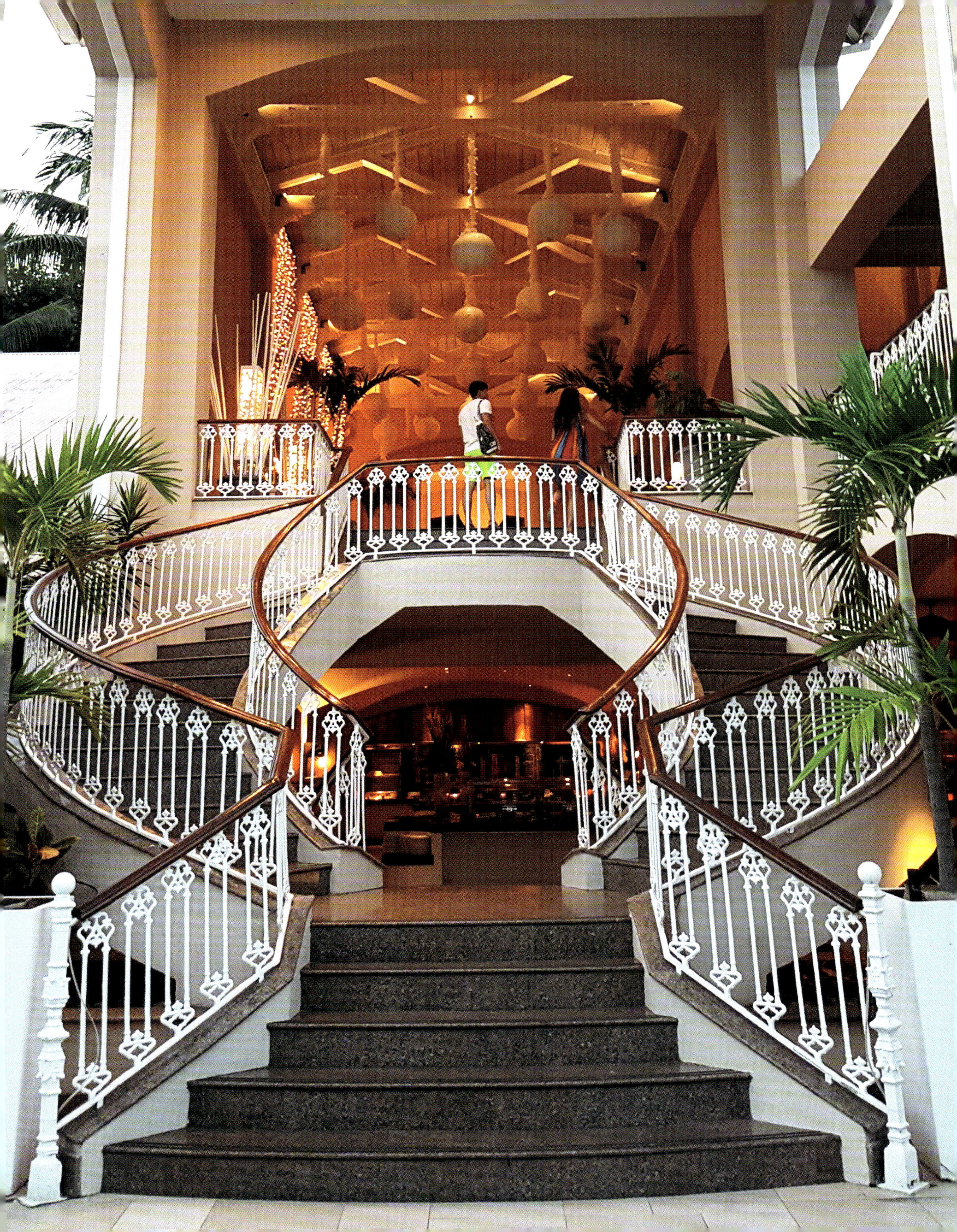

Aerial view of a bedroom wing with manicured lawns in a formal garden planning. The beach in the foreground and views of Le Corps de Guarde and Le Rampart Mountains in the background.

Top: The entrance of the conference centre, framed by ficus trees.
Bottom: The turret roofs of the entrance hall and lounge with its 'raffia' blinds.

Ocean Lodge
Palmar, Mauritius
2002

Ocean Lodge is a luxury boutique hotel on the beach at Palmar on the east coast of Mauritius that responds to the culture and identity of the destination in the hospitality industry. Illustrated by pen and ink drawings, the proposal aims to create an instant connection with place. Individual villas provide more privacy than standard hotel rooms that share common separation walls. Designed on one level with immediate connection to the ground allows private gardens to provide a direct rapport with the scents and sights of the flowers and plants the tropics provide.

Placing the entrance to the suite via the front veranda, like the old houses of the island, reinforces the link with traditional living in Mauritius. The outside has traditional ornamentation and steep timber shingled roofs. The inside offers contemporary amenities with large bedrooms and bathrooms that place the hotel in the higher echelons of hospitality ranking.

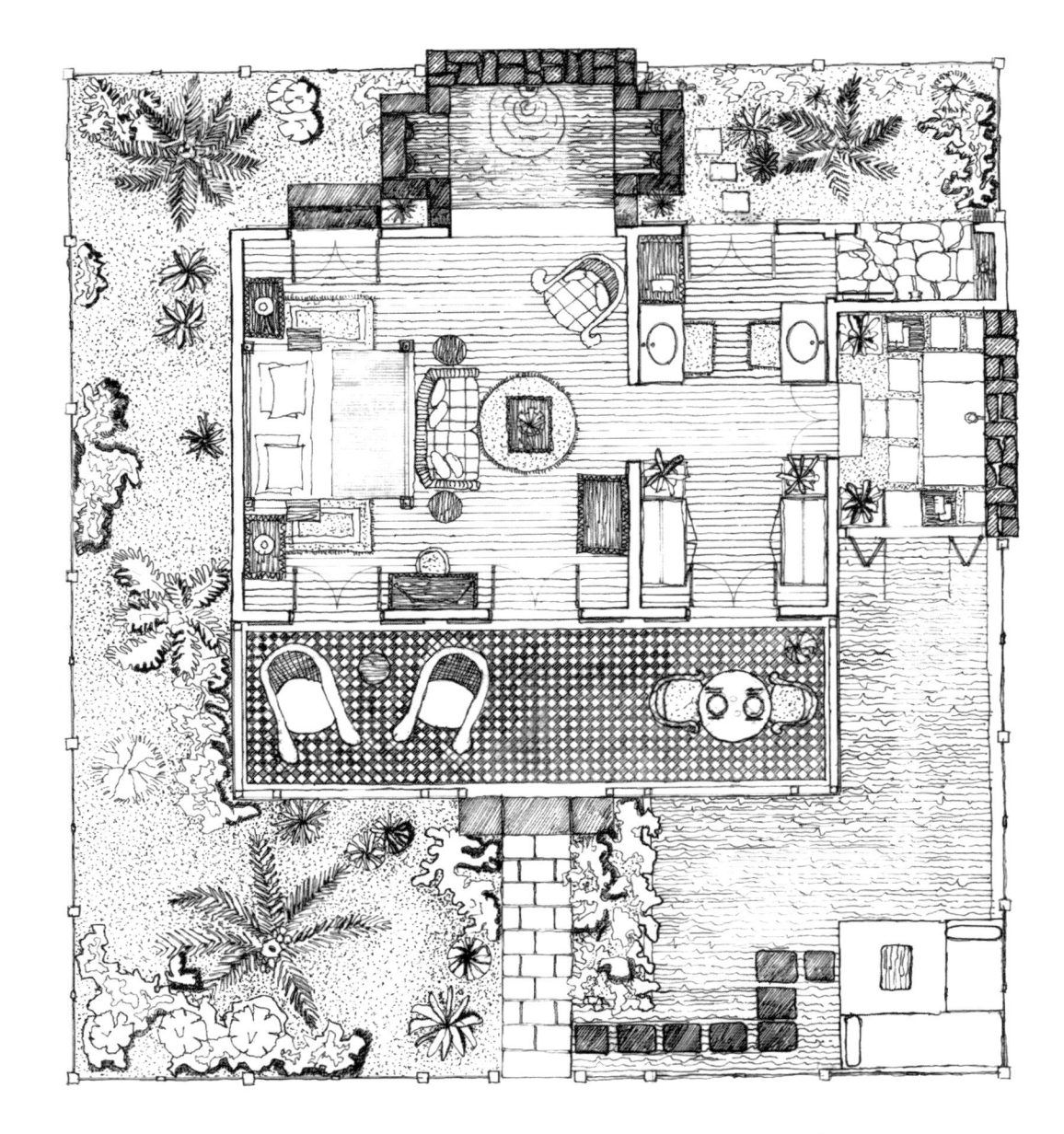

Top and bottom: Plan and elevation of typical guest villa. Technical pen and ink drawing.

Top and bottom: Plan and elevation of guest suite villa. Technical pen and ink drawing.

Indian Resort & Spa
Le Morne, Mauritius
1997–2002

At the foot of Le Morne mountain, next to a site listed by UNESCO, lies the site of the Indian Resort and Spa which runs along the unspoilt beach of the south-western coast of Mauritius. Wary of the need for new construction to make as little a mark as possible on the landscape, the first proposal was for a 150 bedroom hotel on half the area of the site.

Client demands for a 380 bedroom hotel on the totality of the site resulted in a new project which continued the original concept of preserving the existing vegetation, setting all buildings back 50 m from the high-water mark, keeping existing trees, and increasing the landscaping with palm trees to form an efficient wind barrier giving landscaping priority over the buildings themselves. A concept called "the absence of Architecture".

To give cultural identity to a hospitality project in Mauritius, a country where the majority of the population is of Indou origin, the architecture assumes a Mogul theme from which the hotel bears its name. It is designed in the context of the pluri-cultural society of Mauritius, bringing meaning to the destination, and reinforces the link between architecture and culture. The first proposals for the main building illustrate the Mogul architecture whilst retaining a Mauritian beach hotel identity. They were turned down and the main building was redesigned to what is built today. The Mogul architectural theme was retained for some bedroom wings whilst others were simplified to meet a lower budget.

The layout of the master plan starts with the identification of a bend in the site which allowed the public road to continue straight into the site, making it appear as the hotel's entrance driveway. The entrance gate and the gable end of the porte cochère are positioned one behind the other on the road's axis. The white pillars of the entrance were decorated by Tamil workers from mainland India and were recommended to the client by the architect.

The architecture of the main building is a continuous undulating curve that meanders around internal and external spaces in a mixture of flat concrete and pitched roofs in thatch. The concrete ceiling painted white creates a fluid space that evokes a taut tent. The roofs define zoning and break down the scale into a more humane environment of what is effectively a big restaurant, bar, reception, and boutiques for a 380-key beach resort. Inside the central courtyard is a ficus 'multipliant' tree which was transplanted and grown to the desired giant proportions. Myriads of birds come and sing there, keeping the guests in close contact with nature, in an architecture that un-formalises space for a relaxed holiday in the tropics.

Right: The guest bedrooms seen from the garden.

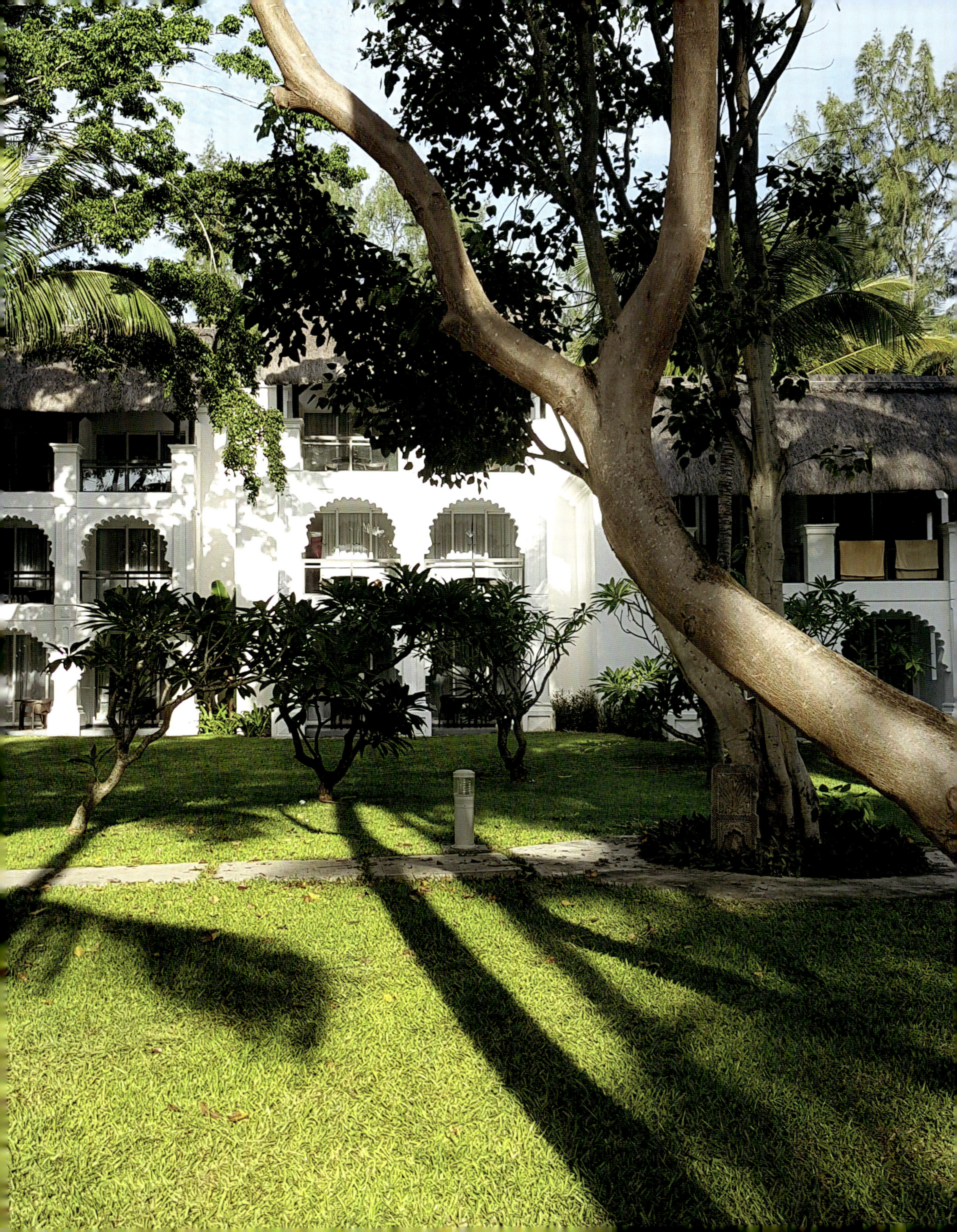

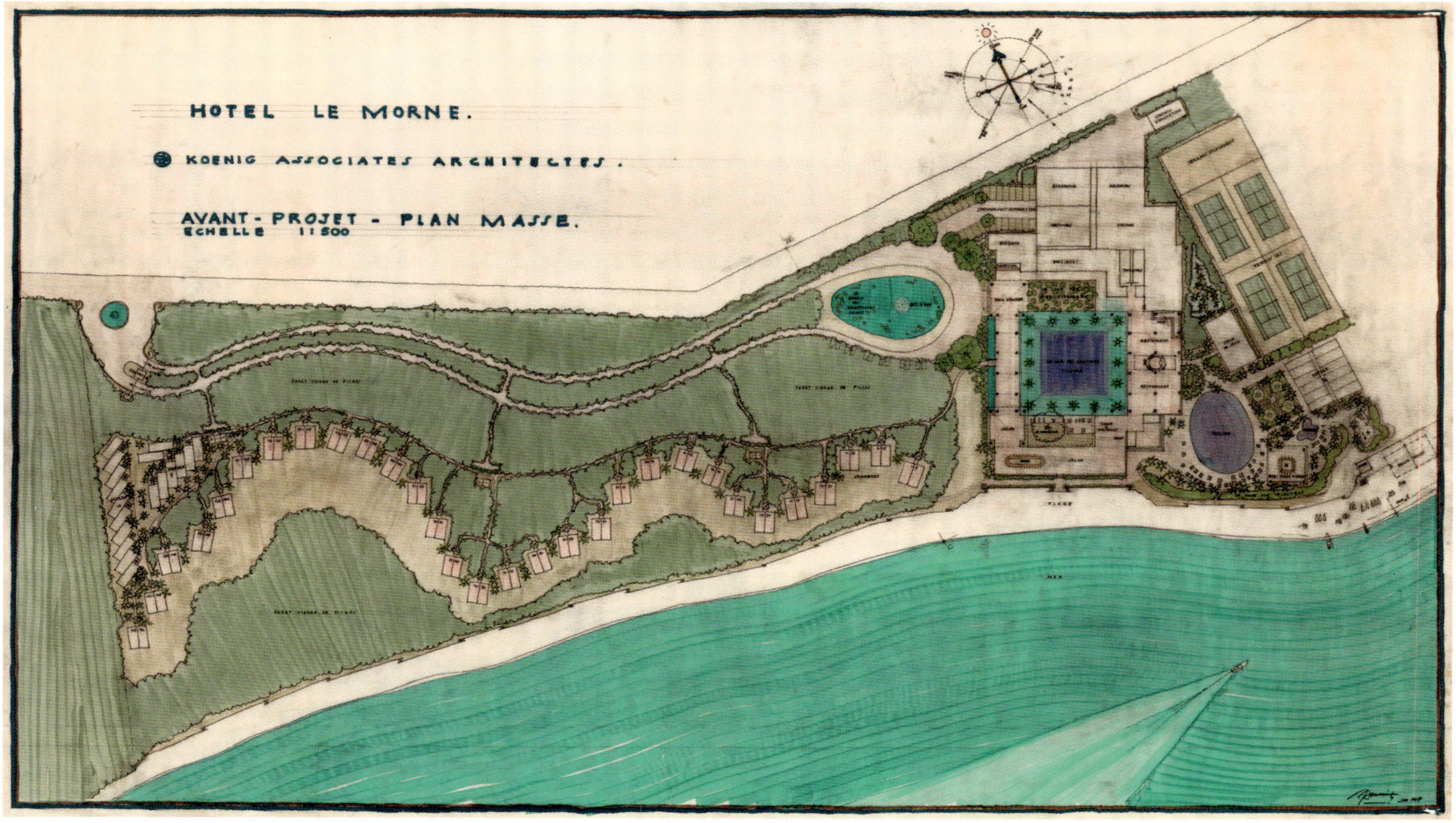
HOTEL LE MORNE.
KOENIG ASSOCIATES ARCHITECTES.
AVANT-PROJET - PLAN MASSE.
ECHELLE 1:500

Top: The main building with its thatched roofs and view of Le Morne Mountain.

Bottom: The buildings are well recessed from the beach behind the existing vegetation.

Top left: The bedroom wings are not visible from the sea.

Bottom left: The first master plan proposal. Drawing by Jean-Francois Koenig.

Top: Main building elevation. Drawing by Jean-Francois Koenig. Centre left, top: Main building section. Drawing by Jean-Francois Koenig. Centre left, bottom: Guest bedrooms elevation. Drawing by Jean-Francois Koenig. Centre right and bottom, Right: Guest bedrooms in the garden.

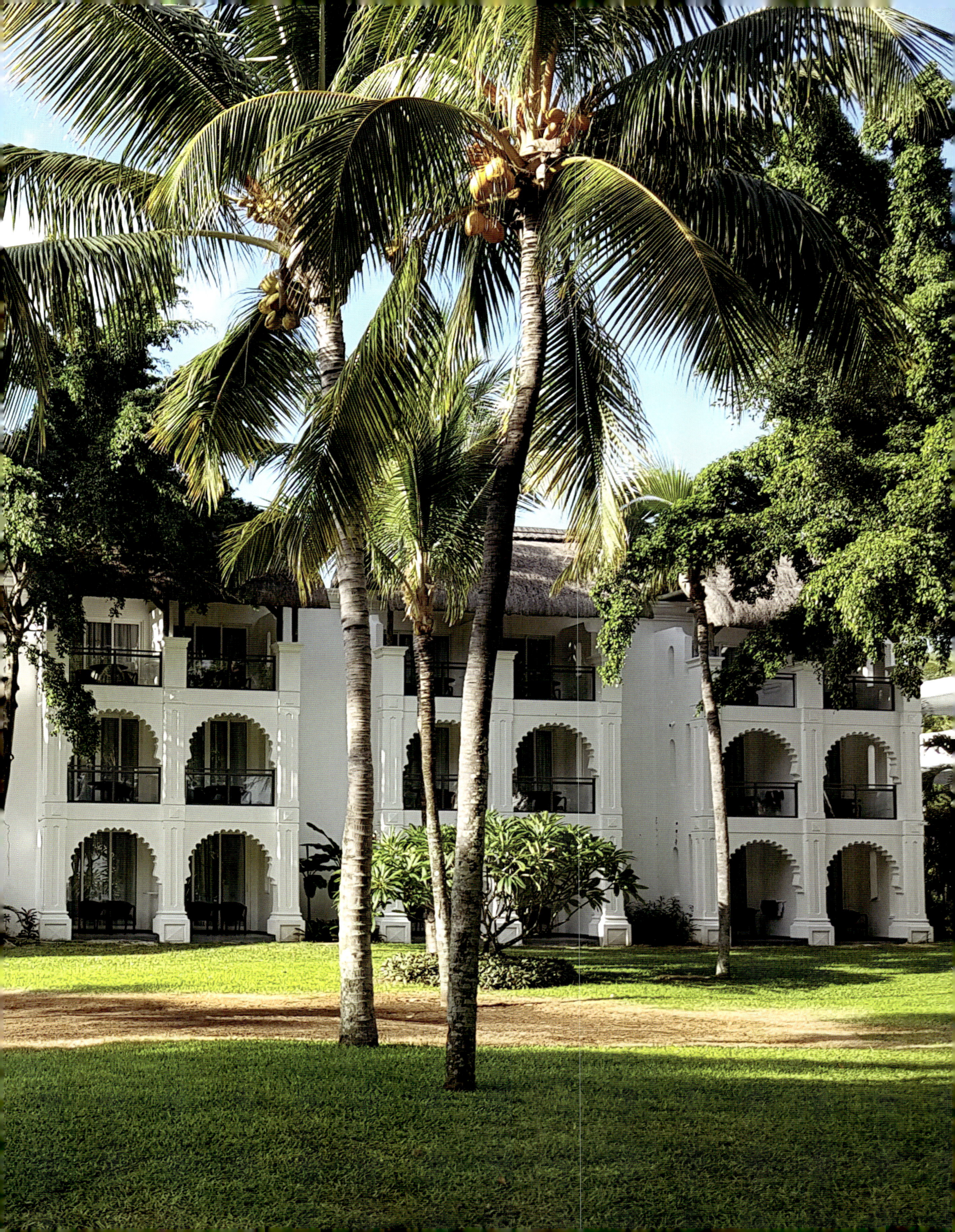

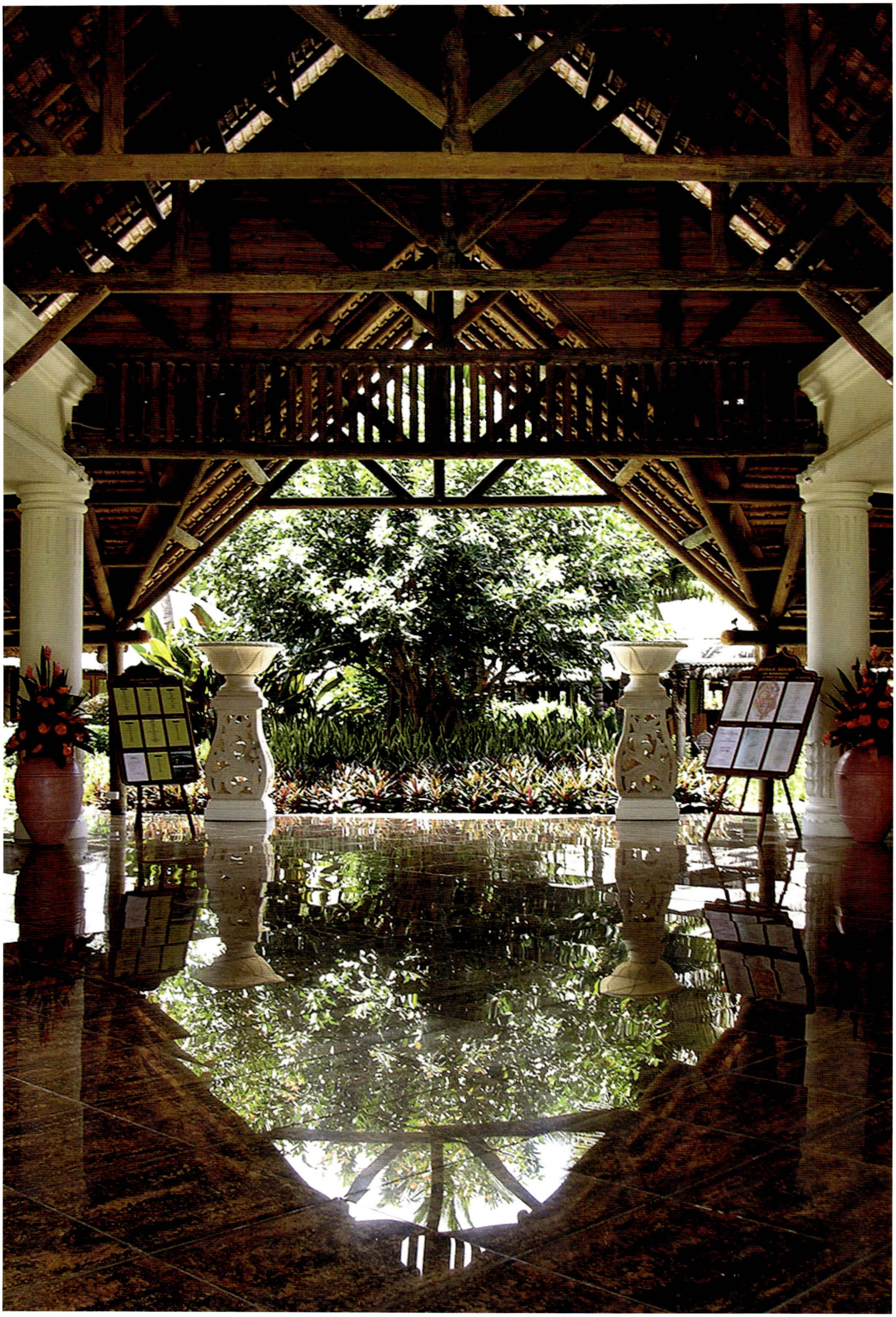

Top: The bar of the main building.

Bottom: Detail in the Tamil-Indian style on the base of the entrance columns. The antique furniture and stone sculptures come from India.

Left: The entrance lobby with view of the courtyard with its ficus tree.

179

Above and top right: "The absence of architecture". The buildings are set back behind and within the landscaping to leave the site as natural as possible.

Bottom right: 'Plein air' painting by Jean-Francois Koenig executed on the site before the start of construction. "Le Morne – face sud", 41 x 55 cm, acrylic on board, won the March 2015 award "Outstanding Acrylic" in the FASO BoldBrush Painting Competition.

181

Les Creolias

Calodyne, Mauritius
2000–2005

Coloured felt-tip drawings illustrate a 5-star hotel for Les Creolias in Calodyne on the north-east coast of Mauritius. Guest experience is defined with open-to-the-sky walk-in showers in private garden enclosures, covered day beds, water features, extension of the inside–outside relationship from front to back of the room 'enclosure', thatch roofs, and weathered-looking stonework integrating with nature.

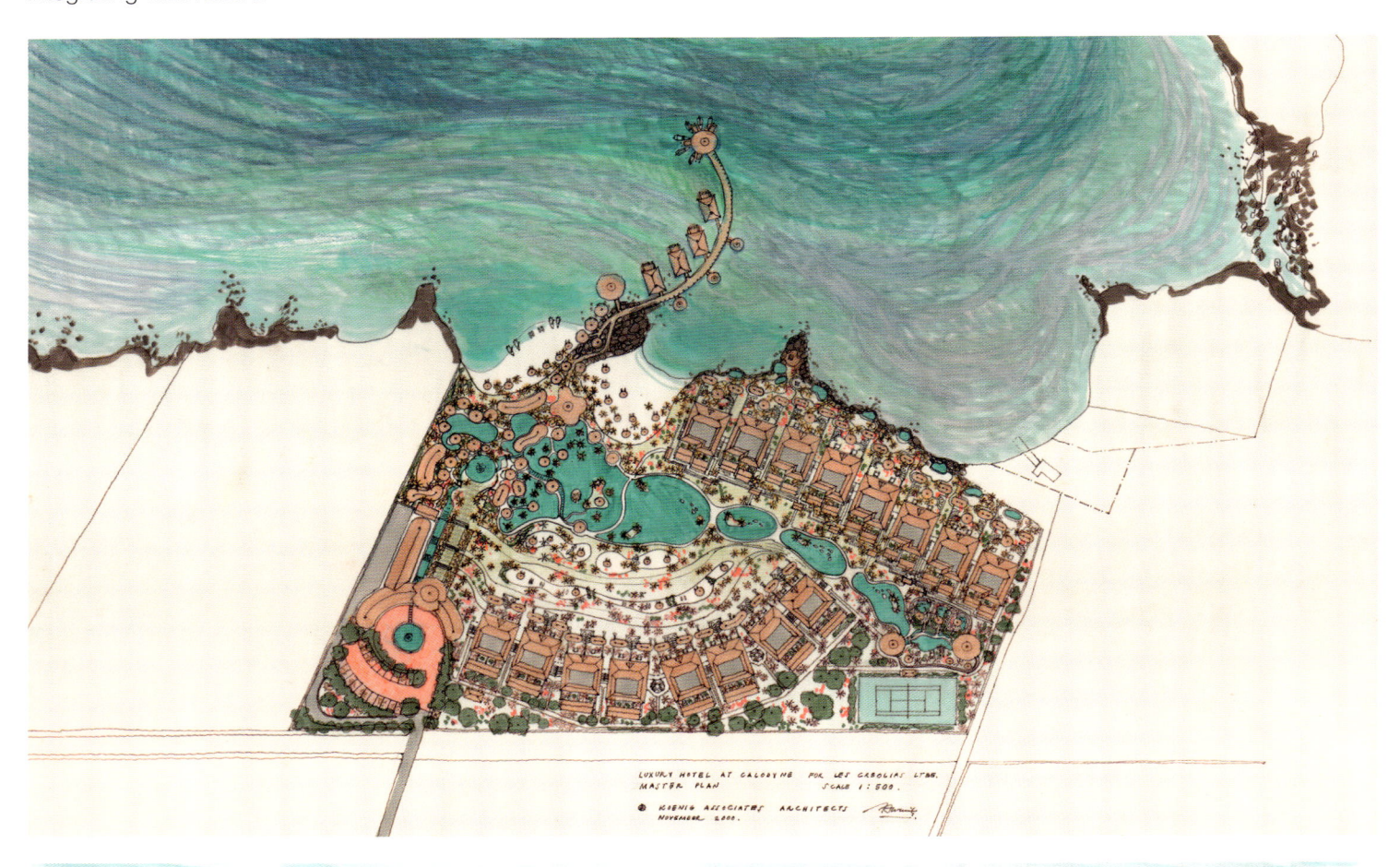

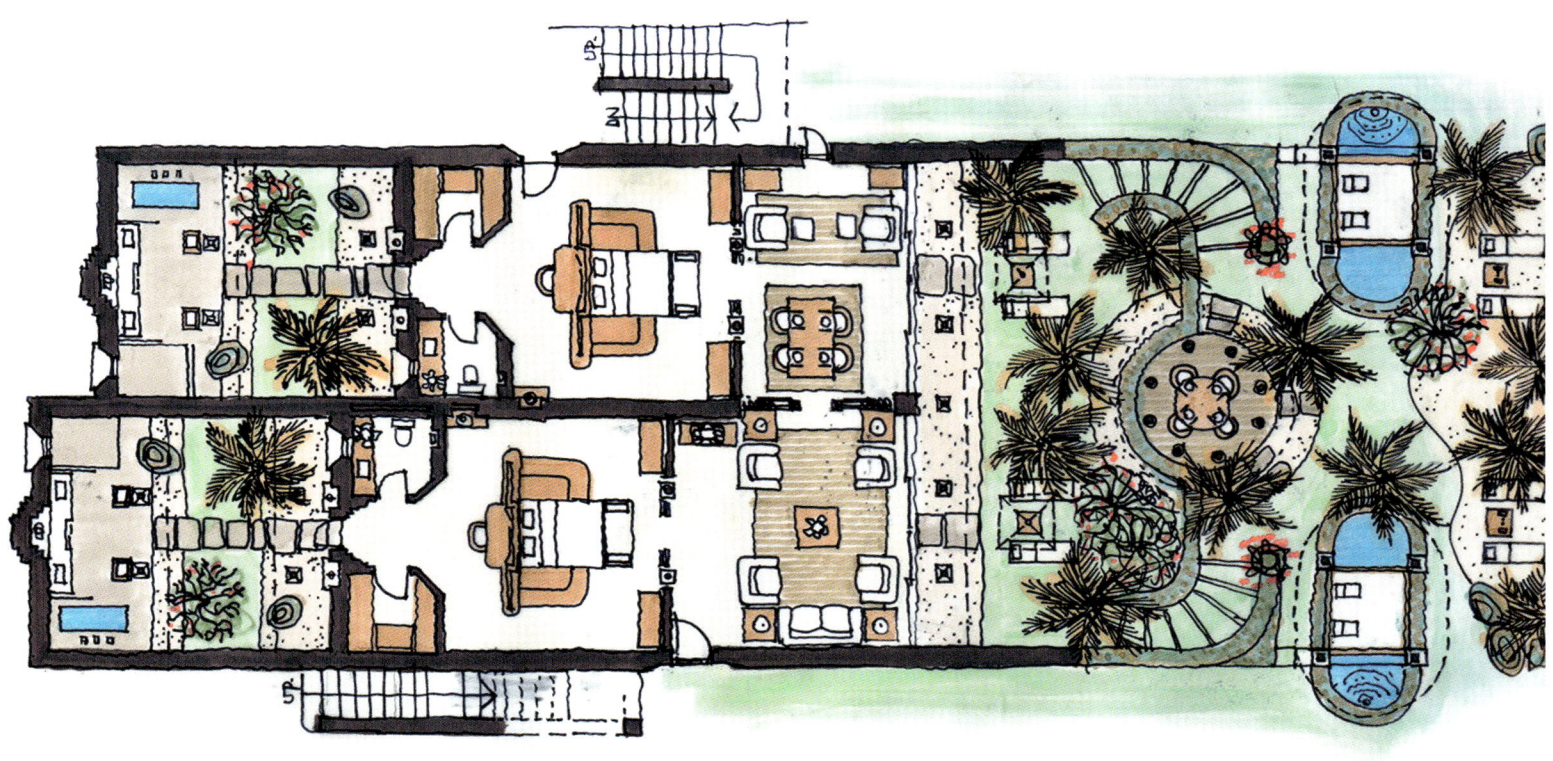

Top: Cross section.

Centre: Ground-floor plan.

Bottom: First-floor plan.

Top left: Master plan.

Bottom left: Elevations.

All drawings in felt-tip markers and pens by Jean-Francois Koenig.

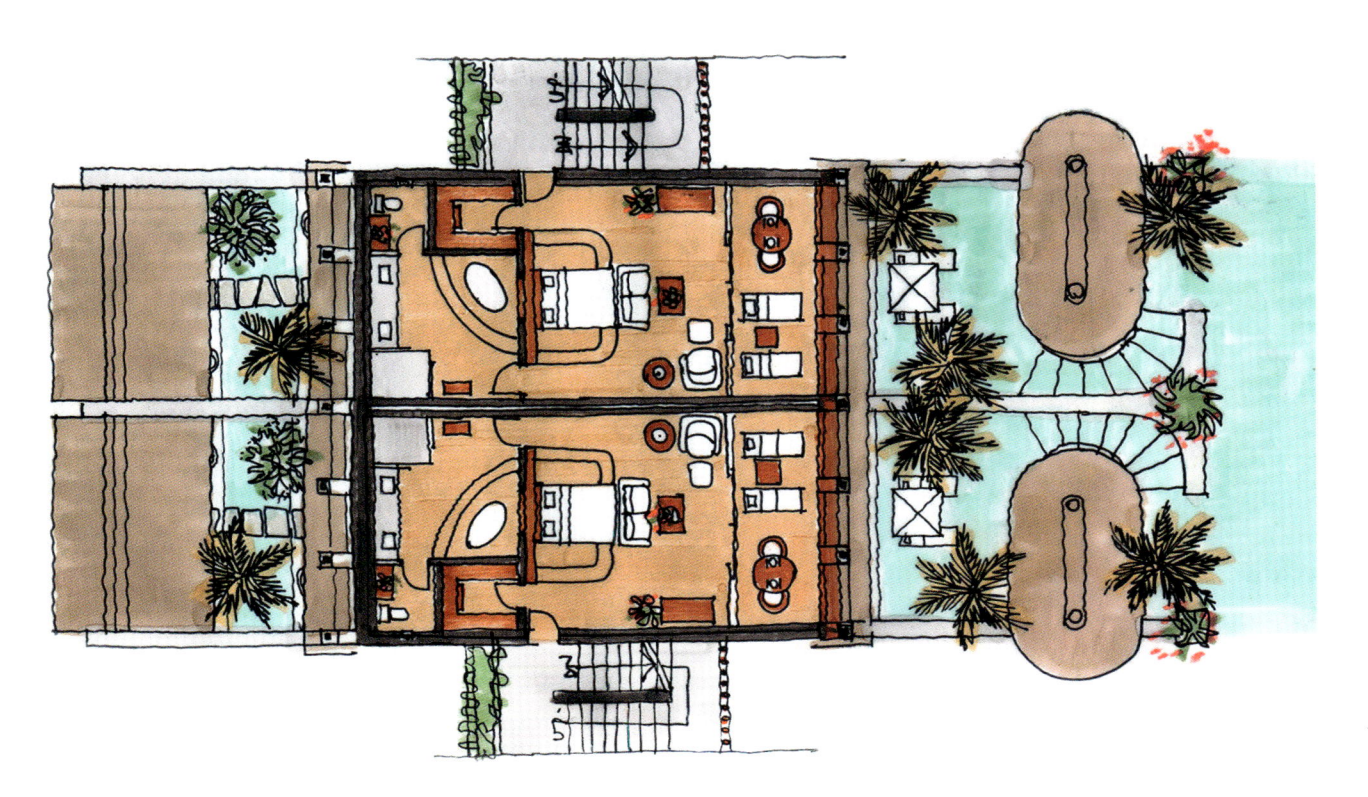

183

Boutique Hotel and Golf
Bel Air St Felix, Mauritius
2003

The estate is situated on the cliffs of the south coast. It has a character of its own and is endowed with natural grassed dunes and three rivers that meander in a series of curves to the sea. The rivers end in cascades over the cliffs. The terrain, with all its natural beauty, lends itself to links golf. A boutique hotel with individual villas in generous grounds make up the proposed master plan of a low-density luxury development.

The separation of the river into smaller streams is turned into a series of small natural waterfalls and running water ponds. The hotel suite consists of an entrance gazebo leading to a large private courtyard containing a day bed gazebo sitting over water cascading into a floor channel that runs to and through a rectangular swimming pool. The floor channel carries through to the inside of the suite and separating the living and sleeping areas of the suite helping air-conditioned cooling and humidity control. It continues outside to fall into stepped ponds.

The walls are in stone, made to look old. Timber shingles, fixed to boarding on rafters expressed internally, make up the roofs that are left to weather naturally. They are supported by solid timber round columns. The floors are in matt beige travertine marble and the choice of materials is one of low maintenance and refinement.

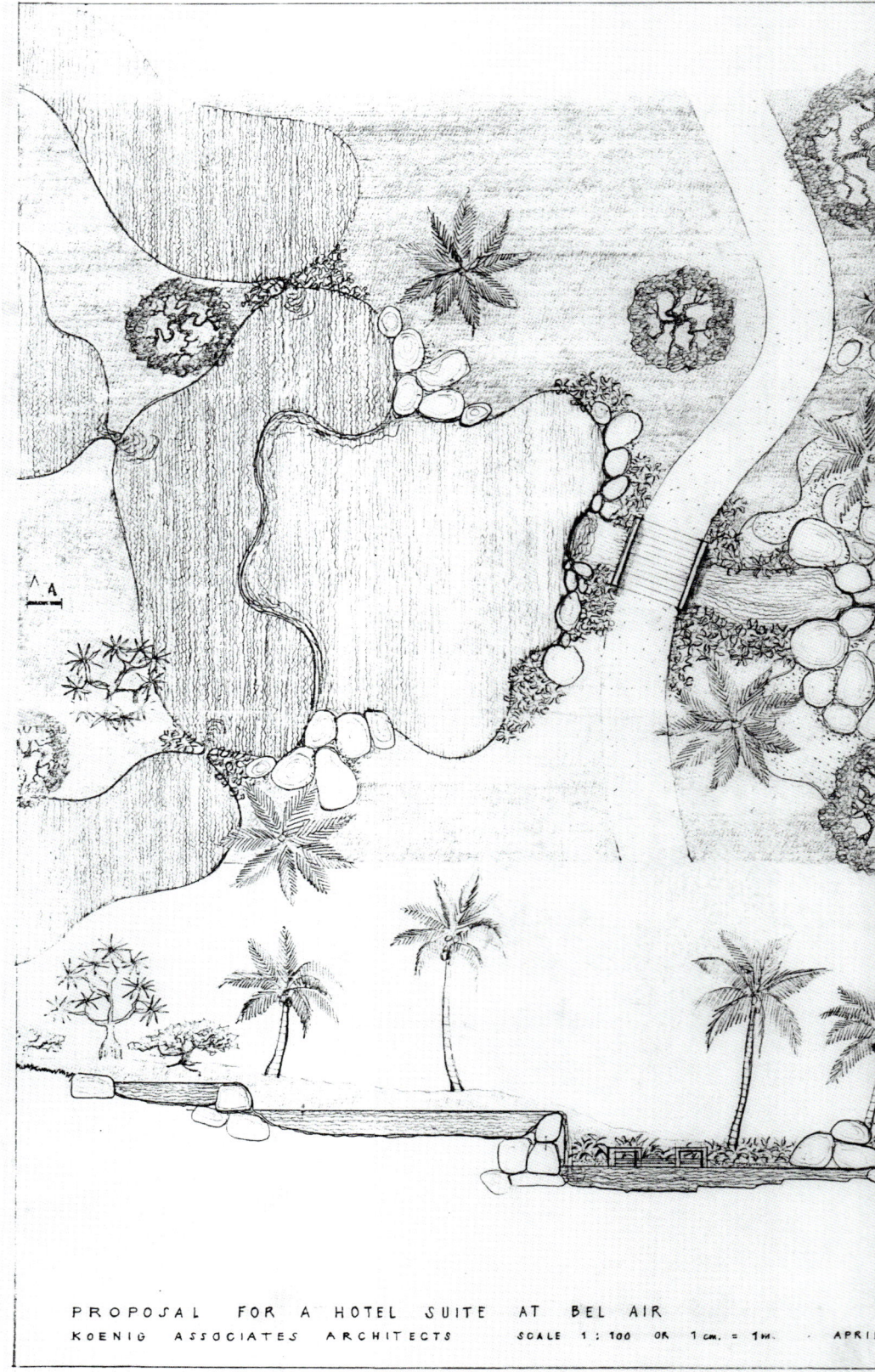

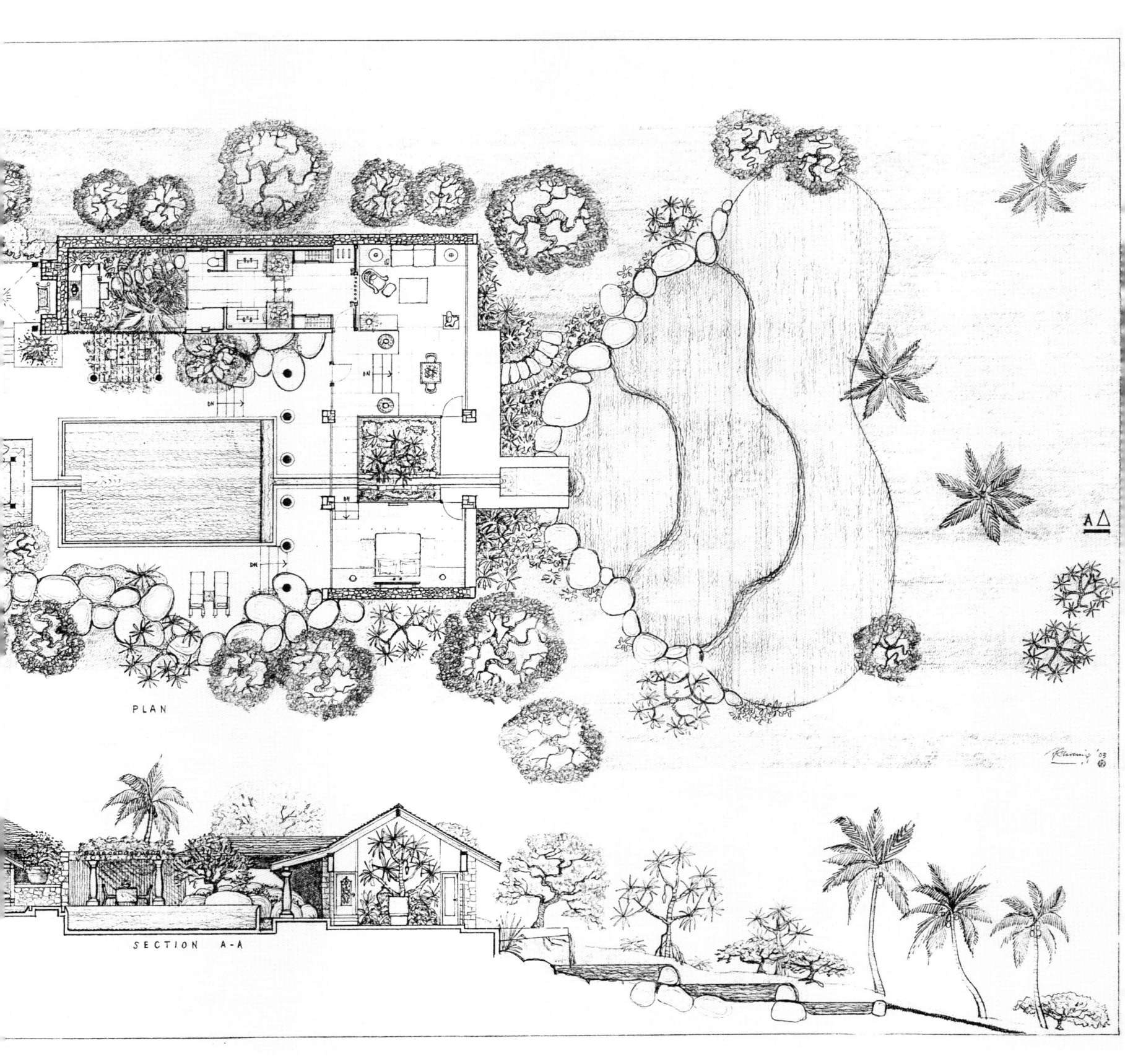

Above: Hotel suite plan. Pencil drawing by Jean-Francois Koenig.
Left: Master plan. Pencil drawing by Jean-Francois Koenig.

La Plantation Hotel
Balaclava, Mauritius
1997–1999

The site is on the banks and the estuary of Rivière Citron in Balaclava on the north-west coast of Mauritius. The hotel is built on the remains of an unfinished structure in a bad state and with a low budget. Extensive landscaping, reflective pools, a pool bar, and entrance lobby were the only additions to the existing structures.

The entrance lobby is a new addition consisting of a long space with a rectangular reflective pool in the middle. The pool adds volume by mirroring the treated pine trusses designed by Koenig without a structural engineer. They are left unvarnished and span 12 m to support a lightweight thatch roof. The roof, like a giant veranda, is open at both ends as well as along its length providing ample fresh air. A grand staircase leads down, on axis, to the pool bar and restaurant below. New concrete columns with classical detailing, painted white, are positioned on the existing structural grid externally, parallel to the existing columns of the body of the existing structure, which consisted of just posts and beams. The floor slabs were not all completed and, to save costs and turn a low budget into an architectural advantage, several were left as is, creating triple volume courtyards open to the sky and planted in the existing ground with lush tropical vegetation and coconut trees.

To the landscaping was added a large reflective pool with transplanted coconut trees in planters. Landscaping is treated as an architectural element, making the pools, weaving in and out in a rectangular pattern become an integral part of the design. The coconut trees unify water and grass in a giant external floor pattern. All existing mature trees are kept and with substantial complementary additions, landscaping is given priority over the buildings themselves.

Main building and pool bar on the left seen from the reflective pool.

Top: Arrival porte cochère.
Bottom: The main building with its thatched roof and treated pine balustrade left unpainted.

Top: The entrance lobby with its treated pine pole trusses left unpainted and its floor reflective pool. The suspension and pedestal lamps in steel and wood respectively are designed by Jean-Francois Koenig. Bottom: The restaurant on the ground floor extends externally with tables placed on islands in the reflective pool.

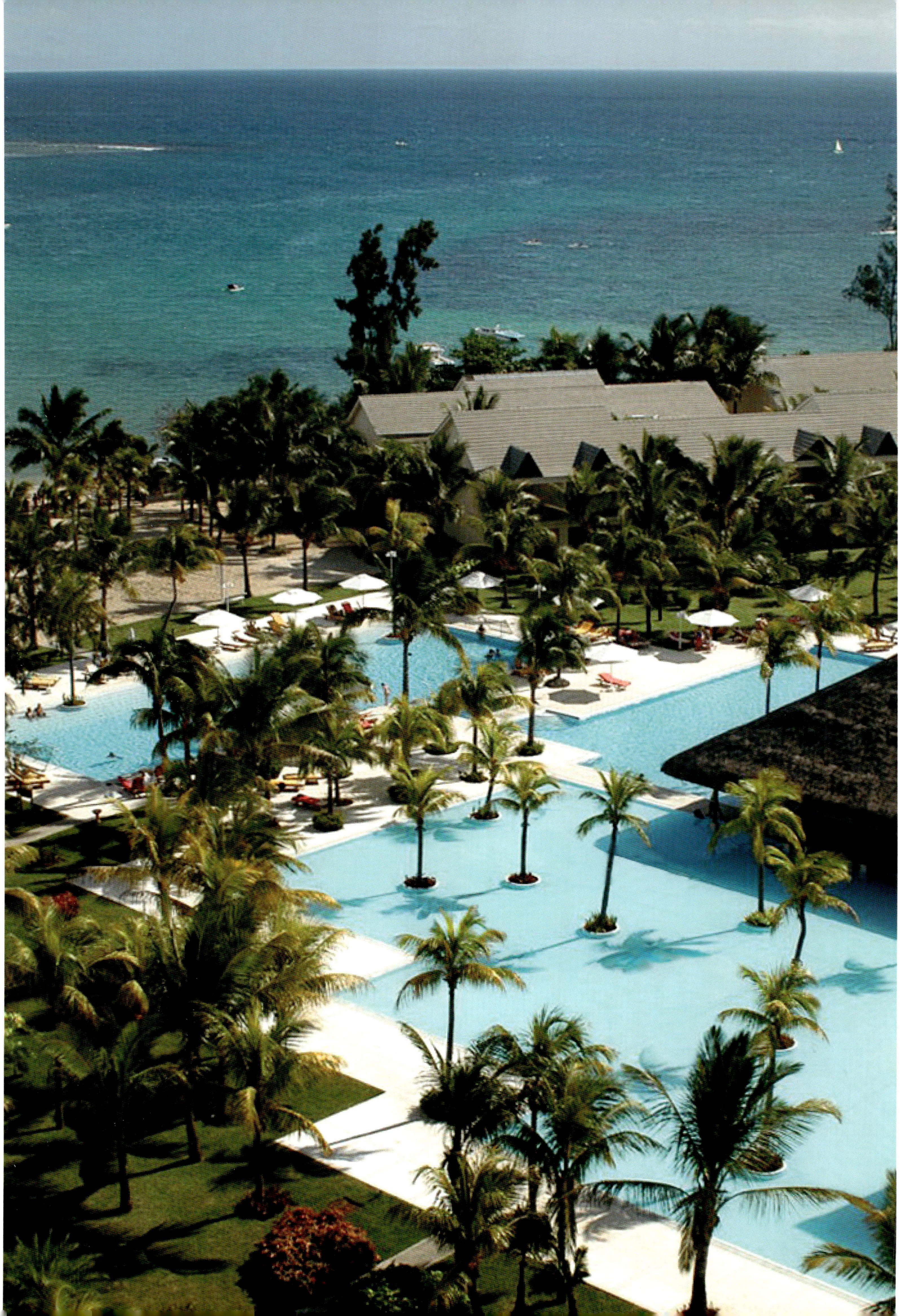

Top: The guest bedrooms set in the landscaping.

Bottom: The banks of La Rivière Citron, which borders the site, before entering the sea and the hotel behind.

Left: Aerial view of the pools and newly planted coconut palm trees.

Holiday Villas
Petite Case Noyale, Mauritius
2000

Planned for the hospitality industry to accommodate large families with children as an alternative to a traditional hotel, four independent villas, two with seven bedrooms and two with three bedrooms, are designed on the slopes of an inland site with sea views in Petite Case Noyale on the south-west coast of Mauritius.

The living areas are under large protecting roofs open on four sides with no walls, windows, or doors. Further eating and relaxing spaces are planned under pergolas heavily planted with flowering creepers to enhance the guest experience of external tropical living. They are on an upper level created as a viewing deck on the roof slab of the bedrooms below. The bedrooms form a heavy inclined stone base on which sit the public zones taking advantage of the sloping terrain to form a higher vantage point to view the sea.

Access and approach are at the back, through landscaped courtyards and reflective pools leading to open indoor–outdoor spaces. The garden contains grown 'flamboyant' trees which bloom in summer with orangey-red flowers. The scents and sights of the colours of the tropics are further enhanced by bougainvillea covered pergolas which flower best on the sunny west coast. The colourful landscape and the architectural solution are responsive to site and context and is illustrated by felt-tip pen drawings.

Right: Site plan. Felt-tip pen drawing on tracing paper by Jean-Francois Koenig.

PLAN MASSE
KOENIG ASSOCIES ARCHITECTES
MAISONS A LES SALINES - ÎLE MAURICE - CORBALIE PRESTIGE PROPERTIES LTD.

1:400
FEV 2000

FACADE · COTÉ MER

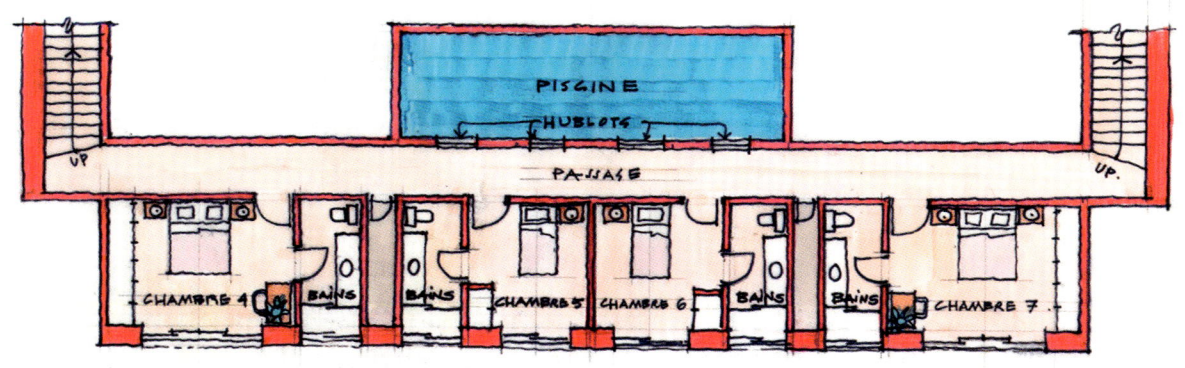

PLAN - NIVEAU · INFERIEURE.

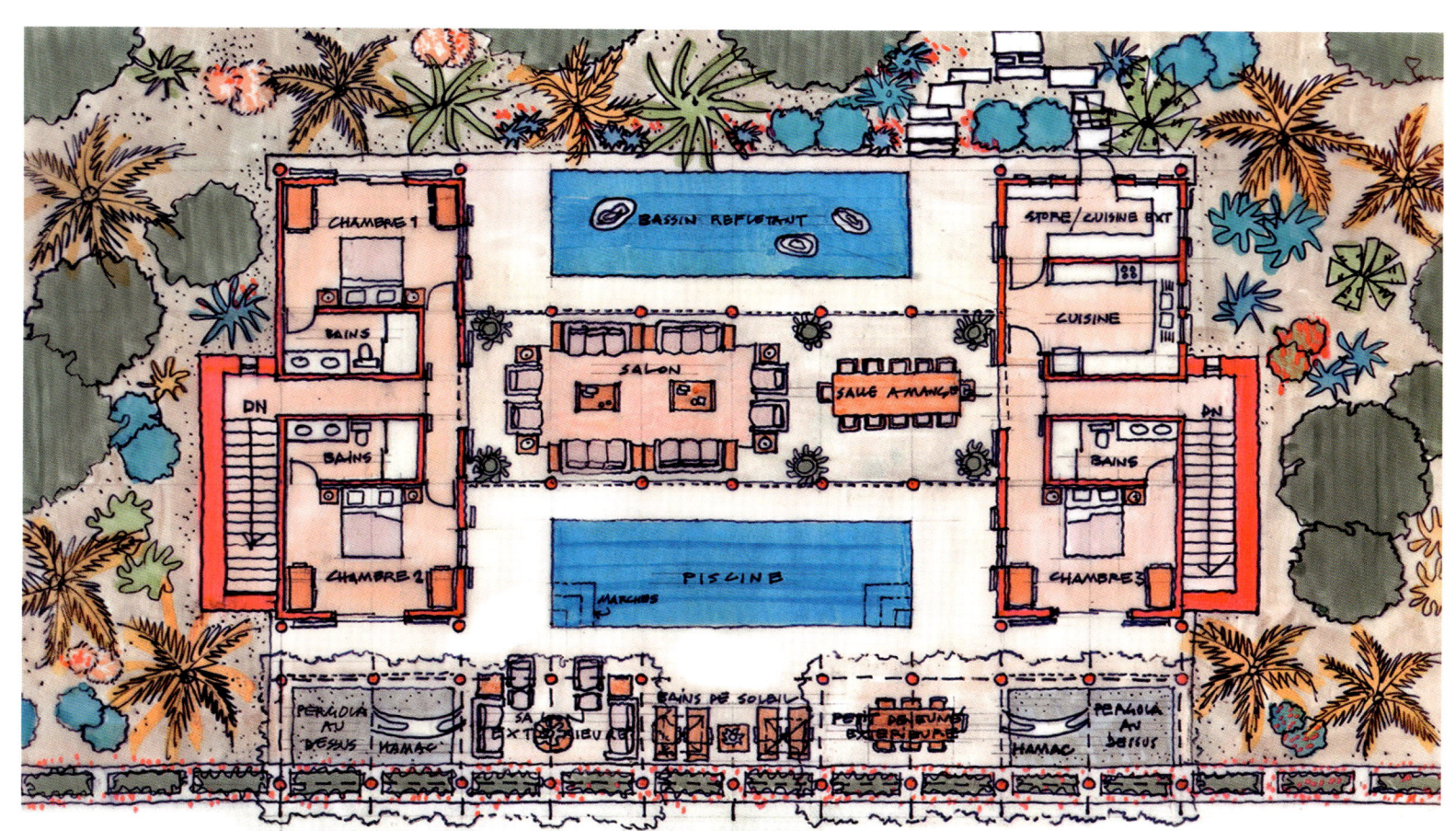

PLAN - NIVEAU SUPERIEURE.

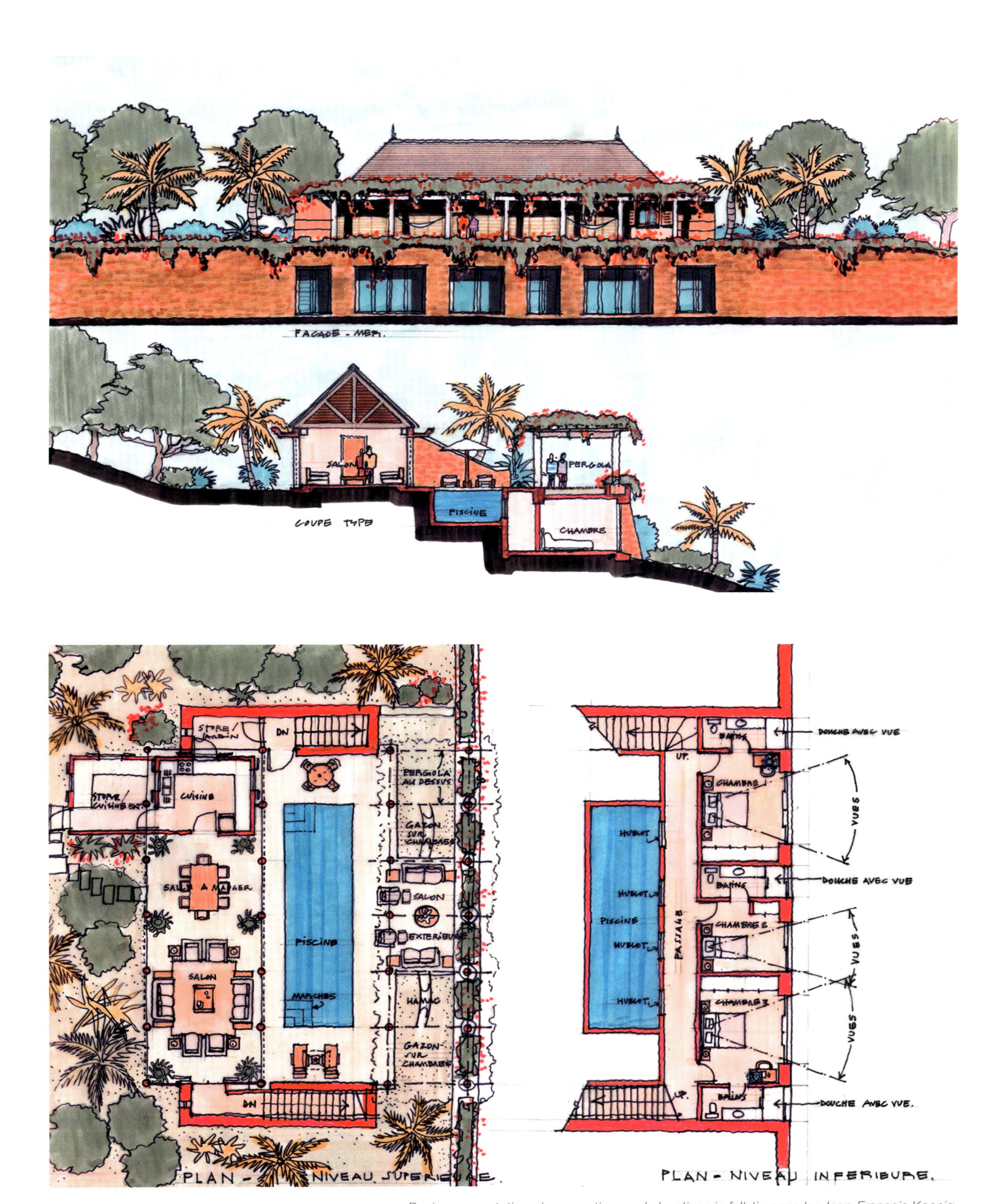

Design presentation plans, section, and elevations in felt-tip pens by Jean-Francois Koenig.

The Palace Hotel

Al Hamra, Ras al-Khaimah,
United Arab Emirates
2002

Designed for Sheikh Saud bin Saqr al Qasimi, the ruler of the Emirate of Ras al-Khaimah of the United Arab Emirates, the Palace Hotel is a 5-star establishment on the coast at Al Hamra. The design is non-typical of what was happening architecturally in Dubai at the time and is what sets this hotel apart. The proposal is an architectural statement, yet retains a certain old charm of the desert with sophisticated class. The architecture is a mixture of old and new but very much 'of the place'. Several features worth mentioning are: the giant 20-storey glass atrium window of the 40 x 40 m plan of the atrium with its Arabian arch and motif inserts; the triple volume walk through entrance with a glass roof shaded by perforated louvres and flanked on both sides with 70 vertical jet fountains intended to cool; the square atrium entrance lobby itself with a central 20 x 20 m glass floor reflective pool acting like a frosted glass light well to the restaurant below; its glass ceiling holding the floor of the exclusive club bar above; the 'mashrabiya' timber screens and balustrades of the bedrooms hanging off the façade of the beige desert-like rough finish of the tower in stark contrast to the high-tech reflective glass cladding of the corners housing fire escapes; the swimming pool with date palm trees providing shade to swimmers on a giant scale; the slide-open roofs of the top-floor grand suites to look at the stars like the Bedouins live in the desert and engrained in the culture of the people; and the 'Arabian crown' of the tower in serrated reflective glass catching light like jewellery. The project is illustrated with coloured drawings in felt-tip pens and photographs of the model.

Sea-facing façade of the main building. Photograph of the model.

Entrance façade of the main building.

CLUB-LOUNGE FLOOR PLAN
LEVEL + 76.6 m

17TH FLOOR PLAN
LEVEL + 54.4 m

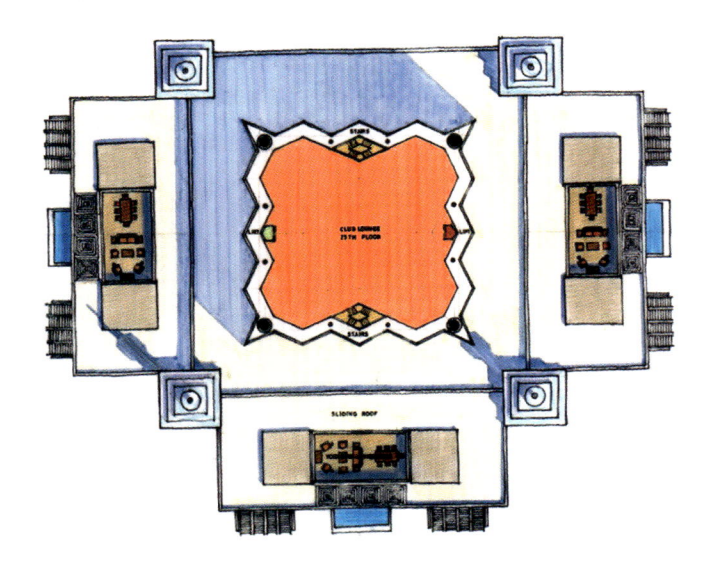

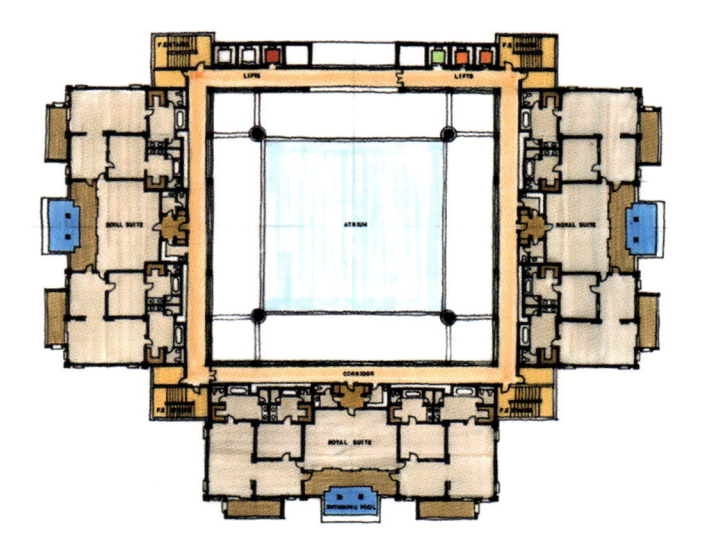

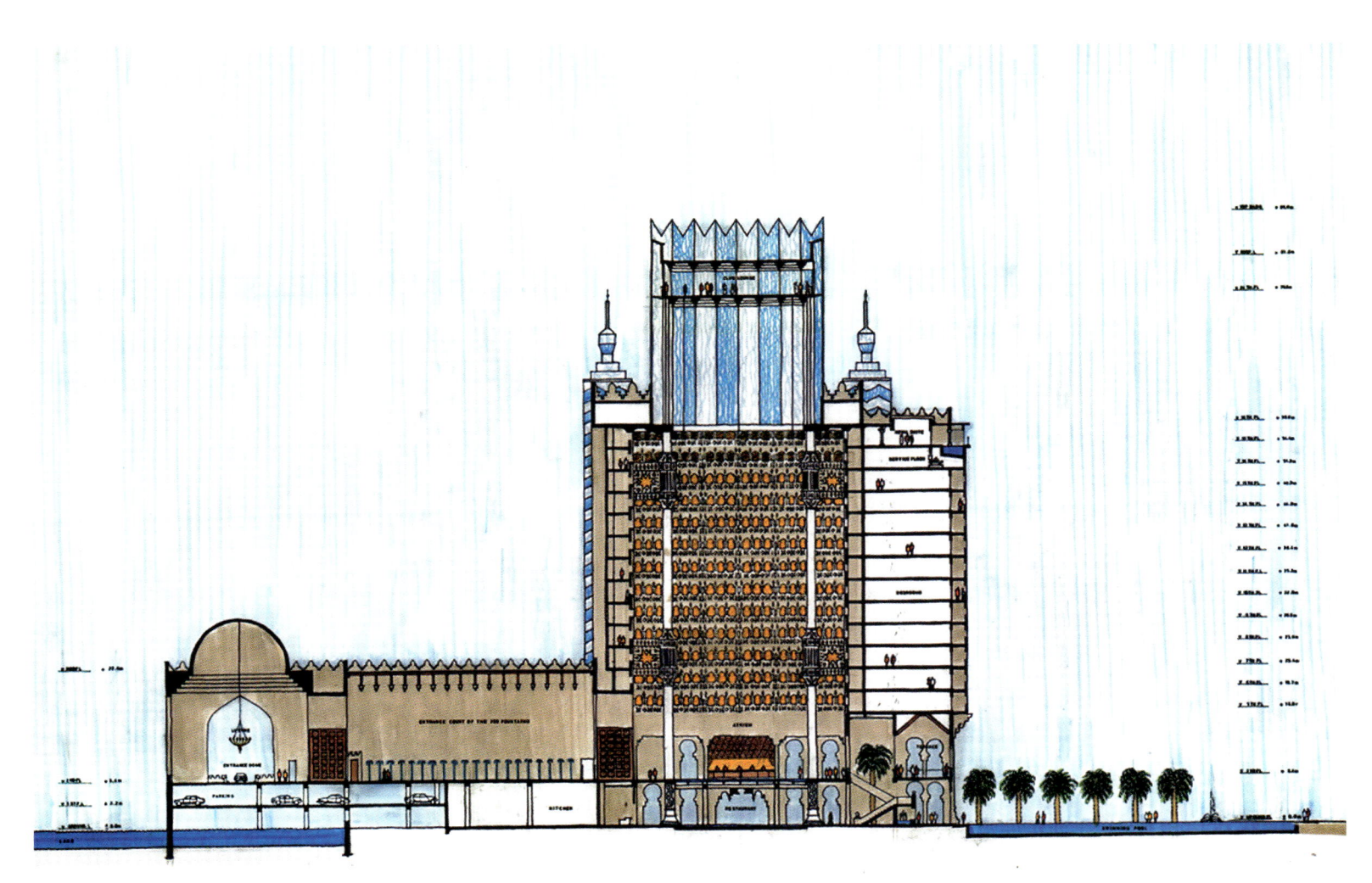

Top left: Top-floor plan of the Club Lounge and roof plan of the bedroom wings with their sliding roofs over the lounge of the Presidential Suites.

Top right: Plan of the Presidential Suites.

Bottom: Cross section through the main building.

All drawings in felt-tip pens on tracing paper by Jean-Francois Koenig.

Skystar
Bangalore, India
2004–2008

The project consists of twin towers for a hotel and apartments on a site next to the Golden Palms Hotel in Bangalore, India, which belongs to the legendary actor and film director Sanjay Khan. Both towers are circular in plan and tapered in elevation to evoke the flame of the Indian oil lamp, used for Divali, the Indian festival for the celebration of the triumph of light in the world. A third similar tower is proposed in a second phase on another site nearby with the intent of creating a trilogy of vertical towers of different heights sending a strong visual signal in silhouette seen from the newly proposed motorway leading from the new airport leading to downtown Bangalore. The project was initiated by Sanjay Khan and evolved in a property development partnership with the company Godrej.

Right: The twin towers.
Below: The trilogy of towers.

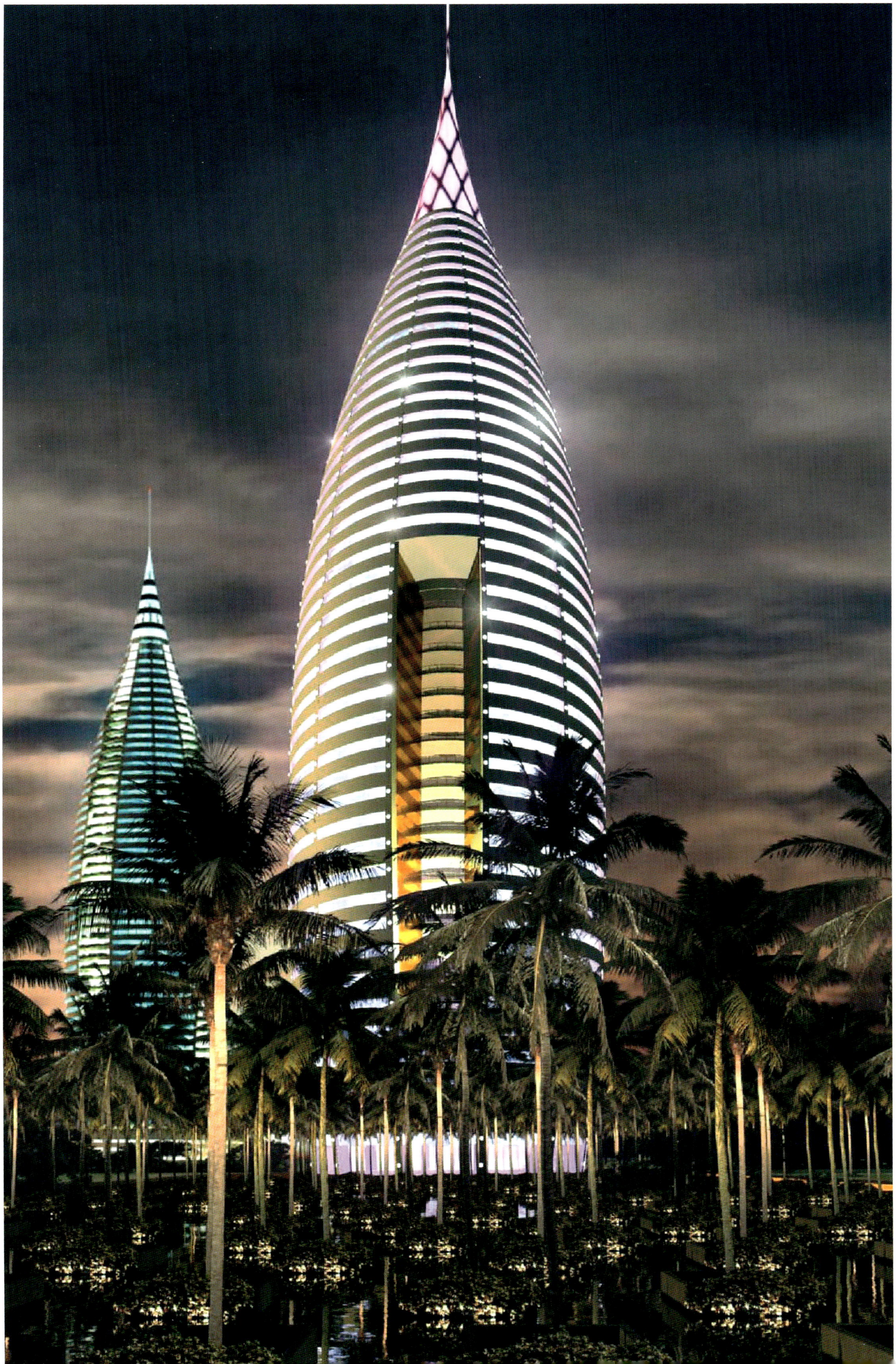

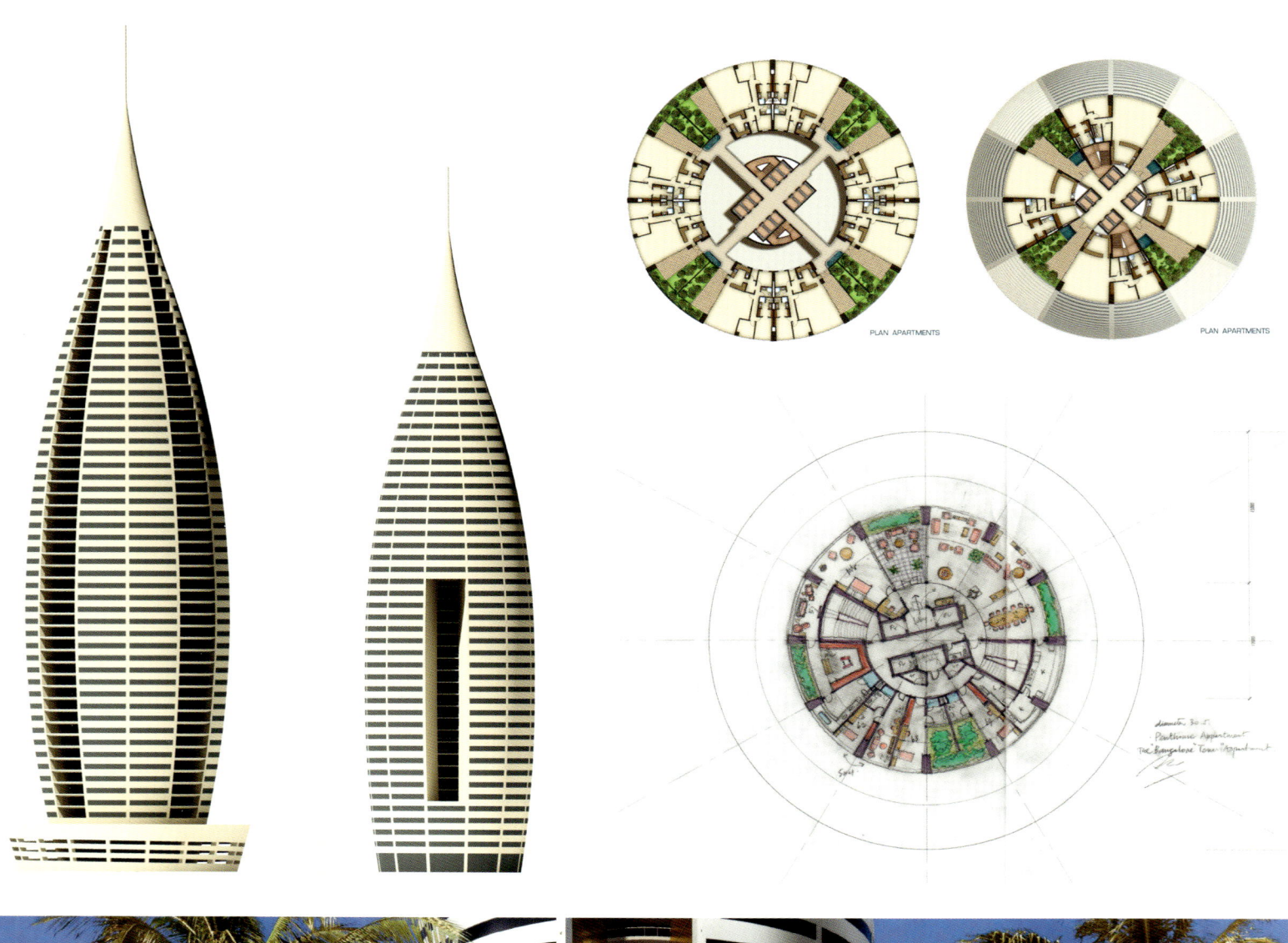

PLAN APARTMENTS
PLAN APARTMENTS

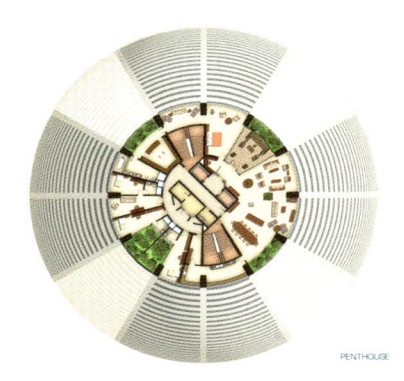

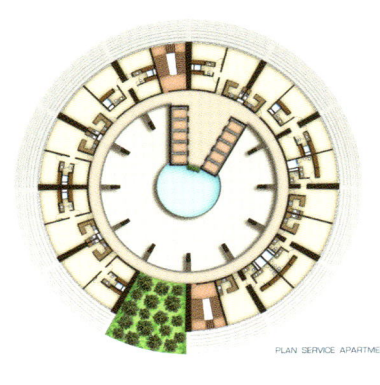

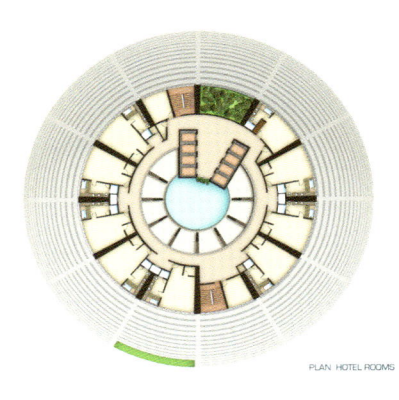

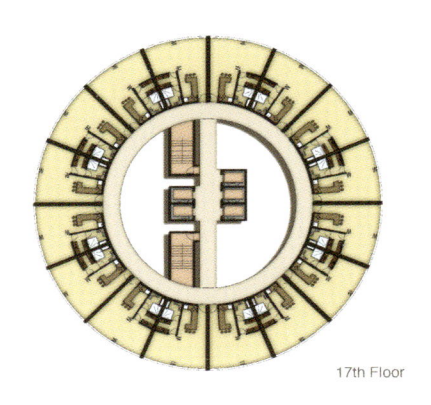

PENTHOUSE PLAN SERVICE APARTMENTS PLAN HOTEL ROOMS 17th Floor

Left/top left: Apartments tower elevation.

Left/top centre: Hotel tower elevation.

Left/top right: Apartments tower. Floor plans.

Left bottom: Front view of the hotel tower with its coconut grove set in a giant reflective pool.

Top left: Apartments tower. Sketch of penthouse apartment.

Top right: Hotel tower: typical floor plan.

Centre: Master plan perspective.

Bottom: Master plan.

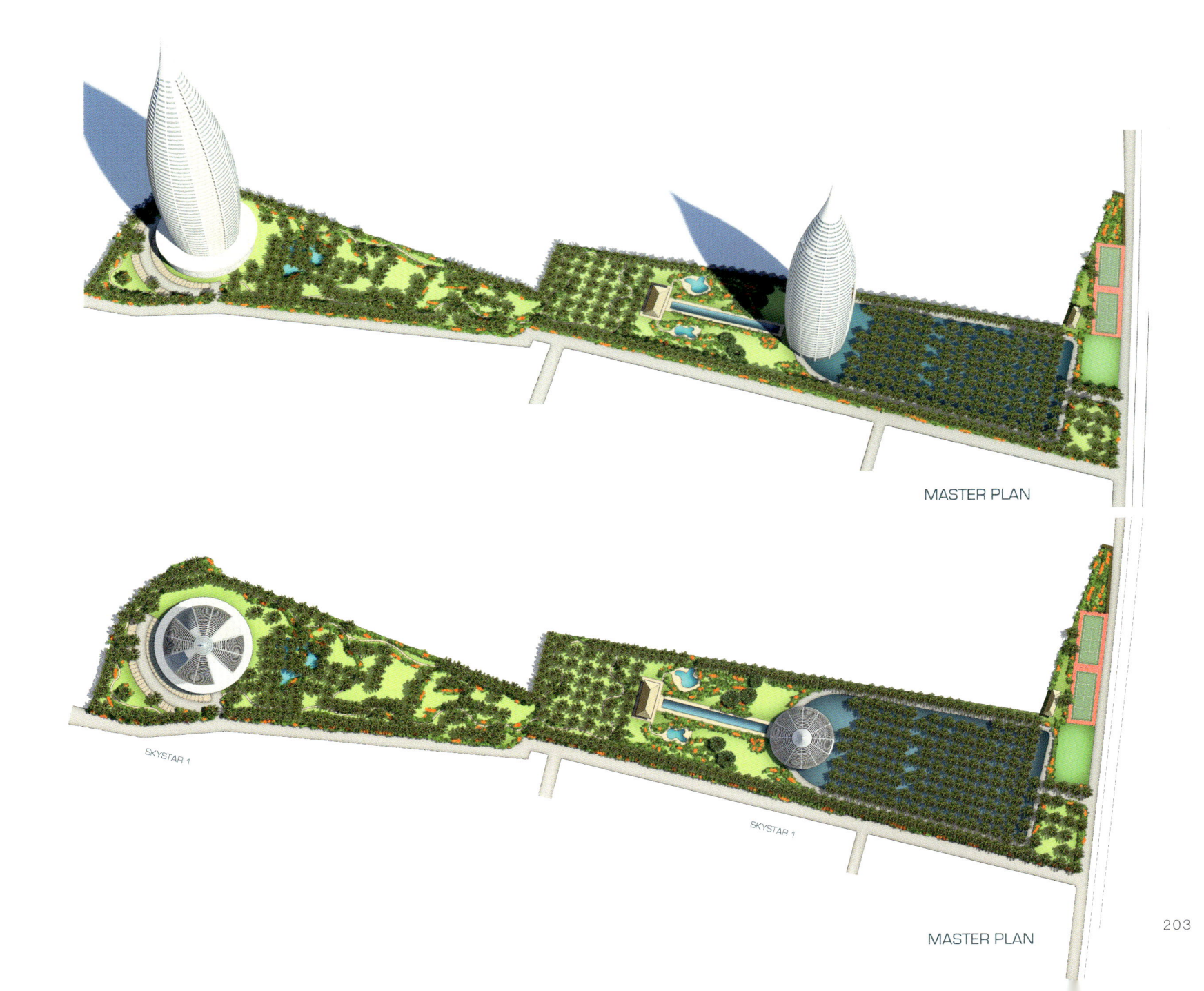

MASTER PLAN

SKYSTAR 1

SKYSTAR 1

MASTER PLAN

203

CHAPTER 3
PUBLIC, EDUCATIONAL, INDUSTRIAL

Mauritius Commercial Bank, Trou aux Biches	206
School for Underprivileged Children	210
Federation Square	211
B+J Mechanical Workshop	218
Baldwins Steel – Canteen and Wash Bay	224
Fresh-Up Factory	230
Springs Brewery	232
Tropic Knits Factory	236
Pre-Mixed Concrete Factory	238

Mauritius Commercial Bank Trou aux Biches

Mauritius

1990–1992

The project is a local branch for the Mauritius Commercial Bank at Trou aux Biches, a coastal village located in the north-west of the Island. Built in concrete, the detailing of the building follows the old traditional architecture of the country, placing it in its context and reinforcing the notion of a local architectural identity.

In contradiction to what could have been normally expected for a bank, which needs to project an image of robust security, the building has a glazed frontage and gable ends. It is built in the spirit of the glazed verandas of old houses found on the higher plateau of the Island where the climate is cooler and verandas were often closed with delicate timber and glass screens. Here the façades are built with solid steel sections acting as a security grill and integrated within them is a pattern of specially designed frosted, transparent, and reflective glass. They give good daylight and the screens project ever-changing patterns of light and shade. The floor is local basalt stone left unpolished and is used both internally and externally. Painted teak shingles, recovered from a demolished building, are reused as the roof cladding.

Right: The glazed gable end of the banking hall.

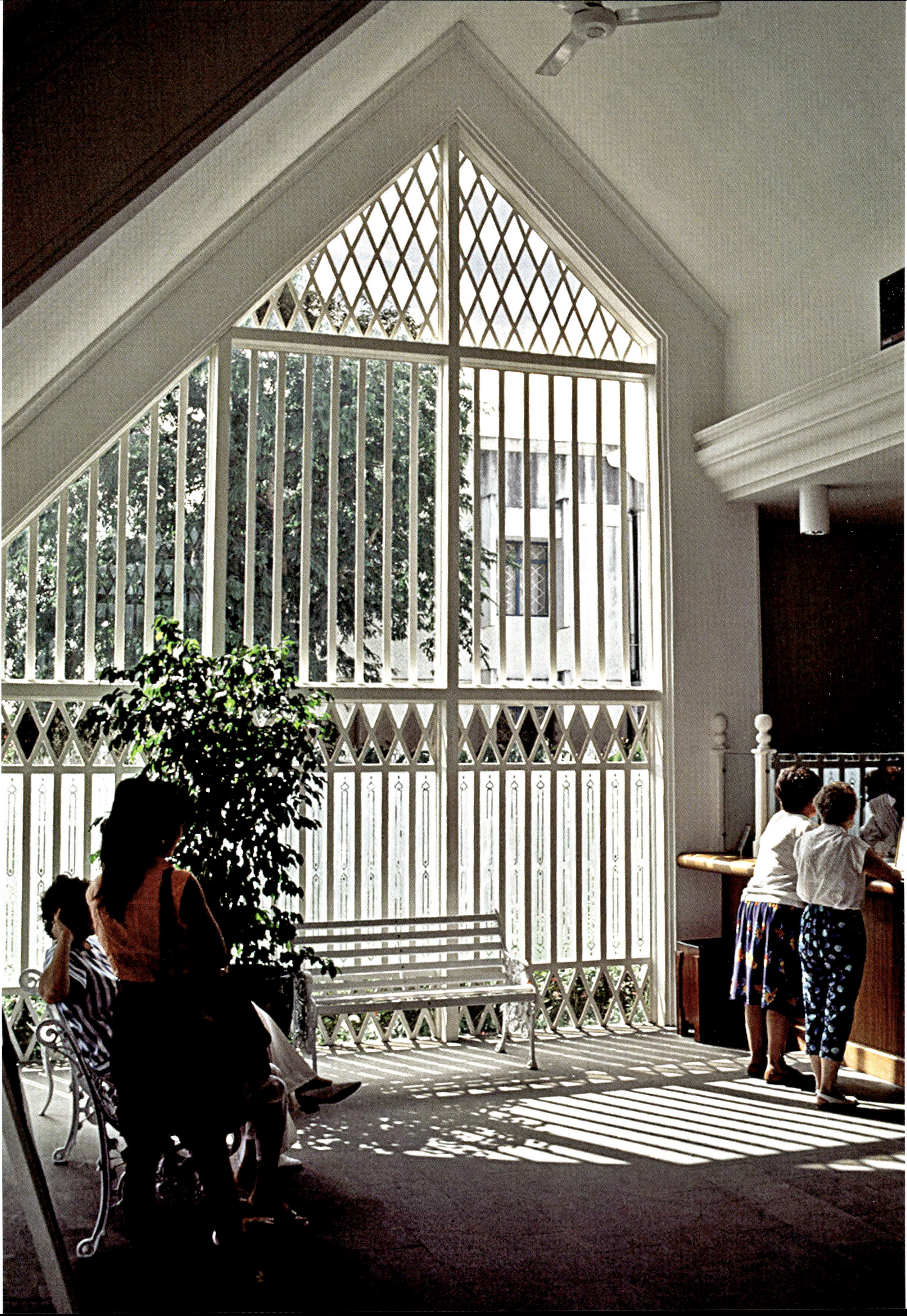

Top: Gable-end and entrance façades. Bottom: View of the entrance.
Right: Detail of the glazing casting shadows on the basalt stone floor.

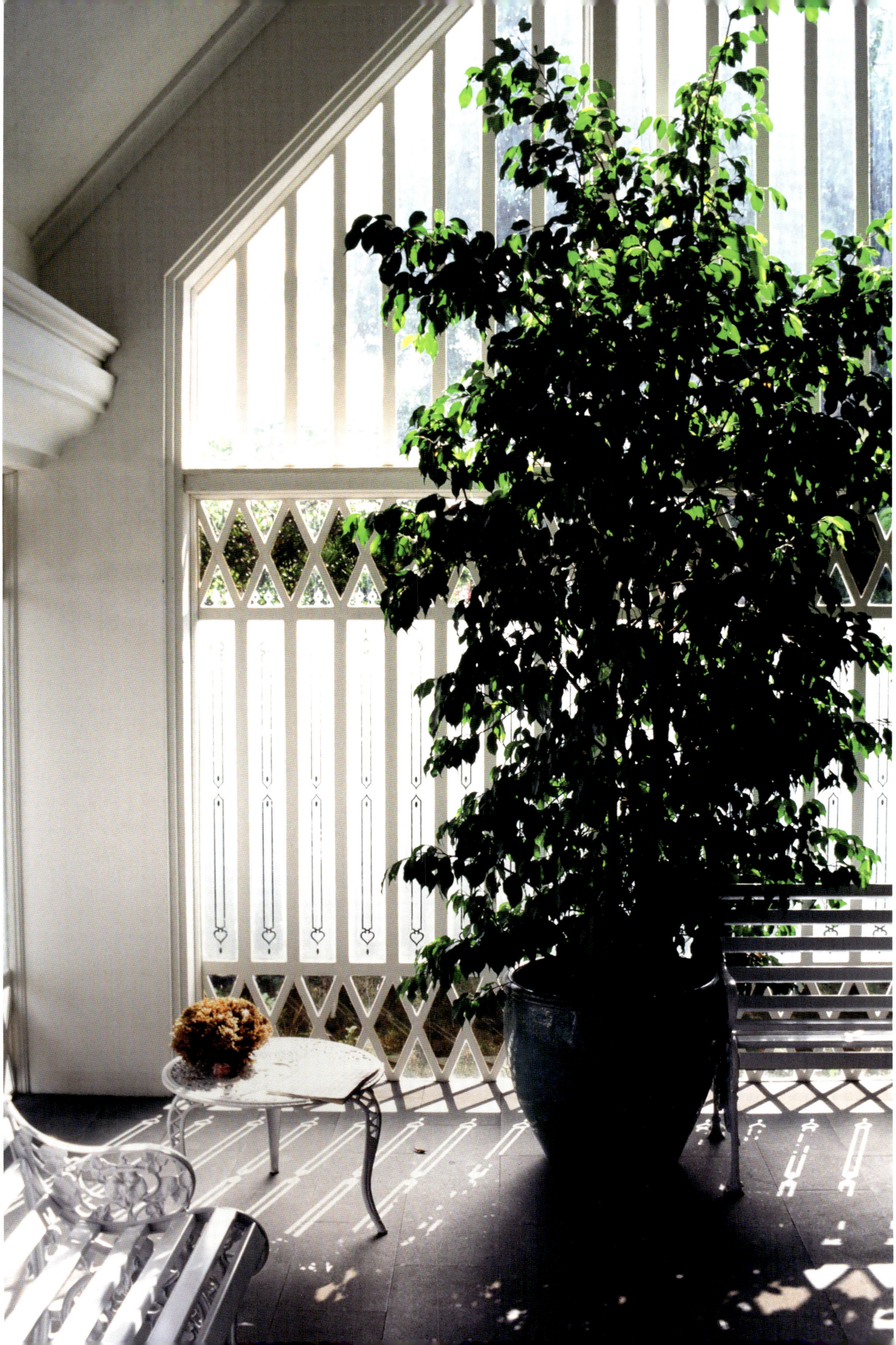

School for Underprivileged Children
Bois Marchand, Mauritius
2009

The school for underprivileged children is a privately funded initiative by individuals devoted to the cause. The architectural contribution consisted of a double storey addition to an existing building giving two additional classrooms. A 300-mm thick reinforced concrete wall giving onto the motorway provides good sound insulation. It is punctuated by irregularly shaped windows to create surprise and curiosity encouraging questioning as part of the learning process.

Below: The façade facing the motorway.

Federation Square
Melbourne, Australia
1997

The project for Federation Square in Melbourne is the submission entry of an Architectural International Competition organised by the State of Victoria, Australia, in 1997. It is situated over railroad tracks opposite Flinders Street Station, Melbourne's central railway station, and close to the Rod Laver Arena, home of the Australian Open Tennis Championships.

The design responds to its site and surrounding buildings with respect to their historical context and the City of Melbourne. The building is set back to create an open public space across the full width of the site and opens a perspective on the front entrance façade of Saint Paul's Cathedral. Positioned on the Cathedral's central axis are two large reflective pools with monumental fountains flanked by a pair of bronze equestrian statues of the founding fathers of the State of Victoria. They, in turn, are on either side of the central axis of the main building facing Flinders Street Station reminiscent of classic 17th-century French urban planning.

The proposal is an entirely glazed building and a contemporary re-interpretation of the great steel and glass structures of Victorian conservatories and railway stations. The giant spans and size of the architecture aims at being lightweight and transparent. It consists of the continuation of the front piazza with trees that carry through into a covered space formed by a low arch of white triangular steel trusses spanning across the width of the site. It is capped by a glass dome of distinctive profile that dominates the surrounding buildings without overpowering them. The whole building would glow at night, illuminating Melbourne's skyline by the River Yarra, to become a beacon and symbol for the City.

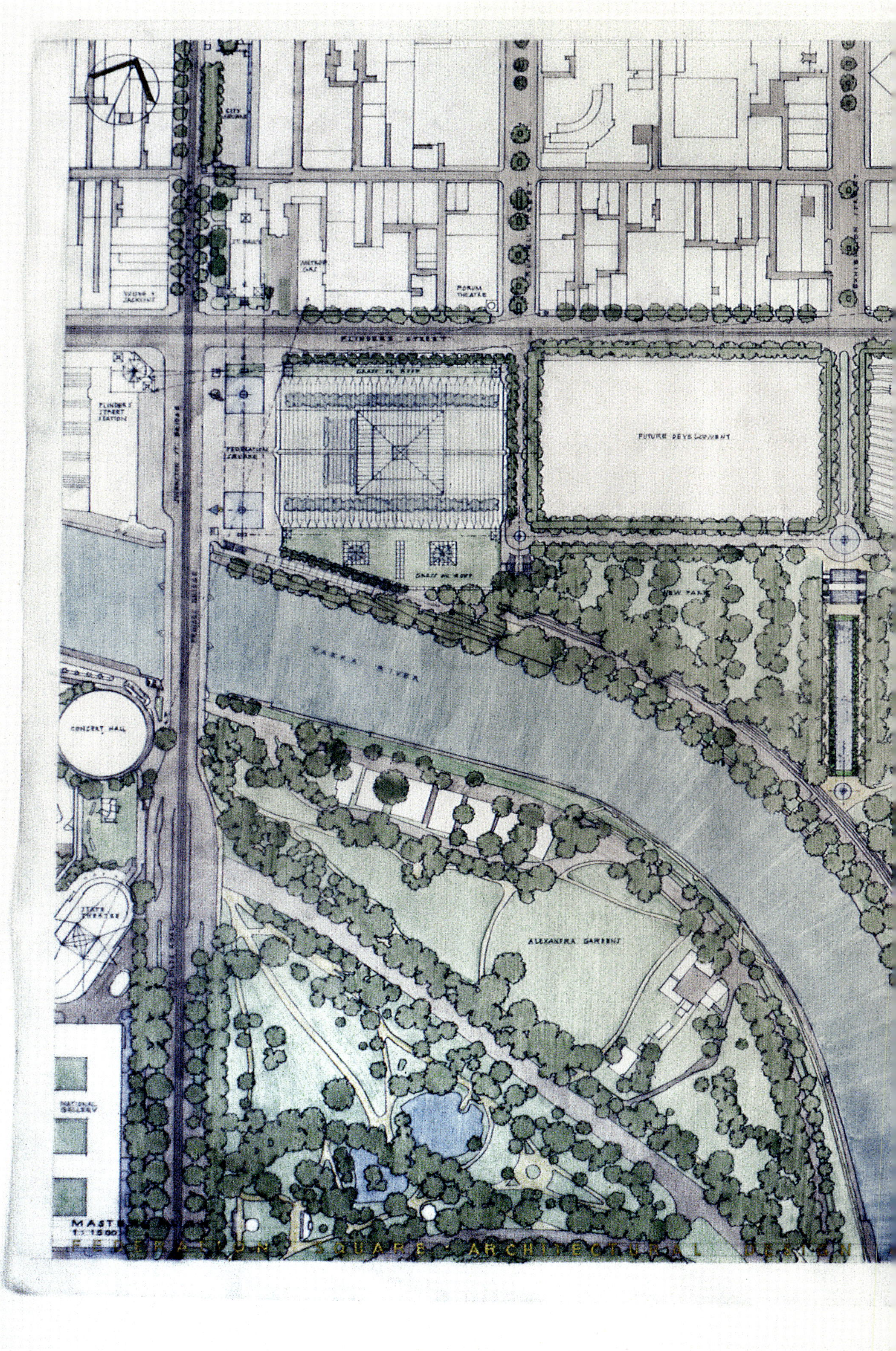
FORUM THEATRE
FLINDERS STREET
FLINDERS STREET STATION
FEDERATION SQUARE
FUTURE DEVELOPMENT
YARRA RIVER
CONCERT HALL
STATE THEATRE
ALEXANDRA GARDENS
NATIONAL GALLERY
1:1500
SQUARE · ARCHITECTURAL

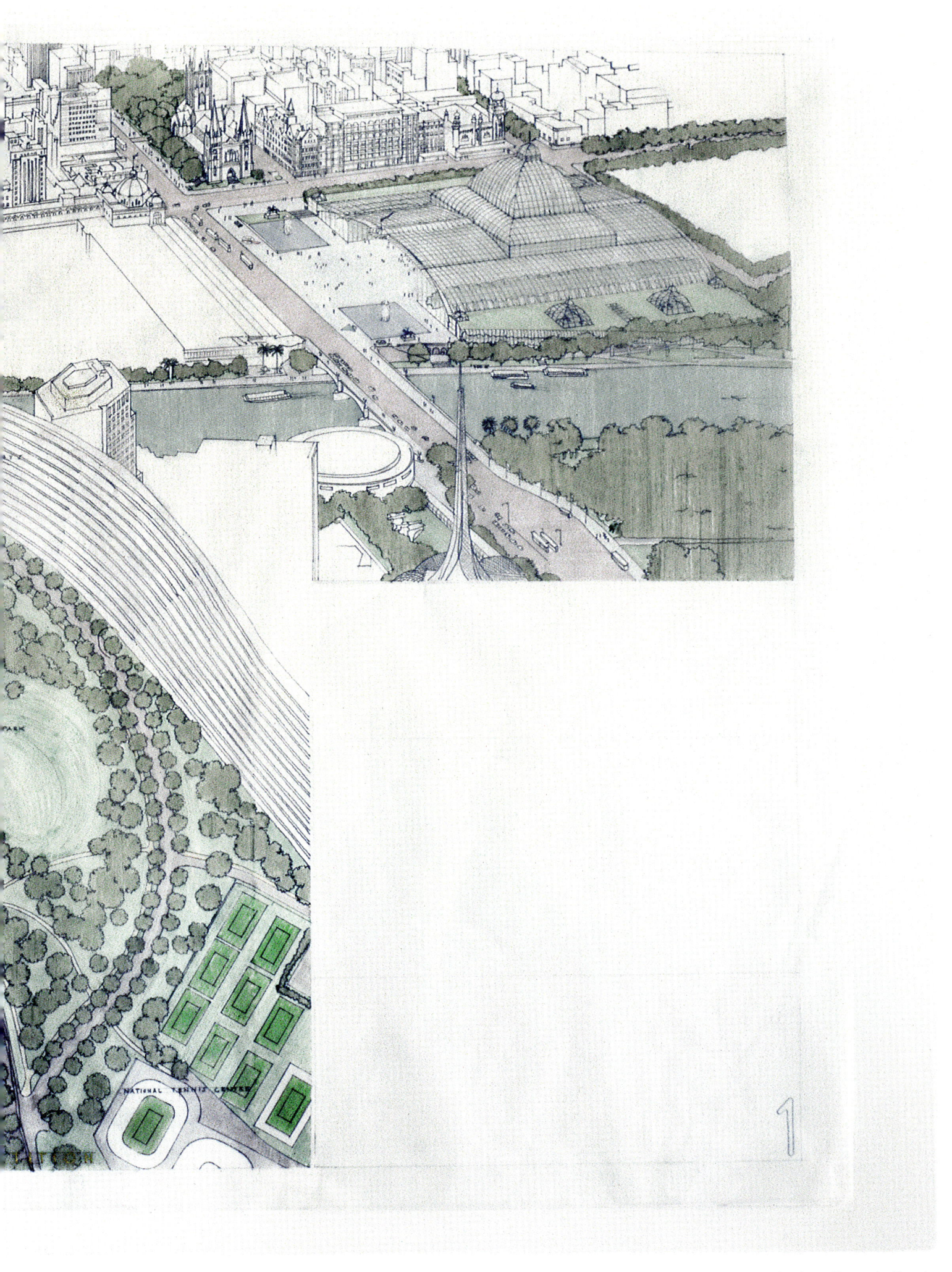

Site plan and perspective. Drawing in pencil and felt-tip markers by Jean-Francois Koenig.

PLAN
DECK - ENTRY LEVEL
SCALE 1:500

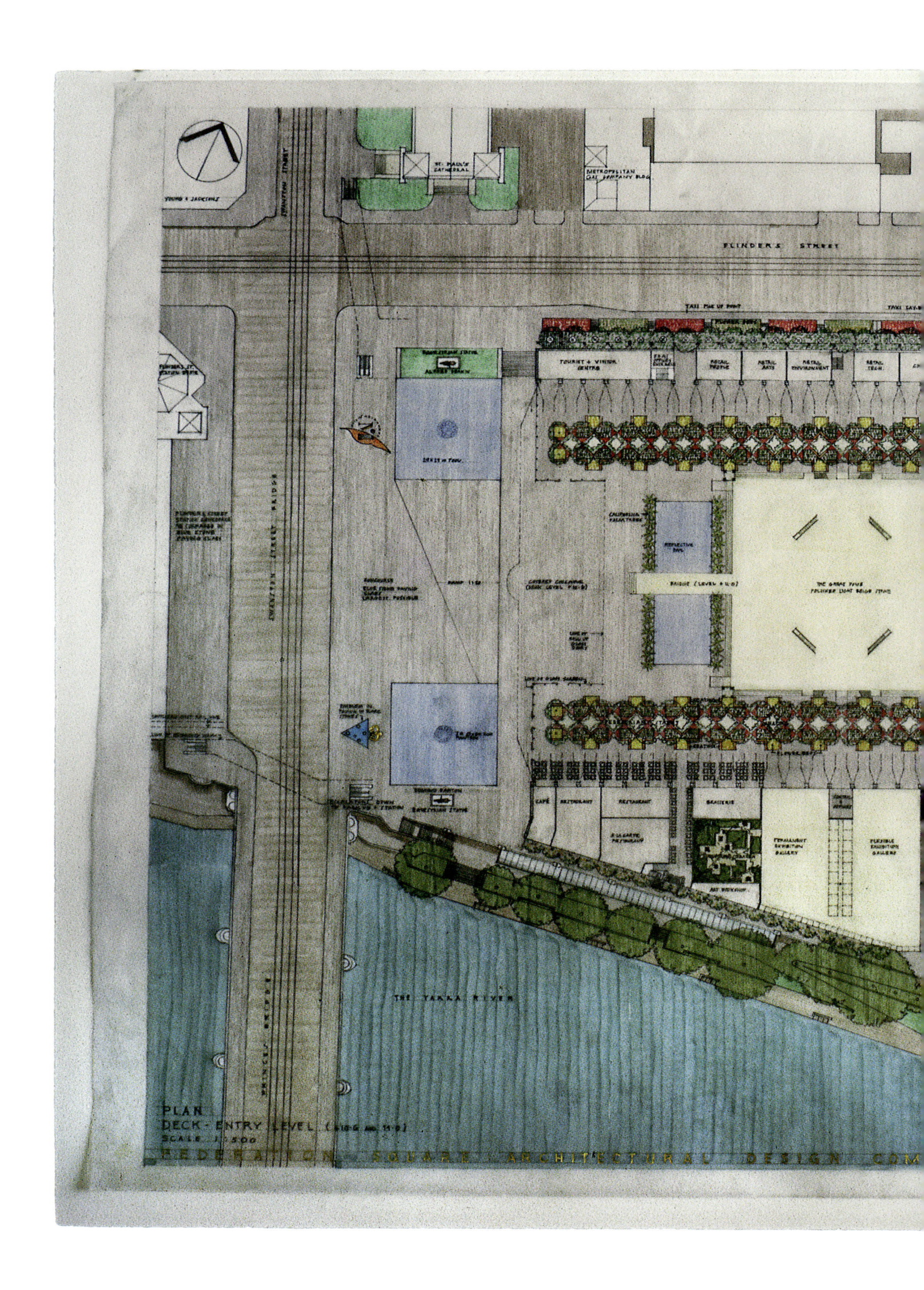

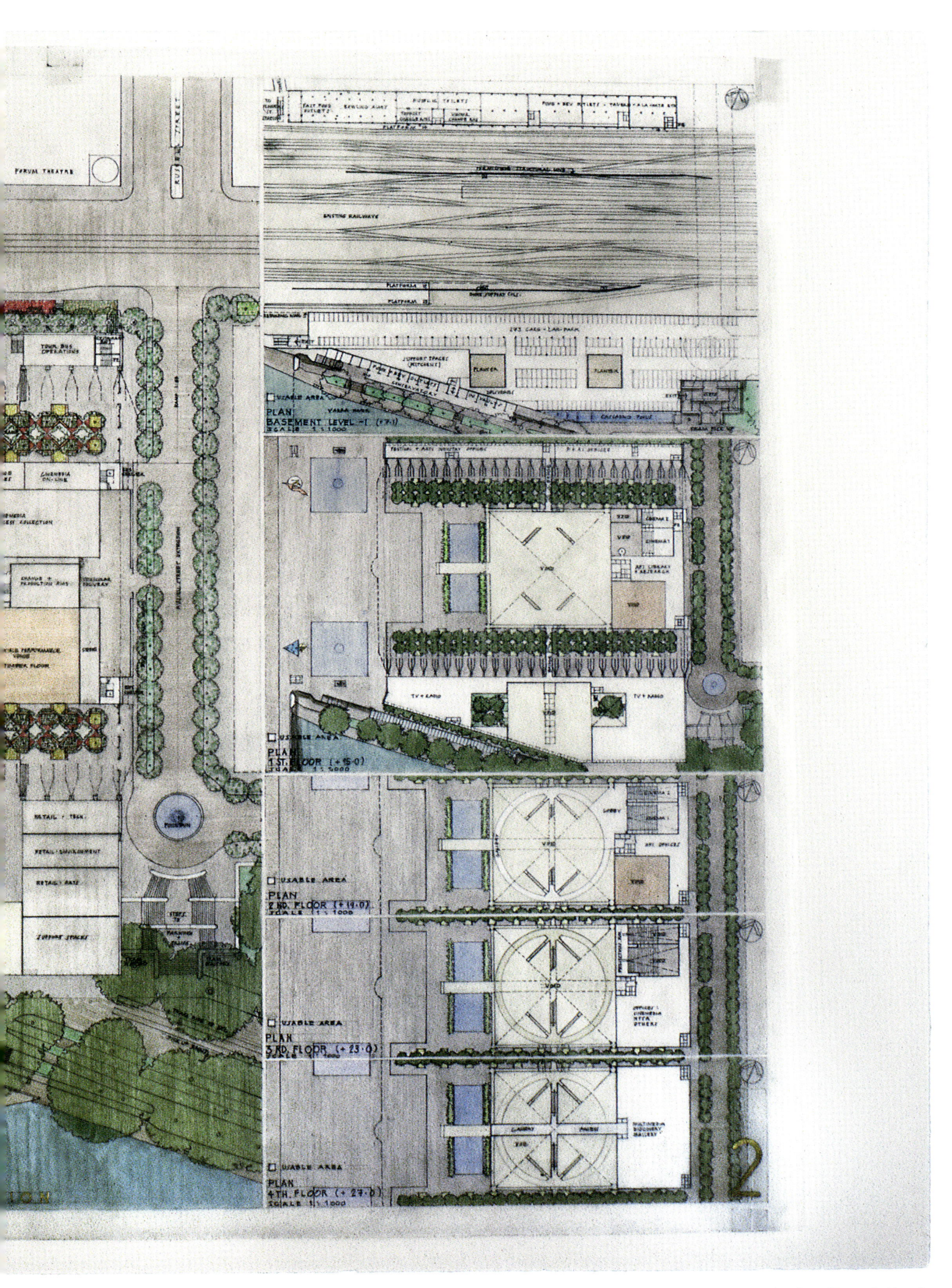

Plans. Drawing in pencil and felt-tip markers by Jean-Francois Koenig.

SOUTH ELEVATION
NORTH ELEVATION
LONGITUDINAL SECTION AA
WEST ELEVATION
FEDERATION SQUARE · ARCHITECTURAL DESIGN

Sections and elevations. Drawing in pencil and felt-tip markers by Jean-Francois Koenig.

B+J Mechanical Workshop
Alrode, Johannesburg, South Africa
1981–1983

The B+J Mechanical Workshop and offices at Alrode, are designed, drawn, and detailed by Koenig whilst working at the multidisciplinary office of Rhodar in Johannesburg, South Africa. They comprise two different buildings which reflect, by the way they are designed, their different functions.

The office is a single storey building with large overhangs for sun and glare protection. Inside, two courtyards enhance the quality of the workplace by shutting out the industrial environment and creating a world within.

The workshop is a 66-m long by 24-m span rectangular building with a 5-tonne travelling crane. The tubular steel roof trusses at 6 m intervals are gently bowed to provide falls in the 'Brownbuilt' sheeting, a profile that can take very low falls. South lights in the roof, continuous side lights in the walls, and end walls fully glazed with bronze acrylic sheeting used horizontally, provide ample natural light. Along with the vertical louvres in the side walls placed in the centre of each structural bay for natural cross ventilation, the continuous louvres at the foot of the end walls as well as in the south lights of the roof, they provide the conditions for a healthy industrial workplace.

Right: Gable-end façade in bronze acrylic horizontal sheeting.

Pages 220/221: Internal view of the Workshop.

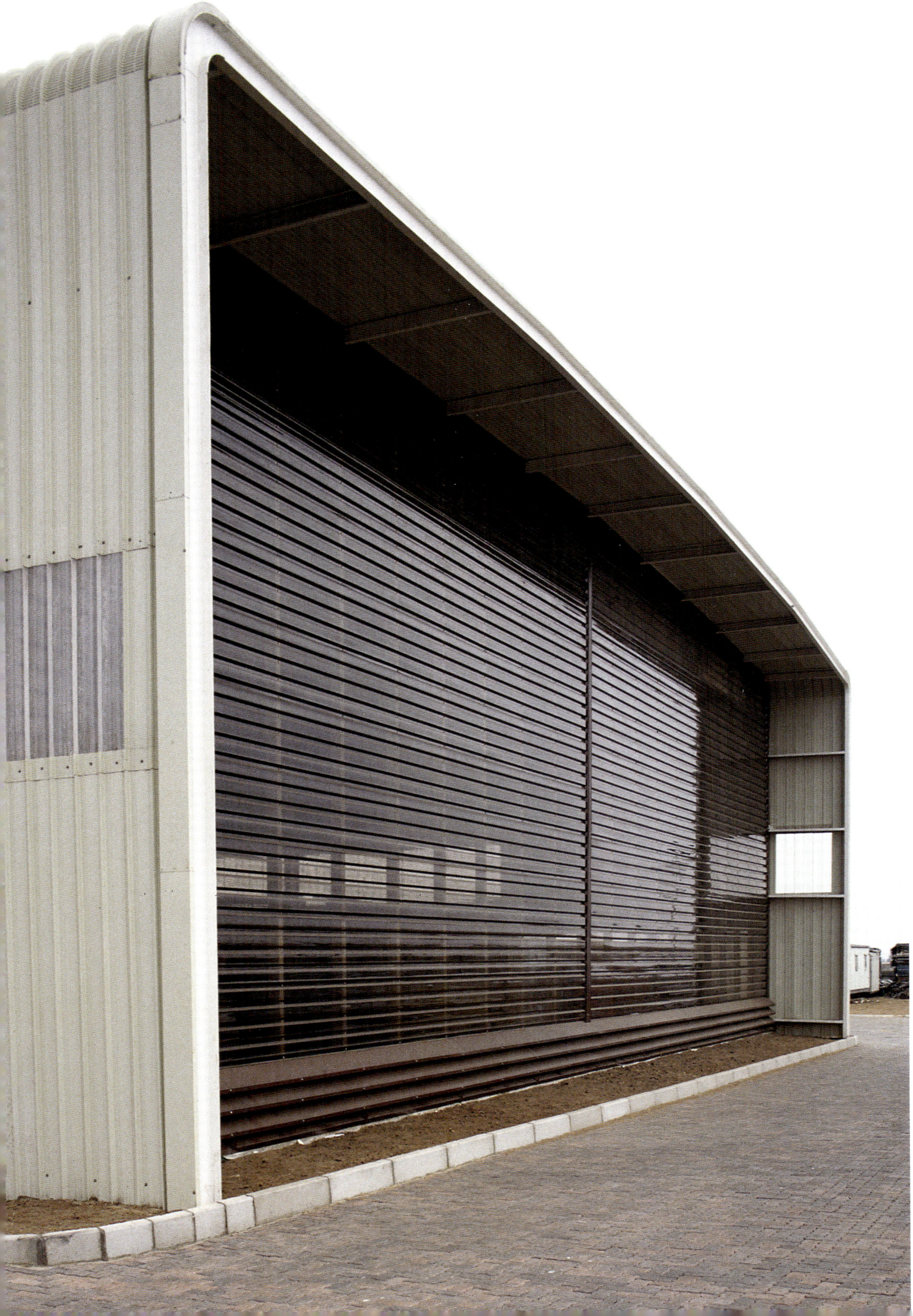

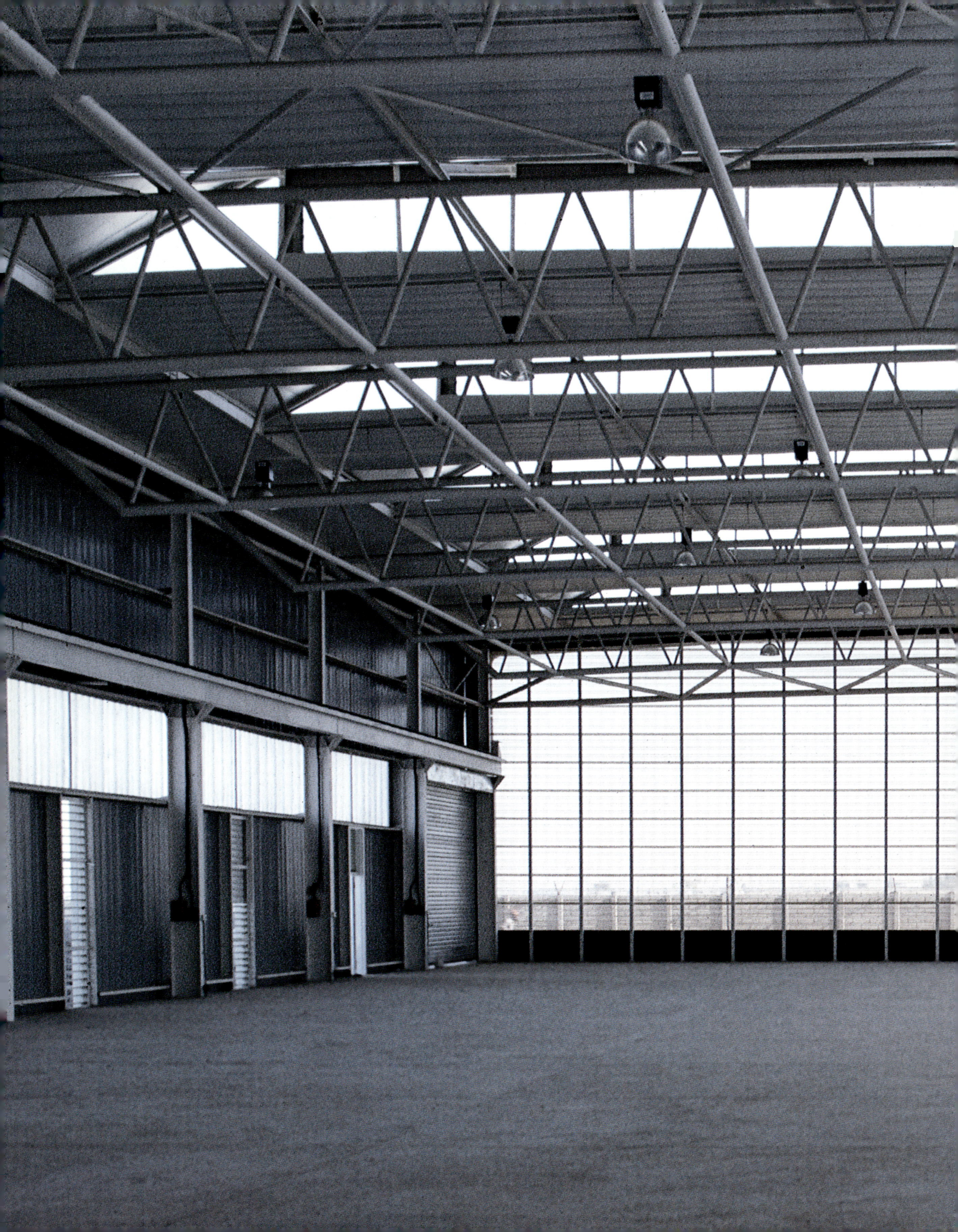

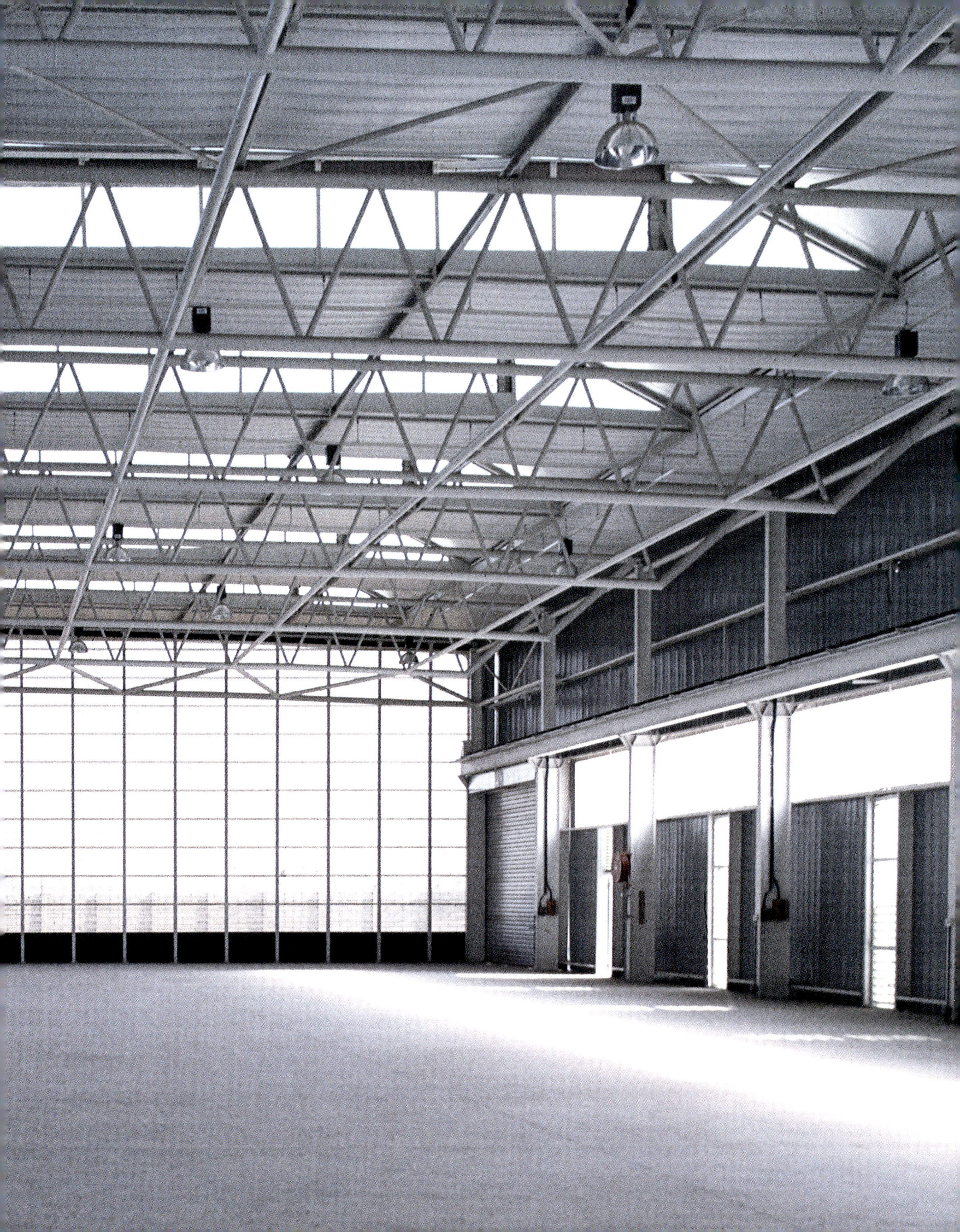

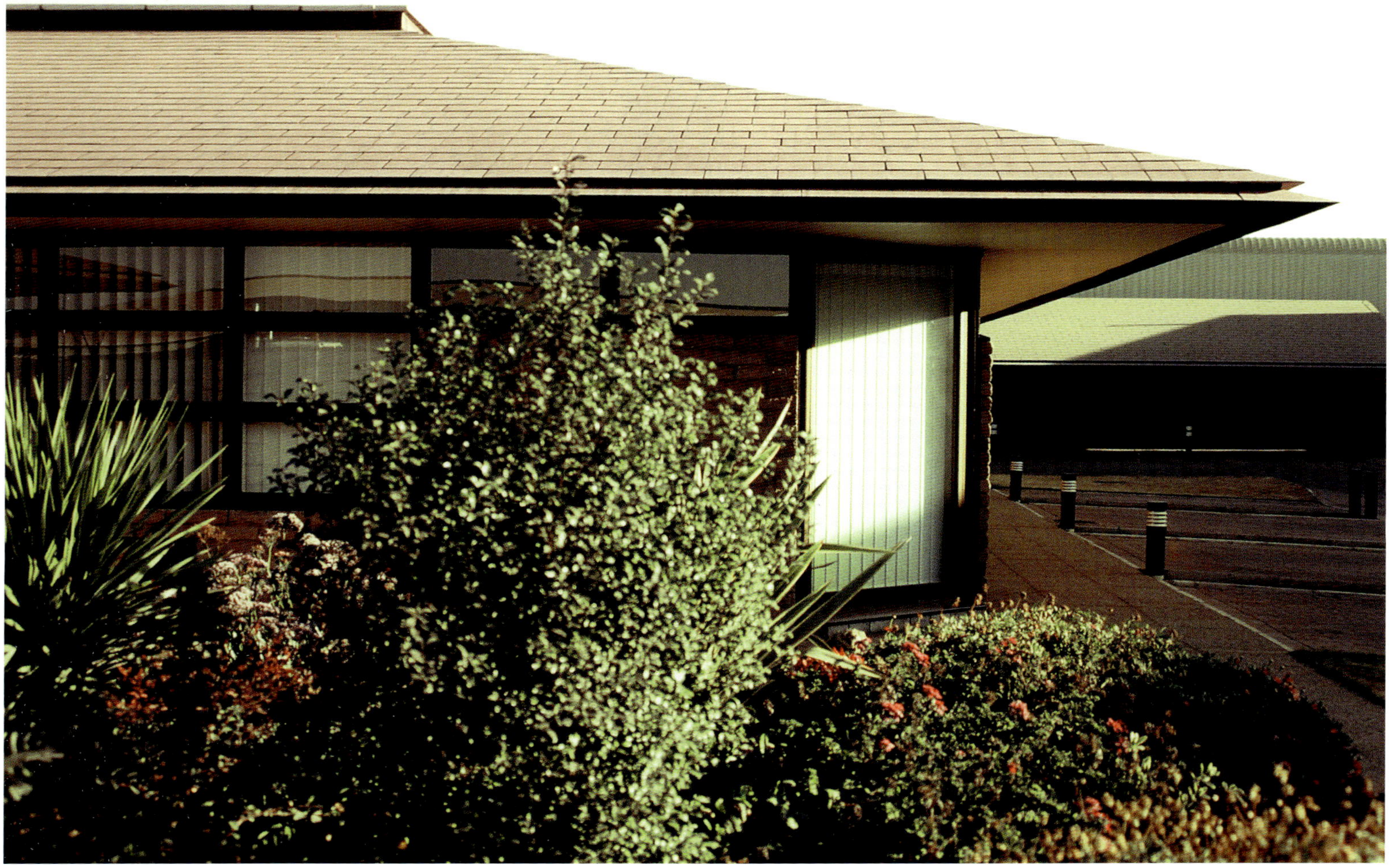

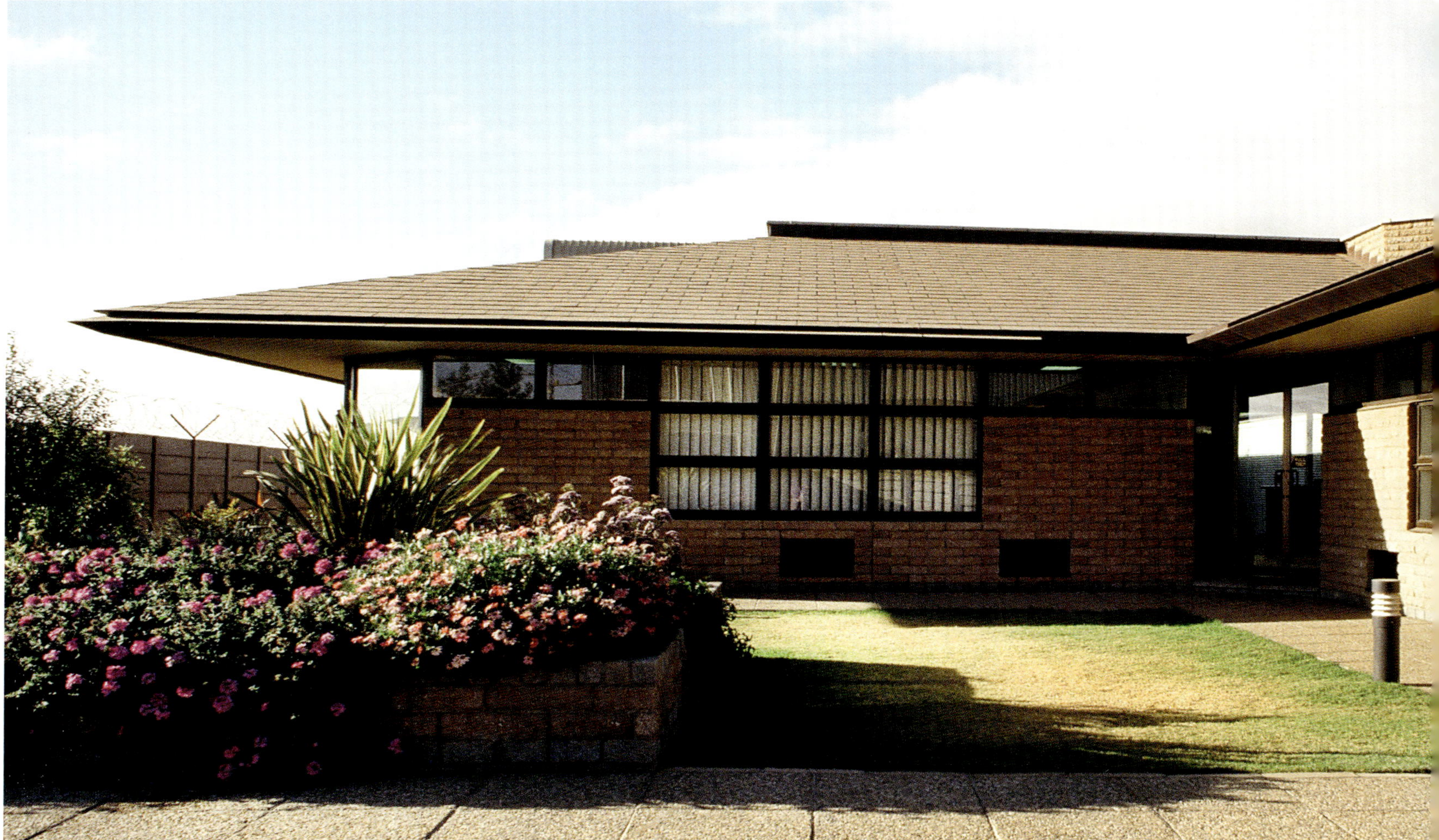

Top left: Cut-away corners of the office building.

Top right: View of one of the twin courtyards of the office building creating a 'world within'.

Bottom: External view of the office building.

Baldwins Steel
Canteen and Wash Bay
Brakpan, South Africa
1982–1983

Two outbuildings for the Baldwins steel factory in Brakpan, South Africa, were designed and detailed by Koenig whilst working at Rhodar in Johannesburg.
The walls of the canteen are in face brick for low maintenance. A high load-bearing back wall is buttressed with brick piers and expressed internally to become columns for the roof trusses. These are composite structures of glue-laminated sapele with steel tension rods, turn buckles, and connection plates to reduce the size of the timber members. Fenestration is in steel painted red and two steel sliding doors meet on a square hollow section column on the corner of the building which opens on a small green space.

Right: Detail of the sapele glue-laminated trusses and their tension cables.

Below: External view of the canteen at night.

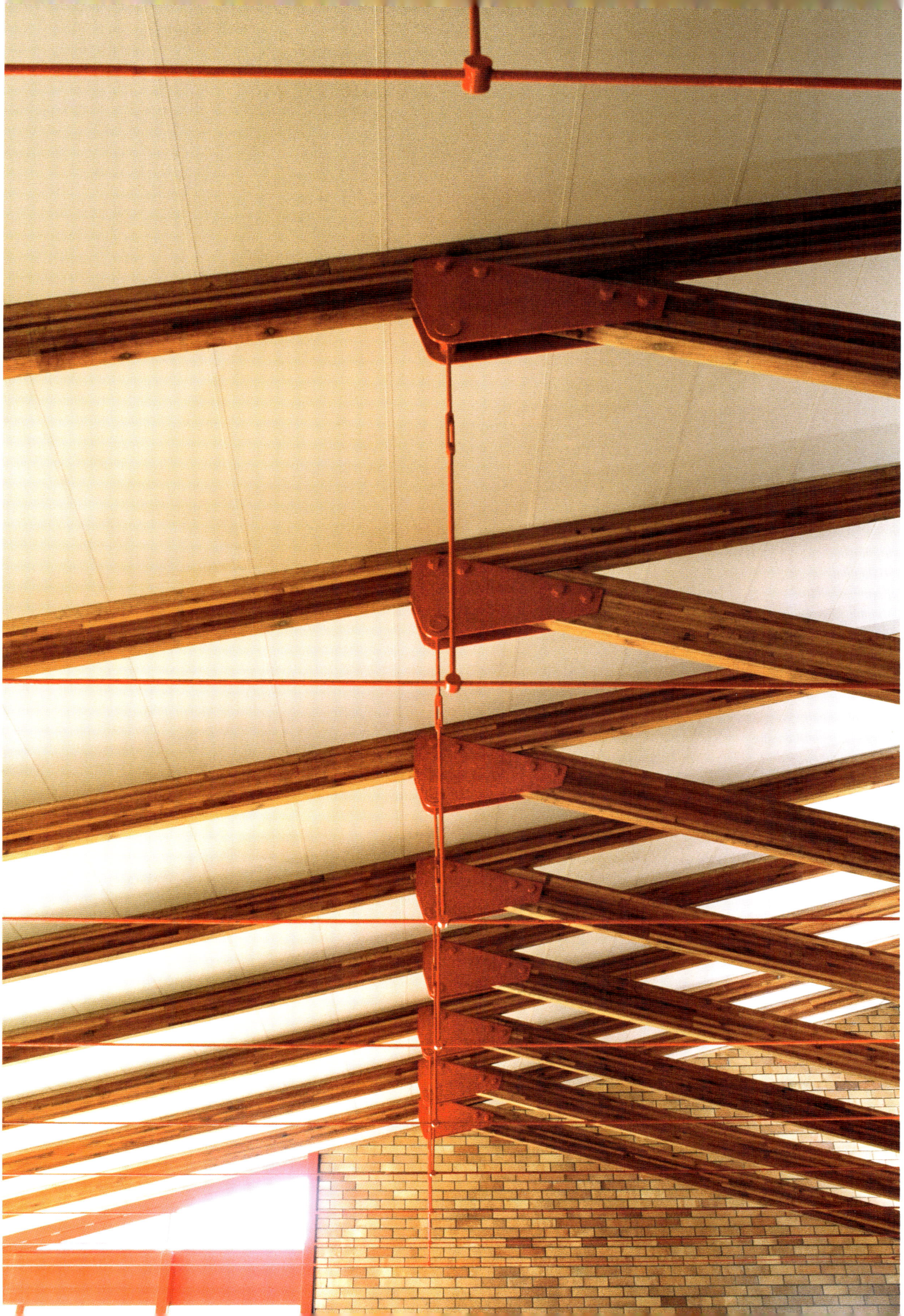

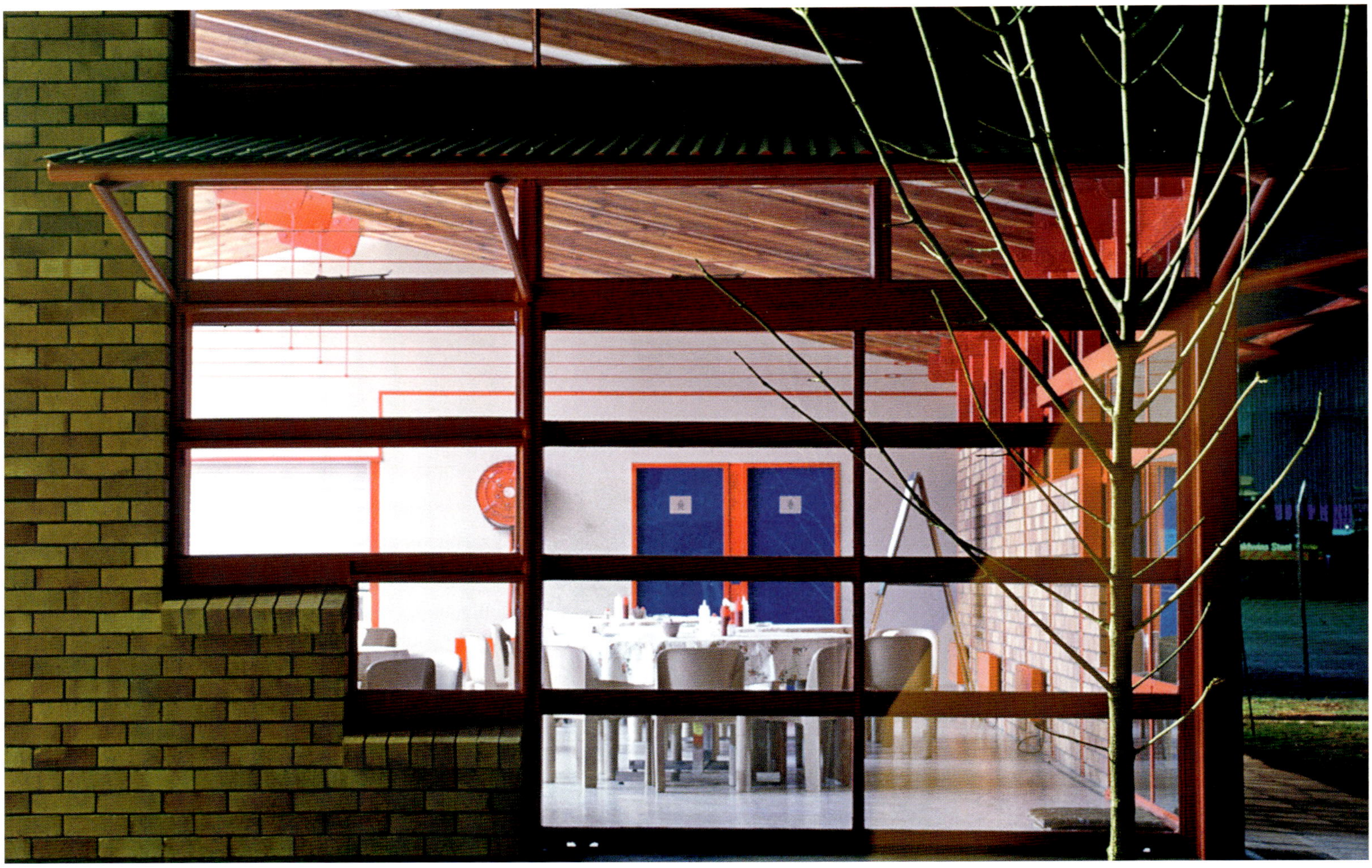

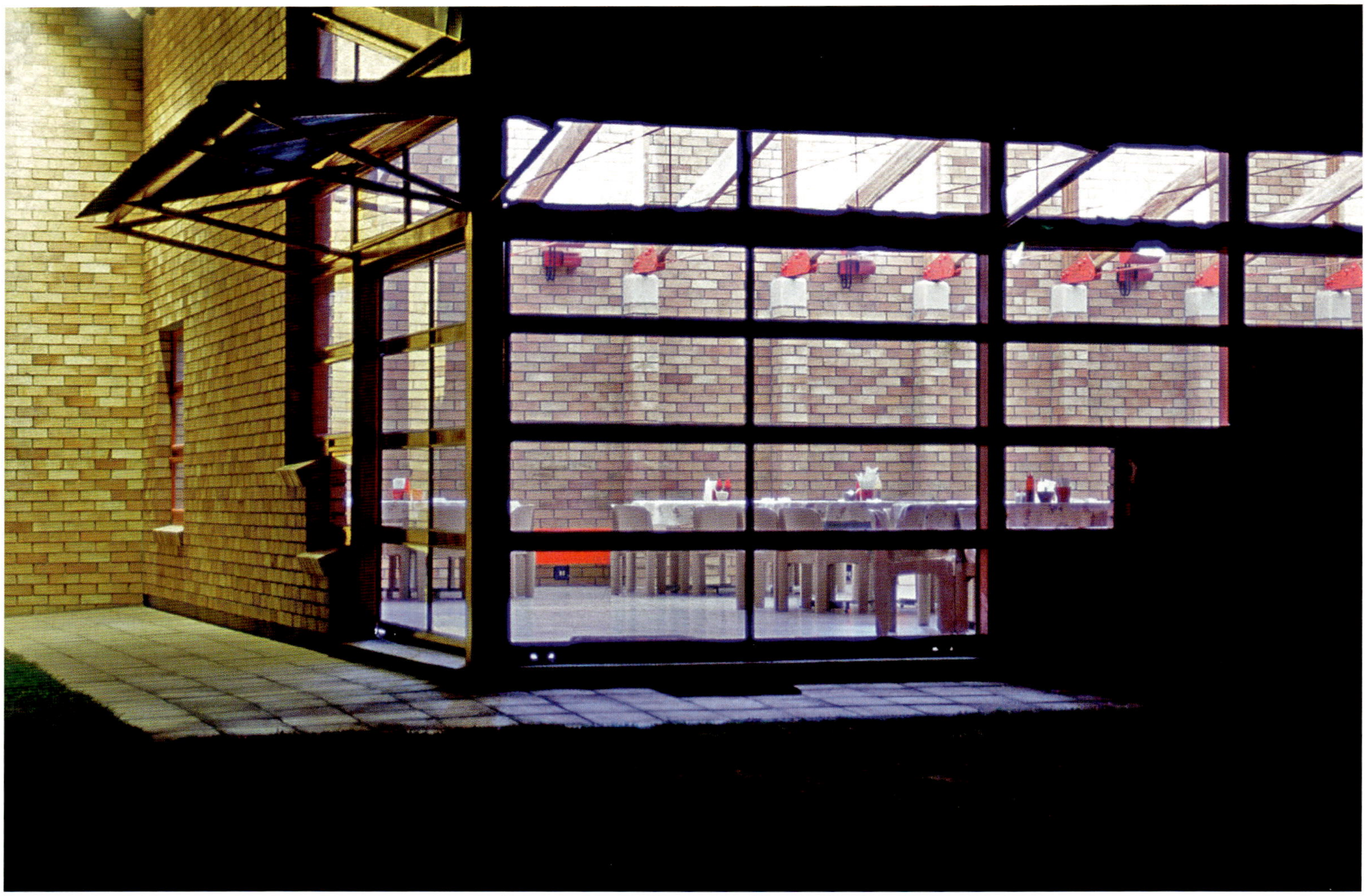

External and internal views of the canteen.

The wash bay is a steel portal frame structure painted red, with a blue sheeting roof, bullnosed on the eaves to eliminate side gutters and flashings and take rainwater down to the ground. The structure rests on low side walls in off shutter concrete which are for water retention and collection. Instead of the traditional Z or rectangular purlins, tubular sections are used for better water run-off. The building acquires its own aesthetic born from its function with attention to detail.

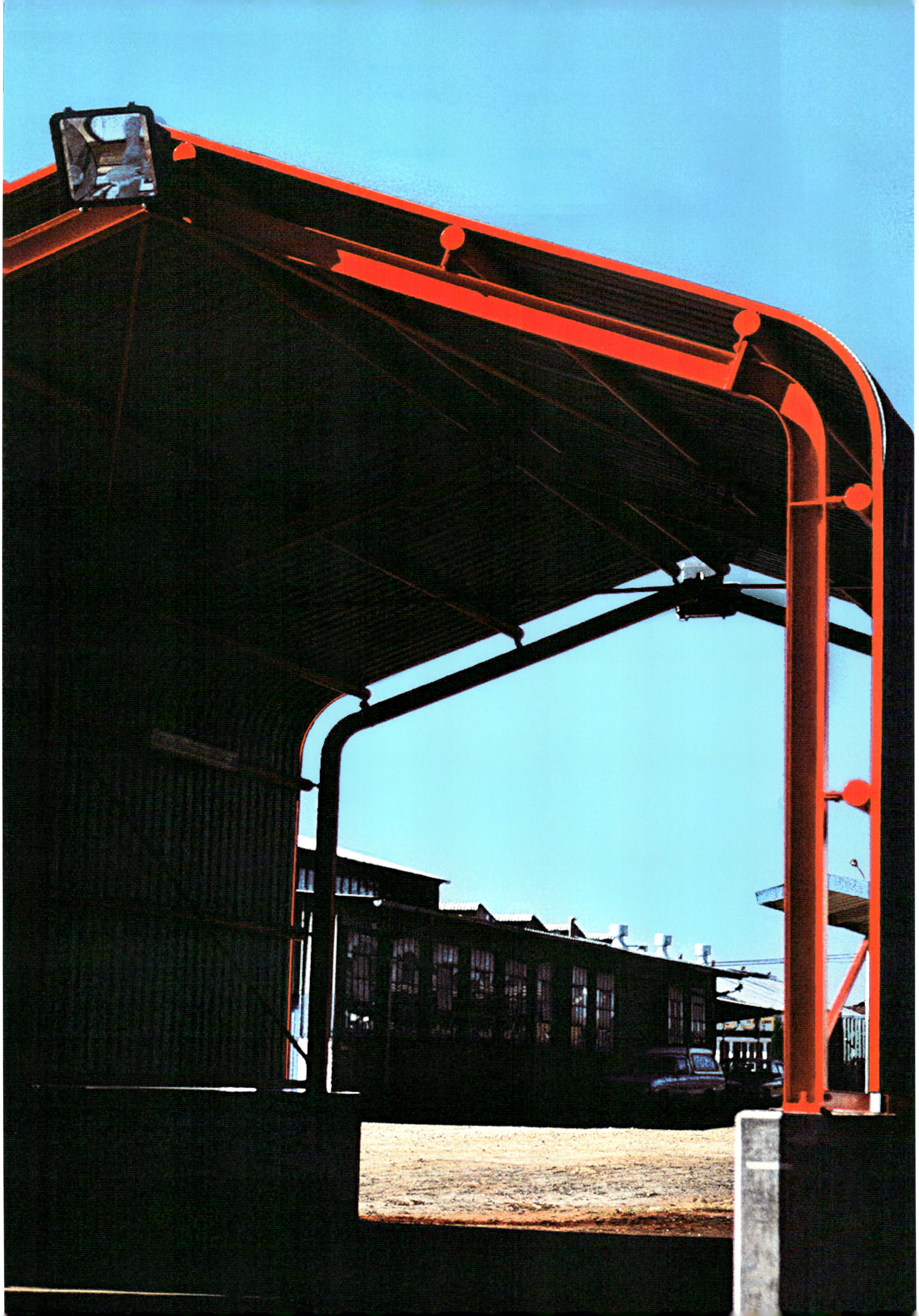

Fresh-Up Factory
Rosselyn, Pretoria, South Africa
1981–1983

The Fresh-Up fruit juice factory in Rosslyn for Willards Foods is the company's production and distribution centre for the Witwatersrand Province of South Africa which incorporates two of the country's largest cities, Johannesburg and Pretoria. The design responds to the linear manufacturing process, from materials kept in cold stores with underground ventilation to keep the substructure and ground from freezing, through manufacturing to warehousing ready for shipping.

Koenig was the architect in a multidisciplinary team of consultants at Rhodar in Johannesburg. He initiated the idea and worked individually in close collaboration with the machine-process engineer from outside the multidisciplinary team to alter and coordinate the stainless-steel pipework of the machinery. The pipework aligns vertically collecting less dust, creating a cleaner and healthier environment whilst being neater and more aesthetically pleasing.

The 'Tetrapack' machines that seal fruit juice in one litre packs at a rate of over one carton per second in an aseptic space were the centrepiece of the project.

Springs Brewery
Witwatersrand, South Africa
1984–1985

The brewery at Springs, Witwatersrand, makes sorghum beer for regional distribution. Koenig was the architect in a multidisciplinary team at Rhodar. The factory is two storeys due to the lack of space on the site. It consists of a manufacturing hall on the first floor which also incorporates the administrative offices. Warehousing is on the ground floor. It is clad in grey horizontal sheeting that incorporates bands of acrylic sheeting and continuous louvres for daylight and natural ventilation.

The external expressed steelwork of the loading bay canopy and the fire escape staircases of the offices are painted bright green. The loading bay canopy is suspended by hangers which also act as support for the sun shades of the office windows above, making dual use of a single structural support.

Corner detail.

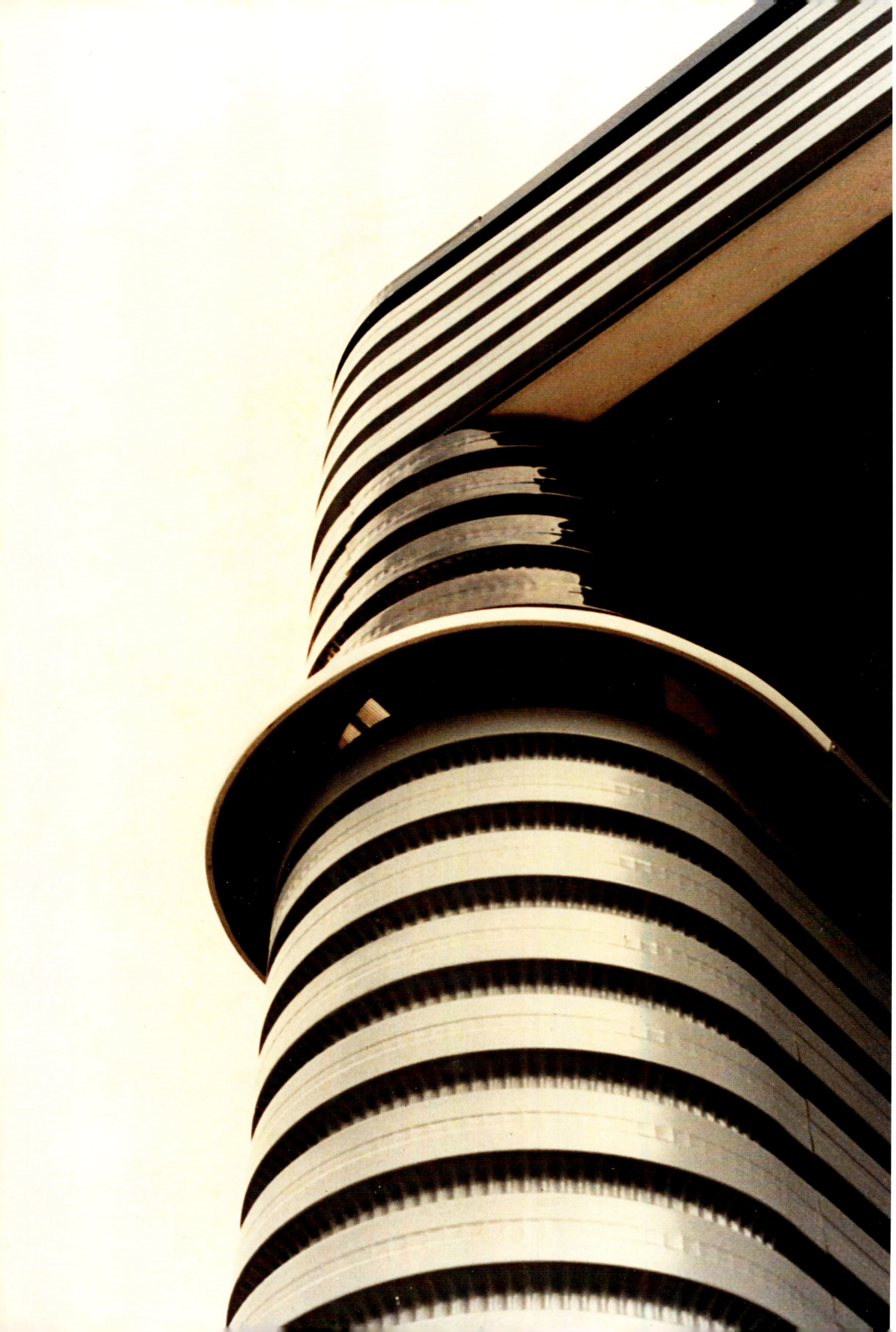

Top: The factory building.

Centre and bottom: The workshop and wash bay building.

Left: Corner detail of the workshop and wash bay building.

Tropic Knits Factory
Forest Side, Mauritius
1997–1998

Tropic Knits is the T-shirt factory of the textile company Floreal Knitwear Ltd., one of the biggest textile companies in the world. It also houses their head office, placed on two levels at one end of the factory, which contains a sales boardroom to receive their international clients.

The double storey front façade is clad in grey horizontal sheeting with tinted glass strip windows. The front porte cochère, in tinted green glass and yellow aluminium, shield from the driving rain of Forest Side's humid weather and continue above the roof to bring natural daylight to the double volume reception.

Right: Reception entrance and porte cochère.

Below: Front façade.

237

Pre-Mixed Concrete Factory
Geoffroy, Mauritius
1992

The concrete manufacturing plant of Pre-Mixed Concrete in Geoffroy, Mauritius constitutes a master plan and the design of four individual buildings performing different functions. Namely, the head office, the Laboratory and mess changing room building, the garage and the control tower, along with the plant silos and sedimentation basins.

The buildings keep architectural unity with a clear expression of structure where the infill panels are either colour-coded blockwork, or dark tinted glass, or pre-painted aluminium louvres.

The site boundary and office access road are lined with flowering 'flamboyant' trees keeping the dusty environment in contact with, and surrounded by, nature.

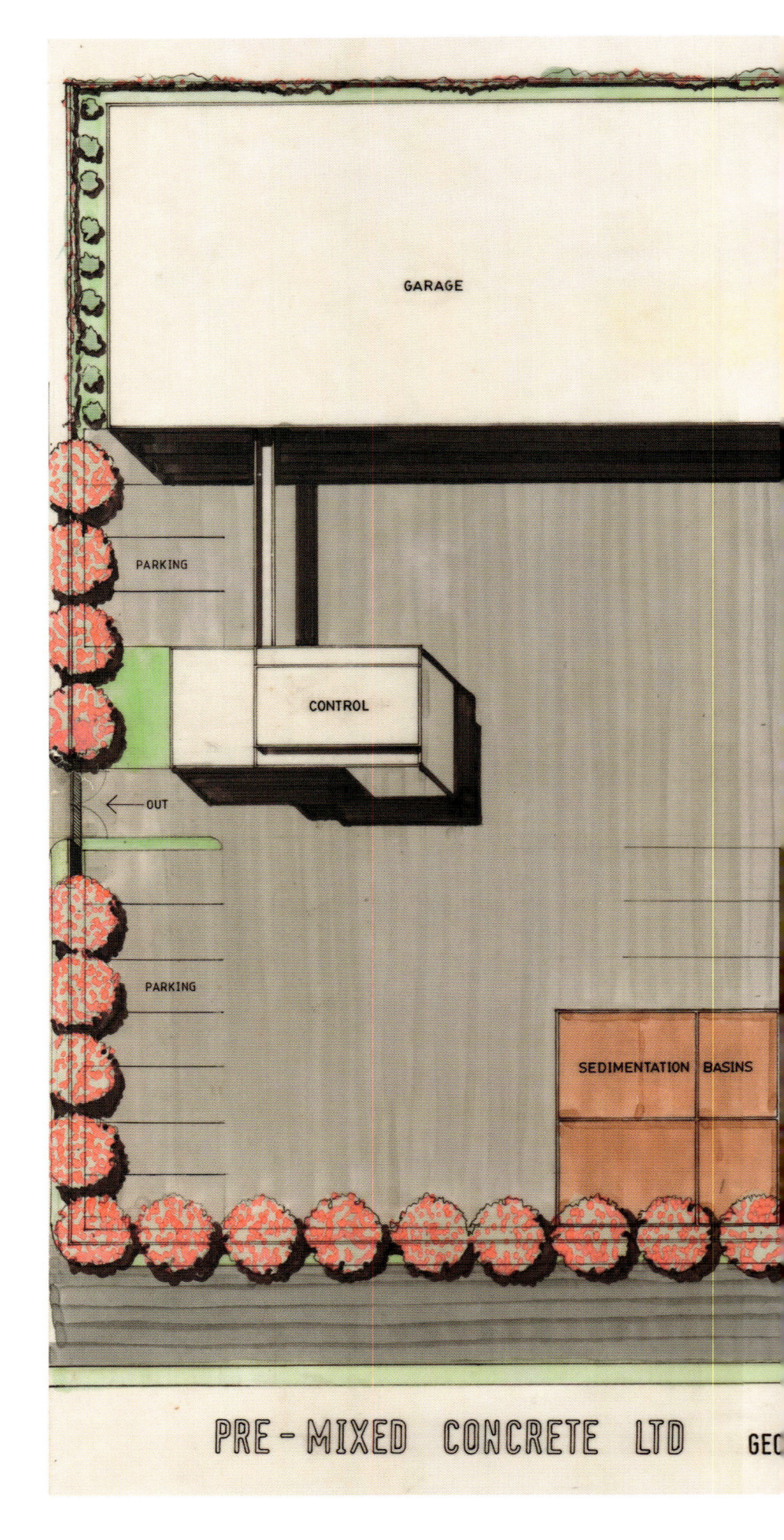

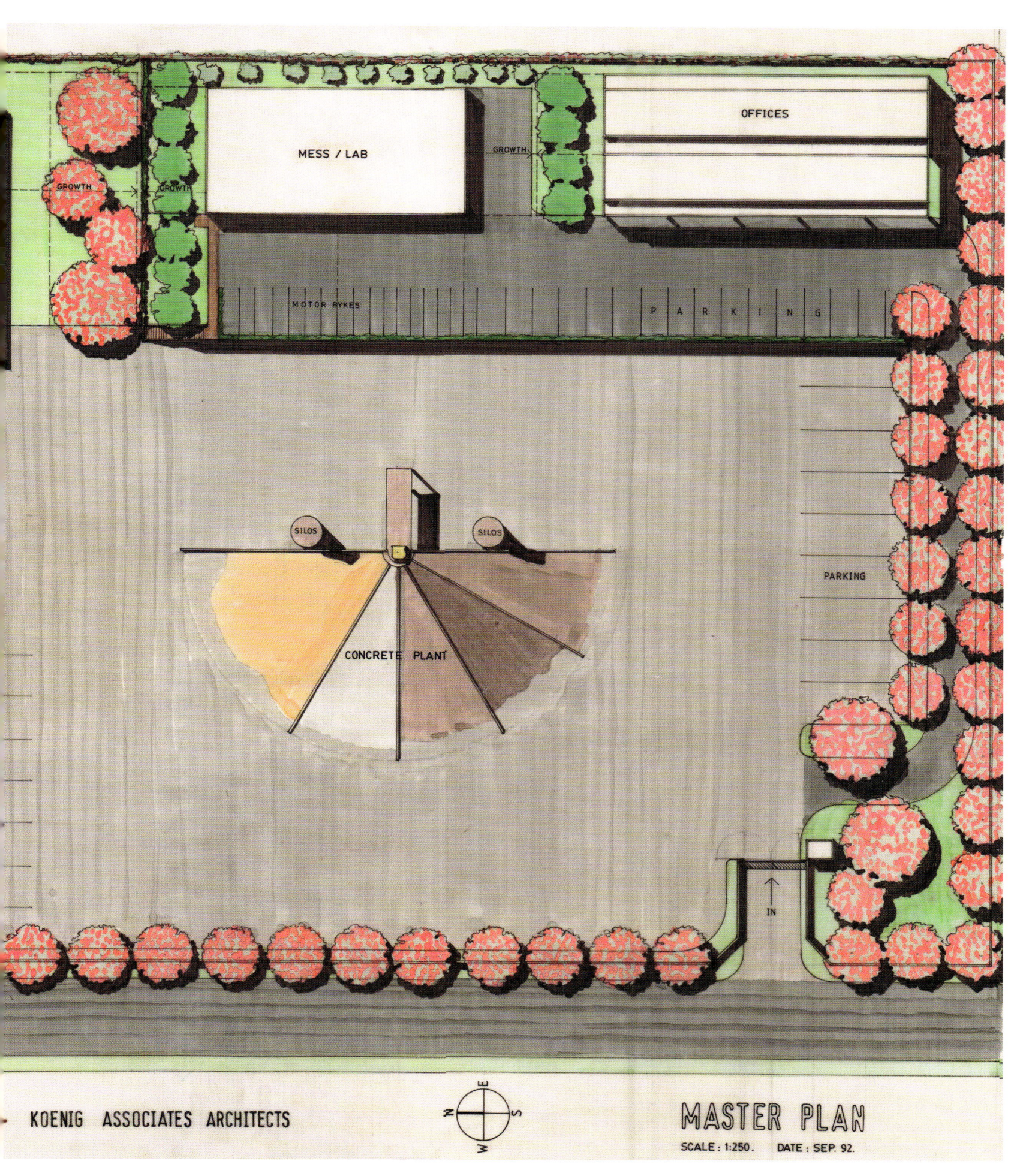

Master plan. Drawing in technical pen and felt-tip markers by Jean-Francois Koenig.

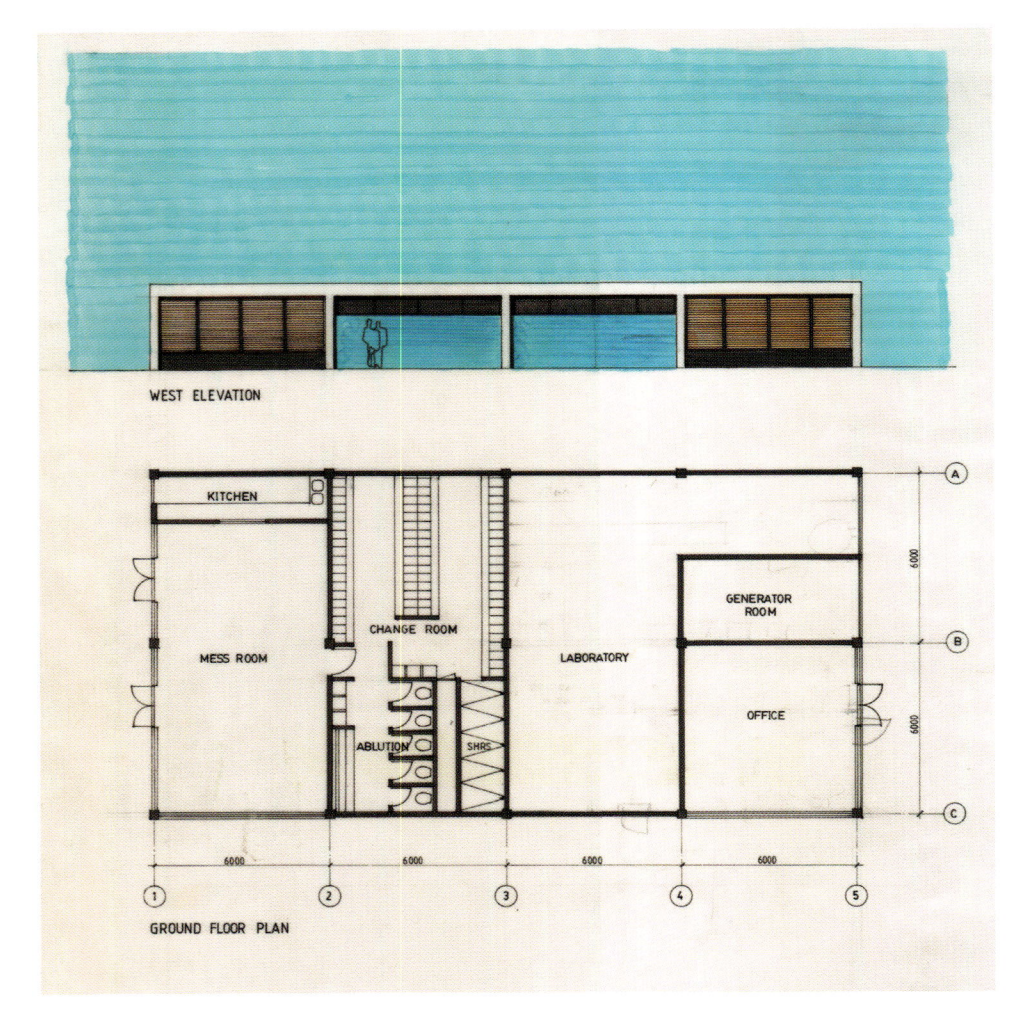

Top: Plan and elevation of the laboratory and mess changing room building.

Bottom: Plans, sections, and elevations of the office building.

Top right: Plans and elevations of the control tower and side elevation of the garage building.

Bottom right: Plan and elevation of the garage building.

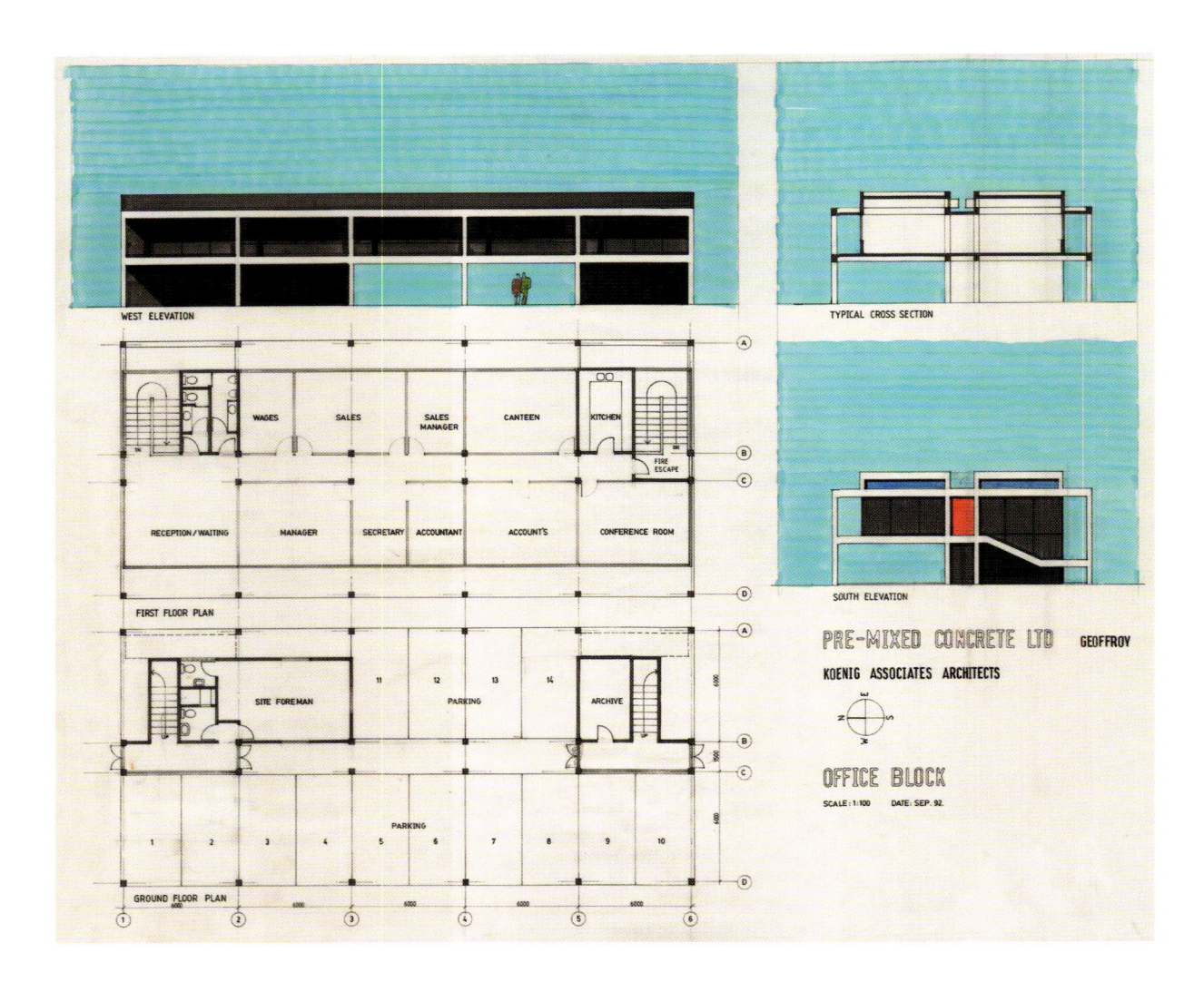

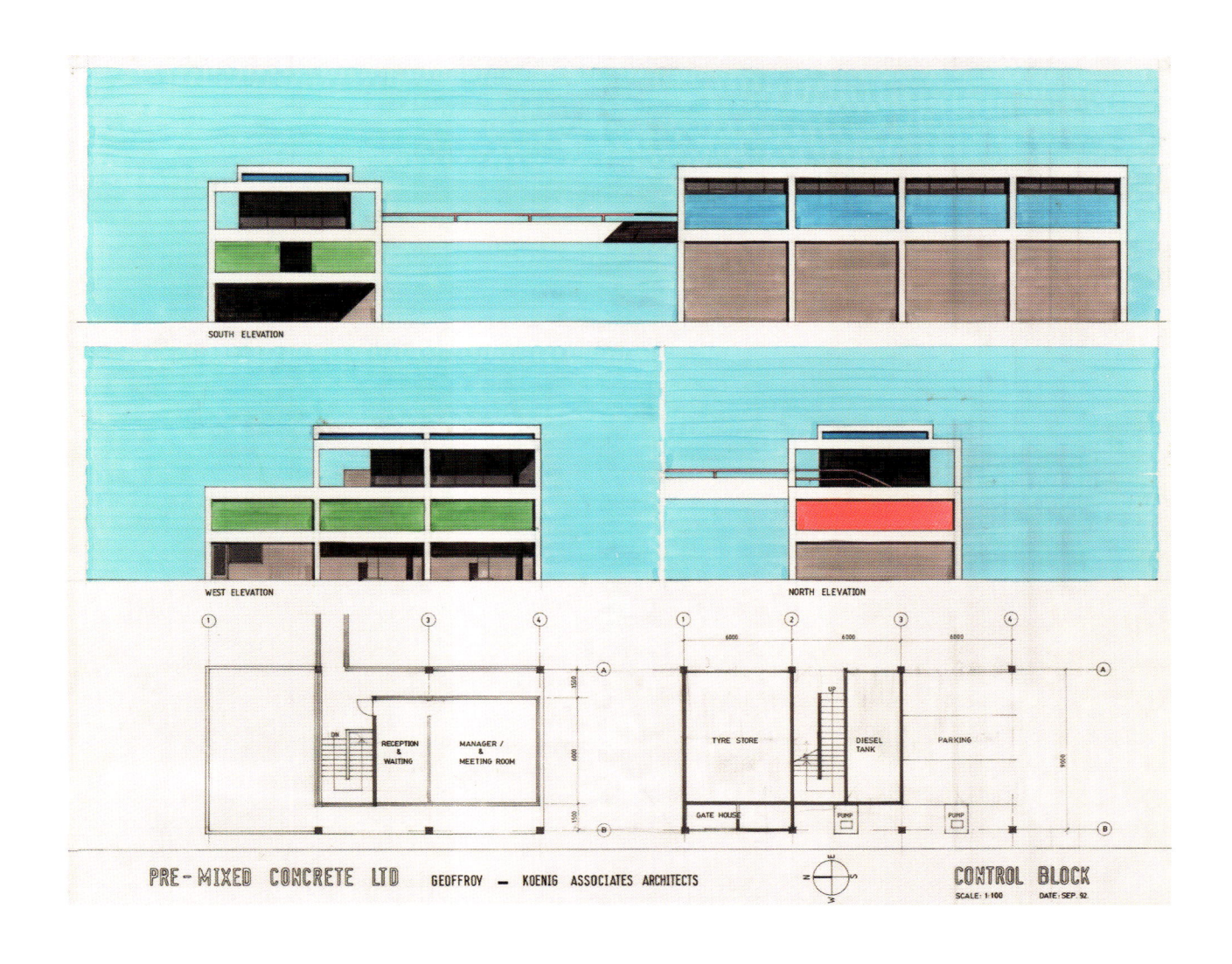

PRE-MIXED CONCRETE LTD GEOFFROY — KOENIG ASSOCIATES ARCHITECTS **CONTROL BLOCK**
SCALE: 1:100 DATE: SEP. 92

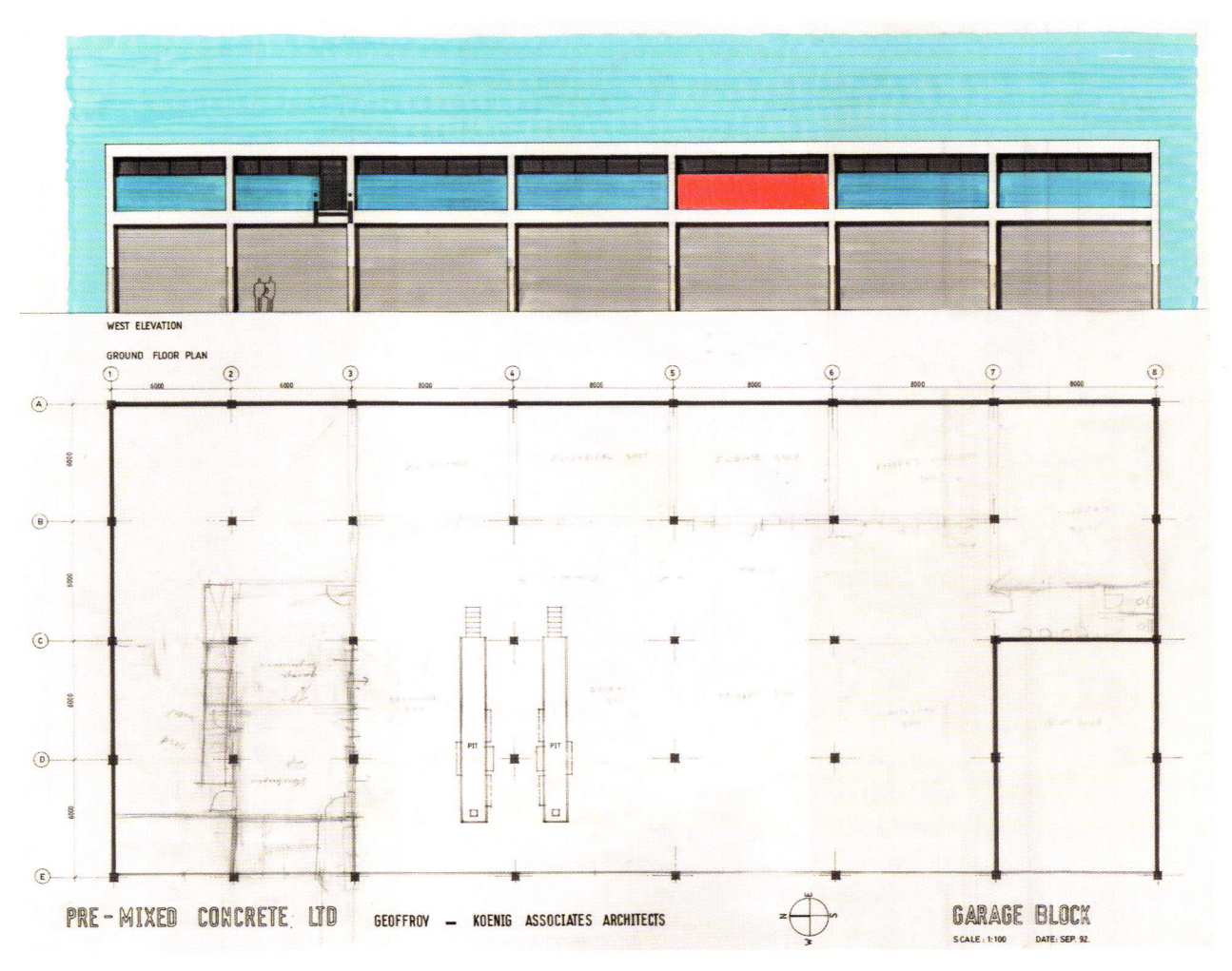

PRE-MIXED CONCRETE LTD GEOFFROY — KOENIG ASSOCIATES ARCHITECTS **GARAGE BLOCK**
SCALE: 1:100 DATE: SEP. 92

CHAPTER 4
OFFICES

Hardy Henry, Bel Air St Felix	244
Oxenham Head Office	252
United Basalt Head Office	254
Sotravic Head Office	258
Mauritius Telecom Headquarters	262
CIEL Head Office	266
Anglo Mauritius Assurance Society Ltd.	270
Mauritius Commercial Bank, Ebène	276

Hardy Henry
Bel Air St Felix
Port Louis, Mauritius
1990–1992

Before the old house was converted into offices for Hardy Henry, Bel Air St Felix, it was part of the residential quarters of the capital city of Port Louis on Rue St Georges. It was built in 1857 and is located adjacent to the financial district in the heart of the city.

The building is in stone on ground floor, and in timber for first floor and roof. Prefabricated wrought iron components were shipped from Victorian England and assembled on site in Mauritius. Columns, beams, and balustrades all arrived ready for assembly. Koenig's first office was located in one of the rooms on the ground floor where he met the French photographer Christian Vesse, a meeting which initiated the book on traditional Mauritian architecture "La Vie en Varangue" (English version "Living in Mauritius", Editions du Pacifique, 1989).

Right: The new courtyard addition at the back of the existing building.

Below: The front façade of the existing house converted into offices.

Pages 246/247: The new courtyard addition around the old mango tree with an entrance from the back street. The pool and fountain are new.

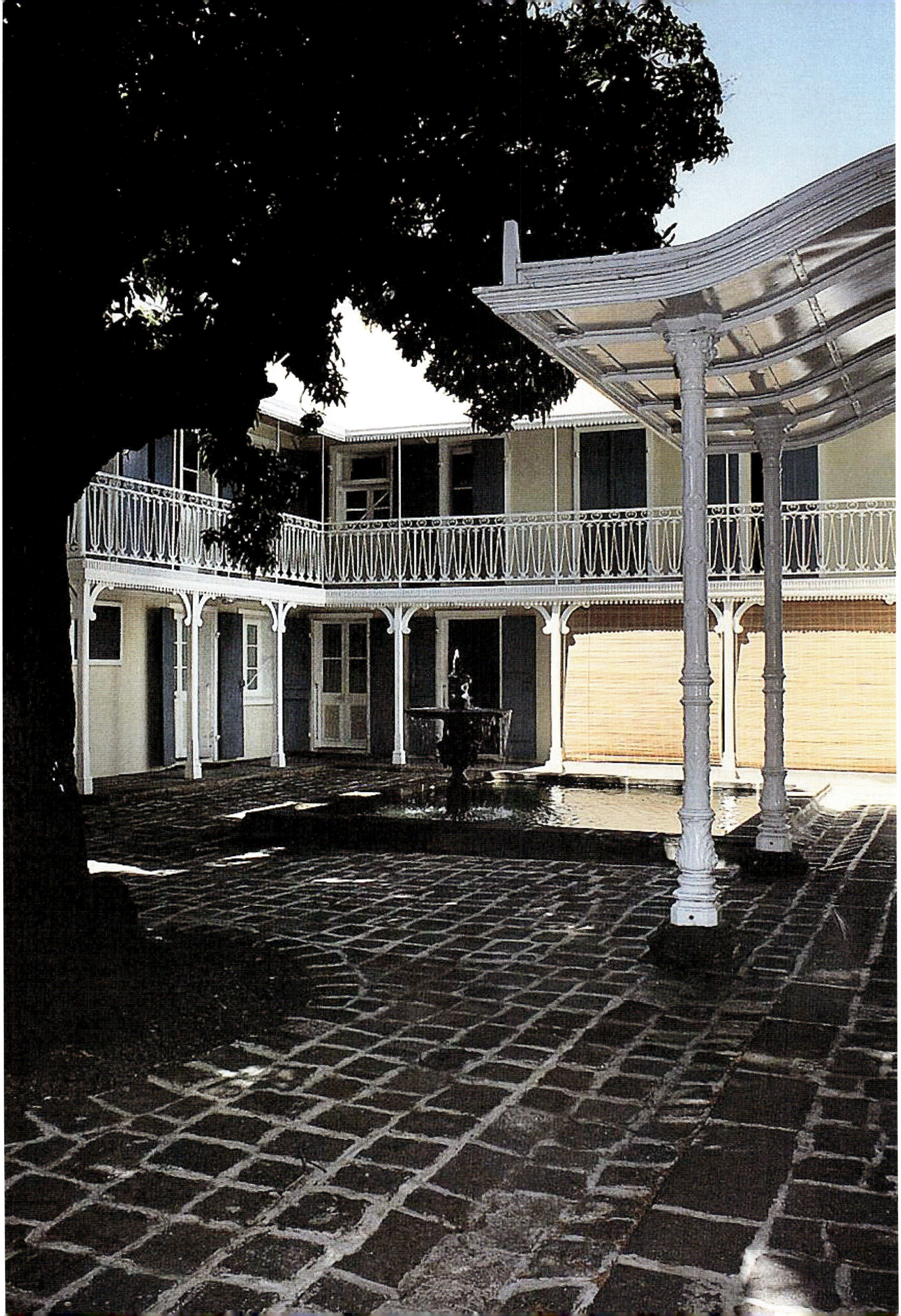

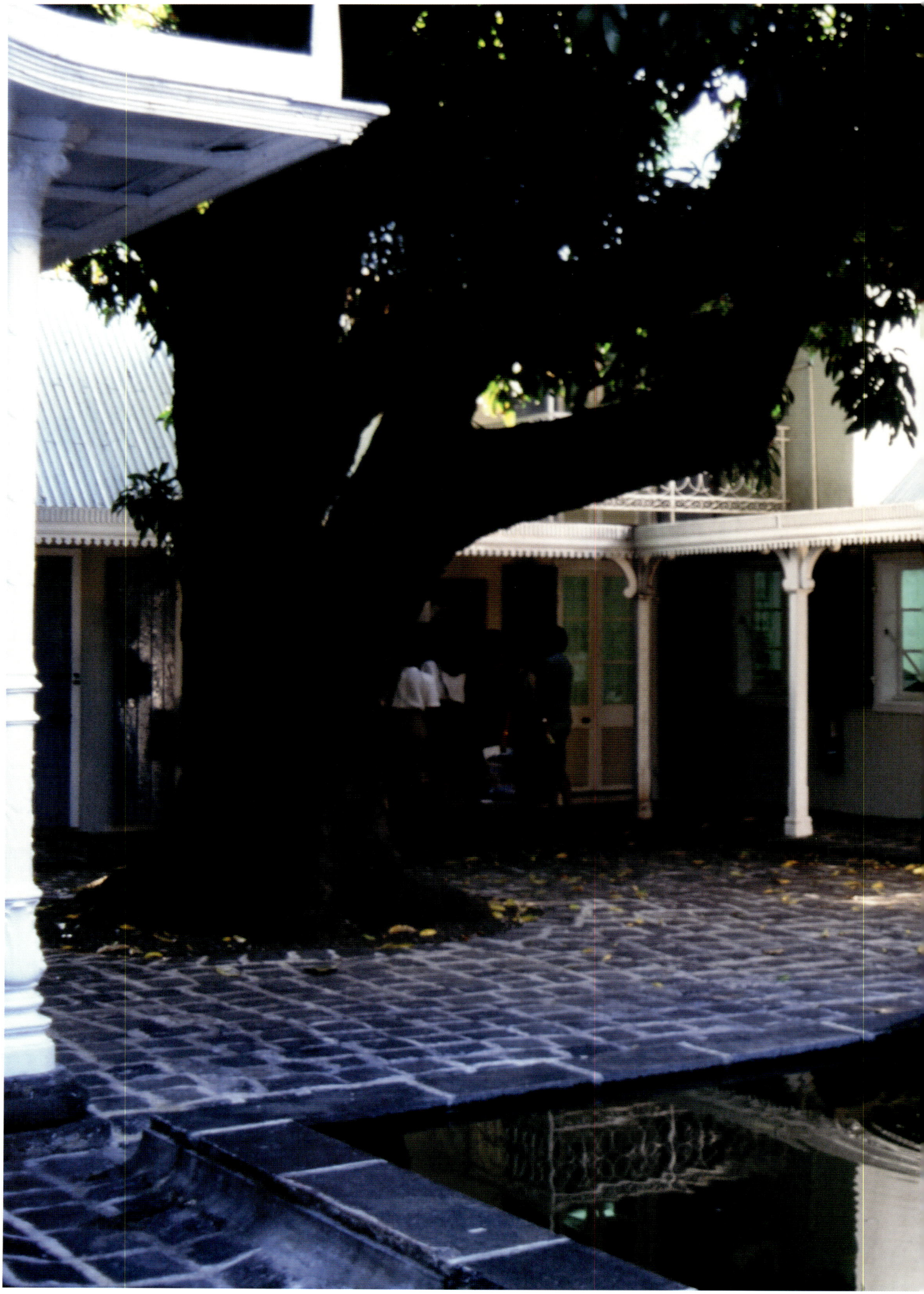

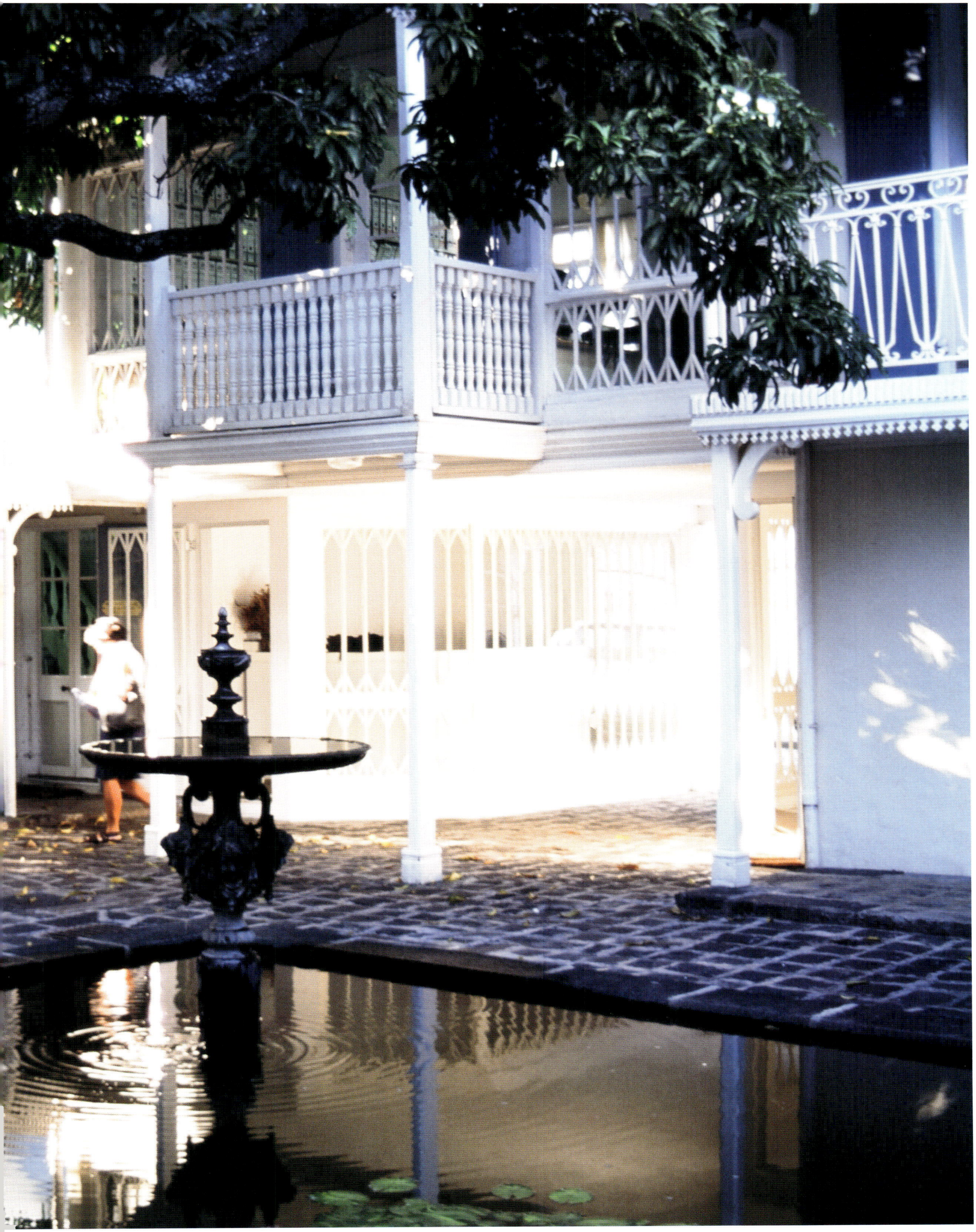

The office extension gives onto another small street, Rue St Louis, at the back of the property. During the extension, many of the old buildings of Port Louis were being demolished. A complete façade in steel was recovered from them with balcony, columns, beams, and brackets, including hand cut stones. These were incorporated in the new construction.

The wrought iron fountain of the new courtyard pool is new and was shipped from France. The result is an extension that creates a courtyard around the old mango tree blending with the existing and indistinguishable from the old. The project survived the financial speculation on land value, preserves the architectural character of Port Louis, bridges the 140-year gap between different periods of time, and saves from demolition one of its most elegant buildings.

The first-floor office circulation balcony, and the new extension, with glazed doors, shutters with their hinges and horizontal lock bars, columns, canopy brackets, and balustrades recovered from demolished buildings in and around Port Louis.

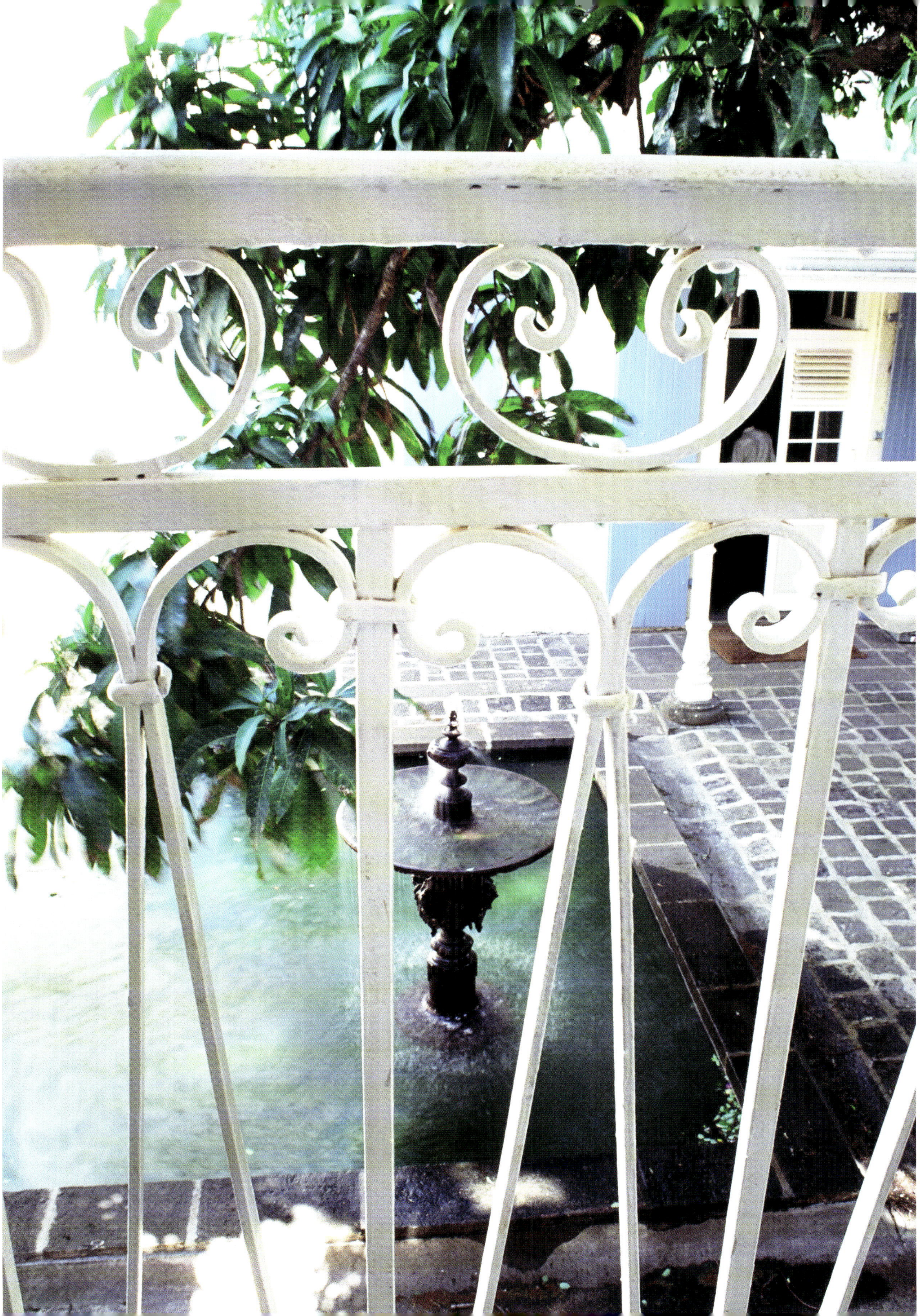

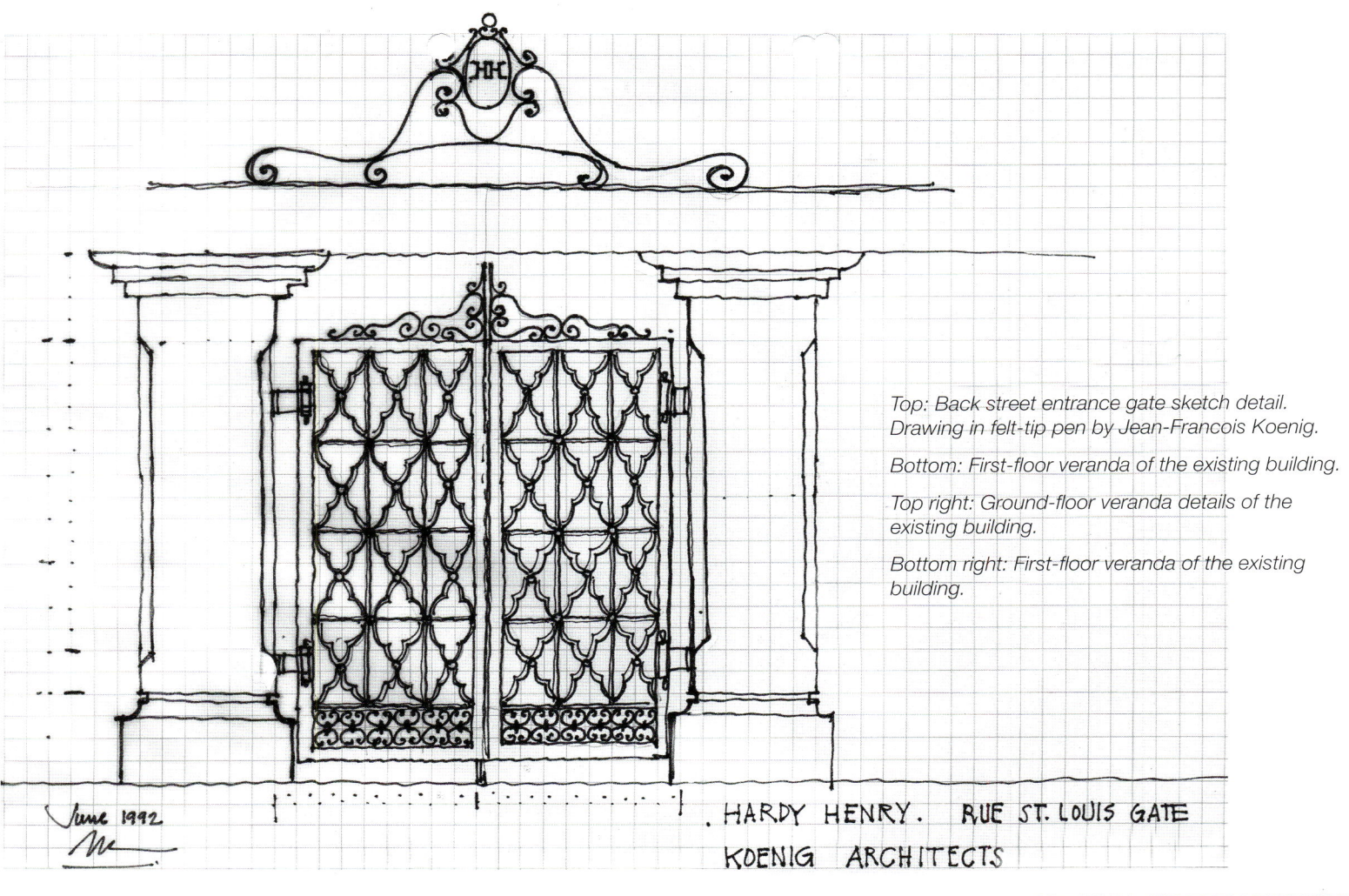

Top: Back street entrance gate sketch detail. Drawing in felt-tip pen by Jean-Francois Koenig.

Bottom: First-floor veranda of the existing building.

Top right: Ground-floor veranda details of the existing building.

Bottom right: First-floor veranda of the existing building.

251

Oxenham Head Office
Trianon, Mauritius
1988

The pencil drawings for Oxenham, a distributor of wines and spirits, illustrate the proposal for a new head office in Trianon in the form of an old house in Mauritian vernacular architecture. It is designed to reflect the image of an established wine estate which is representative of the client's products as well as to create national awareness of the rebirth of traditional local architecture.

The plan is a rectangle of minimalist simplicity with a lightweight steel column and balustrade façade around the four sides of the building acting as a sunscreen, rain screen, and maintenance walkway.

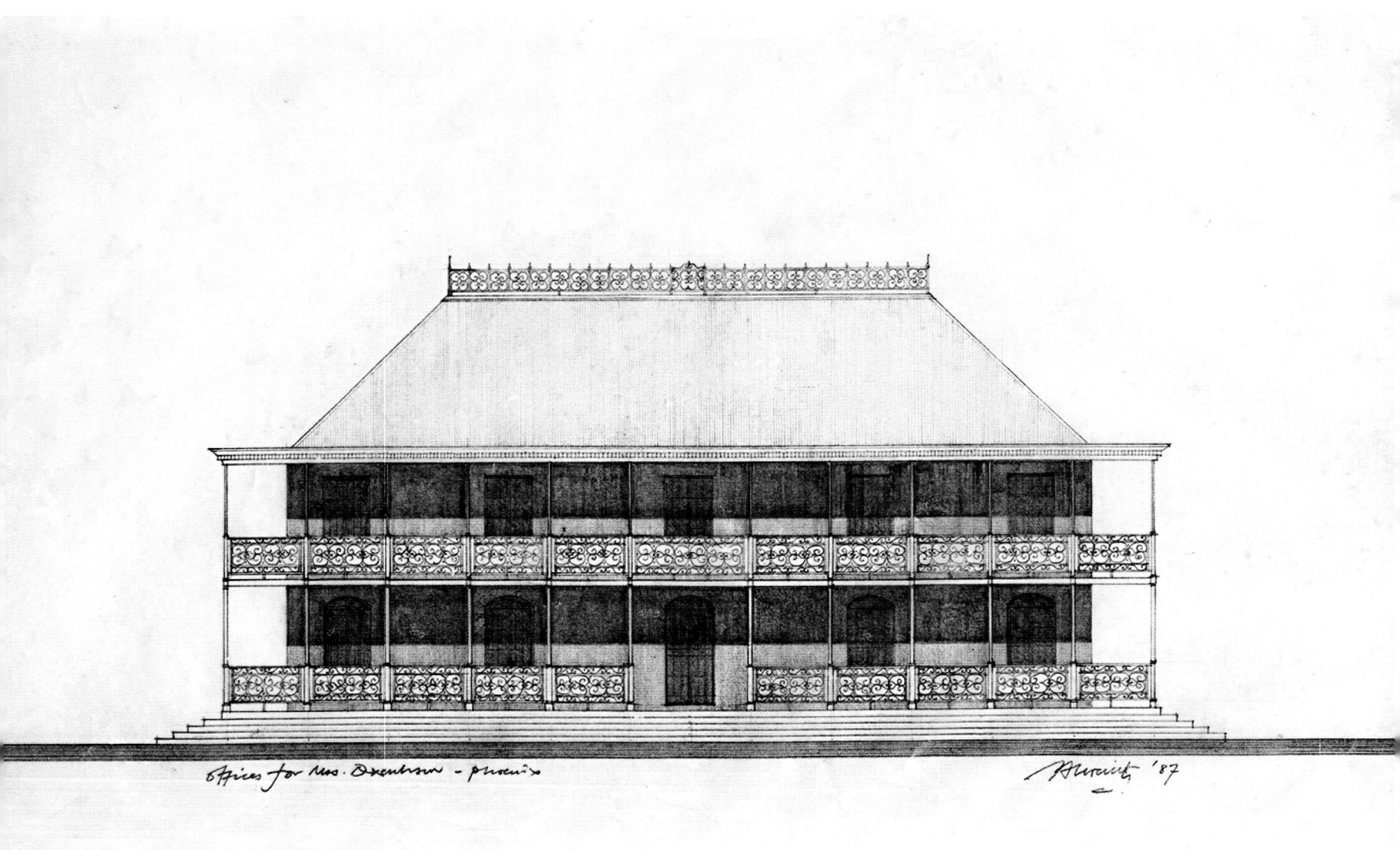

Above: Front façade.

Right: First- and ground-floor plans. Pencil on tracing paper drawings by Jean-Francois Koenig.

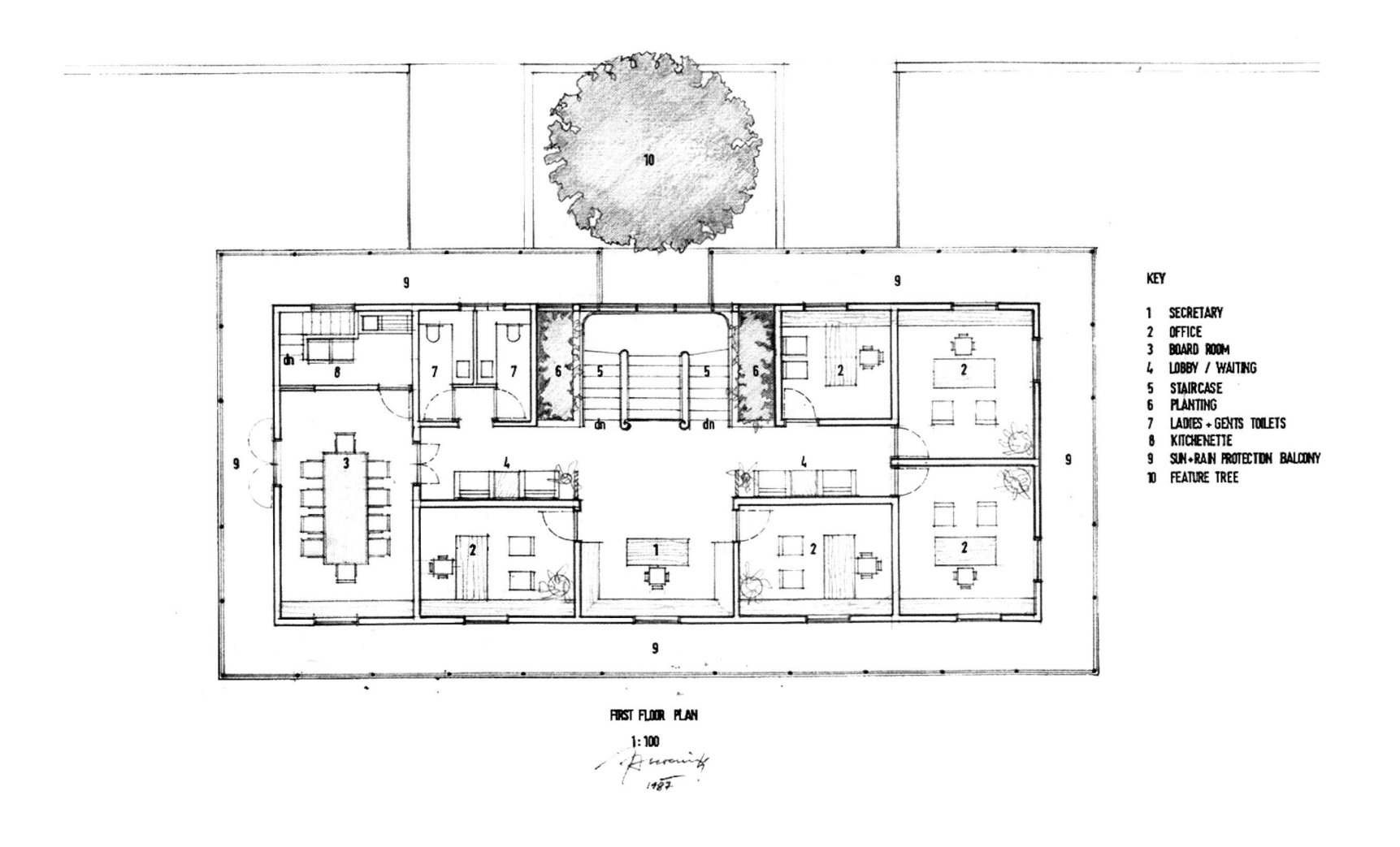

KEY

1. SECRETARY
2. OFFICE
3. BOARD ROOM
4. LOBBY / WAITING
5. STAIRCASE
6. PLANTING
7. LADIES + GENTS TOILETS
8. KITCHENETTE
9. SUN + RAIN PROTECTION BALCONY
10. FEATURE TREE

FIRST FLOOR PLAN
1:100

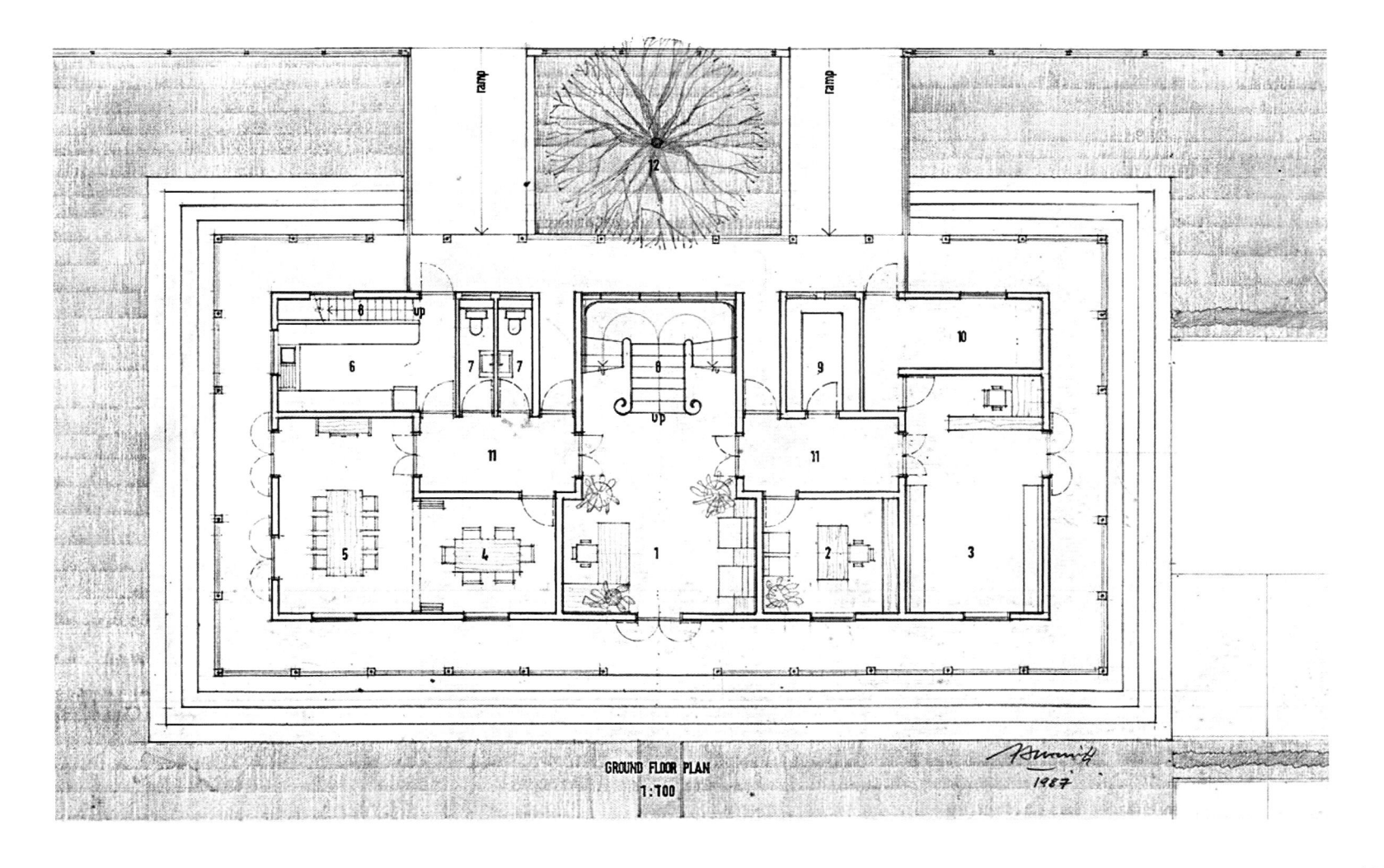

GROUND FLOOR PLAN
1:100

United Basalt Head Office

Trianon, Mauritius
1988–1990

The head office for United Basalt at Trianon comprises two pyramidal roofs on first floor and corresponding lower sloping roofs on ground floor that cantilever 1.9 m to form low lying eaves for sun and rain protection. Raised planters follow the roofs and continuous fenestration all around the building on both levels. They hide individual air conditioning units along a maintenance walkway and reduce the height to the eaves line to accentuate the horizontal proportions of the building.

The plan is a structural tartan grid that defines office and circulation zones. The architecture is a response to construction methods common to Mauritius and its climate. Concrete is the main building material in use, and a low pitch facilitates pouring. The continuation of the straight line of the slope of the roof and the continuation of steel reinforcement in the structural concrete slab balances the large cantilever.

Top: Front façade.
Bottom: First elevation sketches in ballpoint pen on graph paper by Jean-Francois Koenig.

The tropical climate on the high plateau is humid. Walls in painted cement render and especially parapets are vulnerable to staining and mould growth. As offices need shading from direct sunlight and windows and walls need protection from moisture, the resolution of the issues above creates the architectural response of the low lying shallow pitched concrete roof.
During construction in 1988, United Basalt was experimenting with the production of concrete roof tiles for the local market and only one profile in a terracotta colour was available. The dark grey colour, to match the colour of humidity stains, was produced specifically for the job. The low pitched concrete roof with cantilevers and concrete roof tiles was novel in Mauritius at the time of the building's completion and has since been widely used due to its efficiency in solving the problems of tropical climate conditions with a robust solution adapted to cyclones.

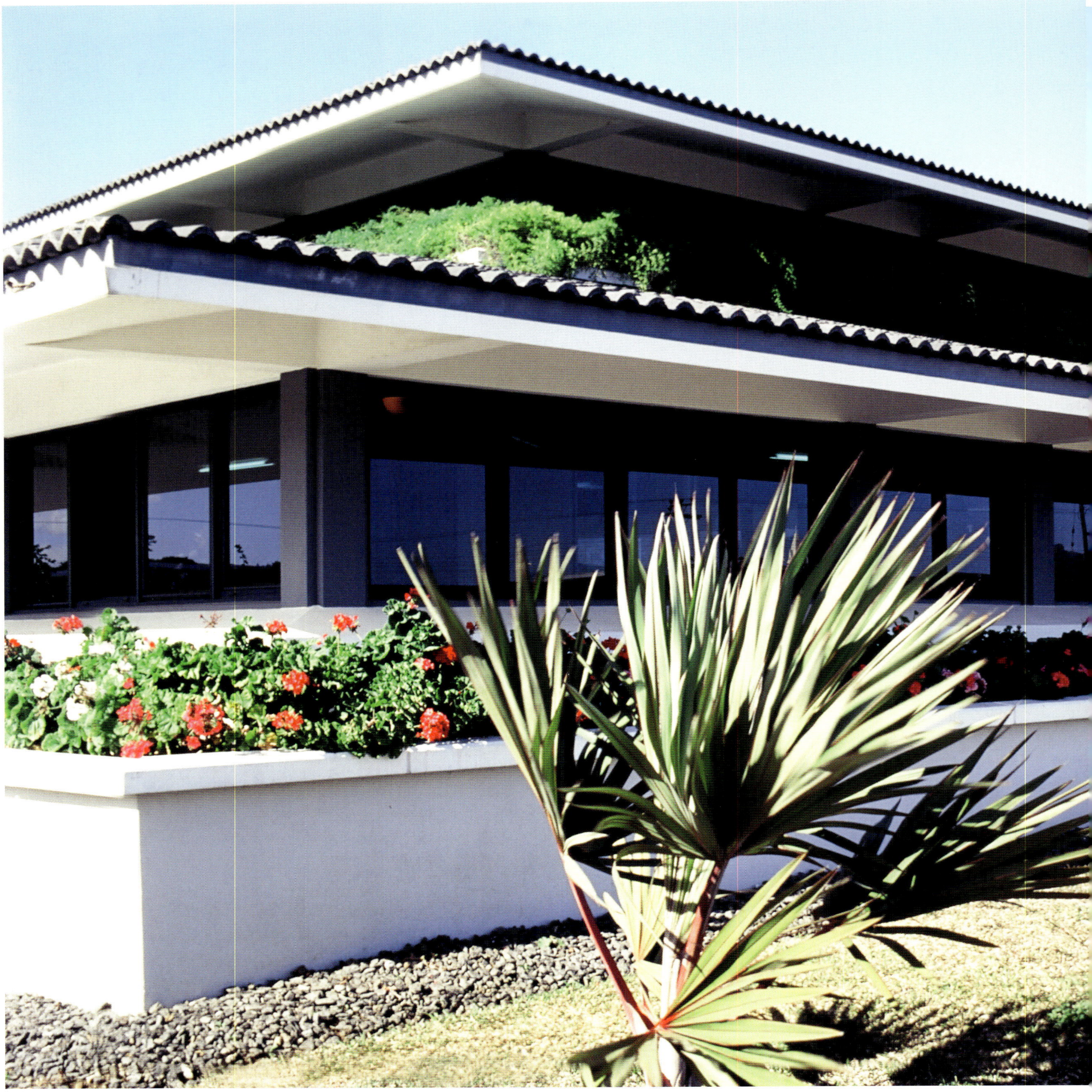

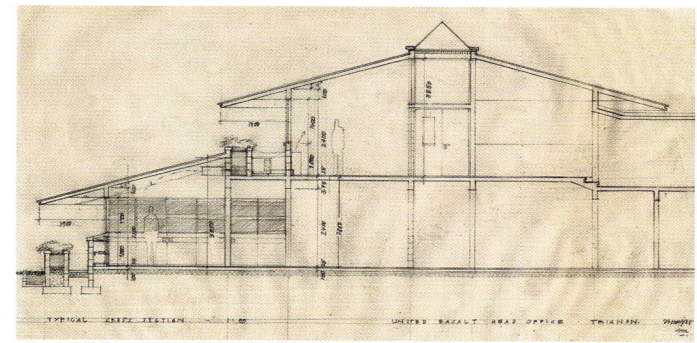

Left: Front face of the building.

Top right: Cross section drawing in pencil on tracing paper by Jean-Francois Koenig.

Bottom right: Staircase detail of tread and riser nosings in machine cut basalt stone specially prepared for the job.

Sotravic Head Office
Coromandel, Mauritius
1992–1995

Sotravic has a parent company specialised in steel construction and, from the outset, it was a given preference that steel, although not commonly used in Mauritius, would be the choice of material for the new building.

The building responds to the sloping rocky site on the edge of the ravine of the "Grande Rivière Nord Ouest" by eliminating extensive earthworks. It bridges the site taking advantage of the fast construction time of steel. The structure is a trussed girder spanning 20 m and expressed in front of recessed blue tinted full-height glass. Blue is the colour of the logo of the companies. Two wings, in a staggered formation, cantilever over the edge of the ravine to offer spectacular views of the landscape.

Right: The building cantilevers over the edge of a ravine.

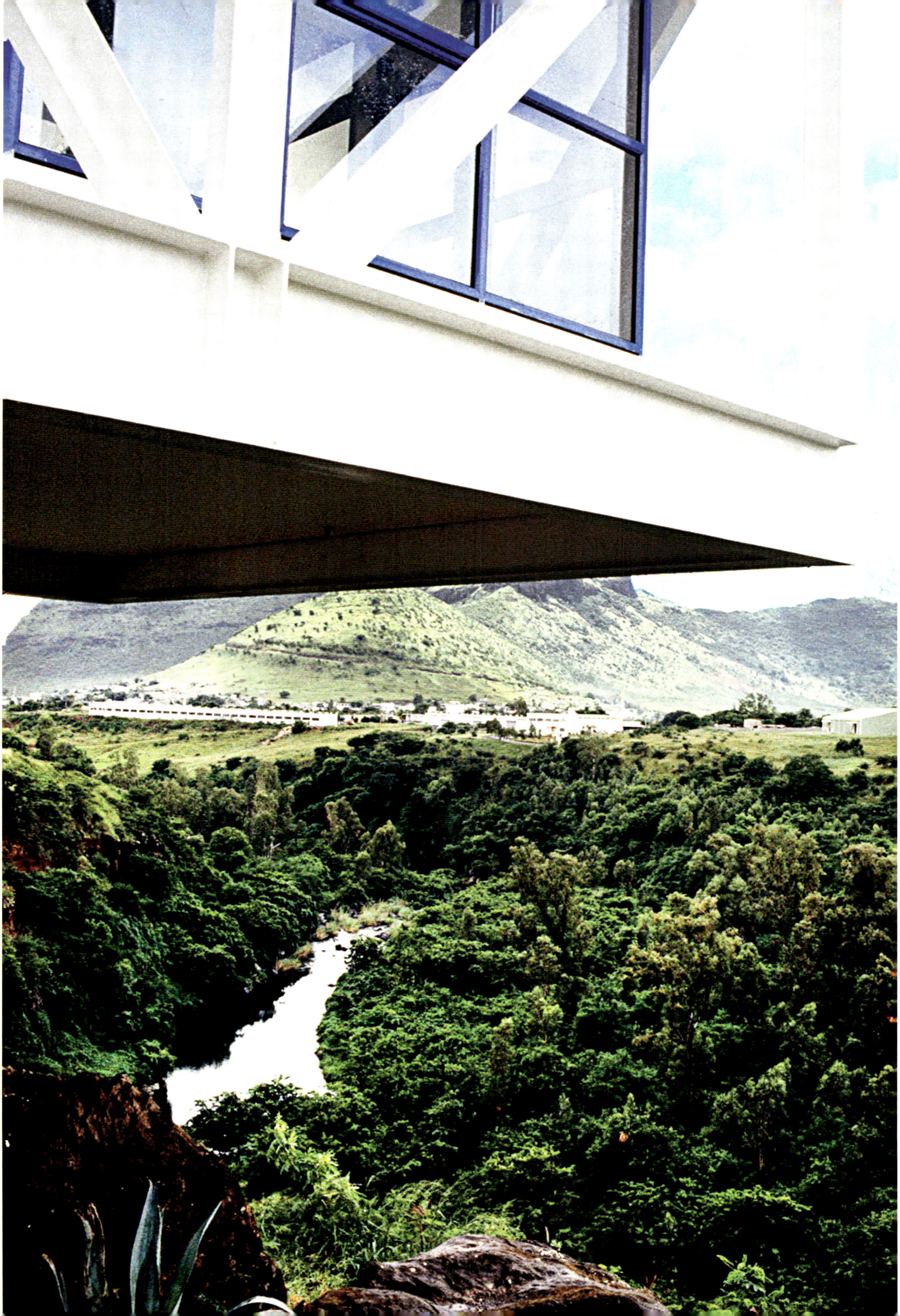

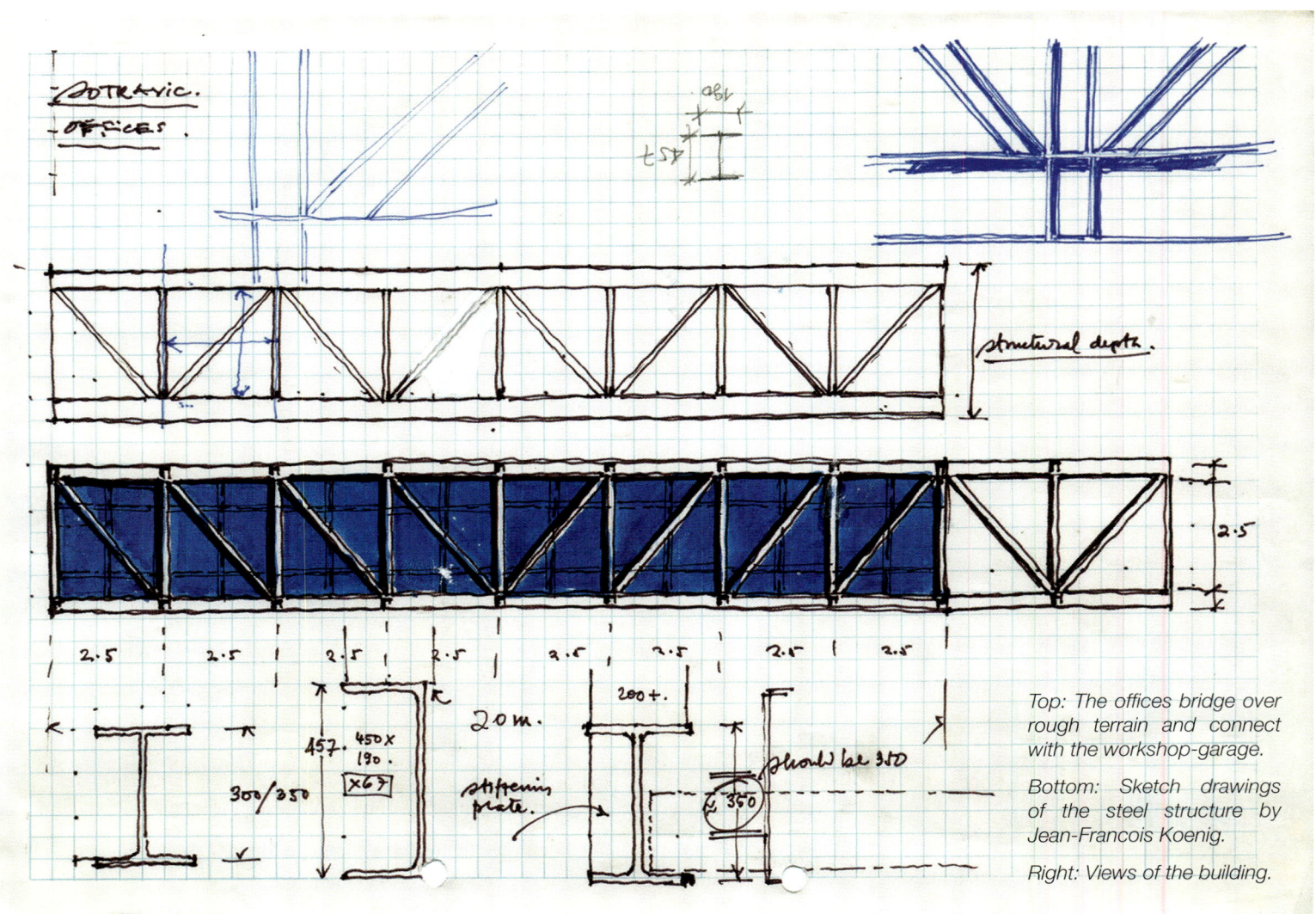

Top: The offices bridge over rough terrain and connect with the workshop-garage.

Bottom: Sketch drawings of the steel structure by Jean-Francois Koenig.

Right: Views of the building.

261

Mauritius Telecom Headquarters
Port Louis, Mauritius
1992–1995

The Mauritius Telecom Headquarters is the winning entry of an international architectural competition for the state-owned company, Mauritius Telecom. At 20 storeys, it was the tallest building on the Island and the first floor-to-floor flush reflective glass façade.

The corners of the tower end in thin edges to accentuate the vertical, culminating with twin masts. The reflective glass mirrors the sky to diminish the impact of the structure on the environment. A naturally lit, triple height atrium on ground floor are for public affairs interface and the confidential office departments are distributed on the floors above.

The Mauritius Telecom building in Port Louis in 1995.

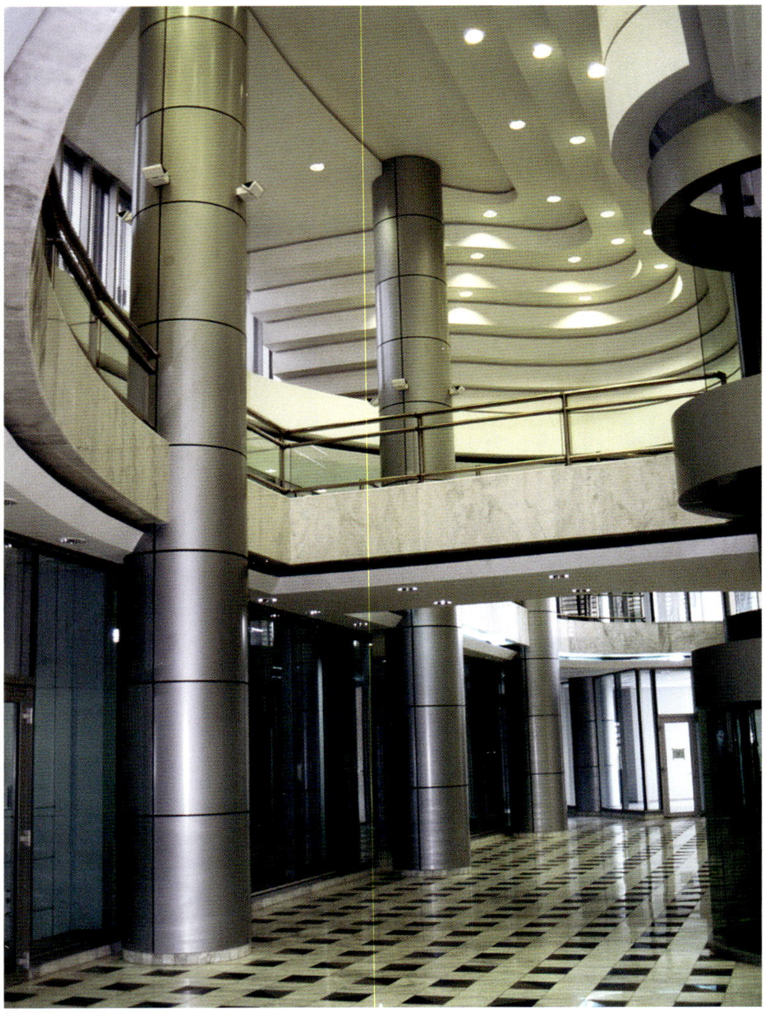

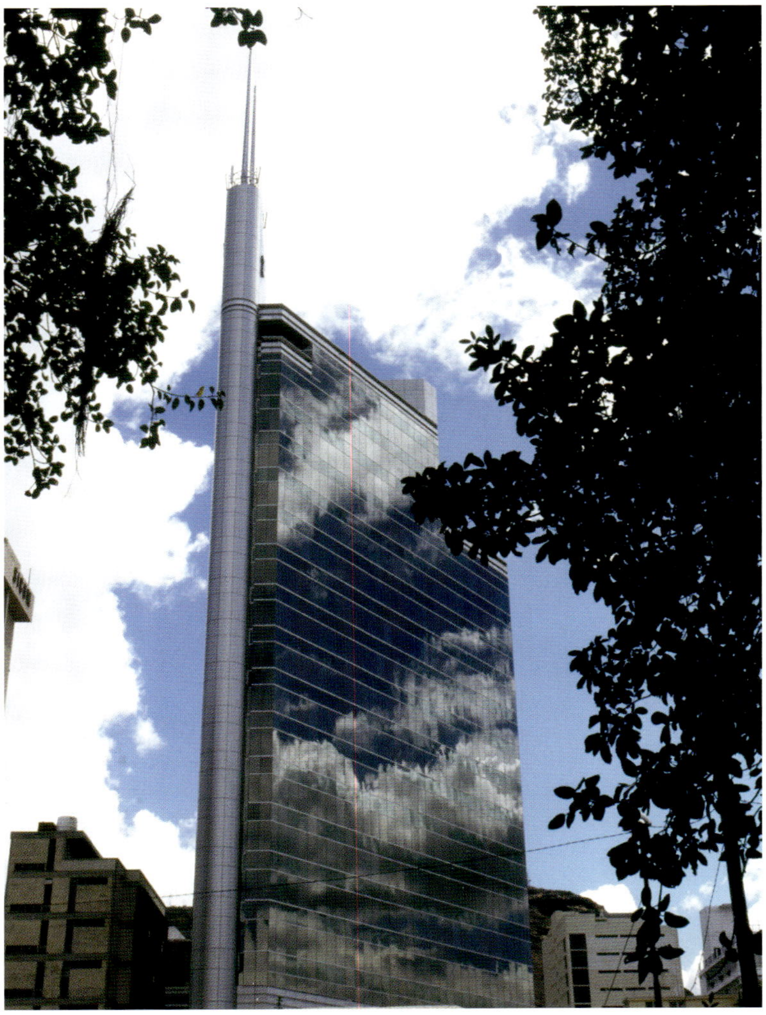

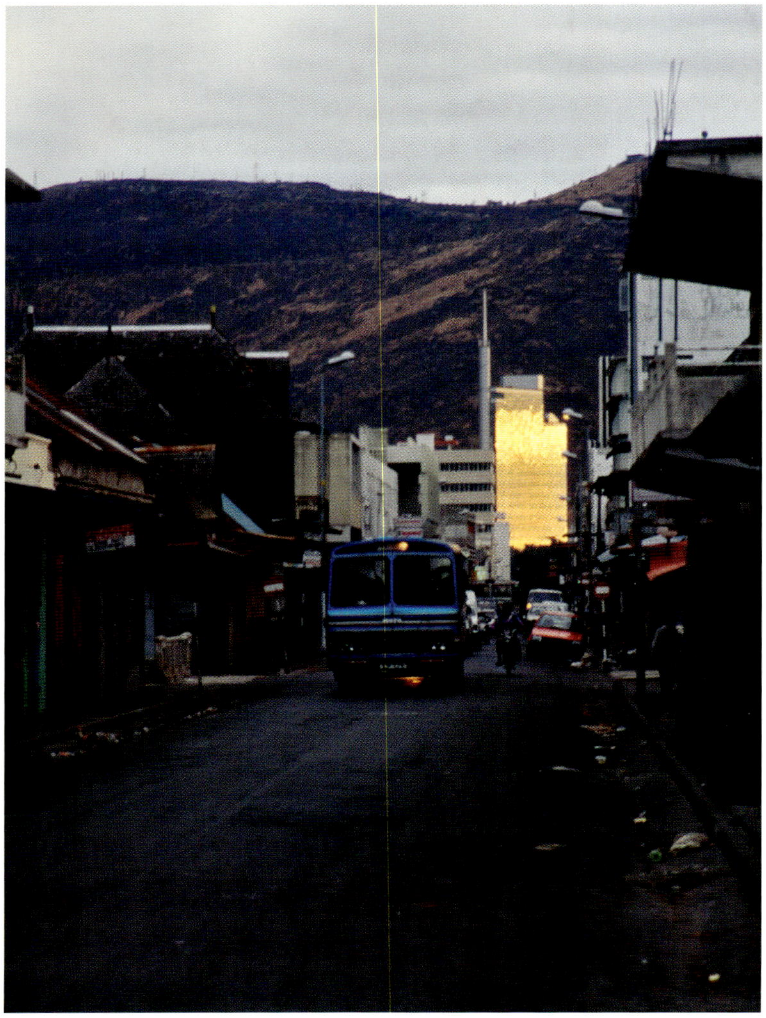

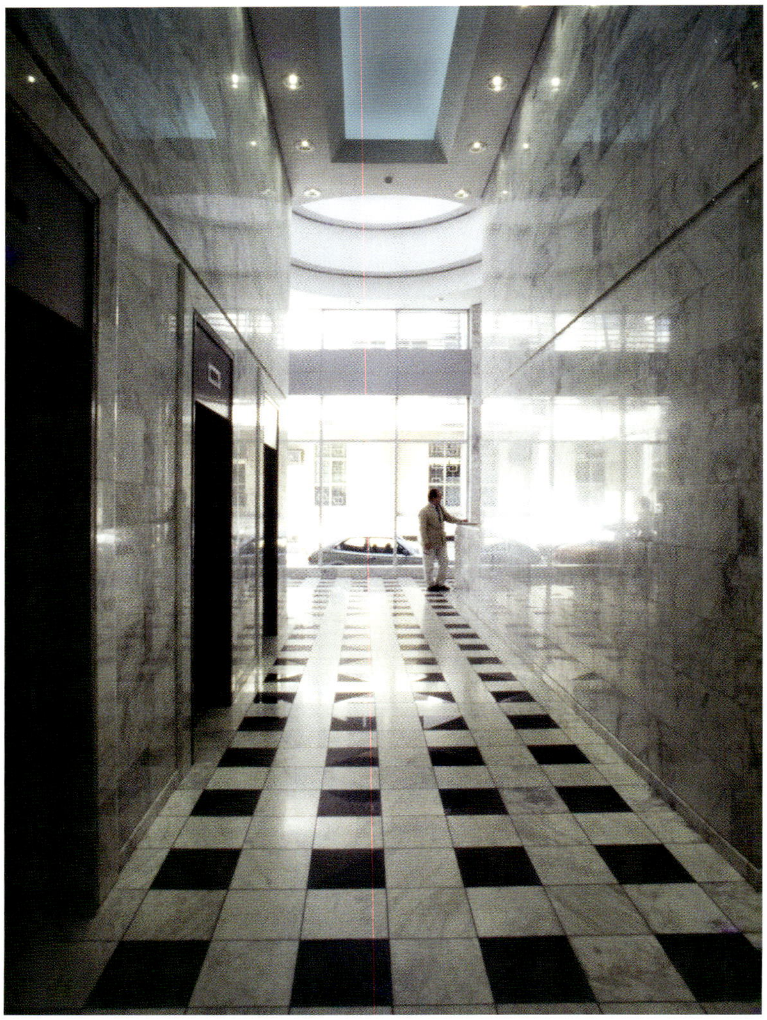

The Mauritius Telecom building.

CIEL Head Office
Ebène, Mauritius
2005–2009

The head office for CIEL is on a site at Ebène in the centre of the country that follows the gentle curve of a ravine overlooking a river below. The plan of the building responds to the shape of the site.

The entrance porte cochère is under a cantilevered structure with a circular pool and fountain. A typical floor plan yields an efficient core to usable space ratio of 11% to 89%. The depth of a typical floor plate is 18 m. The last two floors are interconnected with bridges and internal staircases within a triple volume space which is naturally lit by clerestory windows. The space acts as an atrium bringing management on the top floor visually connected to staff of other departments on the lower floor improving interaction and team spirit.

The façades consist of strip windows in bronze glass with intermittent top hung openings for natural ventilation and 'brise soleils' which also act as maintenance walkways for cleaning the windows above. They consist of a combination of louvres and solid panels with bullnosed ends in metallic grey aluminium.

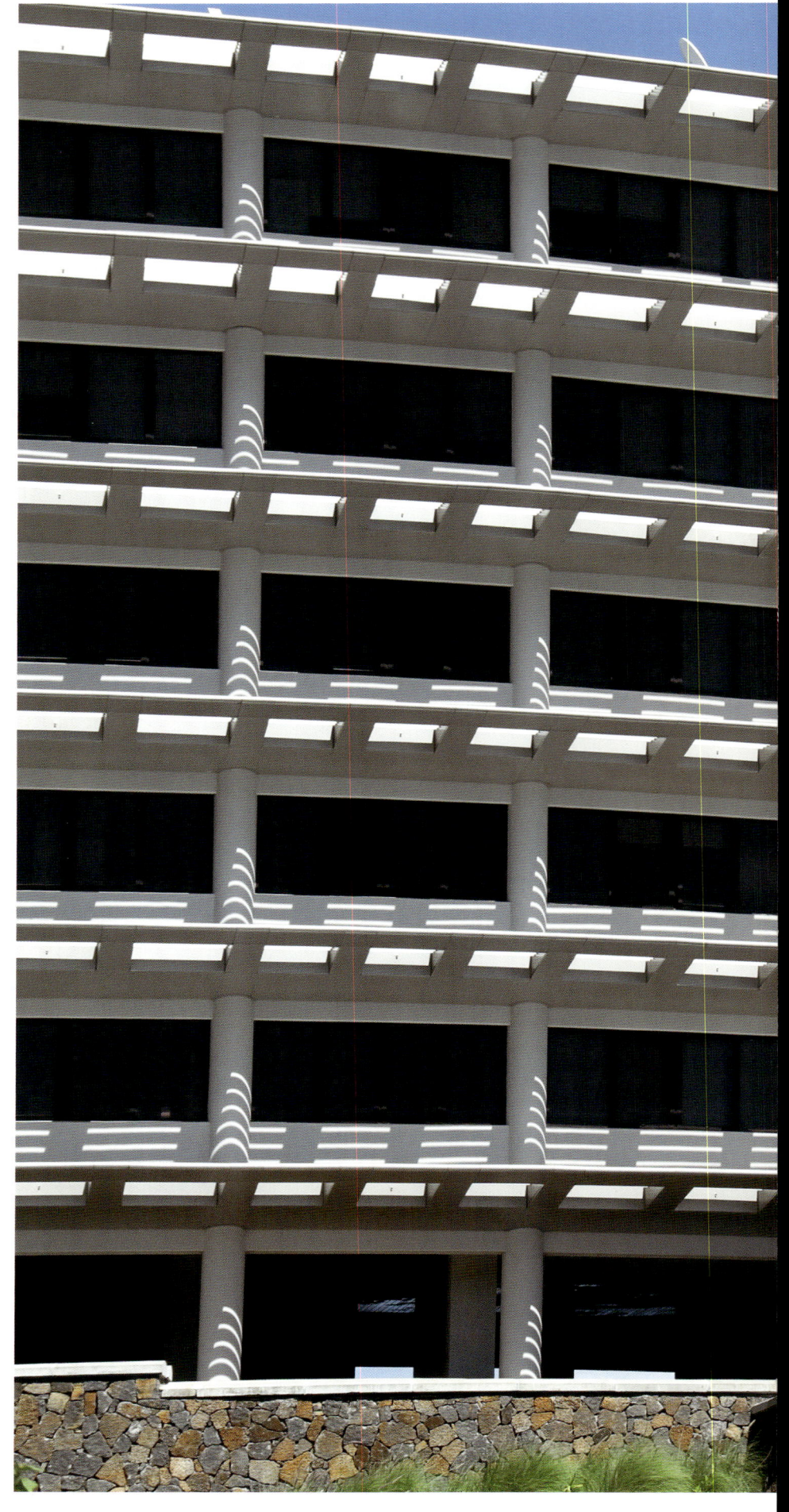

The northern face of the building with aluminium fins acting as both sunscreens and maintenance walkways.

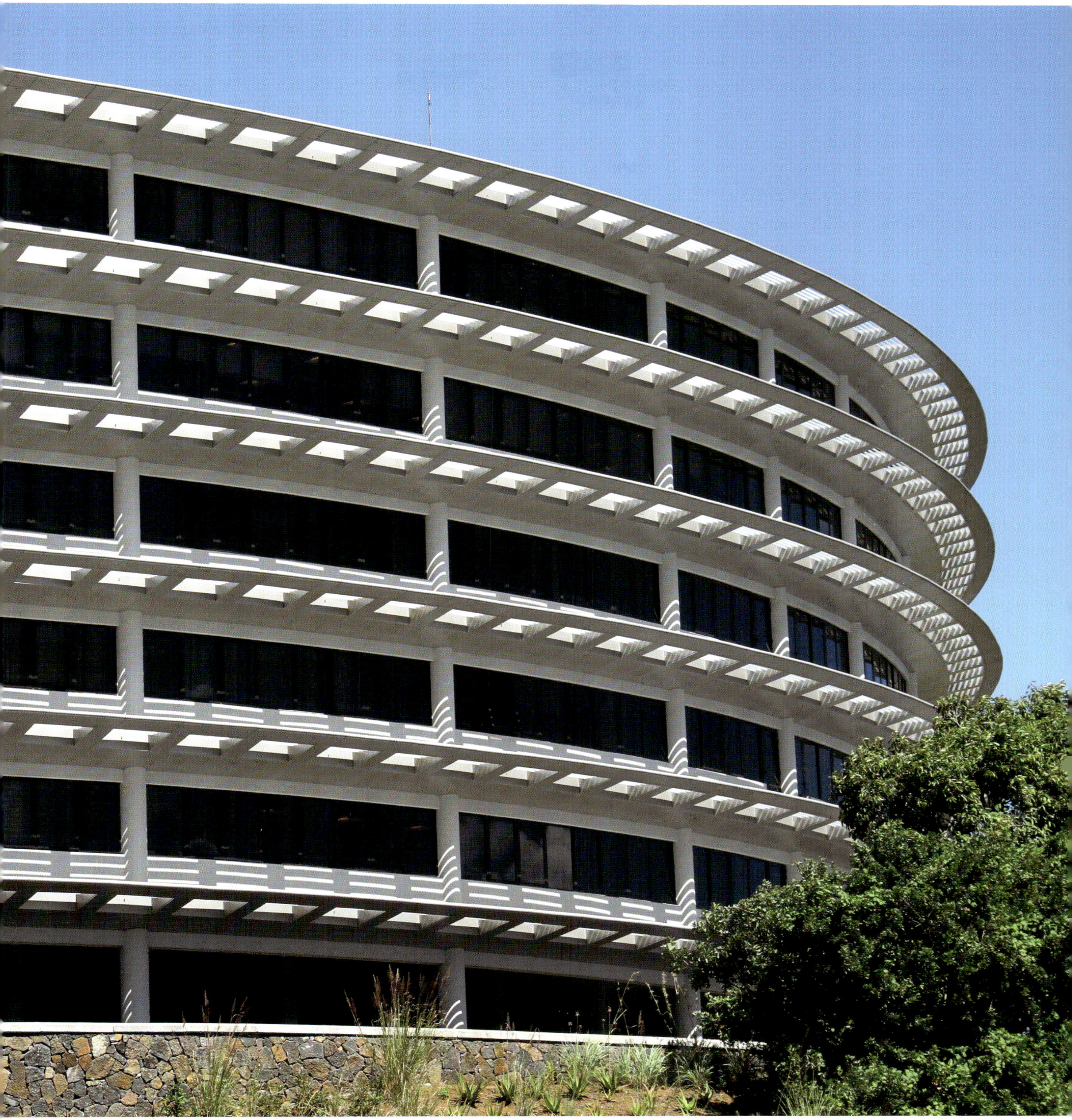

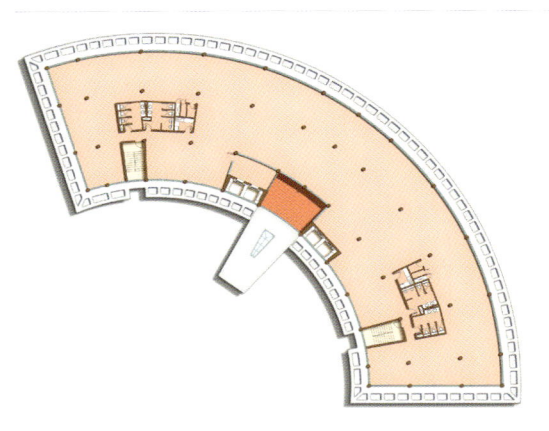

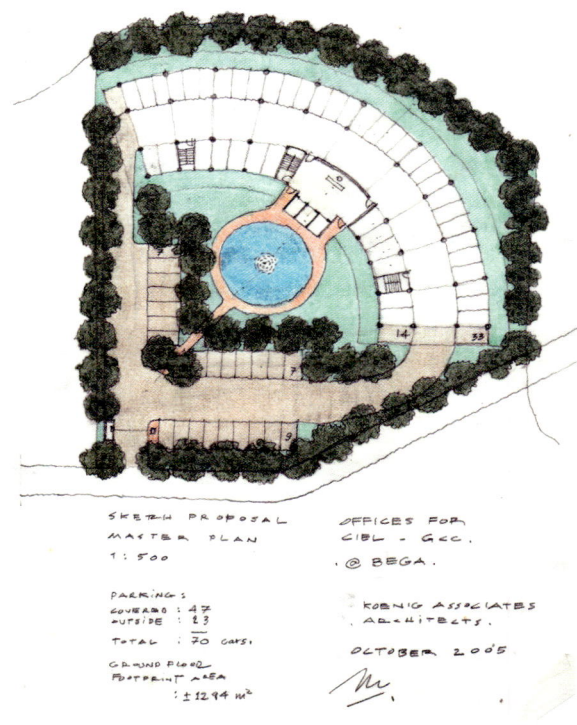

Left: Aerial view of the building and site.

Top right: Drawing by Jean-Francois Koenig.

Centre right: Typical floor plan.

Bottom right: Site plan – ground-floor plan.
Sketch drawing by Jean-Francois Koenig.

Top left: Entrance porte cochère and pool.
Top right and bottom: Views of the clerestory lit atrium.

Anglo Mauritius Assurance Society Ltd.
Port Louis, Mauritius
2006

A master plan study for the future development of prime land in the heart of the capital city of Port Louis opposite the Parliament of Mauritius and the Prime Minister's office for Anglo Mauritius, now the Swan Group, is a project that incorporates all of their properties. These existing properties include a 12-storey Swan Group Centre office building, a 2-storey Swan Insurance building, an 8-storey Anglo Mauritius building, plus land at the back giving onto two streets.

The proposal consists of a new 3-level multistorey car park for 500 cars, the conversion of the 8-storey Anglo Mauritius house into a business hotel with a spa at the top and a glass bottom swimming pool over an 8-floor high atrium fully glazed on the street corner opposite Parliament House and transformed into a garden restaurant, the demolition of the 2-storey Swan Insurance building replaced by a 36-storey double skin glass tower.

The plan of the tower is a 45-degree isosceles triangle. The public is invited to pass through the building at street level to access four levels of shops and food outlets. Offices are on the floors above and include three stacked atria. A club restaurant is on the top two floors with a mezzanine overlooking double height glass and views of the port. The top of the building culminates in a multifunction transmission antenna.

Right: Night view of the double skin glass tower.

Pages 272/273: View of Port Louis with the Mauritius Telecom Tower on the left and the proposed AMAS Tower on the right.

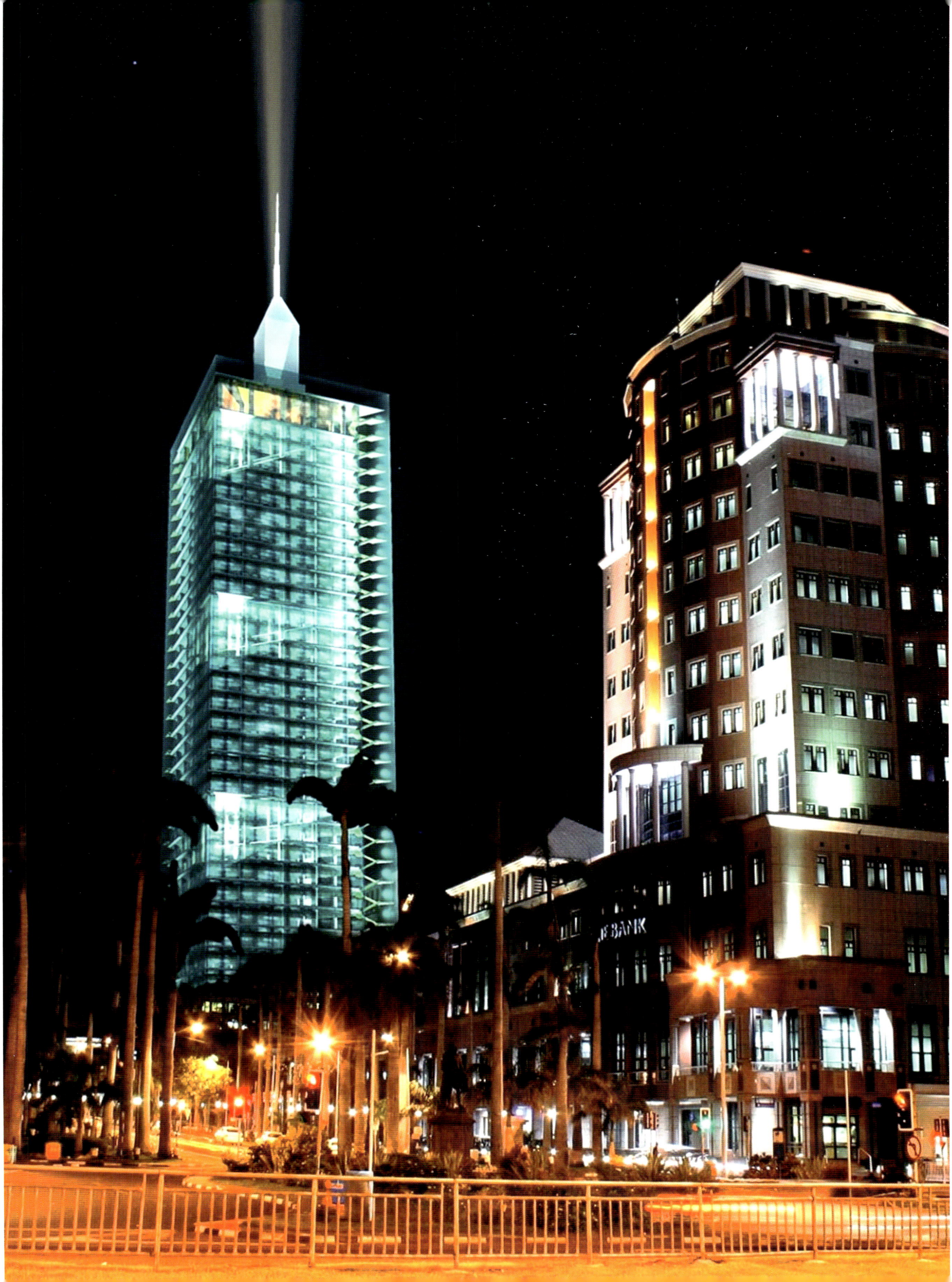
BANK

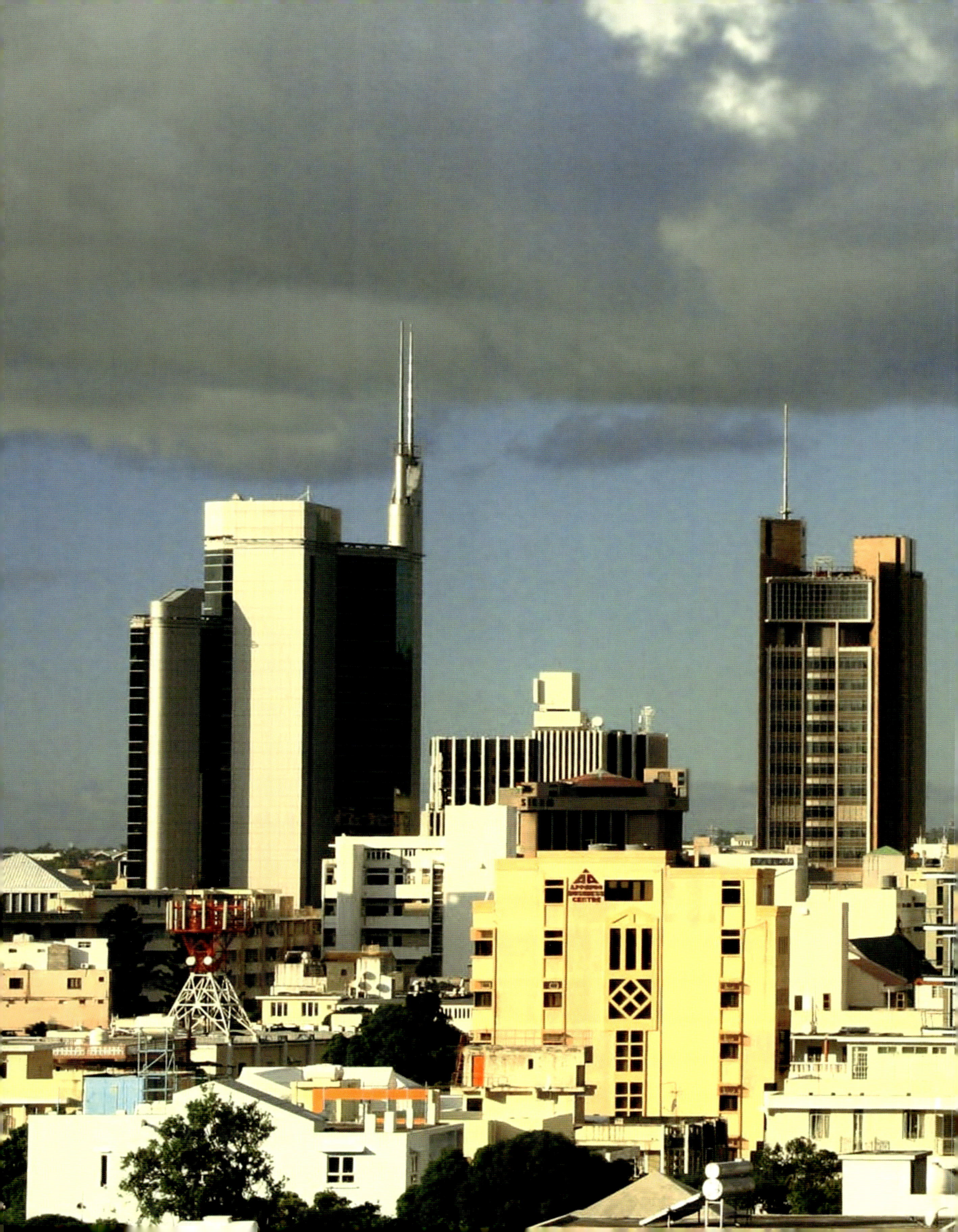

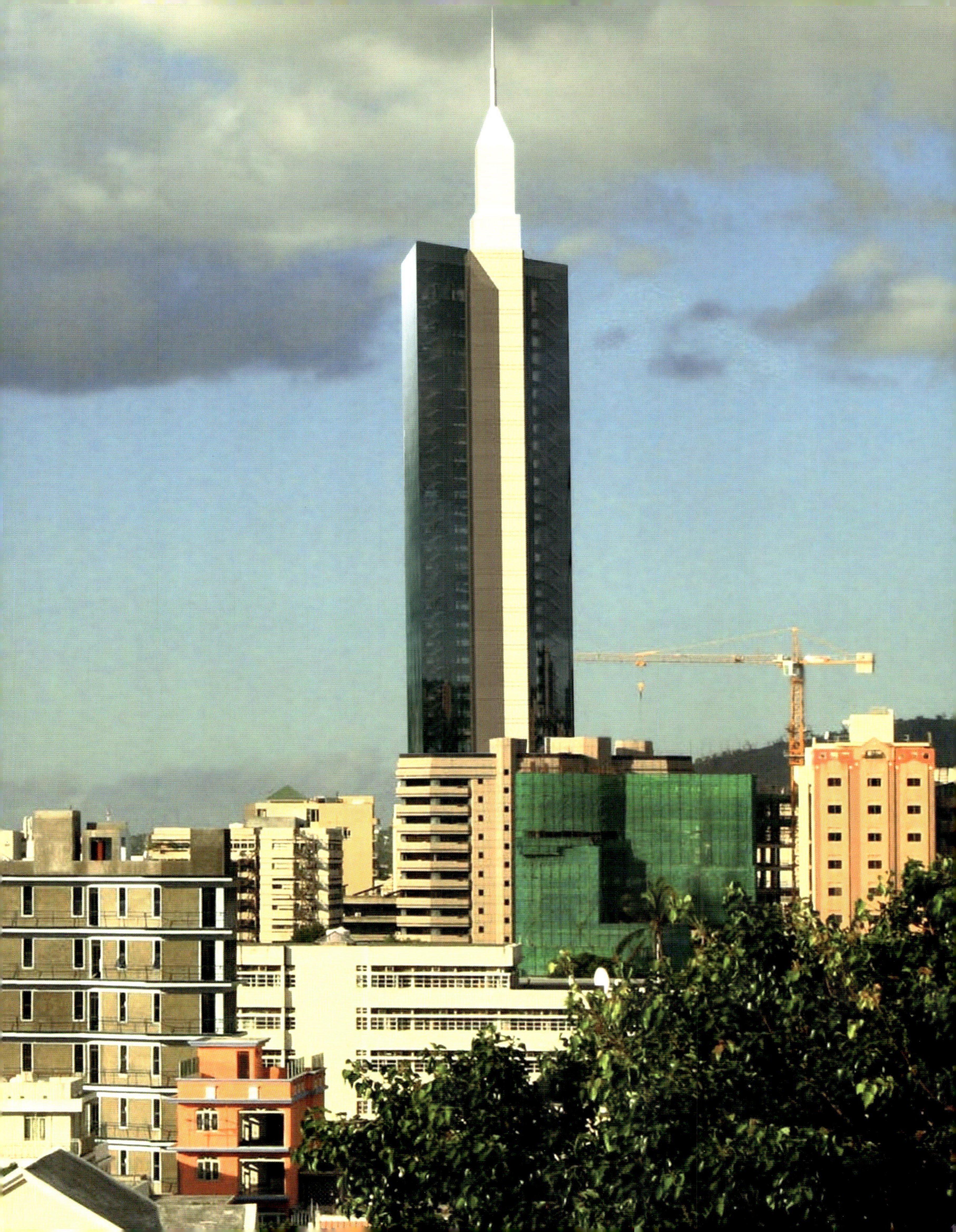

Top: Upper-floor master plan. Bottom: Ground-floor master plan.
Right: Pencil drawings coloured with felt-tip markers by Jean-Francois Koenig.

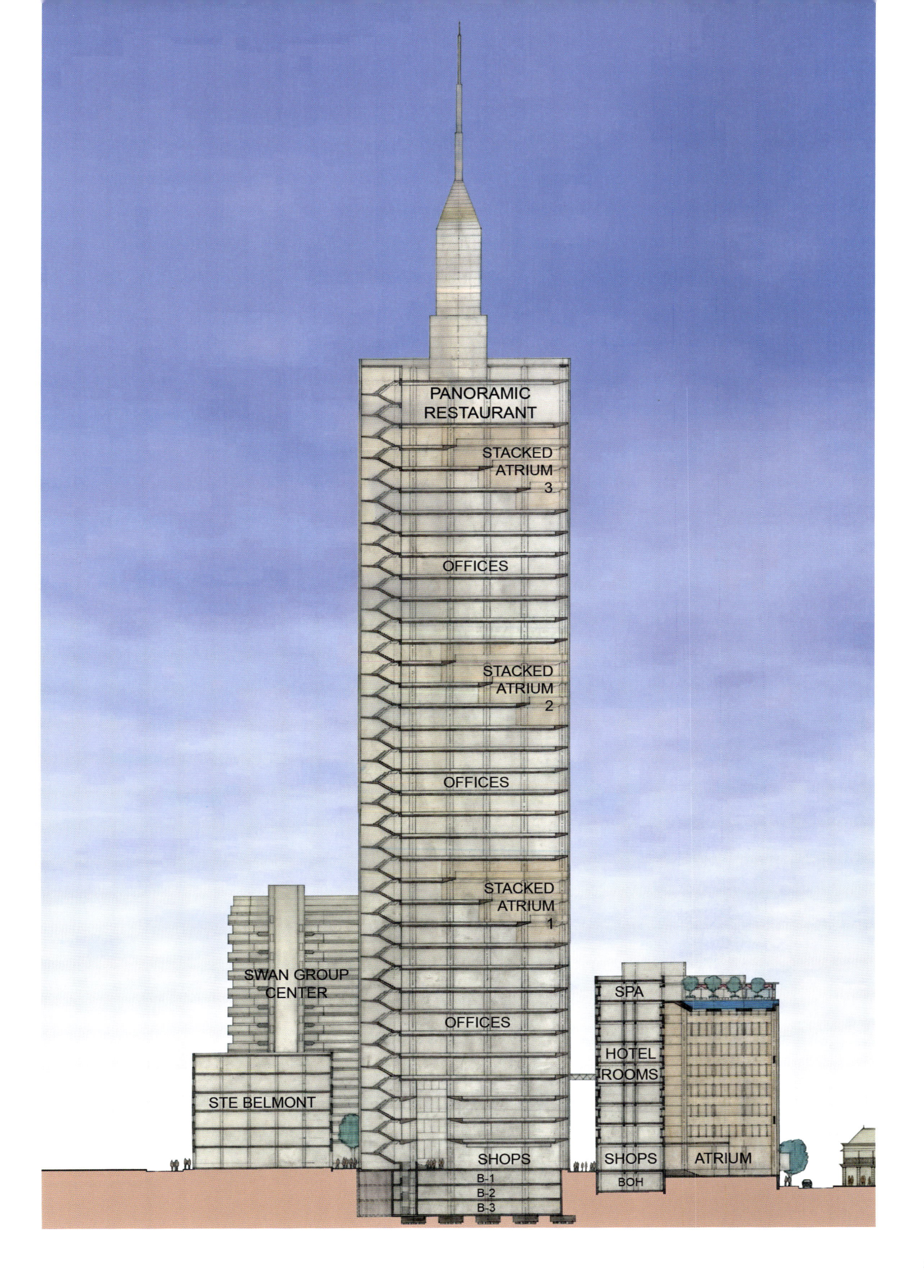

PANORAMIC RESTAURANT

STACKED ATRIUM 3

OFFICES

STACKED ATRIUM 2

OFFICES

STACKED ATRIUM 1

OFFICES

SWAN GROUP CENTER

SPA

HOTEL ROOMS

STE BELMONT

SHOPS
B-1
B-2
B-3

SHOPS
BOH

ATRIUM

Mauritius Commercial Bank Ebène
Mauritius
2006–2012

The building for the Mauritius Commercial Bank at Ebène is located next to the motorway near the St Jean roundabout in the centre of the country to bring the workplace closer to where the staff live reducing travelling time to and from home. It is significant as the first building being derived from its function to be an ellipse in section and elevation.

The form of the building is a response to the brief which consists of the requirement for an auditorium for 275 people, office space, and their amenities. The design intent is a desire to save the unusable low headroom wedge-shaped space usually found under a sloping floor by raising the auditorium off the ground. Space is thus liberated underneath and the auditoriums are expressed in the architecture as a form that follows function.

The need to interconnect departments and people for better interaction and communication between floors is best achieved by internal atriums. In this instance, the concept of stacked atria is reinvented in the form of four mezzanines cascading under a single umbrella roof mirroring the underbelly.

The ellipse is supported by four pillars. The plan is a rectangle 63 m long by 22 m wide. The cores are in two of the northern pillars containing lifts, fire escapes, services, and washrooms. The other two pillars on the southern side are left free for air conditioning plant rooms. The longest floor in the middle of the ellipse yields an efficient core plus structure to office space ratio of 9% to 91%. It holds between 150 and 175 staff in an open plan with same size desks, irrespective of rank, in a democratic 'one size fits all' working environment proposed as an integral part of the space planning. A staff canteen, seating 250 people, is on grade on the shaded south side with views on a man-made pond. When in full use, the building holds 1,025 people.

Photovoltaic panels provide 35% of the building's energy at peak use. The shell is well insulated and can be seen behind five glass rings all around the ellipse. The glass rings run over double glazed portholes that bring supplementary daylight to the internal spaces and highlight the expressed steel structure of the roof. Air conditioning is an all-air system that provides 'free cooling' from thermal storage. It is distributed from within raised floor plenums with no ducts. This improves planning flexibility and makes future change easy. Electrical and computer wiring also come from the raised floor feeding artificial lighting, which is specially designed down-and-up-lighters on poles coordinated with, and integrated into the workstation. There are no suspended ceilings. The underside of the floor slab is the ceiling, left in bare concrete painted white. This contributes to the cooling of the building by releasing cold passing in the plenum above which accumulates in the thermal mass of the concrete slab. The building is oriented true north–south for more efficient sun control. This is achieved by a combination of external sunscreens and internal perforated louvres that drop automatically by sensor control to eliminate early morning and late afternoon low sun infiltration. The full-height glazing of the two elliptical façades provides sufficient daylight well into the centre of the floor eliminating the need for artificial light during daytime working hours.

Right: Detail of the piers clad in travertine and the elliptical shell clad in aluminium.
Pages 278/279: South and East façades.

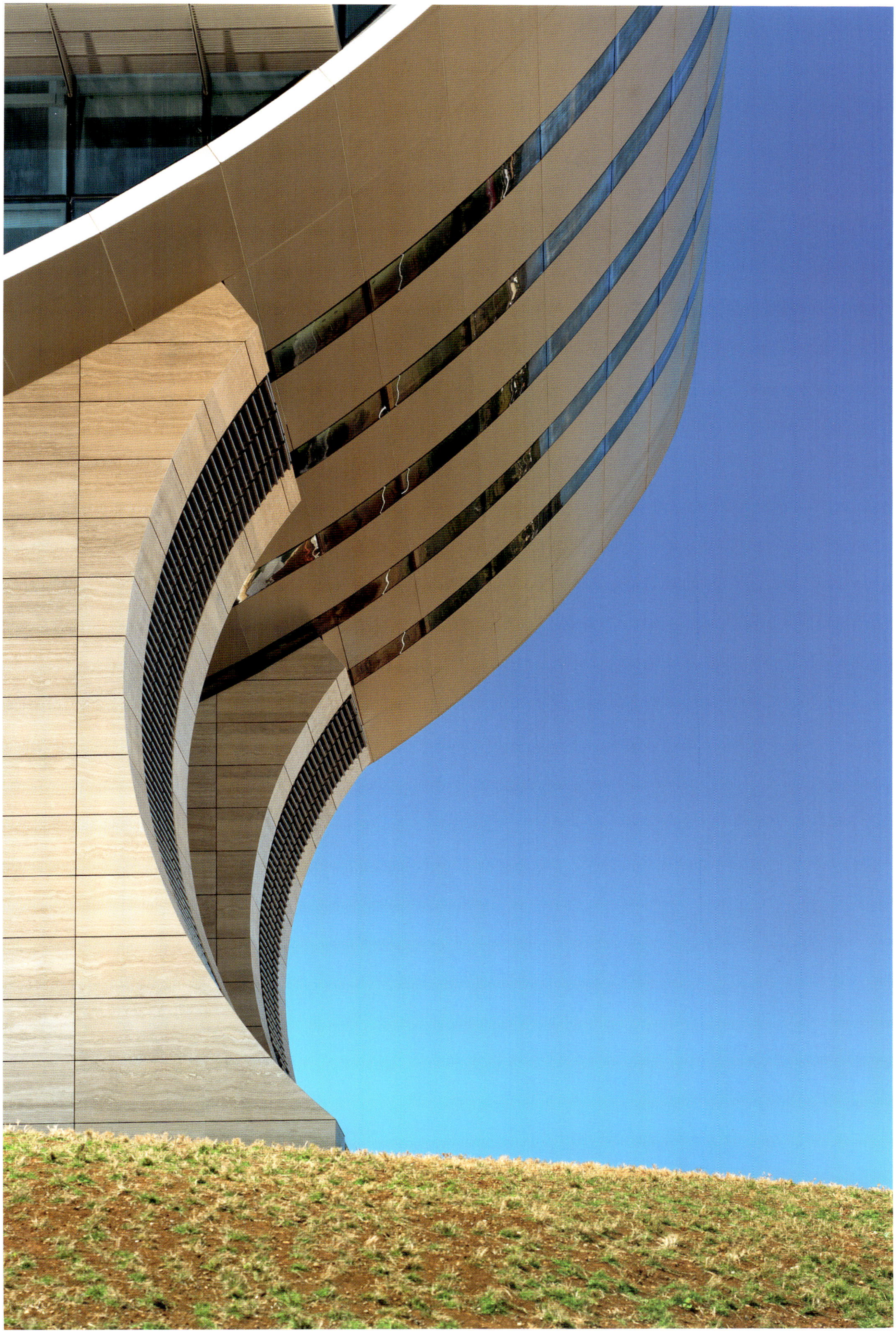

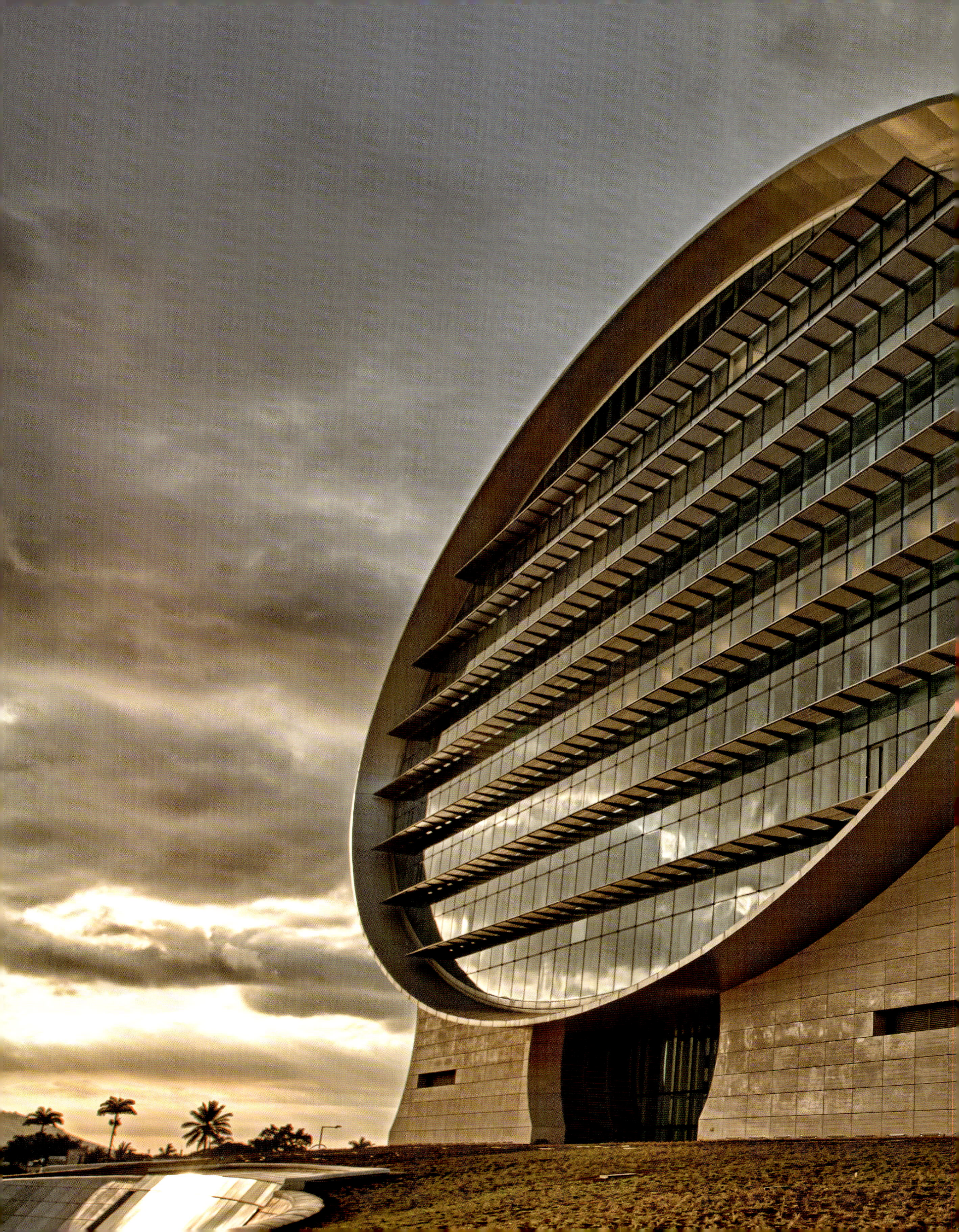

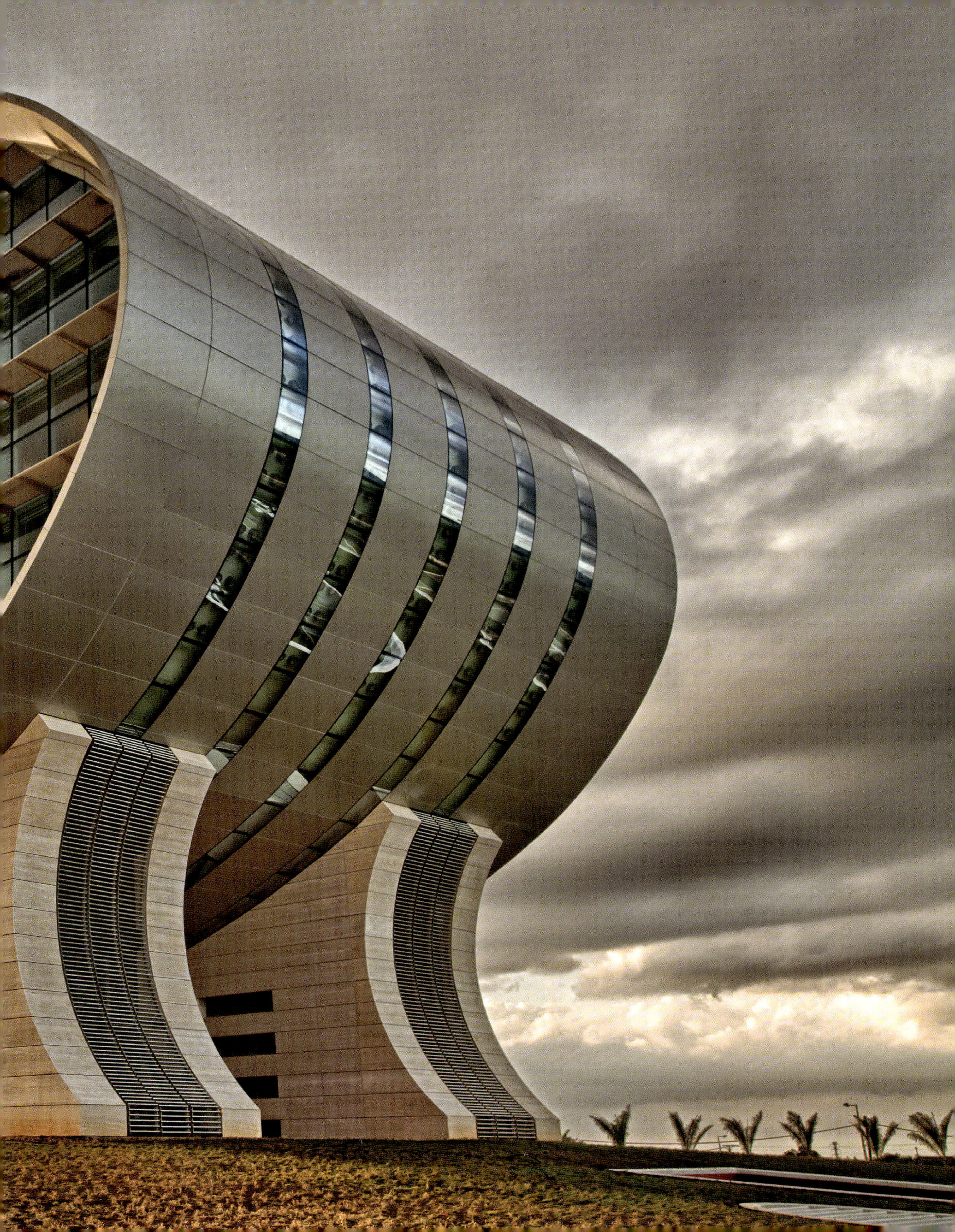

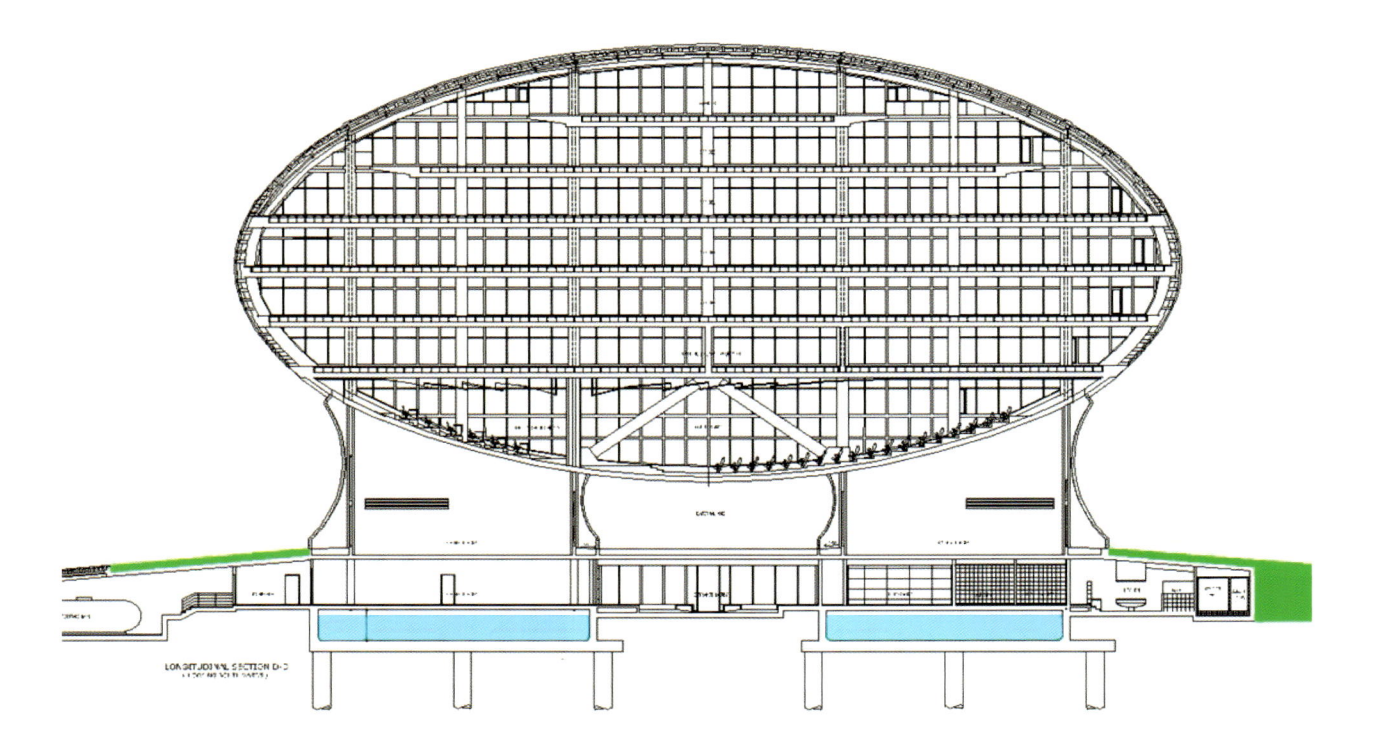

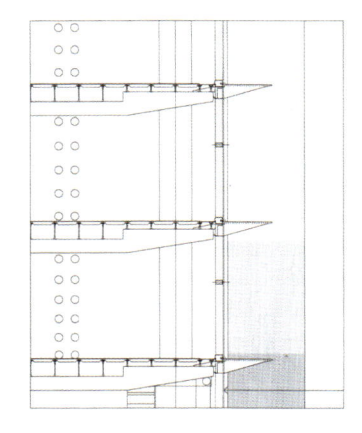

Top: South elevation. Pencil drawing on tracing paper by Jean-Francois Koenig.

Centre: Section through the offices, auditoriums, plant rooms, and the rainwater recuperation tanks sitting on the structural pile caps.

Bottom: Section through south glazing.

Above: Section through the north glazing showing the principle of sun control, working with views out, natural daylight, power and air distribution from the raised floor, maintenance, and thermal mass cooling from the bare concrete ceiling.

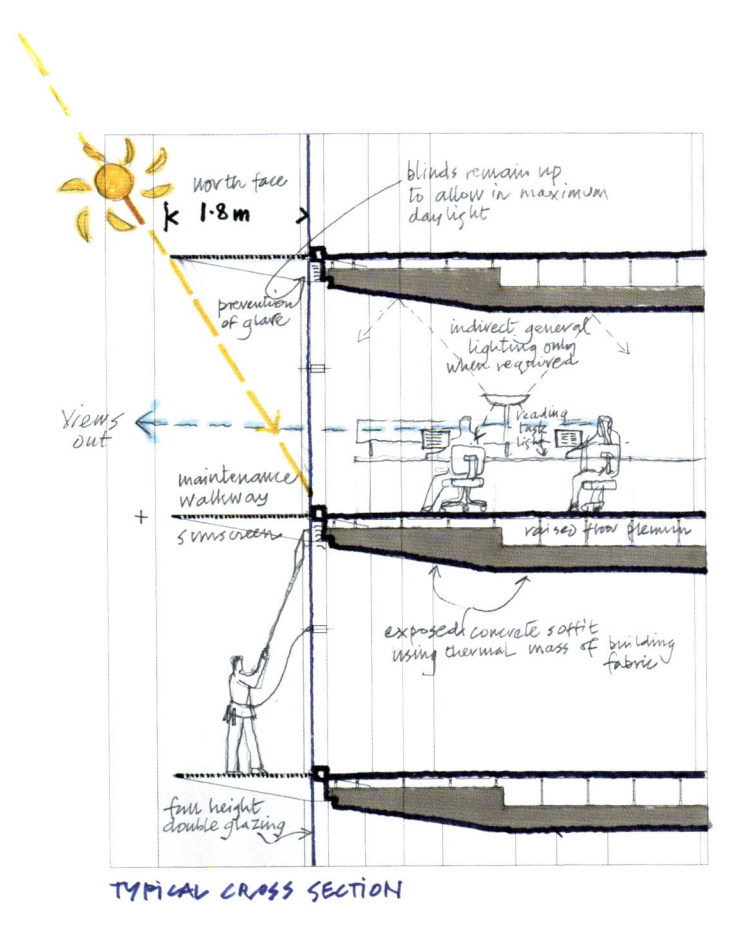

Top right: Working sectional perspective of the top mezzanine floor.

Second image right: Working sectional perspective of a typical office floor layout plan.

Third image right: Working sectional perspective of the auditoriums.

Bottom: Working master plan perspective of the south part of the site.

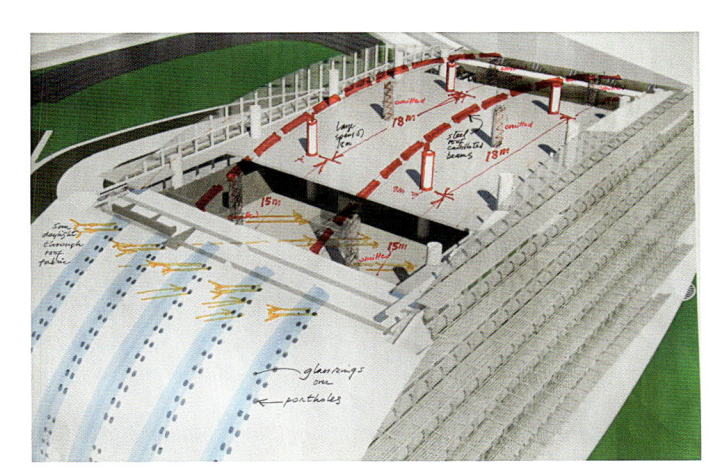

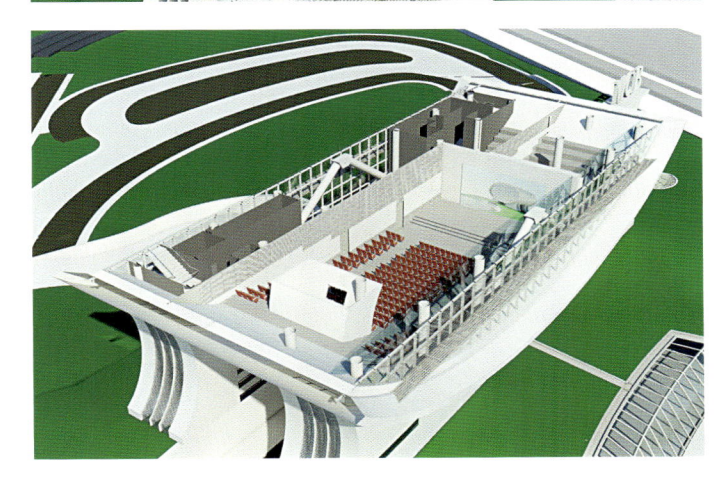

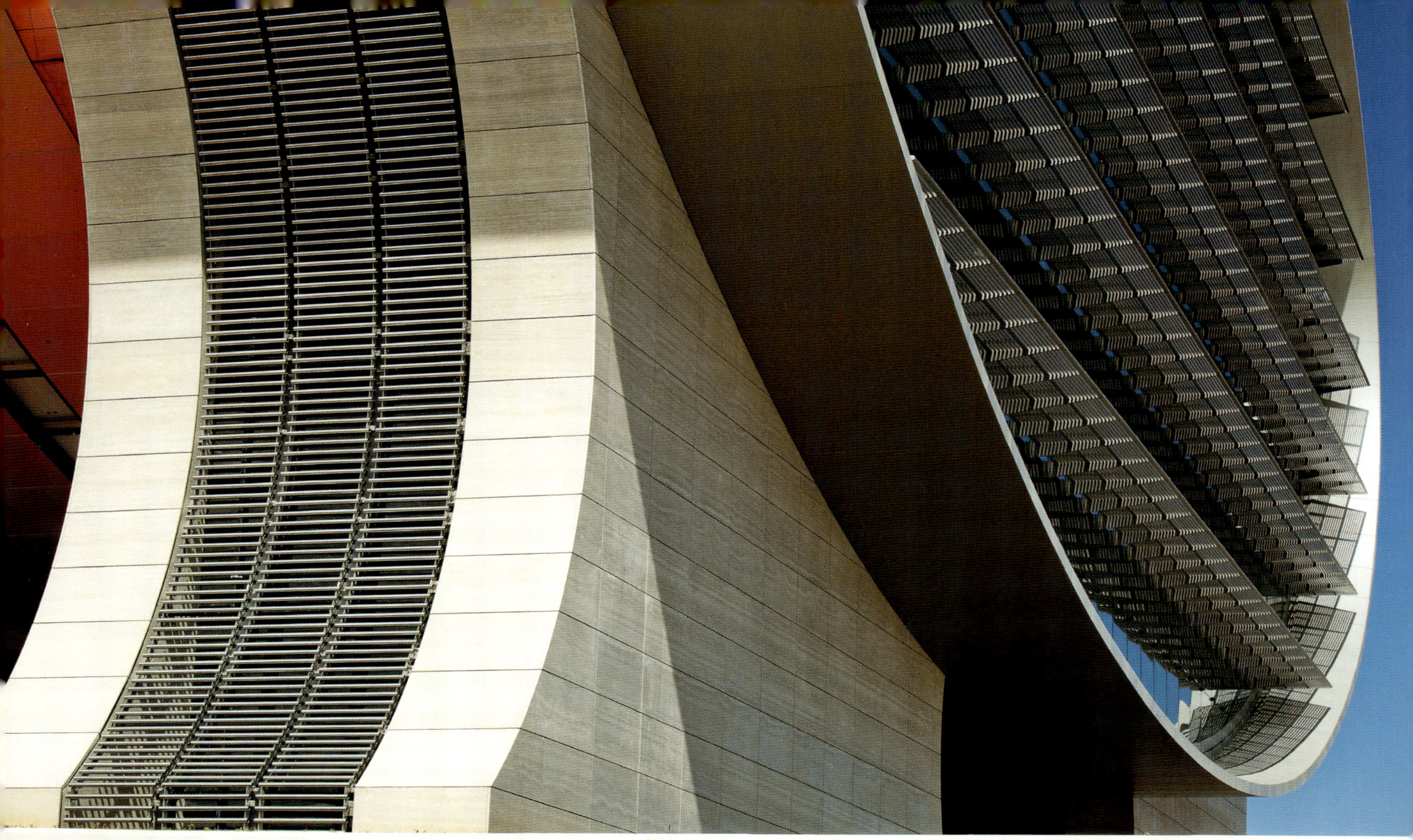

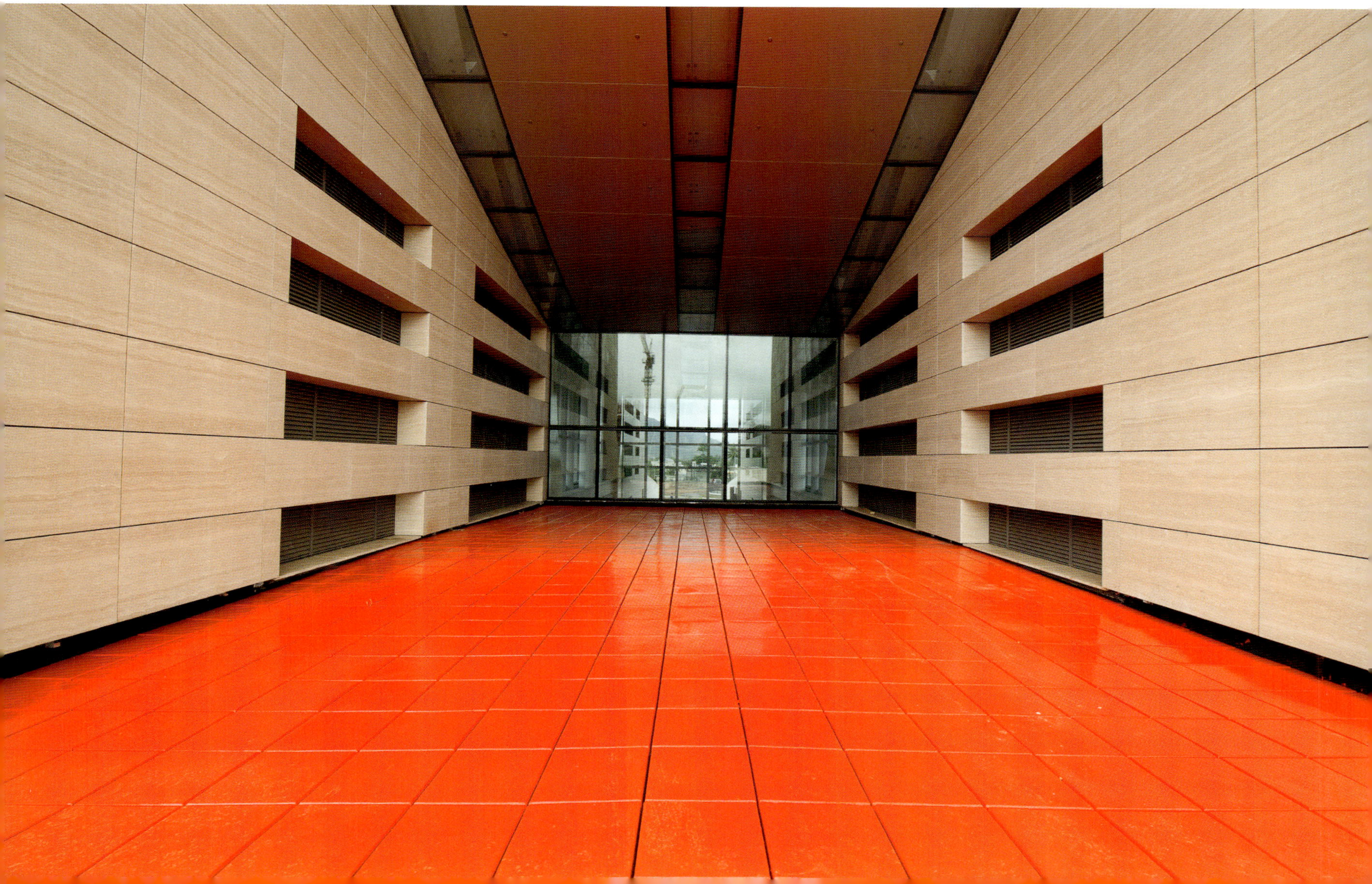

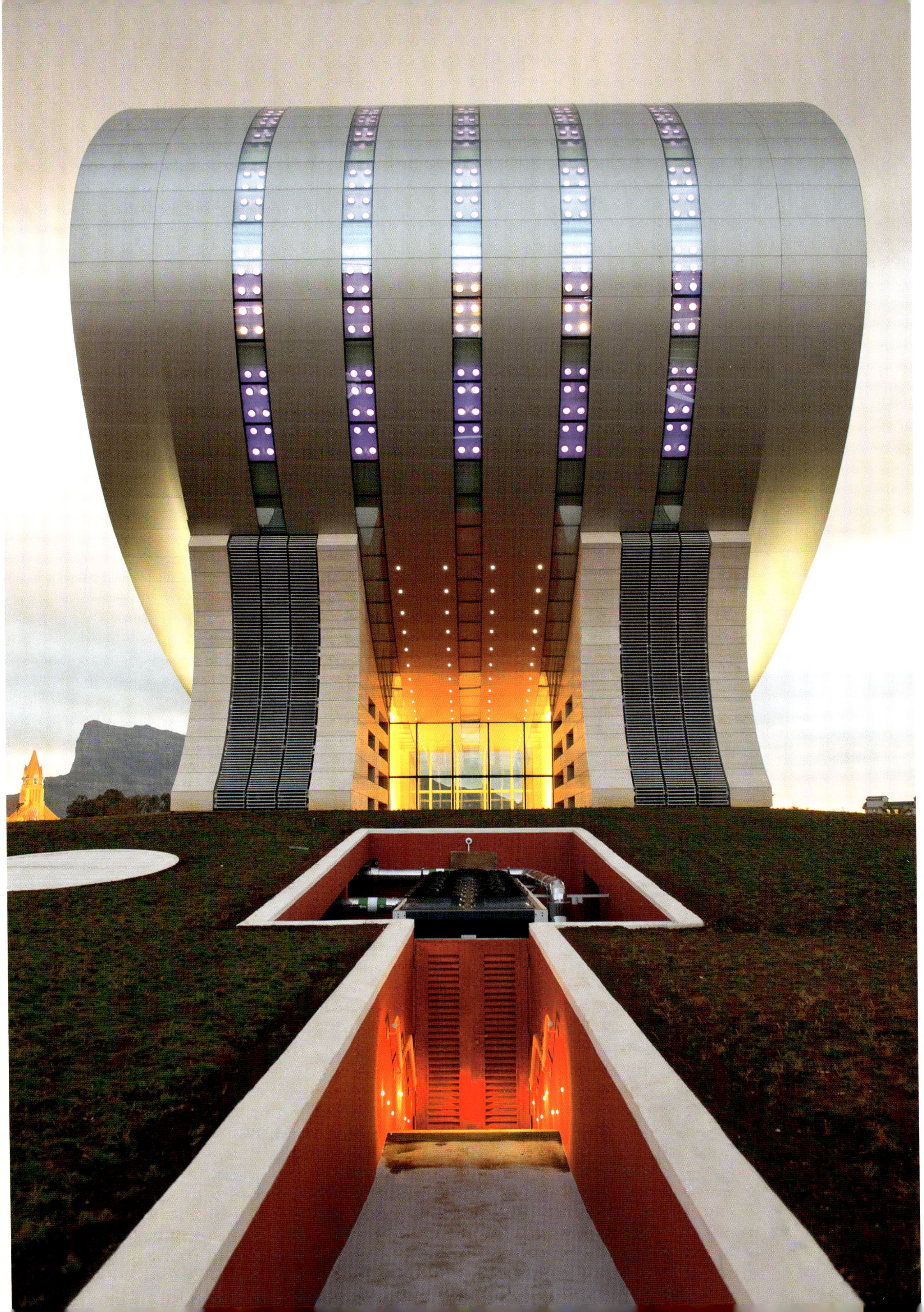

*Top: Working computer-generated perspective of LED night-time illumination from purpose-made desk uplighters.
Bottom: Night-time view of the building under normal working conditions.*

Top: Part view of the south face with the sloping glass walls of the canteen.
Bottom: The staff canteen with views over the reflective pool. The glass is shaded by the building itself.

Top and bottom: The main auditorium with a capacity of 275 seats.

Part view of the northern face with the cast aluminium grills performing the dual functions of sunscreens and maintenance walkways.

Top: The triple height reception lobby with its travertine floor. The underbelly of the elliptical shape of the auditorium's floor runs through the lobby above.

Bottom: The northern porte cochère entrance, the double volume glass window of the lobby, and the curve of the underbelly of the building.

Right: The travertine walls of the piers with the punched louvres of the plant rooms, the recessed external indirect lighting, and the bench.

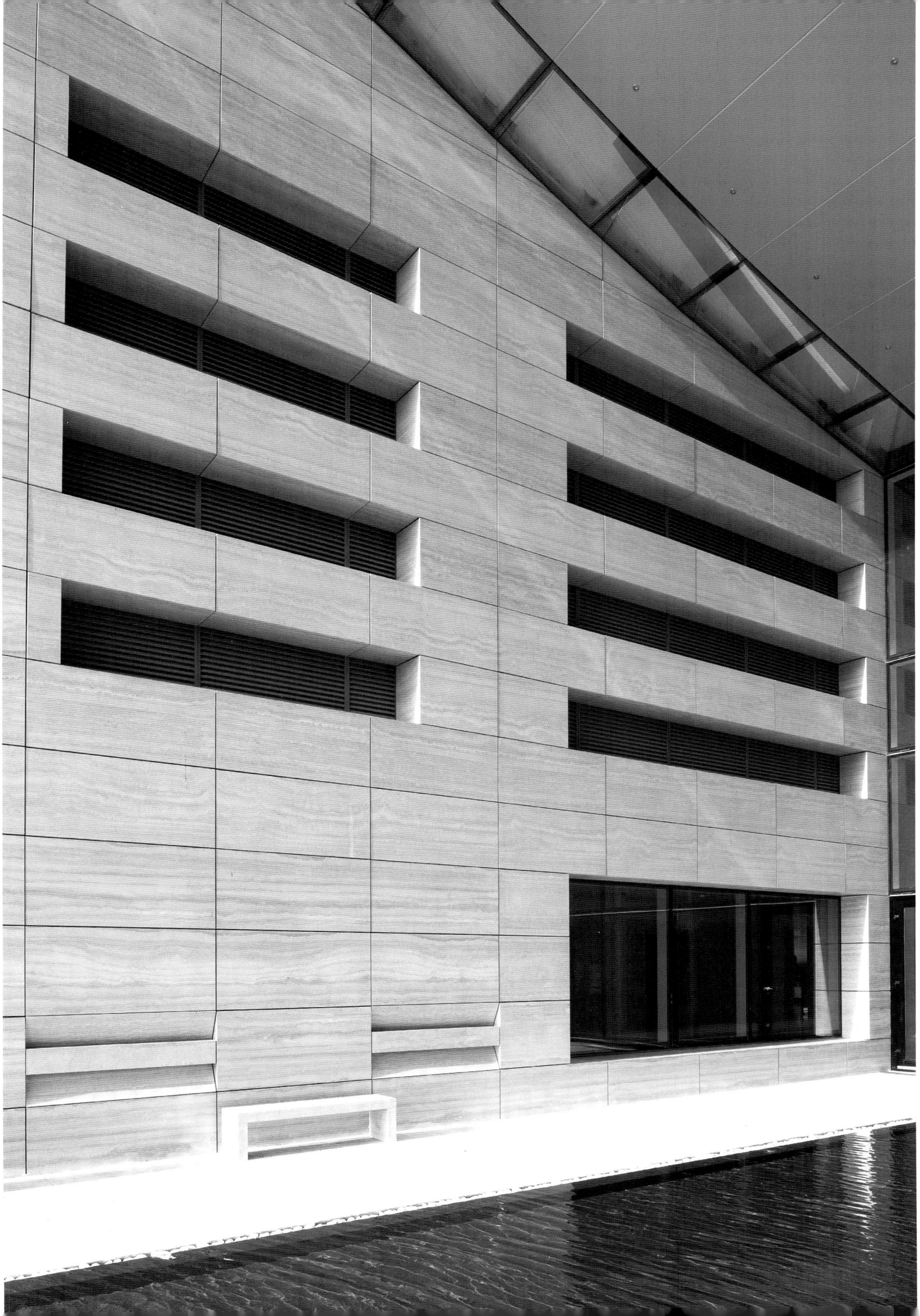

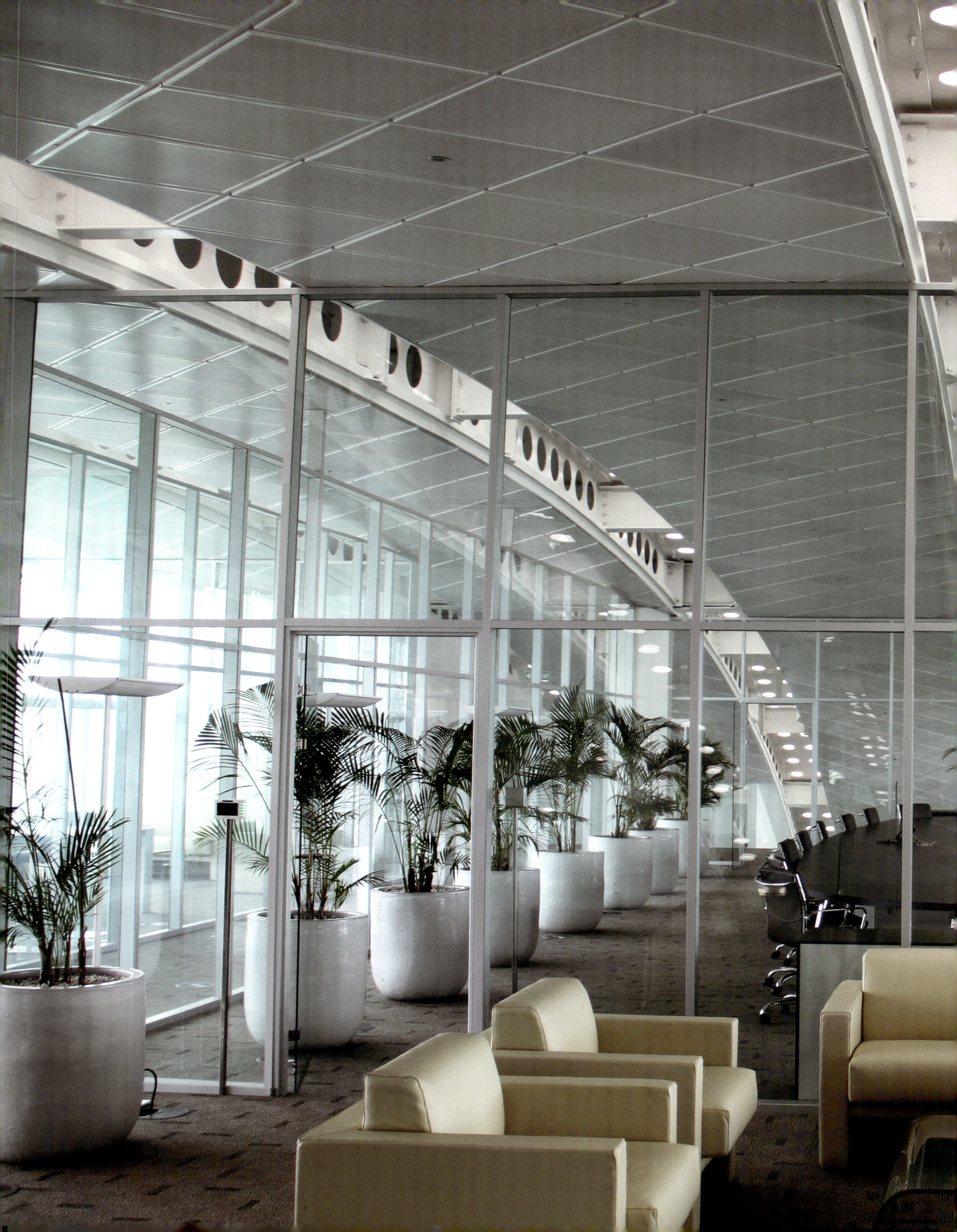

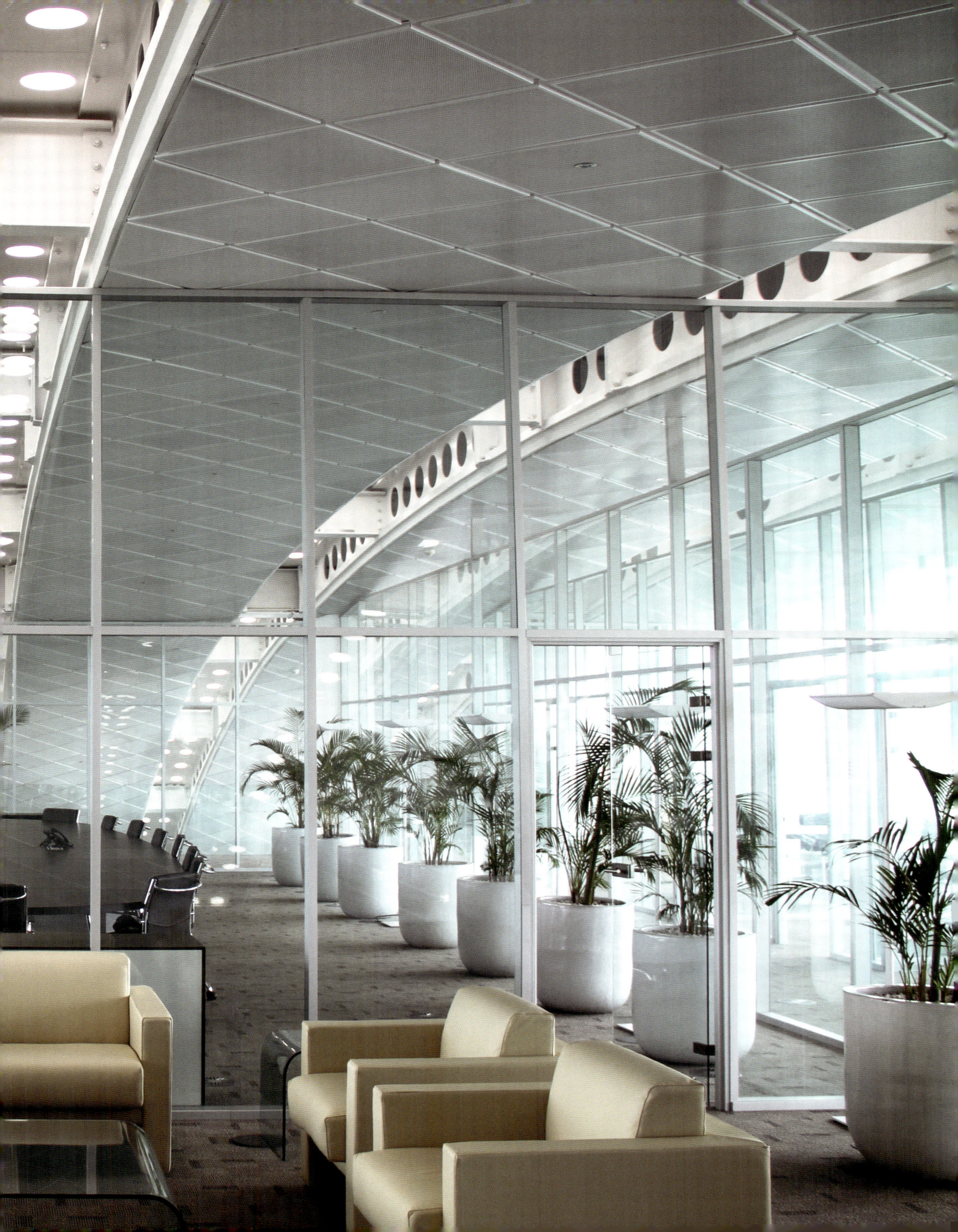

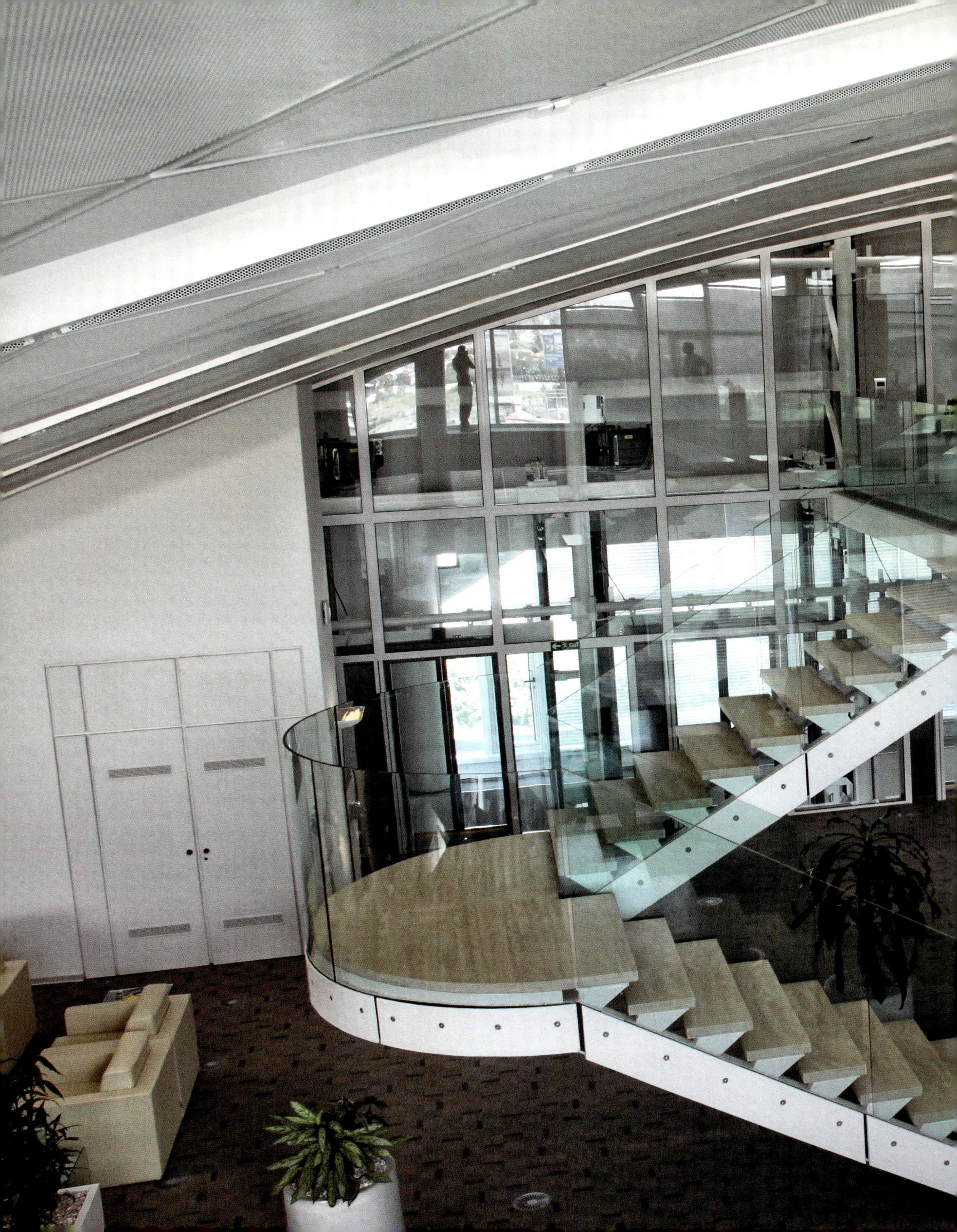

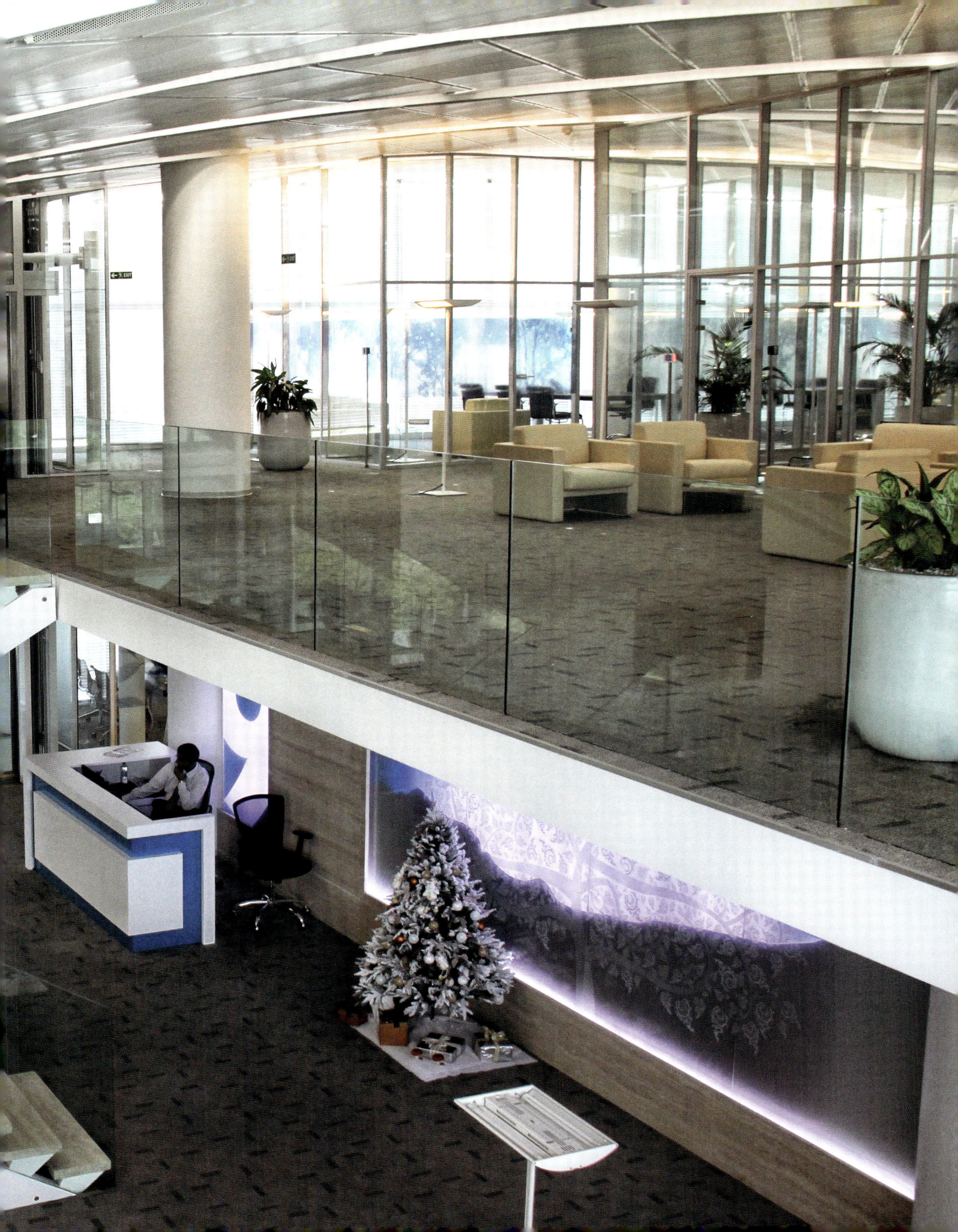

Above: The east and south façades.

Top: The stainless-steel gull-wing doors of the plant rooms.

Centre: Typical office working environment.

Bottom: The porthole windows seen through the glass rings that surround the building.

The pillars supporting the ellipse rest on the first-floor roof of the services and technical rooms. They are hidden by championship golf fairway grass roof planting which forms rolling lawns around the building. Three of the pile cap slabs of the foundations of the four pillars are used as a base for giant rainwater collection tanks. The grey water is reused to flush WCs and urinals, and waste water from wash hand basins and showers is passed through a filtering plant to be recycled back to the grey water tanks.
The building obtained the first Building Research Establishment Environmental Assessment Method (BREEAM) certificate in the Southern Hemisphere.
It represented the best of African Architecture at the Union Internationale des Architectes (UIA) conference 2011 in Tokyo under the heading "Sustainable by Design 2050" and won the joint UIA-KIA competition "100 Architects of the Year 2012".

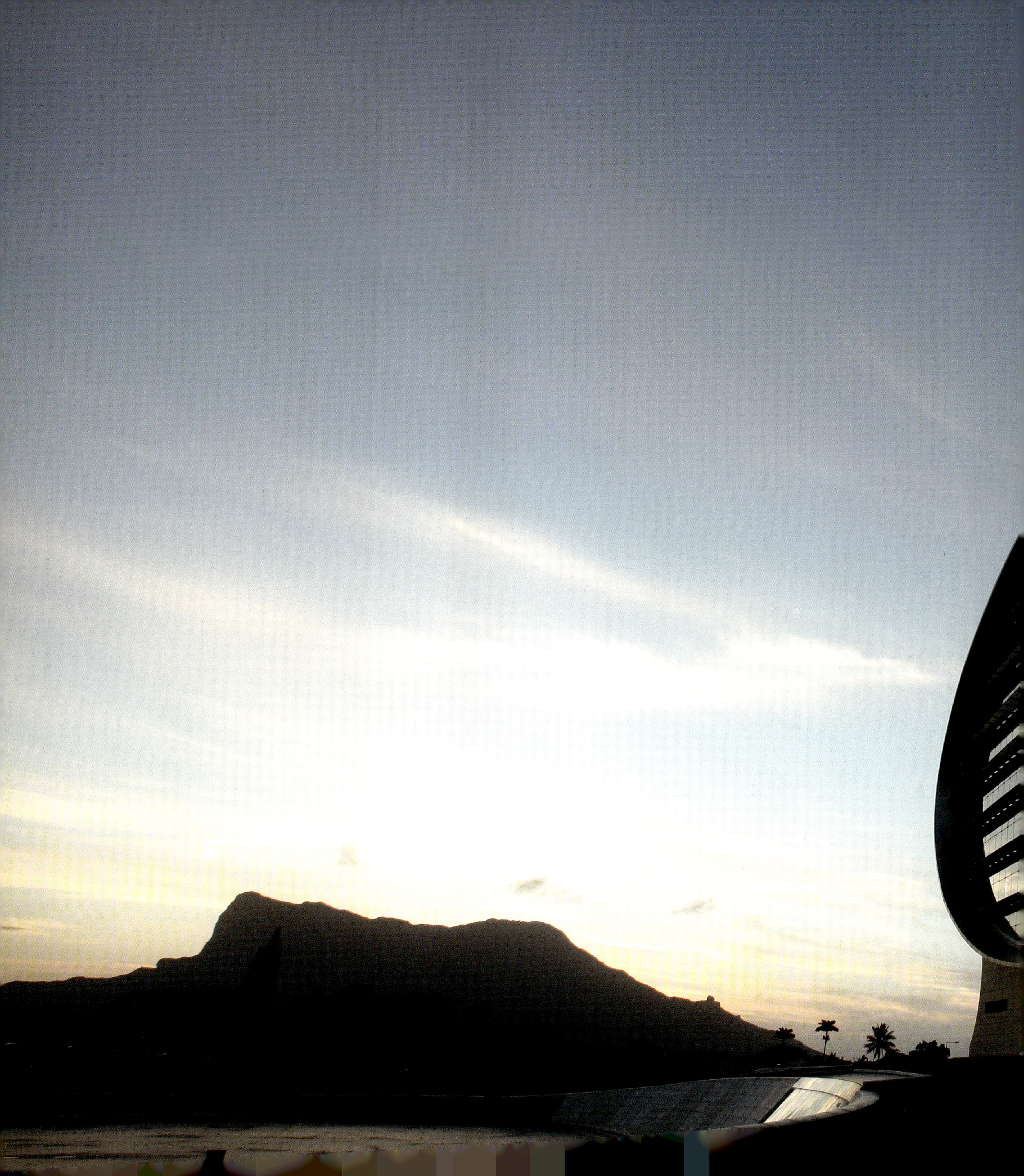

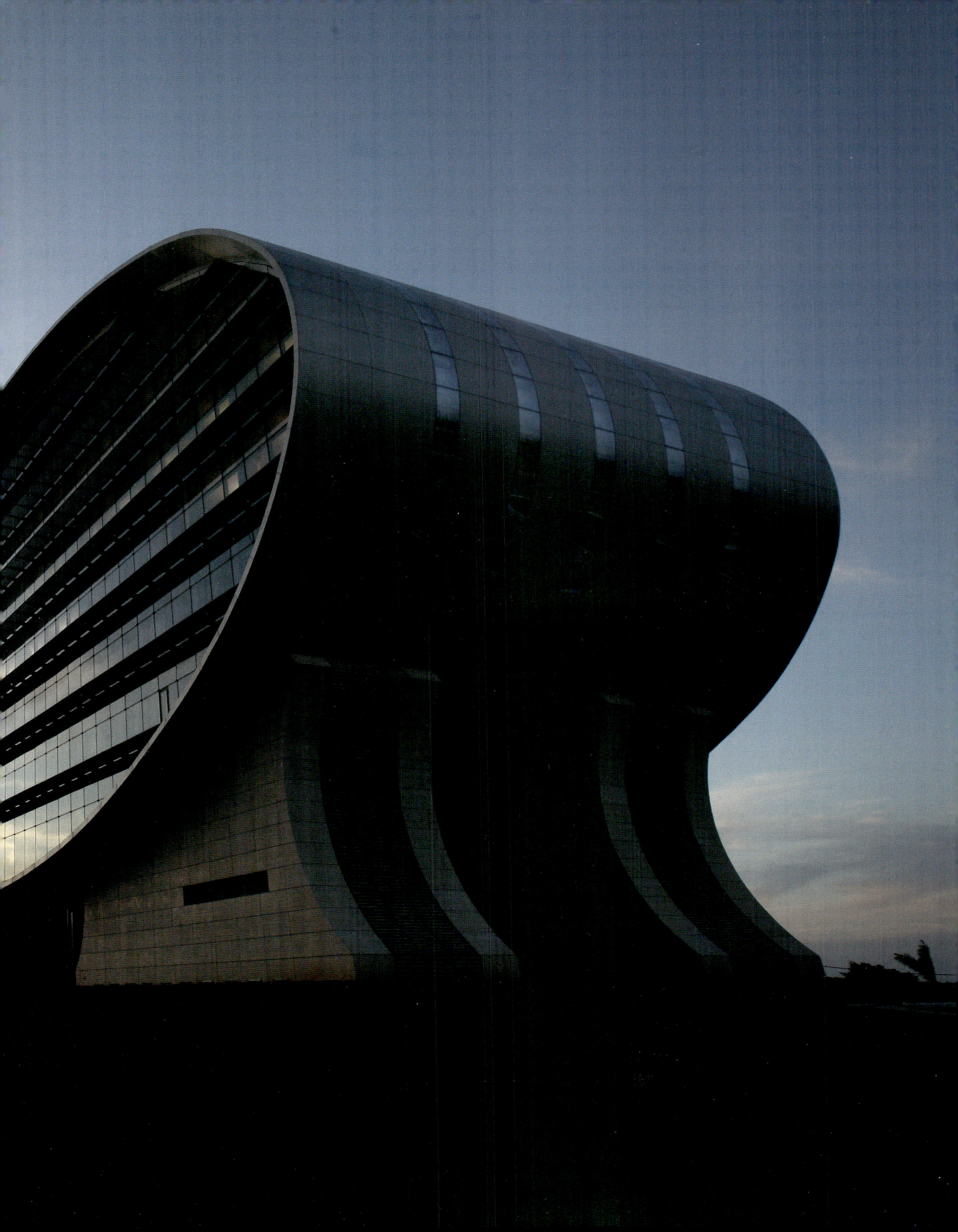

FUTURE

The National Centre of the Arts of Mauritius
Mauritius
2017

This is Jean-Francois Koenig's idea and proposal to build a National Centre of the Arts of Mauritius with an educational and international agenda. It is intended to inspire and elevate culture in the lives of the children of Mauritius, as well as exhibit art from all the countries of the world to reflect the multicultural world we live in, of which Mauritius is an example. The National Art Centre of Mauritius will represent the "United Nations of the Art world".

Art in the domains of Painting, Sculpture, Architecture, and Photography will be exhibited by permanent museum collections in fixed galleries as well as by temporary exhibitions in flexible halls. The Art Centre will also contain a conference auditorium, a museum shop, a restaurant, and a coffee lounge.

The building comprises, in plan, of two interlocking golden section proportioned rectangles of 109 m by 67.5 m making the total internal glass-to-glass length of the building 202 m by 125 m in width. Orientation is due north to control sunlight with half-a-metre high shaped blades that give indirect natural daylight from a glass roof. The glazed areas are interspaced in a tartan grid with concrete in a pattern that reflects the exhibition and circulation spaces below. The building is a single storey structure, for ease of transportation of heavy exhibits. It has a clear floor-to-ceiling internal height of 8 m. The façade is a continuous full-height 8-m high glass wall with an equivalent 8-m cantilevered sunscreen. A reflective pool follows the perimeter of the glass walls mirroring the sunscreens in the water.

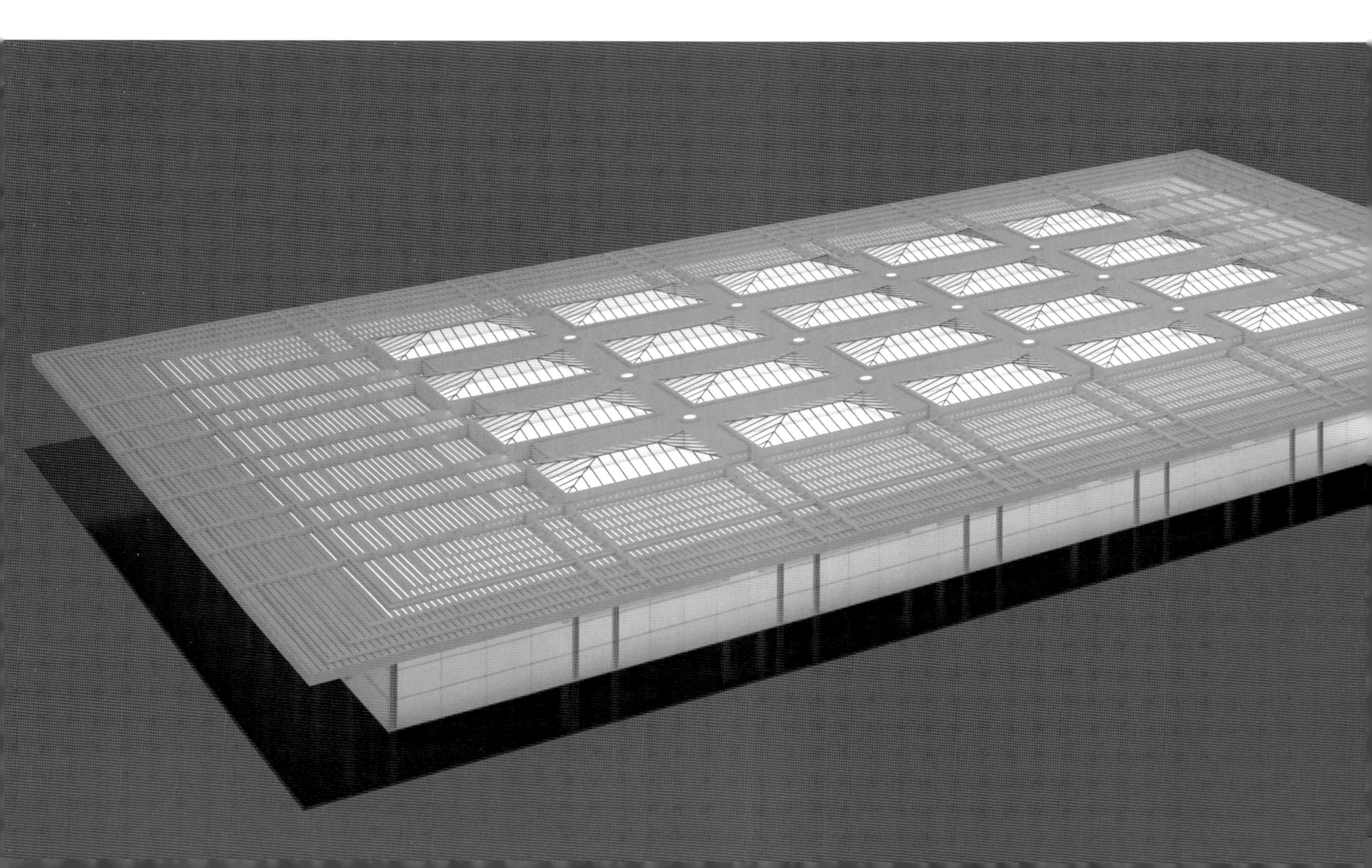

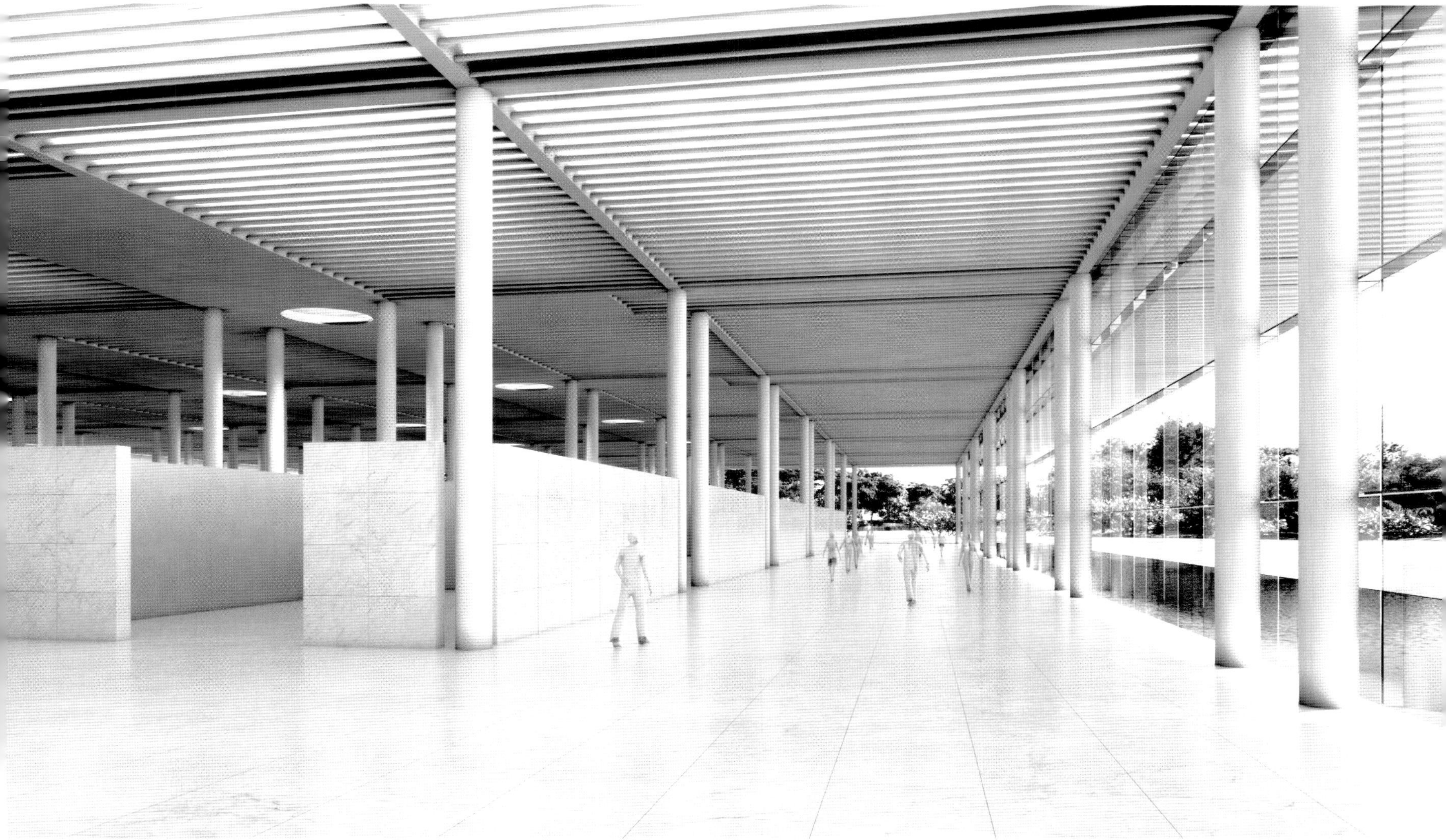

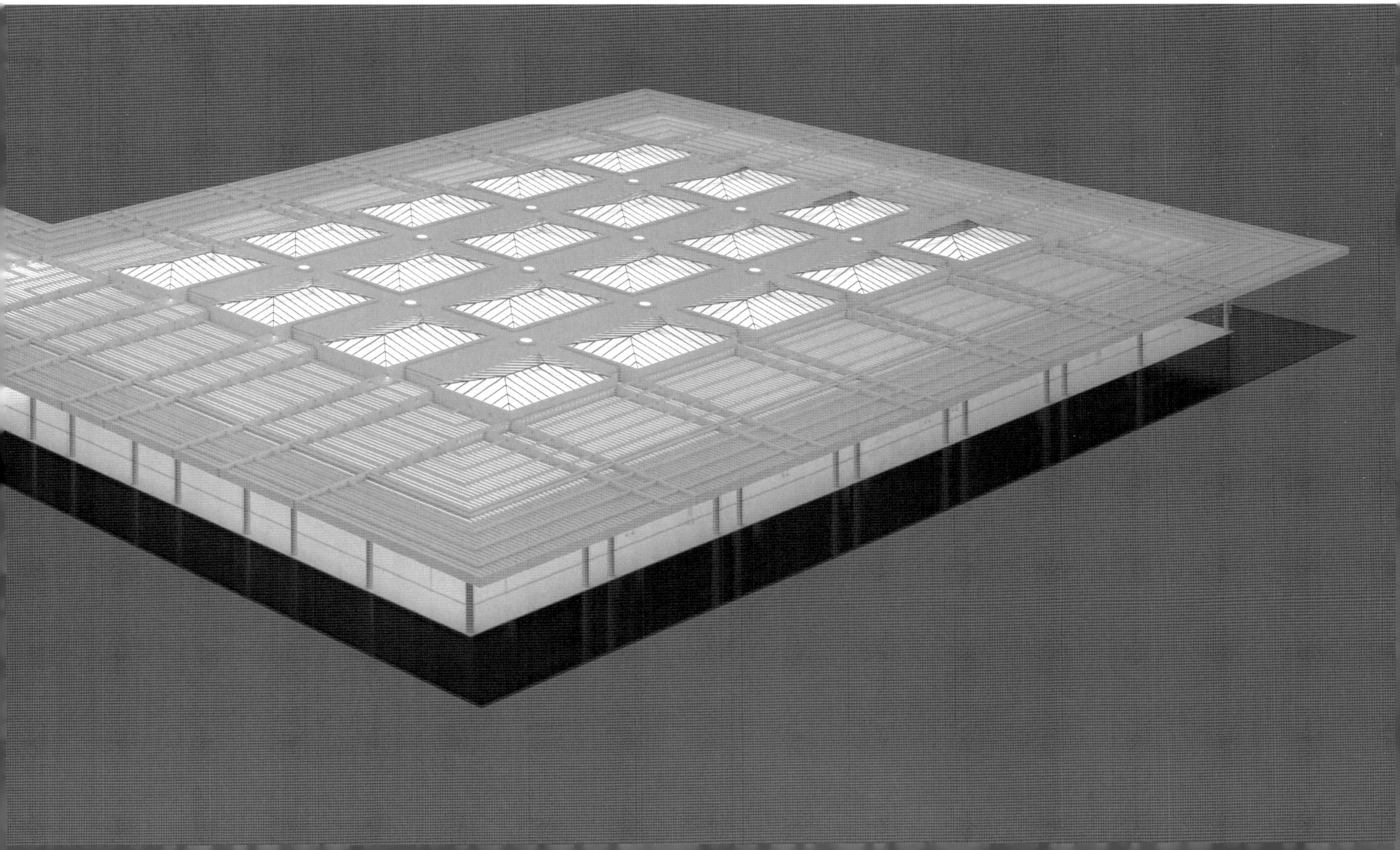

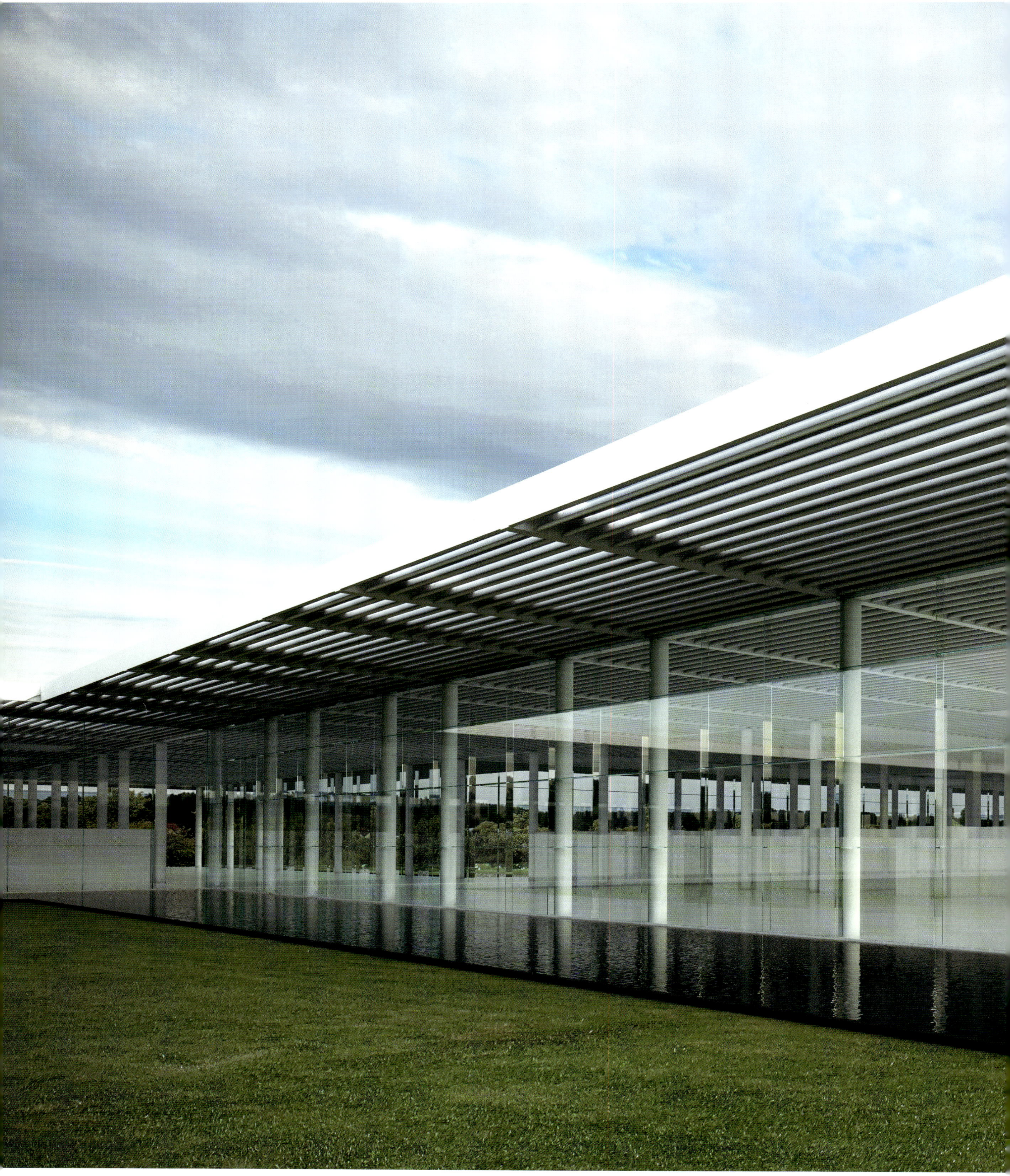

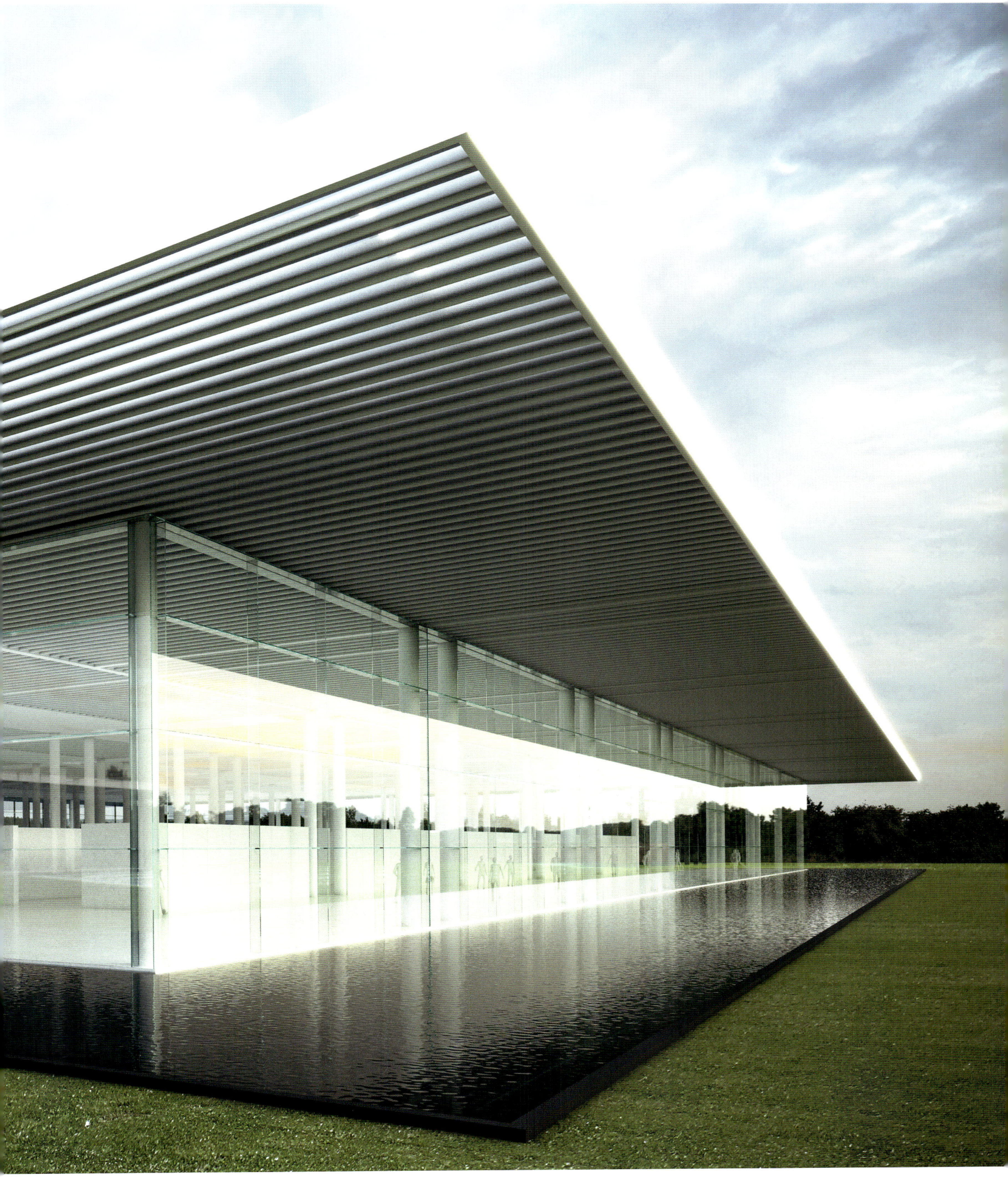

Jean-Francois Koenig
Chronological List of Projects

1980

Jean-Francois Koenig at ZAC Associates:
Ex Service Men Welfare Fund
Port Louis, Mauritius

1981 to 1985

Jean-Francois Koenig at Rhodar
(Multidisciplinary office by Ove Arup and Partners,
RFB Architects, Spoormaker Mechanical Engineers,
SBDS Quantity Surveyors)
Johannesburg, South Africa

Fresh-Up Factory – Willards Foods
Rosselyn, Pretoria, South Africa, 1981–1983

B+J Mechanical Workshop and Offices
Alrode, Johannesburg, South Africa, 1981–1983

Baldwins Steel – Canteen and Wash Bay
Brakpan, South Africa, 1982–1983

Springs Brewery
Witwatersrand, South Africa, 1984–1985

Metal Box Factory
Midrand, South Africa

1985 to 1987

Worked in Group 3
Arup Associates
London, United Kingdom

1987

House at Pointe aux Canonniers
Mauritius

House at Poste Lafayette
Mauritius, 1987–1988

Houses at Swan Properties
Pereybere, Mauritius, 1987–1988

Ile aux Chats House Renovation
Beau Champ, Mauritius

House at Grand Baie
Mauritius, 1987–1989

Les Ternans
Floreal, Mauritius, 1987–1988

1988

Edouard Antelme Houses
Grand Baie, Mauritius, 1988–1989

Petite Victoria
Trou d'Eau Douce, Mauritius, 1988–1990

Bungalows at Montagu
Trou d'Eau Douce, Mauritius

House at River Walk
Mauritius, 1988–1990

Jacques de Maroussem House
Eureka, Mauritius

Pierre Hugnin House
Grand Baie, Mauritius, 1988–1990

Bruno Couve House
Pereybere, Mauritius

United Basalt Head Office
Trianon, Mauritius, 1988–1990

Oxenham Head Office
Trianon, Mauritius

St Ange Chapel
Grand Baie, Mauritius

Klondike Village Vacances
Flic en Flac, Mauritius, 1988–1990

Hotel at Flic en Flac
Mauritius

PSL Flats
Grand Baie, Mauritius

Les Mangliers Hotel
Pointe d'Esny, Mauritius

Arnaud Dalais House
Floreal, Mauritius, 1988–1991

Jean-Francois Koenig
Chronological List of Projects

Swan Group Centre
*Port Louis, Mauritius, 1988–1993
in joint venture with Frank Lincoln
and Stauch Vorster*

Gerald Lincoln House
Pointe d'Esny, Mauritius, 1988–1989

House at Les Salines
Rivière Noire, Mauritius, 1988–1989

Sir Pierre Dalais Billard House
Montagu, Mauritius, 1988–1989

St Joseph's Chapel
Henrietta, Mauritius, 1988–1990

House at Merville
Grand Baie, Mauritius, 1988–1990

1989

IBL Offices
Port Louis, Mauritius

Les Coqueluches Bungalows
Tamarin, Mauritius

Henri d'Argent House
Poste Lafayette, Mauritius, 1988–1989

Le Village Apartments
Pte. aux Cannoniers, Mauritius

Pamela Patten House
Floreal, Mauritius, 1989–1990

IBL Engineering
Plaine Lauzun, Mauritius, 1989–1990

IBL Chemical and Equipment
Cassis, Mauritius, 1989–1992

Gilbert Ferrière House
Poste Lafayette Mauritius

Bois Fleuris Apartments
Curepipe, Mauritius

Christian de Speville House
Cap Malheureux, Mauritius

House at Moka
Mauritius, 1989–1991

IBL White Sand Tours Offices
Cassis, Mauritius, 1988–1989

Christian d'Unienville House
Pointe d'Esny, Mauritius, 1989–1990

1990

Suchem Offices
Port Louis, Mauritius, 1990–1991

Philippe Koo House
Curepipe, Mauritius

Floreal Knitwear Offices
Floreal, Mauritius

Caroline Wiehe Apartments
Grand Baie, Mauritius

Mauritius Commercial Bank
Trou aux Biches, Mauritius, 1990–1992

MECOM Offices
Grande Rivière Nord Ouest, Mauritius

Roger E. Noël House
Grand Baie, Mauritius

Gilbert Bathfield House
Calodyne, Mauritius, 1990–1991

Training Centre Ferney Spinning Mills
Forest Side, Mauritius

Pierre-Guy Noël House
Trou d'Eau Douce, Mauritius, 1990–1992

Beeharry Houses
Bain Boeuf, Mauritius, 1990–1992

IVTB – Sir Gaëtan Duval Hotel & Catering School
Ebène, Mauritius, 1990–1996

Rey & Lenferna Offices
Cassis, Mauritius

Ashok Ramdenee House
Quatre Bornes, Mauritius, 1990–1993

Jean-Francois Koenig
Chronological List of Projects

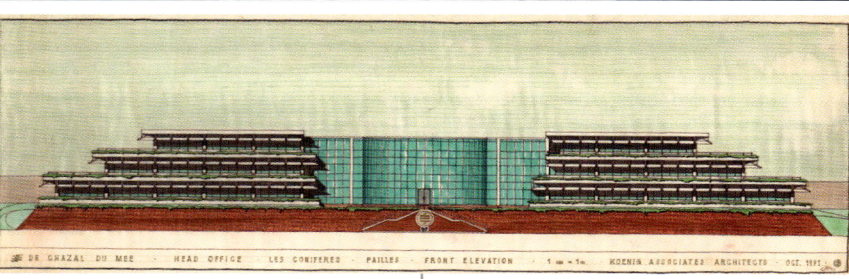

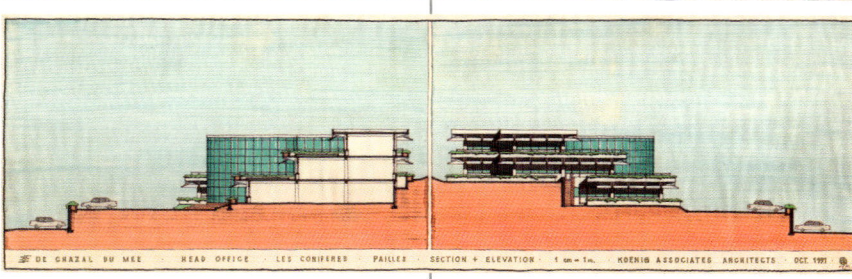

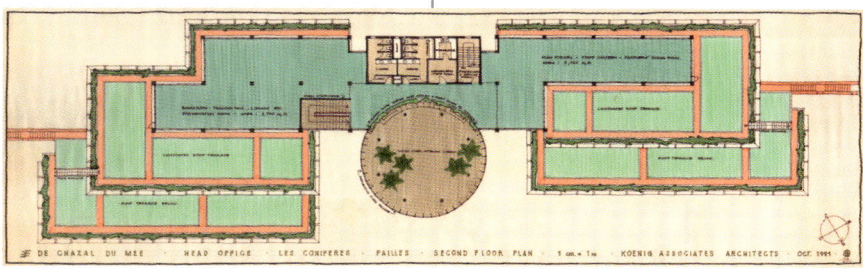

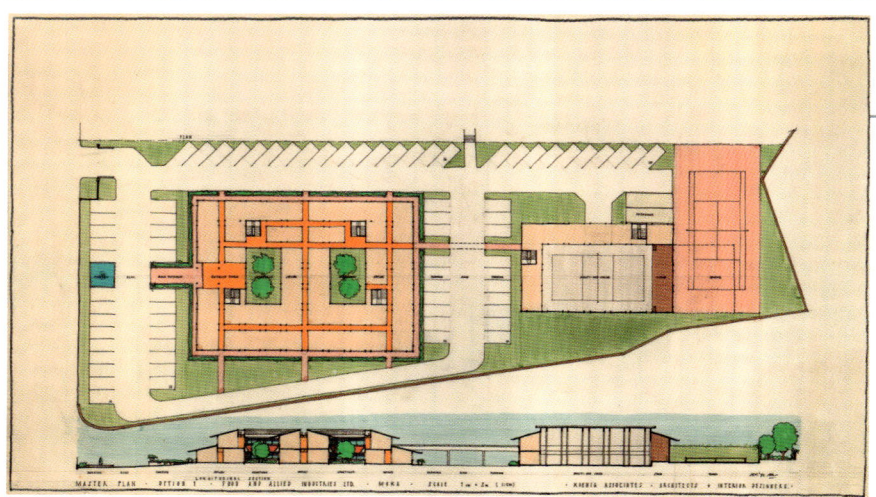

Michel de Speville House
Moka, Mauritius

Medine Sugar Factory Auditorium and Canteen
Medine, Mauritius

S. Bhunjun Houses
Quatre-Bornes, Mauritius, 1990–1994

New Mauritius Docks Offices
Caudan, Mauritius

House at Pereybere
Mauritius, 1990–1993

Mon Désert Alma Offices
Moka, Mauritius

Mauritius Commercial Bank – Lai Tung Building
Port Louis, Mauritius

De Chazal du Mee Offices
Pailles, Mauritius

Dr Chataroo Houses
Blue Bay, Mauritius

Ben Birt House
Ilot Fortier, Mauritius, 1990–1994

Hardy Henry – Bel Air St Felix
Port Louis, Mauritius, 1990–1992

Maxime Leclezio House Renovation
Grand Baie, Mauritius

Claude Leclezio House
Mon Choisy, Mauritius

White Sand Tours Offices at Le St Geran Hotel
Belle Mare, Mauritius, 1990

Food and Allied Ltd. Offices
Moka, Mauritius

Le Ruisseau Rose, House and Office
Les Mariannes, Mauritius, 1990–1995

1991

IBL Medical Trading
Cassis, Mauritius, 1991–1993

Société Anjali Offices
Port Louis, Mauritius

The Mauritius Sugar Syndicate Boardroom
Port Louis, Mauritius, 1991

Thierry Koenig House
Calodyne, Mauritius, 1991–1992
Extension 1998

United States Embassy – McCarthy House Kitchen
Vacoas, Mauritius, 1991–1992

IBL JFK Avenue Offices
Port Louis, Mauritius

Thierry Lagesse House
Cap Malheureux, Mauritius, 1991–1994

Lois Le Vieux – House in the Garden
Beau Bassin, Mauritius, 1991

Jacques Brousse House
Le Morne, Mauritius, 1991–1994

1992

Swan Group – Georges Guibert St. Building Renovation
Port Louis, Mauritius

Hotel Beau Soleil
Rodrigues

Pre-Mixed Concrete Factory
Geoffroy, Mauritius

Sotravic Head Office
Coromandel, Mauritius, 1992–1995

Loïs Le Vieux, The Estuary Housing Estate
Tamarin, Mauritius

Two Houses at Roches Noires
Mauritius, 1992–1997

Heirs Maxime de Speville Apartments
Trou d'Eau Douce, Mauritius, 1992–1995

Ile des Deux Cocos Hotel
Pointe d'Esny, Mauritius

St Aubin Plantation House Renovation
Mauritius, 1992

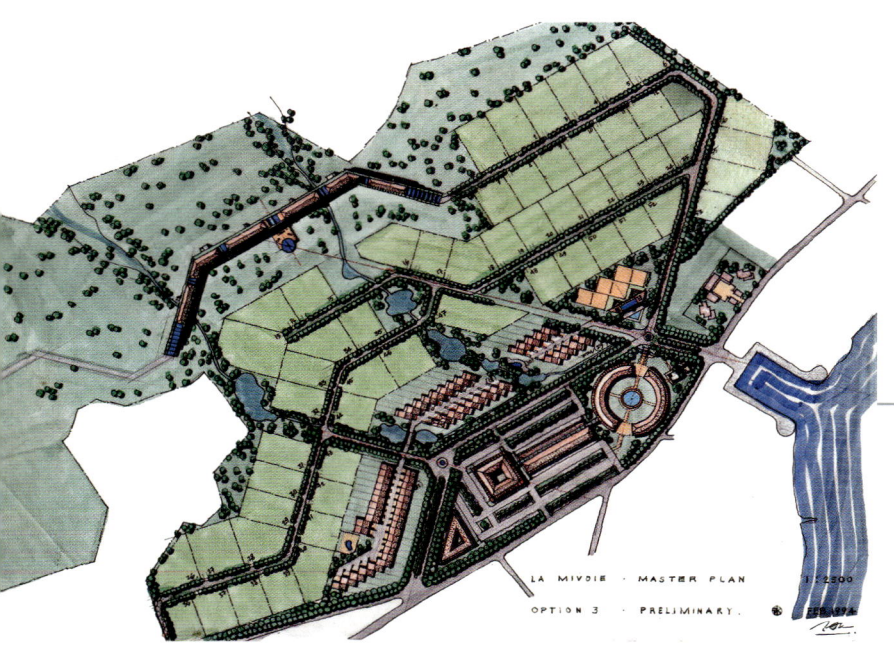

Jean-Francois Koenig
Chronological List of Projects

New Mauritius Docks Master Plan
Caudan, Mauritius

Mauritius Telecom Headquarters
Port Louis, Mauritius, 1992–1995
in joint venture with RFB Architects

1993

Le Ruisseau Creole – La Mivoie Master Plan
Rivière Noire, Mauritius

Anglo Mauritius Offices Renovation
Port Louis, Mauritius

Hypermarket St Jean
St Jean, Mauritius

Mauritius Telecom Teleshop
Cassis, Mauritius, 1993

Mauritius Breweries Ltd. Head Office
Phoenix, Mauritius

House on the East Coast
Mauritius, 1993–1996

Cathedral Square Offices
Port Louis, Mauritius

South Gate Offices
Caudan, Mauritius

1994

De Chazal Du Mee Head Office
Champ de Mars, Mauritius, 1994–1999

Didier Maingard House
La Mivoie, Mauritius

IBL Supermarkets – Winners
Mahébourg, Mauritius, 1994–1995

Place d'Armes Centre
Port Louis, Mauritius

Edinburgh Court
Port Louis, Mauritius

Media Exhibition Centre – Competition: 2nd prize
La Vigie, Mauritius

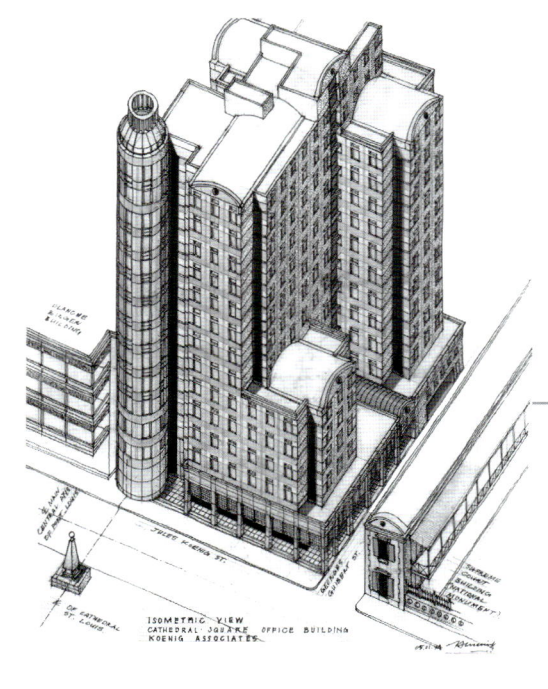

Christian Dalais House
Floreal, Mauritius, 1994–1997

Northridge Clinic
The North, Mauritius

Bahadoor Printing Ltd.
Pailles, Mauritius, 1994–1995

Panagora Marketing Offices
Phoenix, Mauritius

Bel Air Water Bottling Plant
Bel Air St Felix, Mauritius

S. Bhunjun – Le Calodyne Residences
Calodyne, Mauritius 1994–1997

Société de Chazal
Port Louis, Mauritius

Ramdenee Marina Master Plan
La Balise, Rivière Noire, Mauritius

Le Caudan Parking
Port Louis, Mauritius

1995

Le Coco Beach Hotel
*Belle Mare, Mauritius, 1995–1996
in joint venture with Fugleberg Koch
and RFB Architects*

Sugar Beach Hotel
*Flic en Flac, Mauritius, 1995–1996
in joint venture with Fugleberg Koch
and RFB Architects*

S. Bhunjun – Empire House
Poudrière St., Port Louis, Mauritius

1996

Bayshore – Multifunction Complex
Trou aux Biches, Mauritius

Beverly Hills Shops and Offices
Curepipe, Mauritius

St Felix Sugar Estate Offices
St Felix, Mauritius

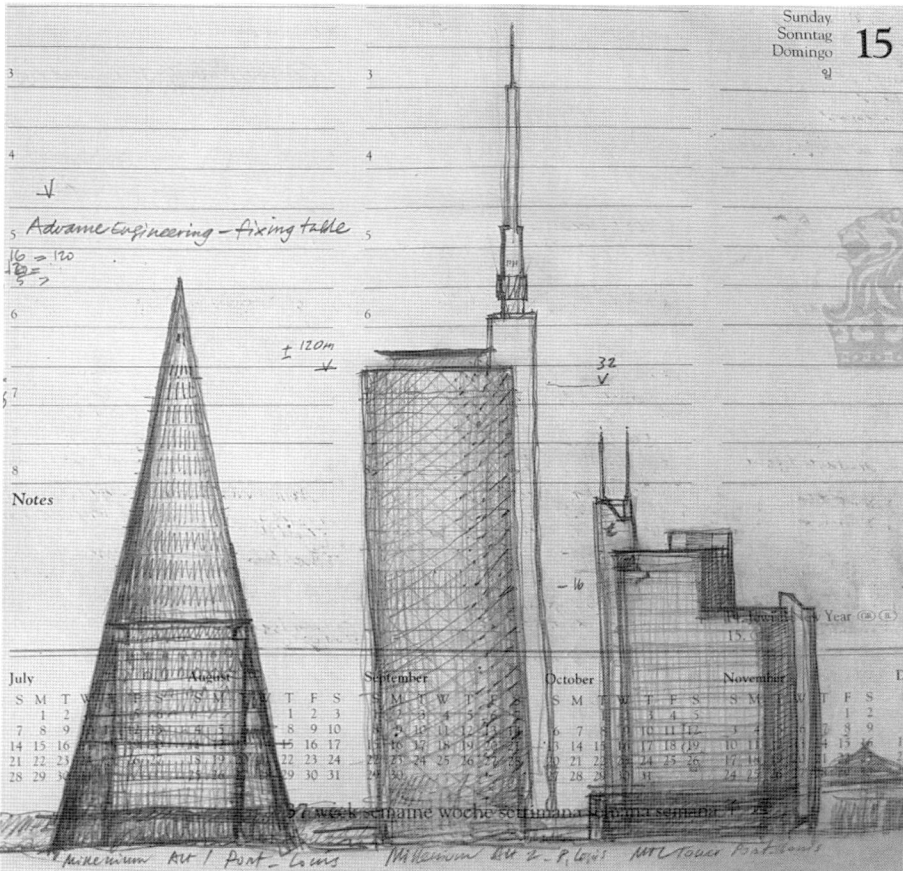

Jean-Francois Koenig
Chronological List of Projects

Gaston Loumeau – Les Terrasses Apartments
Floreal, Mauritius

Prototype for affordable housing in Mauritius

Coopers & Lybrand Offices
Port Louis, Mauritius

Cathedral Square Parking
Port Louis, Mauritius

Le Vieux Moulin
Pereybere, Mauritius, 1996–2000

Millennium Tower
Port Louis, Mauritius

Alex Fon Sing Apartments
Moka, Mauritius

Dr Roy Chavrimootoo House
Quatre Bornes, Mauritius, 1996–2000

Residences Club
Gymkhana, Mauritius

BNPI + Parking
Port Louis, Mauritius

1997

La Plantation Hotel
Balaclava, Mauritius, 1997–1999

Federation Square Competition
Melbourne, Australia

Indian Resort & Spa
Le Morne, Mauritius, 1997–2002

Garden Court Apartments
Cap Malheureux, Mauritius

Tropic Knits
Forest Side, Mauritius, 1997–1998

S. Bhunjun – Phoenix House Offices
Phoenix, Mauritius

Colin Taylor House
Calodyne, Mauritius, 1997–1999

Christian Regnard House
Moka, Mauritius

1998

Tee Sun Factory – Office Extension
Rivière du Rampart, Mauritius, 1998

Gaya Building Extension
Quatre Bornes, Mauritius, 1998–1999
in joint venture with Frank Lincoln

A&IM Interiors
Swan Building, Port Louis, Mauritius, 1998

Vieux Rempart Houses
Belle Mare, Mauritius

Apartments at Pointe d'Esny
Mauritius, 1998–1999

Delphis Bank
Vacoas, Mauritius

S. Bhunjun – Independence House
Phoenix, Mauritius

Albion Wharf Apartments
Caudan, Mauritius, 1998–1999

Mauritius Commercial Bank – Beau Bassin
Beau Bassin, Mauritius, 1998–1999
in joint venture with Frank Lincoln

House at Casa Solar
Grand Baie, Mauritius, 1998–1999

Eddy Yeung House Extension
Moka, Mauritius

Pravind Jugnauth House
Floreal, Mauritius

Les Cocotiers Hotel Renovation
Baie du Tombeau, Mauritius, 1998–1999

Hardy Henry Offices
Pailles, Mauritius

Country Inn Hotel Renovation
Trou d'Eau Douce, Mauritius, 1998–1999

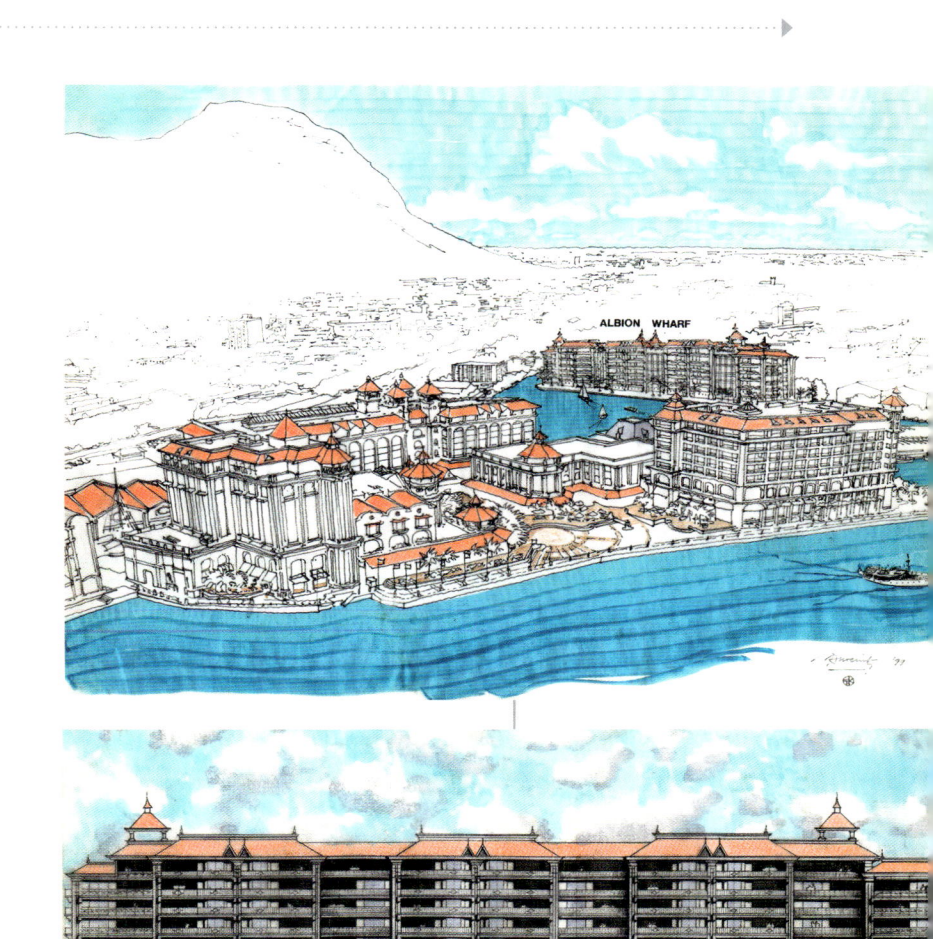

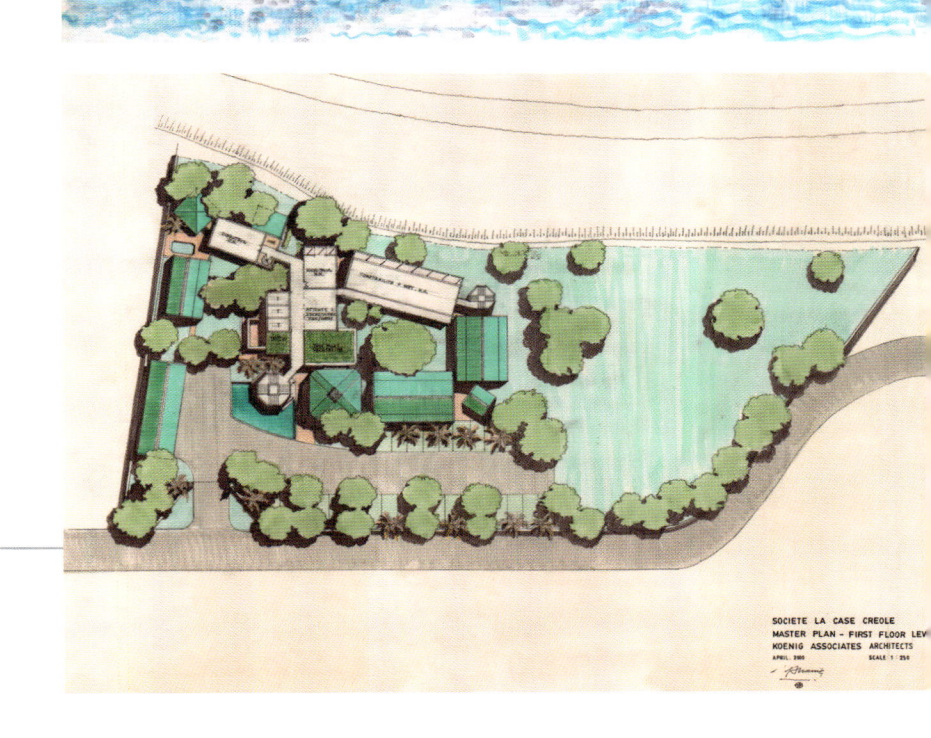

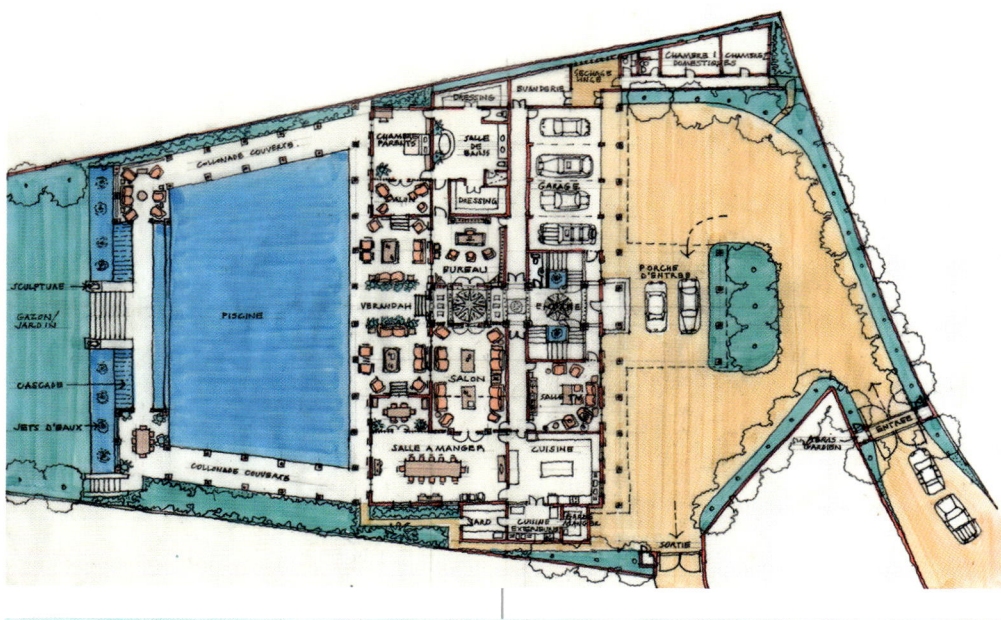

Jean-Francois Koenig
Chronological List of Projects

1999

Mauritius Commercial Bank – Flacq
*Flacq, Mauritius, 1999–2000
in joint venture with Frank Lincoln*

Residences 2000 Housing
Bain Boeuf, Mauritius

Jean-Marc Harel House
Quatre Bornes, Mauritius, 1999–2000

Fatima School Extension
Triolet, Mauritius, 1999

Pierre Noël Bungalow
Grand Baie, Mauritius, 1999–2000

Norland Suzor – Sugar Refinery
Fort George, Mauritius

Hospice Pere Laval
Coromandel, Mauritius

Thierry Koenig House
Grand Baie, Mauritius, 1999–2000

Philippe Goupille House
Roches Noires, Mauritius

Azad Hiridjee House
Tananarive, Madagascar

2000

Holiday Villas
Petite Case Noyale, Mauritius

Bernard Wong House
Floreal, Mauritius, 2000–2001

Queen Mary Apartments
Floreal, Mauritius

Les Conifères Offices
Pailles, Mauritius

Les Eugenias Offices
Pailles, Mauritius

Les Creolias Hotel
Calodyne, Mauritius, 2000–2005

Hong Kong and Shanghai Bank Head Office
Caudan, Mauritius

Le Ruisseau Rose Hotel
Les Mariannes, Mauritius

Domaine du Chasseur – New Boutique Hotel
Anse Jonchée, Mauritius

Les Salines Hotel
Les Salines, Mauritius

2001

Cora Hypermarket
St. Jean, Mauritius

Maurice Lam Apartments
Sodnac, Mauritius

Petite Rivière Master Plan
Petite Rivière, Mauritius

Voile d'Or Resort and Spa
Bel Ombre, Mauritius, 2001–2005

Bhooshan Ramloll House
Quatre Bornes, Mauritius, 2001–2003

Herve Henry Houses
Swan Properties, Pereybere, Mauritius, 2001–2003

2002

Bertrand Desvaux – Le Petit Morne Hotel
Le Morne, Mauritius

The Palace Hotel
Al Hamra, Ras al-Khaimah, United Arab Emirates

Jumbo Hypermarket Riche Terre
Riche Terre, Mauritius, 2002–2003
in joint venture with C.I.A. Internationale

Domaine de Beau Champ
Beau Champ, Mauritius

Felix Maurel – Les Eucalyptus Offices
Pailles, Mauritius

Alex Fon Sing – Trianon Apartments
Trianon, Mauritius

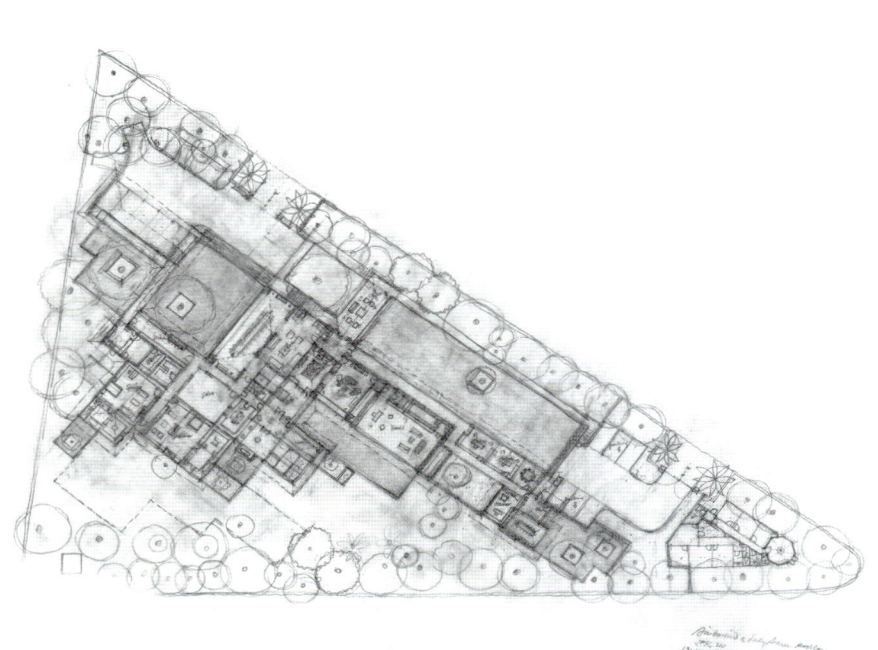

Jean-Francois Koenig
Chronological List of Projects

Beau Rivage Golf Estate Villas
Beau Rivage, Mauritius

Sanjay Cheekhooree House
Flic en Flac, Mauritius

Sir René Seeyave – Centre Point Residences
Centre Point Master Plan
St Jean, Mauritius, 2002–2004

Alex Fon Sing – Parking & Offices
Mère Barthelemy St., Port Louis, Mauritius

Felix Maurel – Four Houses
Pointe d'Esny, Mauritius, 2002–2006

Ocean Lodge Boutique Hotel
Palmar, Mauritius

2003

Ezra Jhuboo – Tecoma Integrated Villas
Tamarin, Mauritius

Boutique Hotel and Golf
Bel Air St Felix, Mauritius

Paddy Rowntree – Twin Family House
Pte. d'Esny, Mauritius

Capitol Hotel & Apartments
Happy Valley, Quatre Bornes, Mauritius

Sir Hamid Moollan House
Phoenix, Mauritius

Hooloomann Offices and Palm Court Apartments
Quatre Bornes, Mauritius, 2003–2006

Mauritius Commercial Bank, Mahébourg
Mahébourg, Mauritius, 2003–2006

Mauritius Commercial Bank - Bel Air
Bel Air, Mauritius, 2003

Le Multipliant Housing Estate
Petite Rivière Noire, Mauritius

Heirs Maxime Leclezio Housing
Grand Baie, Mauritius, 2003–2005

Hotel at Graviers
Rodrigues, Mauritius

Herve Henry – Les Fours a Chaux
Mahébourg, Mauritius

Hotel at Anse Boudin
Praslin, Seychelles

WEAL House Competition
Place d'Armes, Port Louis, Mauritius

2004

Rory Byrne House
Phuket, Thailand

Ruisseau Hortensia
Les Salines, Rivière Noire, Mauritius, 2004–2011

Sanjay Khan-Godrej – Skystar
Bangalore, India, 2004–2008

2005

Three Hotels for Mauritius Property Partnership
*Les Salines, Le Morne and Pte. Jerome
Mauritius*

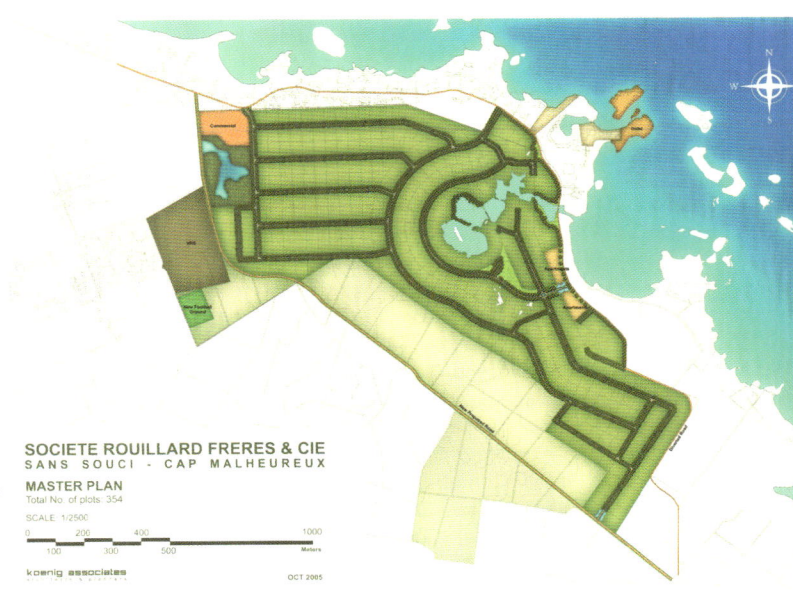

Jacques Tennant House
Pte. D'Esny, Mauritius, 2005–2006

Bois Fleuri Apartments
Grand Baie, Mauritius

Bella Vista Apartments
Moka, Mauritius

Société Rouillard Frères – Sans Souci Master Plan
Cap Malheureux, Mauritius

CIEL Head Office
Ebène, Mauritius, 2005–2009

Le Georges V Residences
Floreal, Mauritius

Narghis Bundhun House
Trou aux Biches, Mauritius

GIBB Head Office
Phoenix, Mauritius, 2005–2007

Emirates Resort Hotel
Cap Ternay, Seychelles

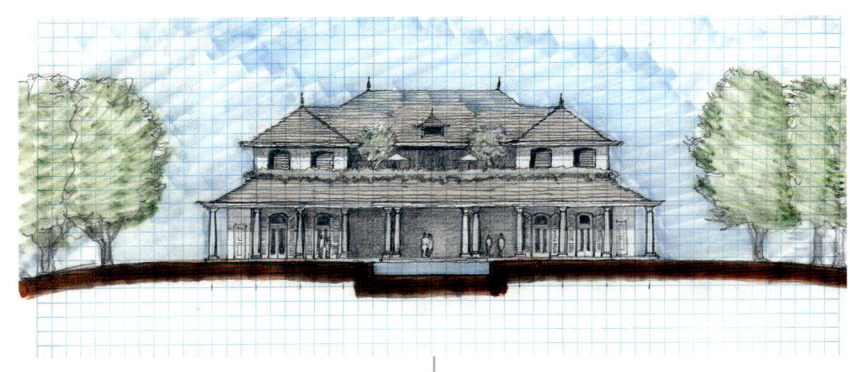

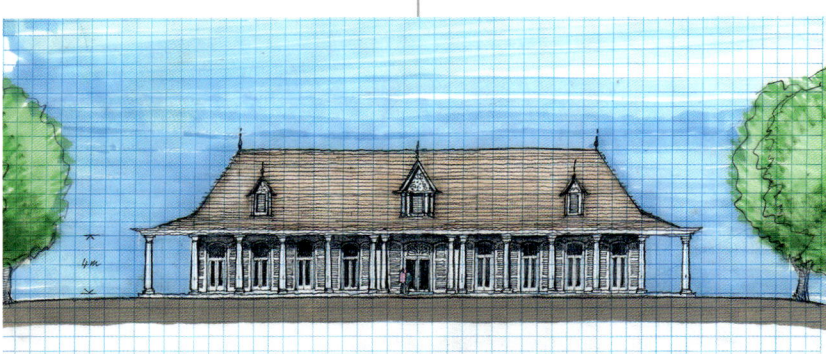

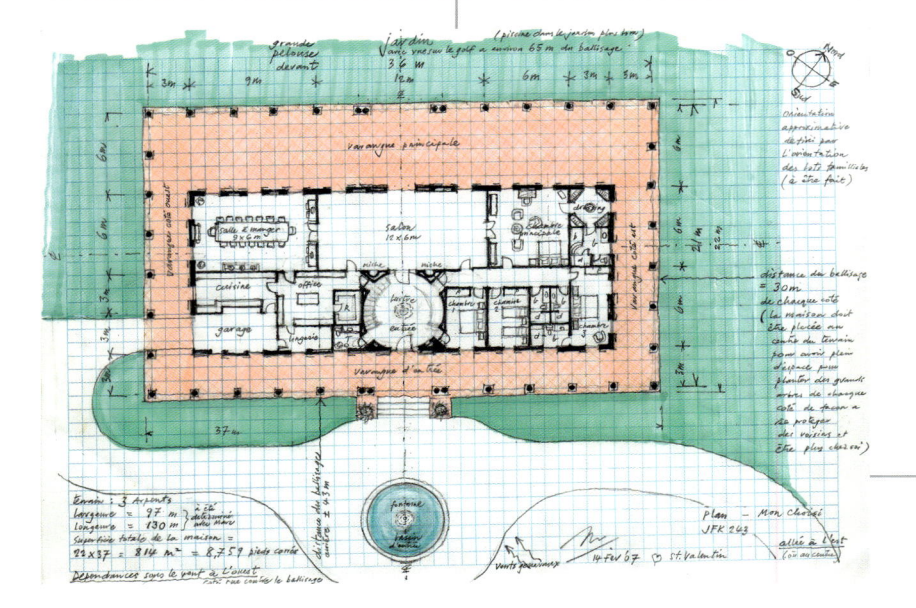

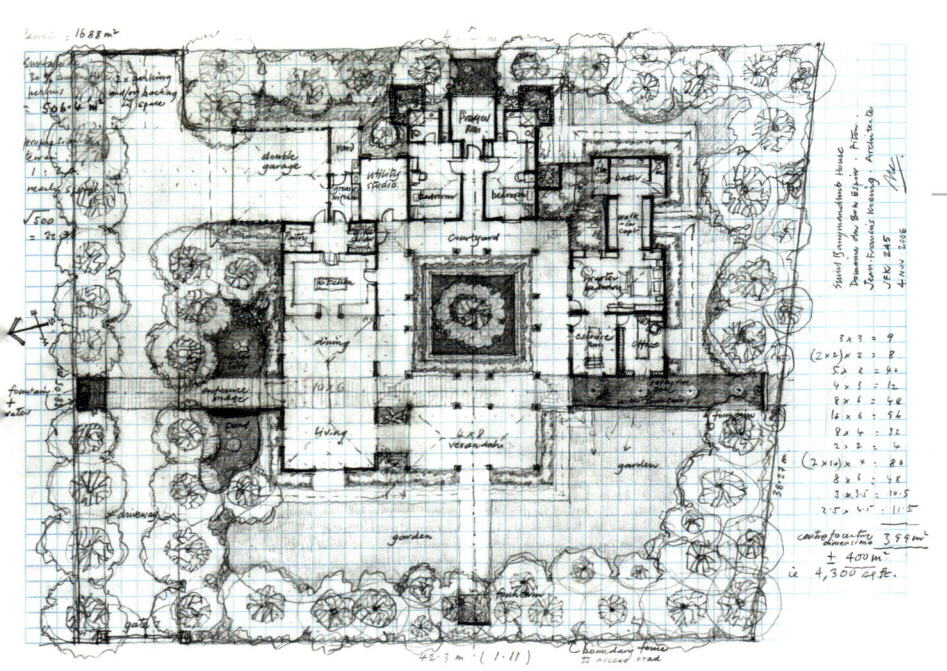

Jean-Francois Koenig
Chronological List of Projects

Two Papillon Hotels
Grand Baie, Mauritius

2006

Jean-Albert Hoareau Villas
La Salette, Mauritius

Yves Tostee – Townhouses
Floreal, Mauritius

Yves Tostee – Hotel at Palmar
Mauritius

Mauritius Commercial Bank
Ebène, Mauritius, 2006–2012

Zaf Bhurtun House
Beau Bassin, Mauritius

Sables d'Or Apartments
Beau Vallon, Mahé, Seychelles, 2006–2013

Valerie Kruegel Apartments
Beau Vallon, Mahé, Seychelles

North Point Hotel
North Point, Mahé, Seychelles

Jean-Albert Hoareau House
La Possession, Reunion Island

Three Houses at Bois Chandelle
Mon Choisy, Mauritius

Luc Pilot House
Les Salines, Mauritius

Dr Philip Wiehe House
Hillside, Labourdonnais, Mauritius

Sunil Banymandhub House
Domaine du Bon Espoir, Piton, Mauritius

Anglo Mauritius Master Plan
Port Louis, Mauritius

2007

Adolphe Vallet Apartments
Floreal, Mauritius

Bertrand Giraud House
Floreal, Mauritius

2008

Gulu Lalvani – Royal Phuket Marina
Master Plan Hotel and Apartments
Phuket, Thailand

2009

Five-Storey Atrium Luxury Shopping Building
City Centre, Bangalore, India

2011

Omnicane – Holiday Inn Hotel
Mon Tresor, Mauritius

2012

House at La Preneuse
Rivière Noire, Mauritius, 2012–2016

2013

Queen Mary Gardens Apartments
Floreal, Mauritius, 2013–2015

Kathy Mason – Denis Island Hotel Villas
Denis Island, Seychelles

Kathy Mason – Hotel at Danzil
Mahé, Seychelles

2015

House and Apartment-Garage Conversion
Vacoas, Mauritius, 2015

Arne Family Apartments
La Saline Les Bains, Reunion Island

2017

The National Centre of the Arts of Mauritius

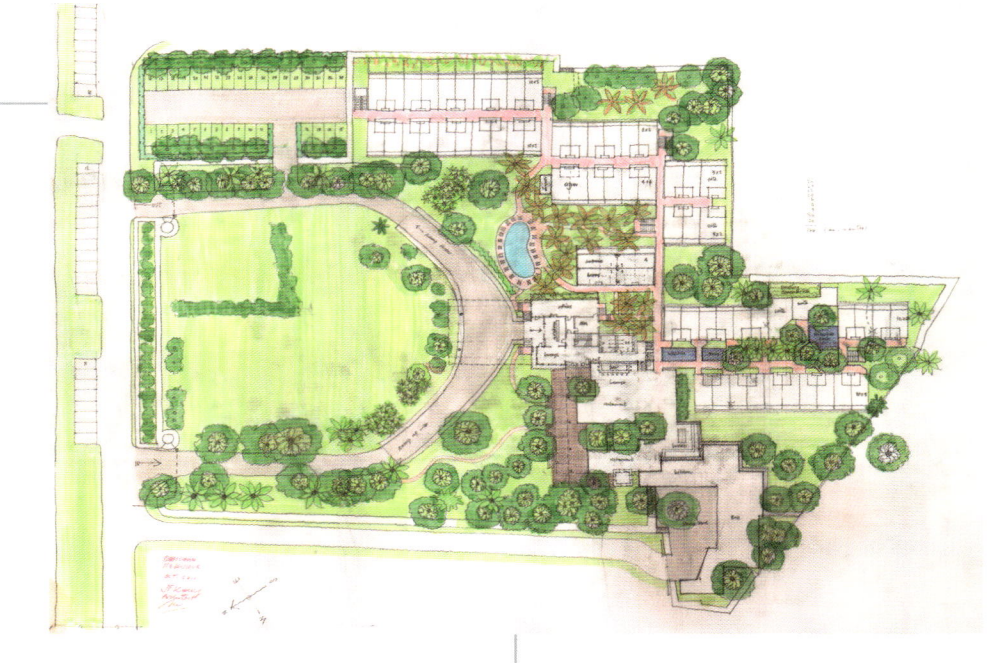

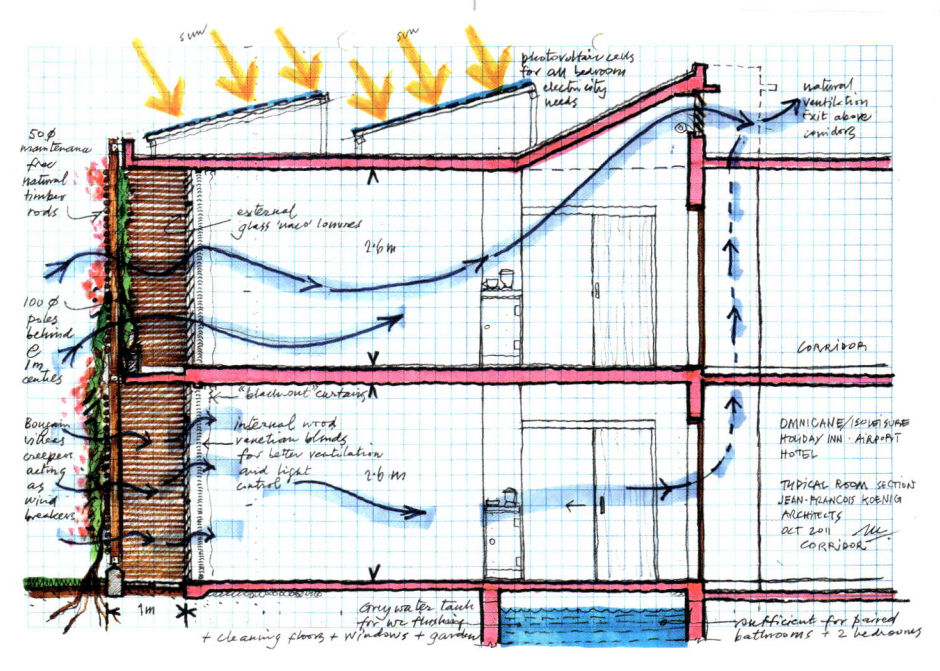

Curriculum Vitae

1954	Born in Mauritius.
1961–1964	Marcellin College, Melbourne, Australia.
1965–1972	St Joseph's College, Mauritius (1970: Senior School Certificate, Cambridge, 1972: Higher School Certificate, Cambridge).
1973	Maurice Giraud Architect, Mauritius.
1973–1976	Thames Polytechnic, London (RIBA Part 1).
1976–1977	Maurice Giraud Architect, Mauritius. Worked on Touessrok Hotel, Mauritius.
1977–1978	Thames Polytechnic, London.
1978–1979	Dr K. Al Kafrawi, Bill Carmen (former partner of DMJM), Ove Arup and Partners, London. Worked on the University of Qatar.
1979	3rd prize in Competition organised by the RIBA "An Image for Britain" judged by Norman Foster, Charles Moore and Derek Walker. Drawings exhibited at the RIBA.
1979–1980	Thames Polytechnic, London (RIBA Diploma in Architecture).
1980–1981	ZAC Associates, Mauritius.
1981–1985	Rhodar, Johannesburg.
1985–1987	Arup Associates, London.
1987	Established Jean-Francois Koenig Architect, Mauritius.
1988–1989	Served on the Committee of the Mauritius Association of Architects (MAA).
1989	Initiated and co-authored the book "La Vie en Varangue/Living in Mauritius", Editions du Pacifique.
2010	Founder member of The Mauritius Green Building Council.
2011	The Mauritius Commercial Bank Building represents the best of the architecture of Africa at the Union Internationale des Architectes (UIA) 24th World Congress in Tokyo.
2012	Elected in "100 Architects of the Year 2012" in a competition organised jointly by the UIA and the Korean Institute of Architects.
2016	Decorated by the State of Mauritius for services rendered to Architecture as Commander of the Order of the Star and Key of the Indian Ocean (C.S.K.).

Credits

Photographs:

Clement Bouic: pages 116 top, 125 right.
Gavin Byrne: pages 13 top, 264 bottom right, 265 bottom left.
Jano Couacaud: pages 124/125 left.
Hans Fonk: pages 62, 63, 88, 89, 90, 91 top.
Martine de Froberville: page 54 bottom left.
Harry Giles: page 18 centre bottom.
Jocelyn Gonzales: page 123 bottom.
Pierre Hausherr: pages 82, 83, 116/117 bottom, 126/127, 128, 129 bottom right.
Michèle Koenig: page 318.
Jean-Paul Le Blanc: pages 5, 7, 284 bottom.
Hasan Mohamedally: Front cover, pages 292/293.
Sophie Montocchio: pages 288 top, 296/297.
Johan Pretorius: pages 20/21, 22, 277, 278/279, 282, 283, 287, 289, 294 top and bottom left.
Tungsten: pages 59, 60, 64/65, 66, 67, 244, 245, 246/247, 248, 249, 250, 251, 254/255, 256/257.
Jean-Francois Koenig: all other photographs.

Digital computer images:

Michael Nadal, Xworx: pages 108/109, 110/111, 112, 200, 201, 202, 203, 269, 271, 284 top, 298, 299, 300/301.

Texts and captions:

Jean-Francois Koenig

IMPRINT

© 2018 teNeues Media GmbH & Co. KG, Kempen
© 2018 Jean-Francois Koenig. All rights reserved.

Texts, captions, and concept by Jean-Francois Koenig
Copyediting by Dr Suzanne Kirkbright, Artes Translations
Proofreading by Inga Wortmann, teNeues Media
Design by Anika Lethen
Editorial coordination by Pit Pauen, teNeues Media
Production by Nele Jansen, teNeues Media
Color separation by Jens Grundei, teNeues Media

ISBN 978-3-96171-075-1

Library of Congress Number: 2017958241

Printed in the Czech Republic

Picture and text rights reserved for all countries.
No part of this publication may be reproduced in any manner whatsoever.

While we strive for utmost precision in every detail, we cannot be held responsible for any inaccuracies, neither for any subsequent loss nor damage arising.

Every effort has been made by the publisher to contact holders of copyright to obtain permission to reproduce copyrighted material. However, if any permissions have been inadvertently overlooked, teNeues Publishing Group will be pleased to make the necessary and reasonable arrangements at the first opportunity.

Bibliographic information published by the Deutsche Nationalbibliothek
The Deutsche Nationalbibliothek lists this publication in the Deutsche Nationalbibliografie; detailed bibliographic data are available on the Internet at http://dnb.dnb.de.

Published by teNeues Publishing Group

teNeues Media GmbH & Co. KG
Am Selder 37, 47906 Kempen, Germany
Phone: +49-(0)2152-916-0
Fax: +49-(0)2152-916-111
e-mail: books@teneues.com

Press department: Andrea Rehn
Phone: +49-(0)2152-916-202
e-mail: arehn@teneues.com

Munich Office
Pilotystraße 4, 80538 Munich, Germany
Phone: +49-(0)89-443-8889-62
e-mail: bkellner@teneues.com

Berlin Office
Kohlfurter Straße 41–43, 10999 Berlin, Germany
Phone: +49-(0)30-4195-3526-23
e-mail: ajasper@teneues.com

teNeues Publishing Company
350 7th Avenue, Suite 301,
New York, NY 10001, USA
Phone: +1-212-627-9090
Fax: +1-212-627-9511

teNeues Publishing UK Ltd.
12 Ferndene Road, London SE24 0AQ, UK
Phone: +44-(0)20-3542-8997

teNeues France S.A.R.L.
39, rue des Billets, 18250 Henrichemont, France
Phone: +33-(0)2-4826-9348
Fax: +33-(0)1-7072-3482

www.teneues.com

teNeues Publishing Group
Kempen
Berlin
London
Munich
New York
Paris

teNeues